Critical
Food Issues
of the Eighties
(Pergamon Policy Studies—39)

Pergamon Policy Studies on Socio-Economic Development

Barney   *Global 2000 Report to the President of the U.S. Entering the 21st Century*

Carman   *Obstacles to Mineral Development: A Pragmatic View*

Franko/Seiber   *Developing Country Debt*

Fritz   *Combatting Nutritional Blindness in Children: A Case Study of Technical Assistance in Indonesia*

Golany   *Arid Zone Settlement Planning: The Israeli Experience*

Goodman/Love   *Integrated Project Planning and Management*

Goodman/Love   *Management of Development Projects: An International Case Study Approach*

Gould   *Bureaucratic Corruption in the Third World: The Administration of Underdevelopment in Zaire*

Grundy/Hughes/McHale   *Evaluating Transnational Programs in Government and Business*

Kidd   *Manpower Policies for the Use of Science and Technology in Development*

Morgan   *Science and Technology for Development: The Role of U.S. Universities*

Morris   *Measuring the Condition of the World's Poor: The Physical Quality of Life Index*

Stepanek   *Bangladesh— Equitable Growth?*

Thomas/Wionczek   *Intergration of Science and Technology with Development: Caribbean and Latin American Problems in the Context of the United Nations Conference on Science and Technology for Development*

Related Titles

Hinich/Staelin   *Consumer Protection Legislation and the Food Industry*

Sinha   *The World Food Problem: Consensus and Conflict*

PERGAMON POLICY STUDIES
ON SOCIO-ECONOMIC DEVELOPMENT

Critical Food Issues of the Eighties

Edited by
Marylin Chou
David P. Harmon, Jr.

Pergamon Press
NEW YORK • OXFORD • TORONTO • SYDNEY • FRANKFURT • PARIS

Pergamon Press Offices:

U.S.A.   Pergamon Press Inc., Maxwell House, Fairview Park, Elmsford, New York 10523, U.S.A.

U.K.   Pergamon Press Ltd., Headington Hill Hall, Oxford OX3 0BW, England

CANADA   Pergamon of Canada, Ltd., 150 Consumers Road, Willowdale, Ontario M2J, 1P9, Canada

AUSTRALIA   Pergamon Press (Aust) Pty. Ltd., P O Box 544, Potts Point, NSW 2011, Australia

FRANCE   Pergamon Press SARL, 24 rue des Ecoles, 75240 Paris, Cedex 05, France

FEDERAL REPUBLIC OF GERMANY   Pergamon Press GmbH, 6242 Kronberg/Taunus, Pferdstrasse 1, Federal Republic of Germany

Library of Congress Cataloging in Publication Data
Main entry under title:

Critical food issues of the 1980s.

Includes bibliographical references and index.
1.   Food supply—Addresses, essays, lectures.
2.   Food industry and trade—Addresses, essays, lectures.
3.   Food industry and trade—United States—Addresses, essays, lectures.   4.   Nutrition policy—United States—Addresses, essays, lectures.   I.   Chou, Marylin, 1933-   II.   Harmon, David P., 1937-
HD9000.6.C73   1979   338.1'9   79-14718
ISBN 0-08-024611-7
ISBN 0-08-024639-7 pbk.

Printed in the United States of America

Contents

v

Contents

Chapter

Foreword

In the past decade, food and agriculture have become important areas of interest for the United States and its citizens. First, there was the extraordinarily widespread belief and the resulting intense campaign of the sixties and early seventies to convince us that the mid-70s and the 80s would be a time of worldwide food shortages and of starvation in many areas. Equally intense, and probably for most Americans of greater immediate importance, are a series of questions which range from the safety of food for human health to the growing contribution of food exports to pay for imports of energy and manufactured goods. Increasingly it is recognized that the United States has a major asset in its comparative advantage in agriculture.

Hudson Institute's work in the food area began in the late sixties, when global grain shortages were causing concern, and in 1973 developed into a comprehensive project addressing this set of issues. At that time many extreme "limits to growth" ideologies were quite fashionable, particularly in intellectual circles. A major tenet of almost all of these ideologies was the idea that world population would grow esponentially, initially overshooting the ability of the planet to feed these growing numbers, much less support tham with the amenities to life. In examining the hypotheses of various kinds of physical limits to growth, the Institute found, contrary to much current thinking, that the world has - and will continue to have - sufficient physical and technological resources to feed itself more than adequately. The problems that are likely to be encountered do not lie in the physical and technological areas, but rather in the "institutional" sphere. The problems are largely social, political and economic and center on how individual countries manage (or mismanage) the food growing, processing and distributing resources available to them. This research, funded partially by the National Science Foundation, culminated in the book, World Food Prospects and Agricultural Potential (Praeger, 1977).

As a result of research on institutional factors impeding countries' agricultural and food supply development, we felt it would be appropriate to "turn down the microscope" several notches and examine short term food issues that are and will be of concern to the food industry, the U.S. government and the public. Many policy issues are neither well formulated nor well understood by Americans, because, in general, a balanced view is not readily available. This is increasingly needed because the lack of understanding of issues, both by the public, as well as by the government and industry policymakers, often leads to faulty, costly decisions and programs. It is also important to temper the adversary position in which the government and the food industry often find themselves.

On the other hand, there is an increasing need to respond to public needs and sensitivities, and to recognize the points of convergence between the food and agricultural sector's activities and more general social concerns. Issues must be well understood, if they are not to be raised to emotional or politicized levels. Hudson Institute's expertise, gained from eighteen years of studying policy issues and advising corporate and government clients on matters of public interest, coupled with the collective expertise and resources of the seven corporate members, consultants, academic specialists and participating government agencies, were brought to bear on the major food and agriculture issues that will face the nation in the next decade.

This is Hudson Institute's second major publication in the area of food and agriculture. We are really pleased with both publications and want to express our appreciation to both Marylin Chou and David P. Harmon, Jr., who developed and implemented the Food, Agriculture, and Society Research Program, from which these papers originated. We believe that this book is an important contribution to better understanding of these issues.

Herman Kahn

Preface

Critical Food Issues of the 1980s is a collection of presentations and papers organized around four major topics. The first section covers the socioeconomic climate likely to face the food industry and the country over the next decade, followed by a discussion in the second section of the changing nature of food and nutrition policies. The third section covers the outlook for technology and the associated impact of regulation - not only for food, but also for agricultural productivity and agricultural chemicals. The book ends with an examination of food and agricultural issues that will have a profound and continuing impact on U.S. agricultural policy.

Critical Food Issues of the 1980s is the culmination of Hudson Institute's Food, Agriculture, and Society Research Program, the objectives of which were two-fold: 1) To focus on and provide alternative solutions to current and near-term food and agricultural policy issues which are likely to have a long-term effect on firms, the government and the public; and 2) To increase public understanding of the economic and sociopolitical aspects of the food and agriculture sector.

The program offered opportunity for discussion, access to information and a vehicle to disseminate findings to both the public and interested parties. Working sessions were used for information exchange and for developing position papers. A very beneficial facet of the research program was the continuing interest and participation of several agencies of the U.S. government. Their participation was invaluable in adding the appropriate degree of balance in both the research and the conclusions that were drawn. In a program of this type it was necessary to insure that the government's side as well as industry's was heard. In some cases, the two viewpoints converged, while in others they ranged from mildly contrary to highly opposed. An example of the kind of issues the group dealt with was the question , "How can government policy encourage innovation and growth in the food industry while at the same time provide realistic levels of protection for the public?" We asked both industry and government to answer this question. We also asked the food industry to answer the question of what role it should play in meeting the public's social and economic demands - specifically when these demands converge with the activities of the food industry.

The editors and authors of this book contend that there are seven key issues and trends for the 1980s:

1) Greater concern over health, diet-related diseases, and the formation of national nutrition policies. This is partly due to increased wealth, greater technical knowledge, higher standards of living and a greater concern for the quality of life.

2) Anxiety over food safety, due to an increasing amount of paranoia or ideology often combined with improved scientific techniques that can detect increasingly smaller amounts of toxic substances. Most of the fear focuses on the possible link of certain chemicals with cancer.

3) A proliferation of regulations and laws designed to enhance food quality and safety. Many of these are based on the premise of "better safe than sorry," and will deter the introduction and acceptance of new food products.

4) New lifestyles and values will demand increasing sensitivity in marketing and promotion to meet the needs and attitudes of consumers at home and abroad.

5) The move toward agricultural self-sufficiency by both developed and developing countries. Adequate food production is a more likely prospect than famine and dire shortages. Food problems will be regional and caused by low incomes, poor distribution, and weather, rather than by inadequate food production capabilities.

6) Increasingly, agricultural crops will be produced for export to offset the higher cost of importing manufacured goods and energy, as well as economic development.

7) Growing interdependence between the developed and developing world will require flexible, multidimensional food policies.

Throughout the book the reader will find several "common threads." A pro-technology message, coupled with a need to understand how science, technology, and economic development proceed, is perhaps the most pervasive underlying "common thread" explicit or implicit in the papers. The participants agreed that one basic requirement necessary to clarify today's misunderstanding of issues is to give the public and members of government a clear picture of the dynamics and accomplishments of science in the food and agriculture area, how scientific progress proceeds, what science can and cannot do today, as well as what we may expect from science in the future. Equally important is the need for the food industry and the scientific community to understand how regulatory agency staffs and elected representatives arrive at decisions based on real or perceived pressures from their constituents.

Another principal common thread is the need to understand the function of agricultural and food chemicals, as well as their benefits and risks. A great deal of confusion, and even fear, over chemicals exists today, which we foresee will grow in the future. This is evident in 1979 in the growing interest in all suspected links between food and cancer. Moreover, there is, and will continue to be, growing public interest in nutrition and changing dietary habits, as our population mix alters and as lifestyles change.

Finally, we looked for policy alternatives as well as consumer attitudes and actions that could be considered "precursors" or "bell-weathers" for the United States over the next decade. One key area is Scandinavia, in particular Sweden, where the government has promulgated a national nutrition policy and is taking strong action in the area of alcohol and tobacco consumption.

Each section of the book opens with the highlights of the papers that follow. The last section "turns up the microscope" a notch, examining the world food outlook for the 1980s and ends with an incisive paper by the USDA's former chief economist, Don Paarlberg, entitled "Coping with Abundance - U.S. Agricultural Policy Alternatives."

The primary objective of the Food, Agriculture, and Society Research Program and of this book is to present a balanced view of the important food and agriculture issues likely to be with us throughout the 1980s. Only in this way can emotionalism and misunderstanding be overcome. The openness of the meetings and of the dialogue, the mix of the participants, the quality of the research, and the understanding that Hudson Institute is chartered to operate in the public interest and has a reputation for objectivity and integrity all helped to insure balance and fairness in the conclusions and recommendations of the research group.

Credits:

Acknowledgments

The papers comprising this book are the result of a year-long cooperative research program initiated by Hudson Institute, with seven members of the food and agriculture industries, specialists, and government agencies. Castle and Cooke, Deere & Company, DeKalb AgResearch, ITT/Continental Baking, Kraft, Inc., Nabisco, and The Quaker Oats Company are the corporations which made possible the Food, Agriculture, and Society Research Program and, as a result, this book. The government agencies that participated were the U.S. Department of Agriculture, Office of Technology Assessment, Food and Drug Administration, Department of Energy, and the Environmental Protection Agency. The views expressed in the following papers are those of the authors. It is to the credit of those companies and participating government agencies that they recognized the need to address the issues in a spirit of openness and frankness.

We wish to thank the Hudson support staff, particularly Carolann Roussel, who coordinated the preparation of the manuscript, Kathy Finch, Stephanie Tyler, Ilse Lehmeier, Blanche Gorton, Annie Small, Connie Targonski, Elaine Shelah, Helen Iadanza, and Anne Marsek for their help in typing the manuscript. We are, as always, indebted to Mildred Schneck and Ruth Paul, our librarians, for their willingness and cooperation in obtaining all the references used; to Ernest Schneider for his editorial assistance; and to Gertrude Tuxen for her steadfast support and encouragement. And finally, we especially wish to thank the staff of the print shop for their help in printing and assembling all the papers and proceedings.

Marylin Chou & David P. Harmon, Jr.
Coeditors
Autumn 1978

I
The Socioeconomic Outlook

Introduction

This first section describes the socioeconomic background responsible for the current attitudes towards business, particularly the food industry. Major trends and issues involving the food industry are analyzed to provide a conceptual framework within which strategies can be developed. Alternative policies, including possible foreign bellwethers, are presented.

Herman Kahn analyzes past, current, and prospective periods of growth, focusing on declining rates of world population and economic growth. He attributes this decline in part to the growing prevalence in advanced capitalist countries of "New Class" values that seriously affect costs and productivity. He describes these values and argues that those who support them are unable to cope with real issues and problems.

In the framework of these new values, Marylin Chou examines how the concern over food safety has gained such prominence over the past decade. She presents the related controversial issues and addresses questions and priorities of the greatest importance. Emil Mrak and Peg Rogers provide perspective on the present leadership dilemma facing the food industry as it is beset by consumer activist attacks. Dean Peterson details the factors and considerations of food price inflation. Of particular interest is the marketing cost component of the total food bill. Graham Molitor describes the causes and cyclical nature of consumerism suggesting that the U.S. can benefit by studying the precursor policies of innovative countries like Sweden. Sweden's policies discouraging use of alcohol and tobacco are presented as examples of "negative marketing."

1 The World at a Turning Point: New Class Attitudes*
Herman Kahn

Below is a tabular representation of the history of the Industrial Revolution dealing with 16 Advanced Capitalist Nations, omitting the USSR. This material is derived from some recently published work by Angus Maddison. The 1886-1913 period was looked back upon nostalgically by Europeans, and therefore became known as La Belle Epoque, roughly the good era. Many people who actually experienced this era would not have agreed with this characterization, since anarchism, nihilism, and other manic movements were prominent during these same years. Indeed, any prolonged period of economic prosperity tends to produce all sorts of social stresses and strains before ending.

		Years	Growth Rate
La Belle Epoque	1886-1913	27	3.3
La Mauvaise Epoque	1914-1947	34	1.8
La Deuxieme Belle Epoque	1948-1973	26	4.9
L'Epoque de Malaise	1974-?	--	3.5

World War I was probably the most senseless war in history. At almost any point it would have paid either side to accept a negotiated defeat rather than fighting on. Thus it was comparatively irrational, especially in contrast to the relatively prudent wars which preceded it. But the Belle Epoque had produced an atmosphere in which people had lost the habit of being sensible and careful.

During the next period, La Mauvaise Epoque (the bad era), growth rates dropped drastically at a time when technology should have caused

---

* Remarks presented at the Food, Agriculture, and Society Research Program meeting, Washington, D.C., March 28, 1978.

them to go up. Growth was perhaps 50 percent below normal for nearly 35 years. It was a turbulent and disastrous era: two world wars, the Great Depression, the Bolshevik Revolution, and the rise and fall of fascism all occurred during these years. Instability was rampant, and growth rates fluctuated wildly.

The world has recently emerged from 26 years of incredible success, which we label La Deuxieme Belle Epoque (the second good era). In no year during the entire period was growth "negative" - for these 16 nations or the world as a whole. No bad years occurred, and few were mediocre. But this is not really a healthy way to live; at the least it produces bad effects.

Two things happened during the Deuxieme Belle Epoque. Not only did the developed world grow faster than ever, but the rest of the world joined in - for the first time. Indeed, the poor nations grew faster than the rich, and faster than the advanced nations had at corresponding stages of development. But many people in the advanced nations have been, and are, preoccupied with the gap which divides the poor from the rich. Concern about this concept is characteristic of rich people, not poor people. Few of us are depressed because we don't live like a Rockefeller or a Rothschild. This is true all over the world. Few in the poor countries would give up a dime of absolute growth in order to close the gap which separates these countries from the United States or West Germany. This is true for peasants, workers, and most businessmen, but it does not hold for intellectuals and government officials.

As the Industrial Revolution trickled down from the developed countries during La Deuxieme Belle Epoque, a "Middle Income" group of nations came into existence. As a result, the nations of the world can now be divided into the three groups below:

	Billions of People	Prospective Economic Growth Rates
Poor	1.2	4+%
Middle Income	1.9	6
Rich	1.1	3+

Before the Industrial Revolution, no nation ever attained an average per capita income above $500. Now almost 2 billion people are making between $500 and $2,000. They would be rich by any standard of history - except ours. Forty-five percent of the world's people, including China, are in this category.

At present, the world - or at least the Advanced Capitalist Nations - is in a period which we call Epoque de Malaise. This is a condition where one feels neither well nor sick, but not badly enough to go see a doctor. However, this era could easily become the Deuxieme Mauvaise

Epoque; one can write a dozen scenarios which would bring about this result. Of course we don't know whether they will happen, and world growth rates for the forthcoming period are also guesswork; our best guess is 3.7 percent for the entire world. It is striking that so many independent studies are coming very close to this estimate, and 3.7 would be a big drop from the 4.9 percent of the 1947-1973 era.

Right now, the poor nations have a total product of $0.3 trillion; they should grow by an average of 4 to perhaps 5 percent. The Middle Income Group is producing $1.6 billion, a quarter of that produced by the rich nations; but this is a big number. These people, who should be growing at 6 or even 7 percent, are still a big market. No nation or group of nations has ever attained a growth rate this high on a sustained basis. The rich nations, which now include the communist members of members of the Warsaw Pact, have a product of $6.4 trillion, and should be growing at a 3+ rate, which is quite a drop from the preceding period.

South Korea is a good example of what the Middle Income Group can do. In 1974, a recession year, they grew by 8.3 percent; in 1975, by 8.8 percent; 15 percent in 1976; and 10.5 percent in 1977. In 1978 the growth is estimated to be 15 percent. The South Koreans accomplish this feat by not having the problems of the nouveau riche.

In addition to grasping this basic picture of the stages of economic development, it is important to understand that the world is running down in some real sense. Thus, the curves showing exponential world population growth rates, which have been so familiar in recent years, omitted the equally dramatic decline of these rates; this is shown in figure 1.1, which puts these trends in a 16,000 year context.

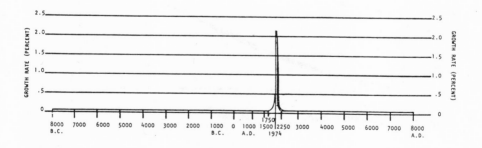

Fig. 1.1. Population growth rate growth in long-term historical perspective.

Source: Adapted from Ronald Freeman and Bernard Berelson, "The Human Population," Scientific American, September 1974, pp. 36-37.

The idea that world population is in the process of decelerating its growth rate is not an idiosyncratic Hudson position. On the contrary, it is conventional wisdom among demographers, including those at the United Nations. It now appears that these growth rates peaked around 1970. The rate probably never quite reached two percent a year. It is now perhaps 1.8 and should continue to drop rapidly. This means that, if momentum is maintained on food output, the world should do very well in terms of supporting a large population.

Gross World Product is also entering a period of declining growth rates. We once thought that the inflection point (where the rates would peak) would occur in the early- or mid-1980s. It now looks as if the high point was reached in or around 1973. It seems unlikely that the world will again witness a growth rate as high as the six percent which was reached five years ago.

This is another way of saying that the world is throwing away 12 years of high growth rates that could occur through 1985, and the reason - to speak bluntly - is stupidity.

The main point is that any effort at extrapolation must take account of the big structural change in the world which is now taking place. Instead of a situation where everything grows at increasing, even exponential, rates, we are entering a period when everything is turning over and heading downward. We must therefore start thinking in entirely different terms. This inflection point - where growth rates change their character - is a unique point in history. Instead of the spike in population growth shown above, we must become accustomed to seeing growth in terms of the logistic S-shaped curve which is typical of most growth (see figure 1.2).

Fig. 1.2. S-shaped curve.

This prospect is about as certain as anything in public discussion today. That is not to say that it will really happen, but it would be very surprising if things went differently. The expectation might best be described as semi-intuitive. Nevertheless, anyone who talks about future exponential growth rates for population or resource consumption will be either a fool or ignorant.

The kind of sobering-up process which occurred during La Mauvaise Epoque (caused by World War I and the Depression) will probably be much slower and less thorough during Epoque de Malaise. The reasons are not difficult to find. For example, the U.S. Department of

Agriculture claims that it is possible to maintain an adequate diet for around $1.50 a day. At the same time, it is not particularly extraordinary for affluent people in this country to pay $140 for a good meal for two couples at a gourmet restaurant.. If $6.00 of this goes for nutrition, then $134 is paying for something else. This amount certainly represents some sort of slack in the system, which is not easy to get rid of. Grain carryover stocks are not the main element of slack. For example, the Soviet Union moved from a diet of potatoes, to grain, to meat. If things were really tough, they could always go back to grain, unpleasant though this would be. If such retrogressions become necessary, or desirable, it will be easier to accomplish them through pricing than through edicts. Given a reasonably well-operating price mechanism, our economic system has an enormous amount of slack in it at the moment.

But this kind of slack in the system does not necessarily provide enough grain for the poor. It is nonsense to refer to this as a problem of distribution; it is a problem of money. If one can get money to the poor to pay for food, delivery can be guaranteed with great assurance, especially since the poor are willing to pay a little more for food than other people, if they have the money. The term distribution is misleading because it seems to imply that shipping is inadequate, when financing is really the heart of the matter. The money problem will be around for a long time, because there are many poor people in all three groups of nations: the poor, the middle income, and the rich. "Poor" has a different meaning, of course, in each group.

Thus, there is a real poverty problem. If food for the poor is not financed, the poor do not receive enough food. Nevertheless, in much of the world, and quite probably in the United States, a minimum living standard is available to any reasonable person.

The foregoing is background to the real problem called "the nouveau riche problem". When a family suddenly makes a lot of money, it often has trouble regulating its expenditures. For an outsider, it is hard to judge whether such a family is living within or exceeding its income. Only detailed accounting can determine this. New York City is a good example of this problem. It is not correct to say that as New York goes, so goes the nation. The accurate observation is that as New York goes, so go Yonkers and Newark. For 10 or 15 consecutive years, the city budget systematically spent more than was coming in, and it even financed short term outgo with long term debt. And even now, New York has not completely mended its ways. Thus, the transport workers are threatening to strike against the subway system. These workers make the valid claim that they are not overpaid in comparison to similar workers elsewhere. But many of these workers are getting maybe twice the income of similar people in the private sector, when fringe benefits are included. The agent who sells subway tokens makes about $18,000 a year, compared to maybe $11,000 for a bank teller - much more challenging work. Thus, paying the subway agent much above $10,000 is a way of giving him some sort of social dividend. This is a luxury. Even though New York City is the richest city in the world, it is living over its income by 20 or 30 percent. Its income dropped, but the city does not know how to cut back. The most obvious way to do so is never to pay more for something or somebody than the market requires; there is no good reason why New York taxpayers, many of whom receive low incomes, should support a subway employee at $18,000 a year. This leads to what is being called the "give-back" problem - the idea that unions should be asked to return, or to concede, advantages which they gained in earlier negotiations. This started in San Francisco two years ago; although it is a strong union town, municipal employees there had to accept a cut in real pay. This was brought about by a revolt of low-paid union workers, who complained that municipal workers were overpaid.

Let's assume that a rather senseless regulation raises the price of food by 10 percent. It has the effect of a sales tax, but no one can spend the revenue. Sales taxes are, of course, regressive. The present system is characterized by an incredible amount of this kind of sales tax. The main reason for this kind of cost-raising is a group which Hudson calls the New Class. The main concept here can be termed lack of reality testing. Figure 1.3 ("Fourteen New Emphases") describes the values of this group.

Why did it take 10,000 years for the Industrial Revolution to occur? Why weren't the ancient Greeks and Romans, or the Chinese, who had a highly developed technology, able to modernize in this way? The reason is that these earlier societies had cultural traits which prevented such a transformation; these didn't differ much from the Fourteen New Emphases. Furthermore, these Emphases are becoming increasingly important in every advanced capitalist nation in the world. This is the reason why Hudson expects the rate of growth of Gross World Product to top out soon, if it has not already done so. The reason that this is likely can be summed up in the phrase, the "social limits to growth." One reason that Hudson doesn't expect physical shortages to inhibit growth is that these social limits will bring about a slowdown long before any serious shortages could have any serious effect on growth. Physical limits won't play any real role unless significant mistakes are made.

For example, Gross World Product in 1978 was about $8.3 trillion; it should eventually flatten out between $100 and $500 trillion - 10 to 50 times higher than today. But if GWP kept going up for 200 years at the pace of the last quarter century, it would be 16,000 times higher in 2178, 300 times more than the flattened-out level. However, there is nothing intrinsically unhealthy about social limits to growth. Thus, if someone is rich, why should he knock himself out to get richer?

But problems can arise in the slowing-down process. Perhaps 10 of the 14 new emphases are probably desirable in themselves. Thus, the question is not one of hostility, but of proportion.

One can distinguish three different attitudes toward these emphases:

1. Discretionary choices

2. Preferential values

3. Moral imperatives

1. <u>Selective Risk Avoidance</u> (Innovators, entrepreneurs, businessmen, and "do-ers" generally must bear all risks and the burden
   of proof as if only they, and not society as well, benefited
   from their profits and efforts)

2. <u>Localism</u> ("ins" vs. "outs," no local disturbance or risks because of needs of external world)

3. <u>Comfort, Safety, Leisure, and Health Regulations</u> (often to be
   mandated by government regulation - sometimes approaching
   "health and safety authoritarianism")

4. <u>Protection of Environment and Ecology</u> (at almost any cost to
   the economy or other programs)

5. <u>Loss of Nerve, Will, Optimism, Confidence and Morale</u> (at
   least about economic progress and technological advancement)

6. <u>Public Welfare and Social Justice</u> (life must be made to be
   "fair" - equality in result, not of opportunity - justice
   should not be blind)

7. <u>Happiness and Hedonism</u> (as explicit and direct goals in life)

8. <u>General Anti-Technology, Anti-Economic Development, Anti-Middle
   Class Attitudes</u> ("small is better" and "limits-to-growth" movements, but enormous resources can be allocated or great economic costs accepted to further Points 1-7 above)

9. <u>Increasing Social Control and "Overall Planning" of the Economy</u>
   (but mostly with New Class values and attitudes made by "input-
   output" theorists)

10. <u>Regulatory Attitudes That are Adversary or Indifferent to the
    Welfare of Business</u> (the productivity and profitability of busi-
    ness are taken for granted)

11. <u>"Modern" Family and Social Values and a De-emphasis of Many
    Traditional (Survival and Square) Values</u>

12. <u>Concern With Self</u> (often accompanied by an emphasis on mystic
    or transcendental attitudes and values, or an expression of the
    "me generation")

13. <u>New Rites, Ceremonies, and Celebrations</u> (both against and in-
    stead of traditional ones)

14. <u>New Sources of Meaning and Purpose, of Status and Prestige</u>

Fig. 1.3. Fourteen "New" Emphases and Trends in U.S. Values

Source: Herman Kahn, <u>World Economic Development</u>, Boulder, Colorado,
Westview Press, 1979, p. 17.

If one can get along without a vacation from home without much trouble, this makes a vacation a matter of discretionary choice. However Frenchmen and young affluent people in the United States put such a vacation on a higher level, that of a preferential value. But some people think of it as a moral imperative: one owes it to oneself or to the world. A better example would be that of someone who would pay the government enough money to save ten lives if he were permitted to kill two people. No government would agree to such a deal because the sanction against murder is a moral imperative. But suppose that an industrialist offers to give the authorities enough money to take two pounds of pollutants out of a river, for every pound he puts in at a certain other point convenient to him. Most Americans would accept such an offer in the interest of a cleaner environment - except for people who see pollution control as a moral imperative akin to not permitting murder. Some primitive people see protecting the environment as a moral imperative, and this is true of more and more people in the Advanced Capitalist Nations. But they are a small minority in the Christian, Jewish, and Moslem cultures.

The Advanced Capitalist Countries are raising a whole class of young, upper-middle class intellectuals who treat many issues as moral imperatives which the rest of society does not see in this light. According to the late economist Joseph Schumpeter, an intellectual is someone who makes up his mind on the basis of second hand information. This definition is not intended to be invidious; in these terms President Carter is certainly an intellectual, since he relies upon briefings and studies by his staff for 90 percent of his decisions. The trouble is that his staff, and the staff of his staff, are all intellectuals. This is simply too removed from the real world. Upper-middle class elites, regardless of whether or not they are intellectuals, are pushing these 14 new emphases in all the advanced capitalist countries. For example, Americans on the east and west coasts are generally unwilling to accept any development or growth which would, or might, inconvenience them personally - in the name of progress for the community or nation. This is not true in the Southwest and Middle West.

The United States is probably the least class-conscious nation in the world; nevertheless, a definite class structure exists and can be identified. The New Class is an emerging sub-group of the upper-middle class. This term "new" in this context means the most recent; that is, the most recent class to come to the fold. Thus, in many a European city there is an "old" church, built about 1200, and a "new" church, built about 1400. It is in this sense that we use the term New Class. Some people, like Daniel Bell, who study futurology, think that the New Class will take over society. Although this seems unlikely, it is true that in about 1970, for the first time, the number of people working in the field of information in this country surpassed those in manufacturing.

New Class people make their livelihoods from language, aesthetic, and analytical skills or the manipulation of symbols. They can be thought of as people who deal with rarefied information (see figure 1.4).

BACKGROUND OF THE IDEA OF THE NEW CLASS

1. NEED TO EXPLAIN THE PHENOMENON OF "POWER WITHOUT PROPERTY" OR POWER WITHOUT "TRADITIONAL AUTHORITY"

2. TERM "NEW CLASS" EMPLOYED IN 1956 BY MILOVAN EJILAS TO LABEL COMMUNITY RULERS.

3. TERM FIRST APPLIED TO UNITED STATES BY DAVID T. BAZELON IN 1967.

4. TERM USED, MORE OR LESS IN OUR SENSE, BY D.P. MOYNIHAN AND NORMAN PODHORETZ IN 1972. INTERPRETED, CIRCULATED AND PUBLICIZED BY IRVING KRISTOL.

5. TERM NOW WIDELY USED--E.G., RECENT ARTICLES IN FORTUNE, THE NEW REPUBLIC, THE PUBLIC INTEREST, THE NEW YORK TIMES, HARPERS, ATLANTIC MONTHLY, ETC.

6. WIDESPREAD BELIEF THAT NEW CLASS WILL BE THE DOMINANT CLASS IN THE FUTURE.

OUR USE OF THE TERM NEW CLASS

THE NEW CLASS IS LARGELY COMPOSED OF UPPER MIDDLE CLASS INTELLECTUALS WHO ARE INCREASINGLY IN POSITIONS OF POWER AND INFLUENCE IN THE UNITED STATES. THEIR SOURCES OF POWER AND INFLUENCE DIFFER FROM THOSE OF THE OLDER UPPER CLASS AND UPPER MIDDLE CLASS ELITE WHOSE BASE HAD BEEN TRADITIONAL PRESTIGE ASSOCIATED WITH WEALTH AND PROPERTY OR HIGH POSITION IN BUSINESS AND GOVERNMENT.

AS A WHOLE, THE NEW CLASS DERIVES BOTH ITS INFLUENCE AND INCOME FROM POSSESSION AND MASTERY OF VERBAL, SYMBOL, AND "PERSUASIVE" SKILLS, SKILLS ENGENDERED MORE BY FORMAL ACADEMIC AND ANALYTICAL TRAINING THAN BY PRACTICAL TRAINING AND EX-PERIENCE. NEW CLASS PEOPLE TEND NOT TO SPECIALIZE IN ENTREPRENEURIAL, ENGINEERING (ESPECIALLY CIVIL AND POWER) OR ADMINISTRATIVE SKILLS. NOR DO THEY, NORMALLY EXERCISE CLERICAL OR MANUAL SKILLS AS A MEANS OF LIVELIHOOD.

WE DISTINGUISH BETWEEN FOUR SUBDIVISIONS OF THE NEW CLASS: TRADITIONAL CONSER-VATIVE, NEO-CONSERVATIVE, TRADITIONAL LIBERBAL, AND NEO-LIBERAL. IT IS THE NEO-LIBERAL SUBGROUP WHICH WE BELIEVE NEEDS MOST TO BE CRITICALLY EXAMINED AT THIS TIME.

IF THERE IS AN EMERGING NEW CLASS, IT SHOULD BE IDENTIFIED BY:

- HIGH FORMAL EDUCATION

- RESPECTABLE SOCIAL ORIGINS

- HIGH PERCENT HAVING "PROFESSIONAL" OCCUPATIONAL STATUS

- HIGH (BUT NOT HIGHEST) INCOME. (IF INVOLVED IN MANUAL SKILLS IT IS AS PART OF THE "VOLUNTARY SIMPLICITY" MOVEMENT OR RELATED TO THE SELF-FULFILLMENT ETHOS. IF LOWER INCOME, THIS MAY BE BECAUSE STILL A STUDENT OR WORKING FOR A LOW PAYING PUBLIC INTEREST GROUP)

- TYPICALLY SOURCE OF INCOME IS FROM A NON-MARKET ORIENTED SOURCE SUCH AS:

  - GOVERNMENT
  - NON-PROFIT ORGANIZATION
  - GRANTS
  - SELF-FULFILLING PURSUITS
  - RELATIVE YOUTH

Fig. 1.4.

The New Class can be divided into five main political components:

1. Traditional Liberals: emphasis on welfare, income distribution, regulation, civil rights, i.e., in FDR, Stevenson, Truman, Humphrey, Jackson, Meany traditions

2. Neo-Liberals: sometimes called "health and safety fascists" or "authoritarians"

3. Traditional Conservatives: emphasis on traditional values and morality; typical examples are speech writers for Reagan and Goldwater, or editors for National Review

4. Neo-Conservatives: have made peace with the New Deal (i.e., traditional liberals), but espouse many traditional conservative programs (Kristol, Bell, Moynihan)

5. Humanist Left: emphasis on socialism, joy, love, creativity, and spontaneity

The neo-liberal segment of the New Class tends to dominate the media and the staffs of regulatory agencies and of Democratic members of Congress. The result is that discussion of many controversial policy issues takes place in neo-liberal terms. This is particularly true of the concept of a gap between rich and poor nations, which neo-liberals tend to feel must somehow be closed. No practical person anywhere believes that relative poverty is nearly as important a problem as absolute poverty. But New Class neo-liberals feel that this is an important problem. A gap is important when two vice presidents want to become president of a company. The New Class is always encountering gaps of this kind, but it has nothing to do with absolute poverty.

In the United States, New Class people are usually raised very badly. At campuses like Harvard and Columbia, almost no undergraduates can understand why anyone would have three guns at home. But in middle America it is normal for a boy to be given his first .22 when he is 12 years old, and more dangerous weapons as he grows older. These are important rites of passage toward maturity for about half the young men of America. But New Class young people are taught that guns are sado-masochistic devices, evidence of latent homosexuality, or similar fantasies. Traditionally, in most societies, adulthood was reached at 12 or 13; this is why confirmation and Bar Mitzvah occur at this age, for example. Voting is not permitted until 18 or 21 because most cultures want the citizen to have five to seven years of adult experience before exercising suffrage.

The kids who know nothing about guns are almost exclusively upper-middle class people. They have almost never had to wait as long as a year before obtaining something reasonable, like a bicycle at the age of ten. Twice a year, at Christmas and at birthdays, the parents get together to buy their kids every material object they could possibly want. As a result, upper-middle class kids miss out on the important truth that life can be unfair, that gaps separate wants from reality.

This goes on past the age of 21. This attitude was evident in the non-negotiable demands put forward by radical youth in the late 1960s. Minority youth made "union type" demands that could be delivered, like better beds, or more scholarships. But the white SDS kids wanted to change humanity overnight.

Upper-middle class kids are often out of touch with reality, especially in the Atlantic-Protestant community and Japan; this is less true in Catholic countries like France and Italy. The strength of George Wallace stemmed largely from ordinary Americans who believed that he was addressing issues that bothered them. This is important because it shows that, in our society, alienation comes from the Right rather than the Left. The fact that Billy Graham is consistently found by the Gallup Poll to be the second most admired man in America suggests that the media do not determine America's attitudes. The average American is much less susceptible to words and symbols than the New Class itself. This shows up in Orwell's 1984, where double-think is a monopoly of New Class types. But the New Class assumes that, since they are affected by propaganda, less well educated people must be even more susceptible to it. However, words are not the lifeblood of most human beings. Since the media are not as important as the New Class thinks, Jimmy Carter is making a mistake when he tries to be a media hero. This is not the best way to get votes.

The trouble is that the New Class isn't dealing with the real issues troubling our society. Thus, the cliche that "New York City is ungovernable" is nonsense. The truth is that it can be governed well or badly. New York, of course, has some serious problems, like unemployment among black teenagers. But this problem has more to do with education than with the recession. Instead of doing something about achievement levels in the schools, HEW is preoccupied with such marginal issues as social balance in faculties and women school principals. This reflects an unrealistic attitude that characterizes many neo-liberal members of the New Class.

This inability to cope with real problems is rather typical of our society today. The snail darter and the Furbish Lousewart are important examples of environmental extremism. They are species of fish and flora which are supposedly endangered by major construction projects. Under present United States law, these projects must be stopped unless these species can be shown to exist elsewhere. In some cases, people are actually exterminating endangered species in order to head off environmental protection problems. Environmental standards will end up being more like the $140 French meal. Since our society is rich, it is willing to pay a high price for clean air and clean water.

It is hard to see how a $2 trillion economy can be operated adequately under current regulatory conditions. For example, no new construction will be permitted after July 1979 in any region of the United States which has neither met prevailing standards for clean air and water, nor come up with a satisfactory plan to do so. This is the law. No one, or almost no one, seems to take this prospect seriously as yet. The assumption is that the law will be changed before the deadline is reached.   But this bizarre kind of thing is not the heart of the problem.   It is simply that <u>current</u> regulations do not permit the economy to operate adequately.   Most of the relevant regulations are mainly environmental, but those on food are subjecting the country to something like a sales tax which is closer to twenty percent than five percent.   Most of these extra costs could be avoided without great risk to society.

When a system is legitimate, the people who run it don't have to worry about basic issues.   This is the job of intellectuals, and this division of labor is useful.   When the system is under attack, however, the people who run a legitimate system may not know how to come to its defense.   Something like this happened when General Eisenhower lost an ideological argument with Marshal Zhukov in Berlin.   Arguments which show the positive side of the gun culture are an example of an issue requiring much sophistication.   Unless the people who run the country are articulate in defense of the programs they favor, the programs may be lost.

This is why winning debates is important.   A typical New Class "public interest" group is articulate and well-prepared to debate any issue which it cares about.   By contrast, the business or government agency which is pressing for action is in a weak position.   They look self-interested and have less time to do their homework.   For this reason, such debates are normally won by the so-called public interest group.   This imbalance might be overcome if the public understood that New Class people have the same biases and narrow self-interest as any other group in our society.   These people are handicapped by the kind of educated incapacity that is outlined in figure 1.5.

If these points are really understood, then the neo-liberal New Class and other groups would be on a more equal footing when it came to controversy.   Thus, being articulate is not the only issue.   This kind of change is already under way; the term New Class, in this meaning, is becoming better known in our society.   This is a step in the right direction, but it's not likely to redress the imbalance between New Class people and the rest of United States society.

Many well-educated upper middle class Americans are unable to understand simple issues clearly which are easily understood by most so-called middle Americans. Some reasons for this phenomenon are listed in 1.

Even in their own fields, experts often show very poor judgment. 2, 3, and 4 list some issues which are generally misunderstood by some groups in United States society.

(1) WHY "EDUCATED INCAPACITY?"

   a. OVERUSE OF ACCUSTOMED SKILLS OR FORMULATIONS
   b. PAROCHIAL PROFESSIONAL EMPHAIS
   c. ORGANIZATIONAL CONSTRAINTS OR COMMITMENTS
   d. MISPLACED GLAMOUR OR INCENTIVES
   e. INSUFFICIENT ABILITY TO MOTIVATE OR BE CREATIVE
   f. IDEOLOGICAL (POLITICAL OR APOLITICAL) BIASES
   g. CLASS AND "ETHNIC" INTERESTS, VALUES AND ATTITUDES
   h. LACK OF REALITY TESTING
   i. WISHFUL OR DESPERATE THINKING
   j. EXCESSIVE GUILT, ANXIETY OR OTHER EMOTIONS
   k. OTHER EFFECTS OF HIGH CULTURE POLITICAL MILIEU
   l. JUST PLAIN IGNORANCE

(2) MISUNDERSTOOD "MIDDLE AMERICA" ISSUES

   a. LAW AND ORDER
   b. BUSING
   c. BASIC ATTITUDE TOWARD NEGRO
   d. GUN LAWS AND OTHER GUN ISSUES
   e. PORNOGRAPHY ISSUES
   f. SEX EDUCATION IN PUBLIC SCHOOLS
   g. SCHOOL TAX REVOLT
   h. ATTITUDE TOWARD FLAG, RELIGION, FIGHTING WORDS, ETC.
   i. ATTITUDES TOWARD VIOLENT PROTEST AND PARTICULARLY DEMOCRACY
   j. HYPOCRISY
   k. GRAFT VS. CORRUPTION
   l. BACKLAST AGAINST NEGROES

(3) MISUNDERSTOOD DEVELOPMENT ISSUES

   a. MISEMPHASIS ON INCOME GAPS AND MAL-DISTRIBUTION
   b. OTHER MISUNDERSTANDINGS OF CURRENT SITUATION--E.G., ALLEGED PREVALENCE OF HUNGER
   c. ALMOST COMPLETE FAILURE TO CELEBRATE SUCCESSES
      1. DECADE OF DEVELOPMENT
      2. GREEN REVOLUTION
      3. MEETING OF DEVELOPMENT GOALS
   d. RELATIVE FAILURE TO RECOGNIZE HOW MUCH EASIER DEVELOPMENT IS THAN UPHEAVAL
   e. SIDEWISE IN TECHNOLOGY ISSUES

(4) OTHER LARGELY MISUNDERSTOOD ISSUES

   a. CURRENT MONETARY CRISIS
   b. MANY INFLATION ISSUES
   c. URBAN SPRAWL
   d. CRISIS OF U.S. CITIES
   e. RURAL INSURGENCY
   f. RURAL COUNTER-INSURGENCY
   g. OTHER LESSONS AND EVENTS IN VIETNAM
   h. LIKELIHOOD AND CHARACTERISTICS OF NUCLEAR WAR
   i. PROBLEMS OF DETERRENCE
   j. POST-INDUSTRIAL ECONOMY ISSUES
   k. TREATMENT OF CRIME, DRUGS, ETC. AS A PUNISHABLE DEVIATION
   l. FREE WILL VS. PREDESTINATION
   m. MASLOW HIERARCHY OF NEEDS

Fig. 1.5. Educated Incapacity

2 The Preoccupation with Food Safety

Marylin Chou

Food safety has become one of the major concerns of the American public over the past fifteen years. A vocal sector of the public believes that the quality of our food has deteriorated because of the use of agricultural chemicals in growing food and of additives in processing food. They suggest that processed foods, because of their sugar, salt, fat, and additive components, are responsible for increases in the major killer diseases. In response to these concerns, there has been a proliferation of government agencies, new regulations, Congressional committees, and industry-wide activity. The U.S. Department of Agriculture's new Food Safety and Quality Service, and the industry supported Food Safety Council are just a few examples of these efforts. This paper examines why food safety has become so important an issue at a time when our food supply is, for the most part, safer than ever before.

How did this emotionalism towards food come about? A number of causes are evident. First, and most important, is that our affluence, our longer life expectancy, and our leisure time afford us the ability to be concerned with quality of life issues such as the environment, pollution, and conservation. Ease of earning a good living with a relatively high degree of security means that people can turn to other pursuits and concerns. Our food supply is no longer completely subject to the whims of nature, because we are able to exercise a measure of control over nature's hazards. Nowhere is this clearer than in agriculture. For instance, our farmers have become so productive that we are far removed from the days when we worried if we would have enough food to take us through the winter.

In fact, our farmers, representing less than four percent of our labor force, produce the food needs of one fourth of the world's population. This increased productivity has occurred mainly since 1950 with greater mechanization, improved seed varieties, widespread use of agricultural chemicals, and a systems approach to farming.

ADVANCES IN AGRICULTURAL PRODUCTIVITY
AND FOOD PROCESSING

Our economy and standard of living have developed to a stage of well being that we can now afford to be concerned about unknowns and risks which may or may not affect us and future generations. Our abundance has given us the ability to focus our concerns beyond the immediate "hand to mouth" need which challenged our great grand-parents. Instead we have the luxury to worry about how today's farming practices may be damaging tomorrow's environment and health. These concerns are legitimate, but represent those which only an affluent society can afford. Today we question whether agricultural chemicals are harmful to our health, while at the same time we enjoy the benefits these chemicals have made possible. Since 1950, the widespread use of chemical fertilizers has increased yields by over 50 percent, and helped to decrease the cost of food. The average American now spends 17 percent of his disposable income on food, compared to 22 percent in 1950 and 70 percent in 1776.

This ability to tame nature has caused today's generation, unfamiliar with her destructive capabilities, to view nature as only good, kind, safe, wholesome and superior. A cult has been built around the theme: "It it's natural, it must be good for you." The desire to return to nature ignores the progress Americans have made from concern over obtaining enough food to survive, to concern over food as it relates to our well being. We have graduated from anxiety over quantity to concern over quality.

The increasing concern over food safety and nutritional quality has resulted in an increasingly widespread misconception that organically grown foods are more nutritious, safer, and of higher quality than those grown with agricultural chemicals. The antagonism toward agricultural chemicals and food additives has led some to condemn all chemicals, including fertilizers, and to call for a return to a "natural" system of food production.

This misconception is dispelled by the fact that plants are only able to take up elements in their inorganic forms. Therefore, organic matter which is added to soil must be reduced by soil microorganisms into these inorganic forms for them to be usable (see chapter 18). The nutritive value of a plant is not determined by whether the fertilizer applied is organic or inorganic. Since plants can only use elements in their inorganic form, the determining factors are genetic makeup, climate, light, location, and the kind and amount of basic nutrients available. Once the plant is harvested, storage conditions are key to maintaining nutrient value. All foods deteriorate in quality during storage: Fresh foods have the shortest shelf life due to microbial decay, as well as chemical and physical changes which reduce quality and nutrient value. Many green vegetables lose 50 percent of their vitamin C in two to three days at 77 F.

Not only have the American farmers' productivity removed our concern for enough food, but also technological advances in food processing have concurrently provided us with unparalleled varieties of food. Moreover, improved transportation and refrigeration have made it possible to eat seafood, fresh fruits, and vegetables, once considered seasonal, throughout the year. In 1941 the average grocery store carried 1500 food items; today, estimates range from 11,000 to 39,000 depending on the size of store or supermarket chain (see chapter 4, p. 61).

Better processes have made foods safer, more attractive, more nutritious, and in many instances less expensive. Basically, food processing aims to preserve food and make it safe from existing hazards. For example, uncooked soybeans contain chemicals that prevent protein digestion and can destroy red blood cells. The heating process destroys these factors. Refrigeration, canning, packaging and other preservation techniques suppress contamination by microbial toxins which might generate toxic substances. Food processing's other achievements in providing convenience or attractiveness are secondary. The canning industry's record of safety is exemplary in that since 1940 it has produced more than 800 billion containers of food with only five known deaths attributable to botulism from that food. (1) During the same period, 700 deaths have resulted from ingesting home canned foods. (2)

Food borne diseases are as much a concern today, as they have been in the past. New York City health authorities estimate that food poisoning is second only to the common cold as a cause of lost time from school and work. (3) What are the sources of food poisoning? Meats, poultry, fish, shellfish and dairy products are responsible for about two thirds of food borne illnesses. Prepared dishes, salads, specialty items and other foods account for the remaining one third. And where is food poisoning most apt to occur? Food service establishments such as schools, hospitals, and restaurants are responsible for 73 percent of the outbreaks, homes for 22 percent and food processing establishments for five percent. (4)

Statistics indicate, therefore, that threats to food safety are more apt to come from mishandling of raw or "natural" foods rather than processed foods. In fact, many "natural" foods contain a variety of substances which are potentially harmful if consumed in large quantities over a short time. Solanine is among the 154 naturally occurring chemical compounds making up the potato. If ten times the normal amount of potatoes are consumed at one sitting, enough solanine is present to be toxic to a human.

Natural foods may be poisonous, either inherently, such as in some species of mushrooms or because of the presence of natural contaminants such as some molds in grains. Moreover, some constituents of natural food interfere with the absorption or utilization of specific nutrients. For instance, clams and mussels, as well as certain species of fish, have enzymes which destroy the vitamin thiamine. Phytic acid present in whole wheat, oatmeal and other cereal grains interferes with the absorption of zinc and iron in unleavened products. If the standards used to test man made chemicals were applied to "natural" foods, many natural foods would be banned. (5) For a chemical substance to be allowed as a food additive, only 1/100 of the dosage used to produce an adverse affect on animals can be used for human consumption.

Because we know more about deliberate additives than naturally occurring toxicants, the Food and Drug Administration has placed additives last as a potential source of food related risks. (6)

1) food borne disease

2) malnutrition

3) environmental contaminants

4) naturally occurring toxicants

5) pesticide residues

6) deliberate additives

The concern over food safety and quality has muddied the distinction between safety and nutrition. Safe foods are not necessarily nutritious; while nutritious foods can also present certain hazards. Vitamin D is considered essential for human health and development, yet only five times the recommended daily intake is toxic in some individuals. As we begin to see a stronger link between diet and health, food becomes a source of suspicion, as do those who produce it. (See figure 2.1 for contrasting viewpoints on safety.)

Another reaon for concern over food safety during the last quarter of the century relates to a new time scale. Whereas in the past, new food processing techniques and additives took centuries to introduce, the time scale of introduction has been reduced to decades or less. The time to judge exposure to these new chemical combinations or new products has simultaneously been shortened. (7) The rise in numbers of new additives has also caused concern, although in recent years the rate has been declining because of stringent regulations. Sixty seven new additives were approved by the Food and Drug Administration between 1968 and 1975 compared to 303 between 1958 and 1967. (8)

CULTURAL CHANGES AFFECTING THE FOOD INDUSTRY

In view of these advances in agricultural and food processing techniques, why has food safety become such an emotional issue in recent years? According to a recent survey "Consumerism at the Crossroads," food manufacturers are heading the list of those industries picked by consumers and activists for future consumer action. (9) Why has the food industry become the number one target? The answer lies in a number of social, cultural, economic, and political changes which have occurred over the past fifty years.

As society has become more urbanized, most people have become more dependent on others to produce their food. This dependency has led to resentment and mistrust of the food industry, and a yearning for

JAMES S. TURNER

DETERIORATING AMERICAN HEALTH?

THE FDA WILL NOT ACKNOWLEDGE THE RELATIONSHIP BE-
TWEEN DETERIORATING AMERICAN HEALTH AND THE LIMIT-
ED AVAILABILITY OF SAFE AND WHOLESOME FOOD. IN
FACT, AMERICAN FOOD CONSUMPTION PATTERNS PLAY AN
IMPORTANT ROLE IN THE NATION'S DISGRACEFULLY HIGH
INFANT MORTALITY RATE, LOW RISE IN LIFE EXPEC-
TANCY, AND SEEMINGLY INSOLUBLE PROBLEMS OF
STROKE, HEART DISEASE AND CANCER.

SOURCE: THE CHEMICAL FEAST, GROSSMAN PUBLISHERS,
         NEW YORK, 1970, p. 67.

DONALD KENNEDY, COMMISSIONER OF FOOD AND DRUGS

I THINK THE PROBLEMS WITH WHICH SCIENCE DOES WORST
ARE THE PROBLEMS OF ITS OWN MAKING. WE HAVE NOT
DEVISED ADEQUATE METHODS TO OPTIMIZE THE TRANSFER
OF KNOWLEDGE FROM RESEARCH TO APPLICATION...

THE MAGNITUDE OF THE EFFORT WE ARE NOW EXPENDING
IN DEALING WITH THE AFTERMATH OF THE REVOLUTION
IN SYNTHETIC ORGANIC CHEMISTRY IS A GOOD EXAMPLE
WE HAVE A TOXIC-CHEMICALS PROBLEM OF TERRIBLE
MAGNITUDE, AND WE MUST NOW TRAIN ARMIES OF TOXI-
COLOGISTS AND ANALYTICAL CHEMISTS TO DEAL WITH
THE ESSENTIALLY UNREGULATED OUTCOME OF OUR
ENTRANCEMENT WITH THAT CHEMISTRY.

SOURCE: "FORUM: THE KEY CHALLENGES," THE
         NEW YORK TIMES, TUESDAY, JANUARY 2, 1979,
         p. C1.

SAFETY IN NUMBERS

FROM THE TOXIOLOGICAL POINT OF VIEW THERE IS
LESS LIKELIHOOD OF ANY EXPOSURE, OR OF HIGH
OR CUMULATIVE DOSE LEVELS BEING ATTAINED IF A
WIDE RANGE OF SUBSTANCES IS AVAILABLE FOR
USE.

SOURCE: THE JOINT FAO/WHO EXPERT COMMITTEE
         ON FOOD ADDITIVES, 1967

CAROL T. FREEMAN, ASSISTANT SECRETARY OF THE
USDA

WE HAVE BEEN SO SUCCESSUL IN USING CHEMICALS
TO INCREASE PRODUCTION, RETARD SPOILAGE AND
PRESERVING FOODS THAT WE MUST NOW BE CONCERNED
WITH THE HEALTH EFFECTS OF CHEMICALS THEM-
SELVES.

SOURCE: REMARKS DELIVERED BEFORE THE ANNUAL
         CONFERENCE OF THE AMERICAN COUNCIL
         ON CONSUMER INTERESTS, CHICAGO,
         APRIL 20, 1978, p. 2.

CHEMICALS IN THE FOOD SUPPLY

CHEMICAL ADDITIVES COMPRISE A SMALL FRACTION
OF OUR TOTAL FOOD CONSUMPTION. THE CONCEN-
TRATION OF ANY SINGLE TOXIC SUBSTANCE IN ANY
COMMONLY ACCEPTED FOOD IS USUALLY VERY LOW.
INDIVIDUAL TOXICANTS OF DIFFERENT CHEMICALS
INGESTED CANNOT BE ADDED UP TO A TOTAL TOXI-
CITY FOR THAT DAY. IT IS POSSIBLE TO HAVE
ANTAGONISTIC INTERACTIONS BETWEEN CHEMICAL
SUBSTANCES IN FOODS, SO THAT THE TOXICITY
OF ONE ELEMENT IS OFFSET BY THE PRESENCE OF
AN ADEQUATE AMOUNT OF ANOTHER ELEMENT, E.G.
IODINE INHBITS THE ACTION OF SOME GOITER
CAUSING AGENTS...

THE REAL CHALLENGE WE FACE IS THE QUESTION
OF THE LONG-TERM TOXICITY OF THE NATURAL
CHEMICAL COMPOUNDS OF OUR FOODS. IT IS MOST
IMPORTANT TO DETERMINE THE EFFECTS THAT
MIGHT RESULT IN NORMAL DIETARY USES, SINCE
THEY WOULD BE EXPECTED TO AFFECT THE LARGEST
NUMBER OF PEOPLE.

THE PRESENCE OF SUCH ABUNDANCE OF TOXIC
CHEMICALS IS REASON ENOUGH TO EXERCISE
CAUTION IN ALLOWING THE ENTRY OF ANY ADDI-
TIONAL POTENTIALLY HARMFUL AGENTS INTO THE
FOOD SUPPLY. THE POSSIBILITY EXISTS THAT
TWO OR MORE FOOD COMPONENTS (NATURAL OR
ADDED) COULD INTERACT SYNERGISTICALLY TO
CREATE GREATER HAZARD THAN EITHER COMPONENT
ALONE. NO PRACTICAL HAZARD BASED ON THIS
SITUATION, HOWEVER, IS KNOWN TO EXIST, NOR
HAVE THERE YET BEEN FOUND ANY OTHER DEFINITE
DIETARY HAZARDS BASED ON TOXICOLOGIC INTER-
ACTIONS BETWEEN NATURAL FOOD COMPONENTS
AND FOOD ADDITIVES OR PESTICIDES.

SOURCE: "NATURALLY OCCURRING TOXICANTS IN
         FOOD," A REPORT BY INSTITUTE OF
         FOOD TECHNOLOGISTS, MARCH 1975.

Fig. 2.1. The food safety controversy.

a return to the good old days and ways. Popular books favoring a return to small self sufficient farms and diets of our grandparents have blamed technology for degrading the food supply. Representative of this attitude is the following statement from Jim Hightower's Eat Your Heart Out. (10)

> Our meek acceptance of giantism, technologies, and of corporate systems, has cost us more than eternally rising prices and deteriorating quality. We are paying with our ability to exercise basic control over something as essential as dinner.

Obviously, it is not only the quality of food which disturbs this group, but the system and technological advances. They are disaffected, alienated, and disappointed with an environment that is becoming increasingly man made, and yet, increasingly frustrating and incomprehensible. They protest against a world that seems "unnatural," inequitable, and controlled by man and machines. (11)

The concept of control seems to be a major concern. The disaffected feel that they have lost control, and they have more faith in nature controlling than man and machines. Because most of this group are under 40 years old, they are too young to know how farmers could lose their crops overnight from plagues, pests, and floods.

Those who feel they have lost control also espouse the concept of "small is beautiful and more efficient." They cannot cope with society or recognize our present economic and social system. Their mistrust and misunderstanding of technology is illustrated in the following quote:

> "Throughout the food economy, efficient and productive people are being displaced by technologies of the oligopolist.... Together they produced massive displacement in the food industry.... First, farm workers were replaced by crop chemicals and harvesting machinery...." (12)

This statement is misleading because it ignores the fact that farmers chose to adopt more productive, labor saving methods. Time and time again effective demand determines the adoption of new technologies. Farmers are willing to risk using new seeds, practices, and machines only when they judge their investment in them to be profitable. These are conscious decisions made by the farmer, not acts foisted upon them by chemical companies or tractor manufacturers.

This disaffected group, in general, lacks scientific background, resists science, and rejects man made goods. For these reasons they refuse to accept the fact that all foods are composed of chemical, and that the body cannot distinguish between natural or synthesized vitamins.

Another characteristic of this group has been an antimaterialistic attitude combined with a concern with the self, sometimes encompassing mystic, and transcendental values. This preoccupation with the self may run counter to traditional inner directed attitudes associated with duty, self sacrifice, the work ethic and achievement. (13)

The negative attitude of this group towards technological advancement and economic growth has caused an erosion of will, optimism and confidence in future scientific developments. (14)   Although there is need for caution and prudent concern, this loss of nerve and morale resulting from hostility to progress can be counterproductive to all. Moreover, the "limits-to-growth" mentality contains certain elements of self fulfilling prophecies. If we are dominated by a feeling of fear, a paralyzing inertia and guilt could prevent us from dealing constructively with technological problems.

SOCIAL CHANGES AFFECTING THE FOOD INDUSTRY

Social changes which have occurred over the last twenty years and trends which may prevail in the coming decade will also affect the food industry.   Family size has steadily decreased, so that we will see smaller family units but increased number of households. In 1977, 66 percent of the adult population (14 years and older) were either childless couples or singles. (15) (See table 2.1 for further details.)

We will continue to see an increasing proportion of working women, comprised of singles as well as working mothers.   Double income households will increase for an increasingly larger number of families. As individuals become more affluent their interests move from quantity to quality -from more "steak" to questioning the effects of "too much saturated fat." By contrast, the poor cannot afford to be concerned over such issues, because they are preoccupied with earning a living. The issues relating to the environment were magnified by the energy shortage. The seventies have seen the American consumer move from a "psychology of abundance" to a new "conservation ethic."

Some of the changes in values account for the hostility business is encountering. Although food safety is not a new concern, preoccupation with food safety was probably triggered by the antichemical movement, which was inspired by the publication of Rachel Carson's Silent Spring in 1962, and furthered by the 1969 Santa Barbara oil spill. Heightening public concern over food safety even further, were incidents related to botulinum toxin in canned liver paste, vichyssoise, and mushrooms, the banning of cyclamates, the linking of monosodium glutamate with brain damage and food coloring with hyperkinesis, and the potential carcinogenicity of nitrates and nitrites in meat products. (16) These incidents started a growing political and public tendency to associate food processing with cancer, and the food industry with denutrification. industry with denutrification.

This concern over quality of life issues is manifested in a new emphasis on comfort, safety, health and vocational self actualization. Rights granted to workers are changing as unions, court rulings, and regulatory agencies demand greater protection.   Some measures are long overdue while others appear excessive, particularly to businesses forced to comply with the changes. It is estimated that total federal regulatory activity, including that aimed at food, involves about 3,000

TABLE 2.1.   1977 U.S. Adult Population

		Percent of Total Population
Total persons, 14 years and over	164,935,000	
married persons living with spouse	96,004,000	58.0%
with children	50,214,000	30.4%
without children	45,790,000	27.8%
single persons (widowed, divorced, never married)	68,931,000	41.0%
with children	5,941,000	3.6%
without children	62,990,000	38.2%
Total persons, between 14 and 15 years old	99,456,000	
married persons living with spouse	50,817,000	51.1%
with children	36,958,000	37.2%
without children	13,859,000	13.9%
single persons	48,639,000	48.9%
with children	4,755,000	4.9%
without children	43,884,000	44.1%
Total persons, 45 years and older	65,478,000	
married persons living with spouse	45,188,000	69.0%
with children	13,256,000	20.2%
without children	31,932,000	48.8%
single persons	20,290,000	31.0%
with children	1,186,000	1.8%
without children	19,104,000	29.2%

Note: All children are aged 18 years and under.

Source: Census Bureau, Dept. of Commerce, Current Population Reports, Series P20, #326.

new regulations proposed annually, and an additional 4,000 regulations changed. During the period between 1973 and 1977, more regulations, laws and rules were issued than in all the previous 30 years. (17) There are some 38 federal agencies and organizations which affect the food business. Of these, at least two dozen have been created since 1970. These regulatory agencies employ over 100,000 people who are concerned with the handling, grading, labeling and packaging of foods, and safety and sanitary standards of farms and processing plants. (18) In addition, there are also state and local governments which have established regulations to cover local situations. While many of these either duplicate, or are in conflict with, federal regulations and hamper productivity and efficiency throughout the food system; others are important in protecting the health and safety of individuals. (19)

These increasing regulations and legislation designed to protect the public have been costly to both business and the public. Funds normally allocated to research and development of new products and processes have been diverted to defensive research to comply with new regulations. One result is that the choice of products and services is reduced for the public. With worldwide concern over feeding an ever growing population with limited resources, new technologies related to processing, packaging, storage, distribution, safety and nutrition need to be developed which are more efficient in conserving nonrenewable and renewable resources, and which may provide food from underutilized sources. New processes could create lower cost substitutes for expensive animal protein, energy efficient foods or packages, or foods that could reduce the risk of various diseases.

The pace of developing new products has decreased due to the risk, cost and time involved. The average cost of introducing a new chemical into the food supply ranges between one half million dollars and ten million dollars and takes at least five years from research to marketing. (20) Only large companies can contemplate such expenditures in developing products which may or may not reach the market. Regulation has increased the risks and costs of innovation to a point where many food companies consider the potential rewards not worth the effort. (21)

The most obvious costs of regulation are the direct ones - the red tape burden of cost and time of data collecting activities of the government and of business for the government, and the cost of complying with government regulations. (For further discussion on the direct and indirect costs of regulation see chapter 18.)

One serious public cost of misdirected regulations is a confusion in our federal research priorities. Only 1.8 percent of the United States federal research and development budget is allocated to food and agricultural sciences compared to 38 percent in 1940. Basic food research is being neglected not only by industry and government, but also at the university level because of the lack of funding. According to Marcus Karel, Professor of Food Engineering at Massachusetts Institute of Technology: "Out of the top 10 schools in chemical engineering, only one was doing anything that could be related to food. Government funding is focusing more on health sciences with emphasis on toxicology and problems related to the environment. Unfortunately, the bank of basic research upon which applied research is drawn is being depleted and not being restored." (22)

According to a recent study by Edward F. Denison, Senior Fellow of the Brookings Institution, the pace of productivity growth and economic growth has been considerably cut by legislative and social changes of the past decade. The increased business costs involved in compliance with environmental and health protection, as well as crime prevention, has not produced an equivalent rise in output. As a consequence, Denison estimates that output per unit of input was actually cut by half a percentage point in 1975. By contrast, the years 1948 and 1969 showed an average annual growth in output per unit input of 2.1 percent. (23) The Council on Wage and Price Stability estimates an annual increase traceable to health and safety regulation of 0.75 percent in the Consumer Price Index.

More research should be aimed at determining answers to questions such as:

How essential are these regulations to the continued safety and well being of the consumer?

What constraints are imposed by various regulations on system productivity?

What are the costs and benefits of the regulations?

How can the implementation of these regulations be improved so as to facilitate productivity? (24)

In the final analysis, the public bears the costs of these new environmental and safety concerns. Since business cannot afford to operate at a loss, the increased costs to business are passed on to the consumer. A sluggish economy also affects the public adversely in terms of jobs and wages.

THE POLITICIZATION OF FOOD

Because we eat food daily, we tend to assume that we know more about food than simply its taste and cost. Yet the understanding of nutrition, food safety and diet related diseases is still in its infancy. Nutrition has become such a popular subject, however, that it has become a political concern similar to taxes, inflation and unemployment. Distilling scientific facts from political rhetoric becomes, therefore, more difficult, particularly when opportunists make claims which cannot be disproved or proved. Because of advances in scientific techniques, we are now able to detect toxicities to parts per trillion, whereas in 1958, when the Delaney Amendment was enacted, we could only detect toxicities to 50 parts per million. Unfortunately, we are not able to understand how much toxicity is harmful to health, or what the tolerance level is, before a substance becomes carcinogenic, terato-genic, or mutagenic.

The result is that some feel we can only be safe by banning any substance that is suspect, in spite of the fact that dosage determines toxicity. Laws and regulations to protect the safety of our food are based, therefore, on what is not known and on the goal of absolute safety. Not only is Congress involved in enacting laws regarding our food safety, but also the Food and Drug Administration, the Department of Agriculture, the Environmental Protection Agency, the Occupational Safety and Health Administration, U.S. Public Health Service, National Marine and Fisheries Services, and U.S. Treasury and the Federal Trade Commission.

Among the better know regulatory agencies involved with food is the Food and Drug Administration (FDA), the function of which is to protect public health and the consumer's pocketbook. It attributes its expanding regulation of the food industry to several developments in our modern society:

> The rapid increase in the use of the plant protein products, while this technology remains in a very active stage of development;

> Increased use of convenience foods, fabricated foods from new ingredients, and substitute foods have resulted in a need to maintain the nutritional quality of diets when there are changes in food patterns;

> The consumer's reliance on formulated meal replacements as a major source of his dietary intake makes it necessary to assure a more complete spectrum of essential nutrients in meal replace-ments. (25)

The rationale behind the proliferation of regulations is "it is better to be safe than sorry." The lack of knowledge enables decision makers to emphasize certain risks while ignoring certain benefits. It also enables them to use hypotheses to further partisan interest - to soothe or instill fear. A responsibly elected official feels compelled to vote for absolute safety, if his constituents believe in this illusory goal. How could he otherwise risk their lives and votes? Because elected officials must consider their own political risk benefit ratios, they usually prefer to err on the side of being supercautious. The result of this caution is increasing social control and overall planning of the economy. (26)

There are many problems involved in government taking a more active role. Most planners do not know how difficult it is to plan comprehensively, completely or effectively. Furthermore, they do not know how controversial many of the goals and objectives are. (27) Moreover, most of the 8,000 regulations proposed annually are designed by Federal technicians, usually lawyers. They have become such a powerful group that they are now referred to as the fourth branch of government. The policies they formulate can be contradictory, uncoordinated, and at variance with their mandates from Congress. (28)

The food industry must also shoulder the responsibility for some of the emotionalism over food safety. To avoid confrontation, most of the industry has assumed, until recently, an almost invisible profile. While the consumer activists have pleaded their case and presented selected data, the industry has hoped that by ignoring the issues of health and safety they would disappear.

Certain marketing strategies have been short sighted, self defeating, and verging on deception. Recent efforts to cash in on the "natural" food fad, with the proliferation of foods "free of the artificial preservatives," have given the consumer the impression that past processing efforts were harmful and that chemicals are unsafe. Some critics of the food industry trace the industry's decline in credibility to the turn of the century when it became more important to determine what to say about a food product rather than to be concerned about what was in it, or for what it was to be used. (29)

According to the study, Consumerism at the Crossroads, all groups queried, except senior business managers, stated that the single most desirable change in the relationship between business and society is better communications, better understanding, and better cooperation between business and consumers. (30) There is strong consensus in this study that the consumer movement has done more good than harm and that consumers get a better deal as a result. (31) The report indicates that many senior managers seemed to be unaware of the strength of the popular support which the consumer movement enjoys, and they appeared to be out of touch with consumers.

Who speaks or represents the general public? According to Consumerism at the Crossroads, neither the consumer activists, government watchdogs, regulators, or business executives can be regarded as representative of the people. Each group has its own characteristic and its own point of view, depending on the issue. The differences between the consumer activists and those of the consumers, however, are often only a matter of degree. The activists are more extreme in their criticism and in their demands of business. They tend to overestimate the extent to which the public worries. Where the consumer may be most concerned about high prices and products malfunctioning, consumer activists are concerned primarily with legislation focused on safety. This concern has resulted in 33 federal agencies and approximately 400 bureaus and subagencies operating more than 1,000 consumer oriented programs. Consumerism at the Crossroads found that consumer activists want more regulation, business wants less, and the public is fairly evenly divided on the issue of how much regulation - not wanting either more or less.

The gulf between perception and attitude of senior business executives and those of the public is greater and more serious. Business executives greatly underestimate the public's concern about advertising claims, about misleading packaging and labeling, about inadequate guarantees and warranties, and about the number of dangerous products (32) Clearly there is need for better communications and understanding between business and the consumers. Consumerism is not a passing fad. The food industry should address legitimate concerns and issues before they become emotionally charged because legislators must respond to public hysteria. The industry needs to recognize that serving the best interests of consumers can be mutually beneficial. A confident public will be reflected by more rational legislation and an atmosphere more conducive to innovation.

DIET RELATED HEALTH CONCERNS

How does our preoccupation with food safety relate to diet related health concerns? Nutrition is the link between diet and health. Only 30 years ago we were concerned about minimum daily requirements to combat dietary diseases. Today we are concerned about establishing maximum levels of nutrients to prevent diseases linked with dietary affluence or overabundance.

Both cancer and heart diseases tend to be diseases associated with industrialized countries. Death rates from cancer are low in developing countries partly because death registration is not compulsory, not all cases of cancer are diagnosed, and many die of infectious diseases at younger ages than those at which most people get cancer. Heart diseases are also more prevalent among those above 50. There are developing countries today which are still plagued by diseases of malnutrition resulting from poor diets as well as spoiled food and contaminated water. Diarrhea is the major cause of death in five South American nations and is one of the five leading causes of death in seven others. (33)

As our population grows older, we are facing diseases associated with aging, namely cardiovascular disease and cancer. These are the major causes of death today, since deaths from infectious and deficiency diseases have decreased. While the total number of deaths from cardiovascular disease and cancer have increased over the last several decades, the mortality rate expressed on an age adjusted basis has not increased significantly, and, in fact, for cardiovascular disease, has shown a significant reduction. (34) (See table 2.2) Moreover, the incidence of deaths from ten of the fifteen leading causes of death has decreased in the past twelve years. (35)

At the present time there is substantial controversy over the causes of coronary heart disease. Among the many possible causes of heart disease are cholesterol in the diet, saturated fatty acids, hypertension, lack of fiber, obesity, lack of exercise, cigarette smoking, stress, and hereditary factors. Because as many people died of heart disease with low blood cholesterol as did those with high blood cholesterol, many scientists question whether the whole population should be told to reduce their cholesterol intake. Based on the lack of evidence, they believe that dietary intervention should be recommended to only those individuals, between 5 and 20 percent of the population, who have elevated blood lipid problems. There are also some who believe it is the quantity of fat, and not the nature of the fat we eat which makes the difference.

Just as the causes of coronary heart diseases are related to a variety

TABLE 2.2. Leading Causes of U.S. Deaths (per 100,000 Population)

	1960	1965	1970	1972	1973	1974	1975	1976*
DISEASES OF HEART	515.1	510.9	496.0	497.1	494.4	478.2	336.2	338.6
CEREBROVASCULAR DISEASES	108.0	103.7	101.9	102.5	102.1	98.1	91.1	88.1
MALIGNANCIES	149.2	153.5	162.8	166.0	167.3	170.5	171.7	174.6
ACCIDENTS	52.3	55.7	56.4	55.4	55.2	49.5	48.4	46.8
INFLUENZA & PNEUMONIA	37.3	31.9	30.9	30.1	29.8	25.9	26.1	29.3
DIABETES MELLITUS	16.7	17.1	18.9	18.6	18.2	17.7	16.5	16.3
CERTAIN DISEASES OF EARLY INFANCY	37.4	28.6	21.3	16.2	14.5	13.6	12.5	11.1
CIRRHOSIS OF LIVER	11.3	12.8	15.5	15.6	15.9	15.8	14.8	14.5
ARTERIOSCLEROSIS	20.0	19.7	15.6	15.6	15.5	15.3	13.6	13.4
SUICIDE	10.6	11.1	11.6	12.0	12.0	12.1	12.7	11.7
HOMICIDE	4.7	5.5	8.3	9.4	9.8	10.2	n/a	n/a
TUBERCULOSIS	6.1	4.1	2.6	2.1	1.8	1.7	1.6	n/s

* Projected

Note: THE NUMBER OF CANCER DEATHS PER 100,000 HAS INCREASED DUE TO CANCER OF THE LUNG WHICH ROSE FROM 18 DEATHS PER 100,000 IN 1950 TO 53 DEATHS PER 100,000 IN 1975 FOR MEN; AND 4.0 DEATHS PER 100,000 IN 1950 TO 13.0 IN 1975 FOR WOMEN.

Source: STATISTICAL ABSTRACT OF THE U.S., U.S. DEPARTMENT OF COMMERCE, BUREAU OF THE CENSUS; 1976, GOVERNMENT PRINTING OFFICE, WASHINGTON; p. 65.

of factors, so is cancer. Not only may genetics and environment play a major role, but also the degree to which foods are processed, the role of fats, carbohydrates, protein, fiber, tobacco and alcohol in the diet, food storage and preservation practices, deficiencies or surpluses of trace elements and vitamins, the ingestion of naturally occurring carcinogens, and the type of preparation some foods receive, are all considered as possible causes of cancer.

The current fear of cancer, is caused by the realization that we have been widely exposed to an increasing number of synthetic chemical compounds over the past 20 to 25 years and that cancer has the characteristic of latency. From this, some have drawn the conclusion that we may well experience a blossoming of "environmental" cancer. The estimate that 60 to 90 percent of all cancer is related to "environmental" factors is often interpreted to mean that most cancer is caused by synthetic chemicals or air pollution. In fact, these estimates of environmentally induced cancer include all types of cancer not resulting directly from heredity. Environmental factors include smoking, diet and alcohol, which some believe account for more than half of all cancers, as well as health and hygiene, and pollution. Direct occupational exposure is believed to cause from one to five percent of all cancer. (36)

Despite the widespread concern over cancer, statistics indicate that only the death rate from lung cancer, is on the increase, while the age adjusted death rates from other types of cancer have leveled off or even declined (See figure 2.2). Death from cancer of the stomach has declined more than 50 percent for both United States males and females since 1930.

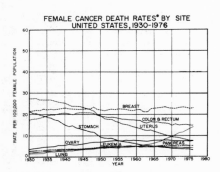

*Rate for the female population standardized for age on the 1940 U. S. population. Sources of Data: National Vital Statistics Division and Bureau of the Census, United States.

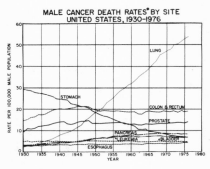

*Rate for the male population standardized for age on the 1940 U. S. population. Sources of Data: National Vital Statistics Division and Bureau of the Census, United States.

Fig. 2.2.

Source: 1979, "Cancer Facts and Figures," American Cancer Society, New York.

We have devoted our past efforts in nutritional education to assuring an adequate diet - one with sufficient proteins, vitamins and minerals. Now we are proposing that much of our ill health today may be due to overnutrition - not simply eating too much but eating too much of specific nutrients, such as fats, salt and sugar. What needs to be emphasized is that the foods are not causing cancer or heart disease, but the excess quantity may be a contributing factor. We need to learn to adjust our food intake to our energy use. Neither our jobs nor our recreation are as physically demanding as are those of our ancestors. Moreover, we live and travel in air conditioned or heated surroundings so that our energy needs have greatly decreased.

The Senate Select Committee on Human Nutrition's labeling of coronary heart diseases and cancer as diet related diseases killing Americans in epidemic proportions has also helped to heighten the public's concern over food safety. Yet, as a nation, we are healthier than ever before. Life expectancy for Americans is not the longest in history, 73.2 years, because we have overcome the major infectious diseases, such as tuberculosis, pneumonia and malaria, and we have virtually eliminated dietary deficiency diseases. Within the last 50 years, average life expectancy has increased by 20 years.

In response to the criticism that our food supply has deteriorated, and that this is responsible for an epidemic of degenerative diseases, Professor A. E. Harper, Chairman of the Department of Nutritional Sciences at the University of Wisconsin, has refuted this by comparing our present nutritional and health status to what existed 60 years ago. With the exception of magnesium, we have greater quantities of essential nutrients in the food supply than we had during the early part of the century. In viewing vital statistics, infant, childhood and maternal mortality rates are at all time lows, although infant and maternal mortality rates are not as low as in countries where comprehensive health care is available to all. The major cause of death for those between ages one and 45 is violence - accidents, suicide and homicide. Only after age 45 do cardiovascular diseases and cancer become the major causes of death. (37)

The previous examples indicate how affluence, manifested by increased agricultural abundance, food variety and improved health, has allowed us to be concerned over what appear to be dangers in our food supply. Our perspective of danger of safety is affected by how removed we are from imminent food shortages and death from infectious diseases and plagues. This removal has been achieved through scientific developments and technological achievements. Yet, ironically, one of the major causes for concern over food safety stems from failure to understand the scientific process.

CONCEPTUAL PROBLEMS WITH ABSOLUTE SAFETY AND RISK/BENEFIT ANALYSIS

The concern by the public for absolute safety represents another misunderstanding of terms. Absolute safety cannot be achieved because nothing is absolutely free of risk. While risk is a measure of the probability and severity of harm to human health, safety is a value judgment, based on personal and social values, of the acceptability of risk. (38) A substance as harmless as water is safe until you drink too much in a very short period of time. Vitamins and minerals are essential to maintain good health, but excessive amounts of some vitamins can be harmful. The amount and duration of time in which the substance is consumed are two factors that determine the degree of safety or risk.

Also, reactions to substances differ according to many variables, such as whether the subject is animal, human, male, female, old, young, healthy, or frail, allergic or non allergic. To determine the safety of any food is to test for the hazards we consider likely today. If the substance in question appears free from those hazards, it is considered safe at the moment. Moreover, the bioavailability of specific nutrients in different processed and unprocessed foods varies according to the individual ingesting the substance. Safety, therefore, is a relative attribute that can change from time to time, because other hazards may arise in the future. Foods free from of carcinogens may be considered safe today, but new fears regarding mutagens may classify them as unsafe tomorrow. On the other hand, with increasing scientific knowledge, substances once considered harmful, may, in small doses, actually be beneficial. This is the case of the substance selenium.

The counterpart to risk is efficacy - the measure of the probability and size of beneficial effects. The corresponding value judgment is the benefit - the desirability of the efficacies.

Although it is impossible to measure safety, it is possible to measure risk. Statistical tools are used to weigh or assign probabilities to the chance of being exposed to a situation, chemical, etc. as well as the chance of harm from the exposure. Furthermore, one can compare risks by relating them to exposure by a common denominator. The most familiar comparison is that of accidents for different modes of travel expressed as rates per hundred million passenger miles.

Because we now recognize that many problems cannot be resolved by common sense management, we increasingly turn to more rigorous, orderly means of problem resolution. One such means, albeit very primitive today, is risk benefit analysis. The objective is to quantify all relevant variables in order to calculate the optimum solution for the given situation. The problem is that so many of the variables do not lend themselves to accurate measurement. What dollar value does one put on human life or beauty of surroundings?

In the case of agricultural chemicals and the environment, there are many such intangible "externalities." They are intangible because they are human feelings about such future dangers as environmental disruption, mutations and genetic damage; or the variable(s) may be tangible, but not quantifiable because of lack of reliable data or absence of any data. This is particularly true when dealing with environmental effects.

Unfortunately, risk/benefit decisions related to food cannot be made until we develop scientific technology which enables us to fully understand the risks involved. For example, the levels of hazard in the use of materials such as food additives is extremely low, and for many substances information is lacking. Furthermore, benefits are difficult to evaluate because they cannot be measured, and what may be a benefit to one person is not necessarily a benefit to another. How does one measure benefit in terms of palatability or aesthetics? Where may economic gains be expressed in dollars, in what unit can convenience or nutrition be expressed?

In determining health related risks, however, it is possible to distinguish between those which are controllable and those which are not. Controllable risks are those for which risks have been clearly proven, and for which one can exercise control, such as obesity, smoking, and alcohol abuse. Uncontrollable risks involve the unproven and uncontrollable gray areas such as diet, environment, synergistic reaction, and antagonistic effects of two or more chemical compounds, delayed effect hazards, age, sex, and genetics. Therefore, people who overeat, smoke, and drink alcohol in excess have made individual decisions on risks and benefits and have undertaken to assume the risks.

As foods once considered safe are banned by legislation or regulation, consumers lose confidence in regulatory bodies such as the FDA and USDA, as well as in science. Unfortunately the public fails to recognize that more accurate information and evaluations are possible as scientific evidence accumulates, and new techniqes of analysis are developed. The evaluation process is an on going one which draws on scientific competence and experience, mature judgment and full possession of all existing data. Moreover, there is need for flexibility and periodic assessment. For example, unexpected new evidence or new techniques may prove today's view of a given risk benefit balance wrong. Risk benefit analysis, however, does help state the issues clearly by organizing relevant information, identifying variables, tangible and intangible, and by defining alternative courses of action. Furthermore, as the public better understands risk, industry will have a strong new responsibility to quantify benefits in terms that are real and rational. (39)

Risk benefit analysis, if equally comprehensive in all respects and if carried out recognizing the dynamic context of natural systems, can be very valuable in comparing similar materials. This is extremely important because "comparison of parallels" is a powerful means of anticipating future problems.

The recommended banning of saccharin in 1977 forced many consumers to attempt for the first time to weigh risks and benefits in light of existing information. For the overweight and the diabetic, the objective of total safety was abandoned. People were willing to accept the risks to obtain benefits that could not be obtained in less risky ways. There was recognition that the size of the dose can make the difference, and that substances which cause cancer in animals do not necessarily cause cancer in humans.

Bernard Cohen, a physicist at the University of Pennsylvania, recently attempted a risk benefit study of saccharin, comparing the risks resulting from obesity and bladder cancer. Using the statistics from saccharin studies in Canada, he estimated that one can of diet soft drink a day reduces average life expectancy for an overweight person by two days. The weight gain from an extra calorie a day for a lifetime also reduces life expectancy by two days. With these estimates, Cohen concluded that if a diet drink reduces caloric intake by more than one calorie a day, then its benefits outweigh its risks. (40)

A scientific report on saccarin released by the National Academy of Sciences in the fall of 1978 concluded that saccharin does cause cancer in laboratory animals, and is probably a "low potency" cancer causer in people. The report, commissioned by the Food and Drug Administration, suggested that saccharin may be more dangerous as a "promoter" of other carcinogens than as a cancer causer itself. The report recommended that more research is needed to assess just how much of a risk it poses for people, how it promotes other substances' carcinogenicity, and how it affects the unborn. (41)

THE TECHNOLOGICAL GAP

As mentioned earlier, more sophisticated techniques have enabled us to detect minute quantities of toxic substances. For some perspective on the measurement capabilities of these techniques, one part per billion is the equivalent of one inch in 16,000 miles, or one minute in 2,000 years. A part per trillion would be equivalent to one grain of sugar in an olympic sized swimming pool. (42) This measurement capability has made possible higher standards of safety at a time when more additives are being used to meet the demands brought on by urbanization and the desire for variety, convenience, and foods tailored to lower calories and fat content. In some instances knowledge of the presence of traces of impurities has given the impression that danger pervades the entire food supply. Unfortunately this impression has caused needless anxiety since our bodies have the ability to deal with certain levels of toxicity.

At the present stage of scientific knowledge, our ability to detect toxicities is far greater than our ability to comprehend how much toxicity is harmful to human health. This lag has caused our attention to focus on a host of unanswered questions regarding additives, such as:

1. Is there a safe minimum level of any particular chemical used as a food additive, and is there a safe level of cumulative exposure to such chemicals?

2. Can two or more components (natural and/or synthetic) interact synergistically to create greater hazard than either component alone? (43)

3. What might be the long term effects over 20 to 30 years of exposure to very low levels of known carcinogens?

There are also a number of problems about testing techniques (not the least of which is that the ethical consideration limiting the use of human volunteers in biological research has virtually eliminated studies to determine possible harmful effects of food excesses)

1. The validity of animal test results applied to humans;

2. The fact that people are biologically different and may respond differently to various chemicals;

3. The variability of the human diet, that is, some people ingest more than the accepted daily intake;

4. Infants and elderly may be more sensitive to a particular chemical;

5. Additives are tested on healthy animals, people with disease may respond differently;

6. The chemical might react with other components in the human diet not present in an animal's test diet and form a new chemical that may be more hazardous;

7. The microbial flora in the intestines of a human and a test animal are different. These microbes could possibly change the chemical into a more or less toxic form, or even into a nontoxic form. (44)

In an effort to deal with these unknowns, government regulations have been tailored to try to manage uncertainties. The 1958 Food Additives Amendment to the Federal Food, Drug and Cosmetics Act of 1938 contains a clause, often referred to as the Delaney Amendment. The Amendment, which has the objective of absolute safety and tries to deal with what is not known, states: "No additive shall be deemed to be safe if it is found to induce cancer when ingested by man or animal, or if it is found, after tests which are appropriate for the evaluation of the safety of food additives, to induce cancer in man or animals." (45) The Delaney Amendment has raised questions among those who feel that it is too restrictive. They argue that unusually large amounts and unrealistic methods of animal testing are not necessarily relevant to human tolerances. Moreover, they believe that a safe level of the substance can be selected with confidence on the basis of current knowledge.

In view of what is not currently known, the Delaney Amendment and subsequent legislation pertaining to food safety, have been based on three fallacious assumptions, namely: (46)

1. Appropriate tests and techniques exist for the evaluation of hazard.

2. A zero effect level can be established.

3. A risk benefit ratio can be calculated so that decisions concerning the use of specific substances can be made objectively.

The establishment of a zero effect level involves the phenomena of thresholds. The primary question is whether there is a threshold for carcinogenic action in humans, below which the human body can take care of itself, or whether the presence of one active carcinogenic molecule endangers cellular organization.

Because medical evidence regarding nutrition, food safety, and dietary links to diseases is in its infancy, definite answers are not yet available. Yet we are a society accustomed to simple, direct answers. And when nutrition is everyone's concern, policy makers are caught between giving answers based on consensus or acknowledging what is known and not known. When answers based on consensus, premature conclusions can assuage the public but destroy future credibility. Herein lies one of the main differences. Policymakers implicitly deal with probabilities to determine costs and anticipated benefits; while scientists are more concerned with conclusive proof. This difference can further confuse the public because not only do scientists disagree openly, but they do not take positions until they are satisfied that the evidence has substantiated their theory. The lack of understanding of how the scientific process works combined with the pressure of adversary interests often cause political and social decisions to outweigh scientific fact. Tentative research results, such as the dietary cholesterol hypothesis, and the relationship of sugar to heart disease, become manipulated for political purposes and get presented as proven facts.

A scientist reaches a conclusion by evaluating all the pertinent evidence to attempt to prove his theory is correct. When evidence negates or discredits his theory, the hypothesis has to be revised to be consistent with the actual observation. For the policymaker and public this can cause confusion. Yet it is the nature of science that scientific data is always being generated in the development of new knowledge. As it progresses, new evidence based on new technologies may be revealed. Pronouncements about discoveries of toxic substances in fish, meat or other foods cause consumers to believe these substances are new and all pervasive in the food chain. These substances may have existed in these foods for a long time, but improved scientific techniques and increased observations have been responsible for detecting them.

There is also a difference between how the public and scientists perceive safety. The public demands safety so that their life and the life of their descendants can be healthy, happy and complete. (47) As people become less vulnerable to diseases and other natural hazards, the risks from man made hazards gain importance, and people worry about adverse effects they were unaware of until a few years ago. (48) The only form of safety the scientist can offer is that which is free from the hazards he can measure with traditional approaches, whereas the public demands that safety ensure the broader quality of life.

To establish scientifically defensible criteria for food, research in food safety in the coming decade needs to be directed towards developing rapid procedures for detecting and quantifying food poisoning organisms and their toxins as they affect the host, as well as sensitive analytical methods to determine the extent to which environmental contaminants enter our food, and sensible methods for measuring their effect on man. (49)   As the technological gap narrows, hopefully the preoccupation with food safety will be placed in perspective.   Thus, we should be capable of understanding the benefits as well as the risks of various food components as they relate to health, recognizing that safety is only one factor influencing food choice, and diet is only one of many factors affecting health.

NOTES

(1) "The Risk/Benefit Concept as Applied to Food," A Scientific Status Summary by Institute of Food Technologists Expert Panel on Food and Nutrition, Institute of Food Technologists, Chicago, March 1978, p. 1.

(2) Food Borne Bacterial Poison, USDA, Animal & Plant Inspection Service, Washington, D.C., September 1976.

(3) E.M. Foster, Director, Food Research Institute, University of Wisconsin, "The Microbiological Safety of Processed and Raw Foods," Grocery Manufacturers of America Meeting, September 15, 1976, p. 2.

(4) John G. Ayres, "Food-Borne Infections in the Food Supply" paper presented at Grocery Manufacturers of America Press Briefing, Milwaukee, Wisconsin, October 21-22, 1976

(5) Richard L. Hall,   "Safe At the Plate," Nutrition Today, November/December 1977.

(6) Dr. Alexander M. Schmidt, "Food and Drug Law: A 200 Year Perspective," Nutrition Today, Volume 10, No. 4, 1975, p.32.

(7) Sanford A. Miller, "Additives In Our Food Supply," paper included in Hearings before the Select Committee on Small Business, U.S. Senate, on Food Additives: Competitive, Regulatory, and Safety Problems, January 13, 1977, Washington, D.C., p. 539

(8) Statement by Sherwin Gardner before the Select Committee on Small Business, U.S. Senate, on Food Additives: Competitive, Regulatory, and Safety Problems, January 13, 1977, U.S. Government Printing Office, Washington, D.C., p. 130

(9) Marketing Science Institute, Associated with the Harvard Business School and Louis Harris Associates, Consumerism at the Crossroads, conducted for Sentry Insurance, May 1977

(10) Eat Your Heart Out, Crain Publishers, Inc., N.Y., 1975, p. 235.

(11) Robert J. Wolff, "Who Eats for Health?", The American Journal of Clinical Nutrition, April 26, 1973, p. 443

(12) Jim Hightower, Eat Your Heart Out, p. 235

(13) See paper "The World at a Turning Point: New Class Attitudes," by Herman Kahn, "Fourteen New Emphases and Trends in U.S. Values," p. 16

(14) Ibid., p. 5.

(15) Census Bureau, Department of Commerce, Current Population Report, Series, p. 20, #326.

(16) Gabriel Lauro, "Product Development Today," Food Technology, July 1977, p. 73.

(17) Ibid.

(18) Emil Mrak, Paper presented before the California Agricultural Leadership Program, November 2, 1978, p. 2.

(19) Guy H. Miles, "Alternative Food Delivery Systems," prepared for National Science Foundation, September 1977, p. 28.

(20) Theodore P. Labuza, Food and Your Well Being, West Publishing Co., St. Paul, 1977, p. 368.

(21) Charles Niven, "Where Should We Go From Here in Improving the U.S. Diet?", Food Technology, September 1978, p. 92.

(22) "The Future: 15 Experts Analyze Events," Food Engineering, June 1978, p. 104.

(23) "Effects of Selected Changes in the Institutional and Human Environment Upon Output Per Unit of Input," Survey of Current Business, January 1978.

(24) Miles, "Alternative Food Delivery", p. 29.

(25) Jay Geller, "The Regulations Affecting Product Development," Food Technology, July 1977, p. 79.

(26) Herman Kahn, "Some Current Cultural Contradictions of Economic Growth: The Twelve New Emphases," p. 30.

(27) Ibid.

(28) Frank McLaughlin, Acting Director of Office of Consumer Affairs, HEW, "Government Influence on the Food System," February 2, 1978, New York Cooperative Extension Conference.

(29) Sanford Miller, "Additives in Our Food Supply," Hearings before the Senate Select Committee on Small Business on Food Additives: Competitive, Regulatory and Safety Problems, January 13-14, 1977, U.S. Government Printing Office, Washington, D. C., p. 546.

(30) Consumerism at the Crossroads, p. 60.

(31) Ibid., p. 50.

(32) Ibid., p. 28.

(33) "'Turista' Is Bad Joke to Travelers, Death to Locals," New York Times, October 3, 1977.

(34) Gilbert A. Leveille, "Establishing and Implementing Dietary Goals," paper presented at the 1978 Food and Agricultural Outlook Conferences, Washington, D. C. , November 17, 1977.

(35) Dr. Cortez F. Enloe, Jr., "Takin' Away Me Dying," Nutrition Today, November/December 1977, p. 14.

(36) "The Chemical Facts of Life," News Bureau, Monsanto Co., St. Louis, p. 7.

(37) A. E. Harper, "What Are Appropriate Dietary Guidelines," Food Technology, September 1978, pp. 49-50.

(38) William W. Lowrance, Of Acceptable Risk, National Academy of Sciences, 1974, p. 8.

(39) Paul F. Hopper, "The Future," Food Engineering, July 1, 1978, p. 156.

(40) Bernard L. Cohen, "Relative Risks of Saccharin and Calorie Ingestion," Science, March 3, 1978, Vol. 199, p. 983.

(41) Rich Jaroslovsky, "Latest Saccharin Findings Boost Chances U.S. Will Act to Impose New Curbs on Use," Wall St. Journal, November 6, 1978.

(42) G. Edward Damon, "A Primer on Food Additives," FDA Consumer, May 1973.

(43) According to the Institute of Food Technologists, in their report "Naturally Occurring Toxicants in Foods," no practical hazard based on this situation is known to exist, nor have any other definite dietary hazards based on toxicologic interactions between natural food components and food additives or pesticides been found.

(44) Food Additives Amendment of 1958, Section 409 (c) (3) (A) , 21 U.S.C. Section 348 (c) (3) (a) (1964).

(45) Rita Ricardo Campbell, Food Safety Regulation, American Enterprise Institute for Public Policy Research, Washington, D. C., 1974, p. 6. and Theodore P. Labuza, Food and Your Well Being, Avi Publishing, Westport, Conn., 1977, p. 377.

(46) Sanford A. Miller, "Risk/Benefit, No-Effect Levels, and Delaney: Is the Message Getting Through?" Food Technology, Feb. 1978, p. 94.

(47) Ibid, p. 94.

(48) Lowarance, Of Acceptable Risk, p. 10.

(49) James R. Kirk, "Research Priorities in Food Science," Food Technology, July, 1977, p. 70.

3 Leadership and Responsibility in the Food Industry

Peg Rogers
Emil M. Mrak

The primary responsibility of the food industry is to provide food that is safe, nutritious and acceptable at a reasonable cost/benefit ratio. Today the food industry must reassess its role. Obviously, contemporary expectations and the new demands for corporate performance now far exceed those of merely furnishing safe, nourishing food to sustain life to an ever increasing urban population.

Some serious observers question the reality of such an identifiable structure as the so-called food industry. Food is unlike the products of the steel industry, Bell Telephone, or the textile conglomerates. The raw material source, the inherent problems with nature, the processing and preservation, the complexities of distribution, and the impact of the final product are so diversified that many of the food businesses have very little in common with each other. The confectioners are not pressured by many of the problems facing the miller, the meat processor, or the citrus grower. The food industry is an archipelago, composed of separate islands, each of which is self-contained and narrow in its thinking. Yet all of these companies are bound by some of the same regulations and the same everincreasing demands of political and social expectations.

In the United States, 92% of the people are totally dependent upon the 8% who are engaged in the agri-food industries. This 92% has become effectively separated, not only in physical distances, but in philosophy, understanding and appreciation of the complexities in the sphere of their supplier. Nowhere is this expressed more forcibly than in the excesses of criticisms and regulations that have characterized the past decade. The blessings of modern food production no longer appear miraculous to the cynical eye of many of today's society. The crippling bonds of spoilage, growing seasons and great distances have all but disappeared, but in their place are now the public hostilities and government interventions that divide and conquer the food industry.

Indeed one of the anomalies of this decade is the low esteem the public holds for the food industry at the very time when the food supply is most abundant. Yet any corporate executive who comes forth to defend either his product or his profit is likely to have his legitimacy questioned. An outraged public seldom reckons with pricing factors such as raw materials, nature and government. Few institutions throughout history have been so miserably unpopular as food processing companies today.

This public attitude seems to puzzle many top managers, most of whom are between 50 and 60 years old and who grew up in the Great Depression. In those days many people were in desperate need of food, clothing and consumer goods. In contrast, few of today's generation have ever experienced such comparable need. Consequently many of today's food manufacturers find it difficult to appreciate the climate of hostility in which their products are examined.

Many executives dismiss these consumer criticisms as a temporary socioeconomic phenomenon, and some company men are reluctant to revise their depression day thinking despite today's realities of an "adversary culture." Only the enlightened chief executive recognizes that he must manage in an entirely different environment where the old rules are distressingly vague and patently inadequate. Furthermore, the past decade shows that criticism and fear are rewarded by government grants and increased regulatory costs.

Though one commentator described the giant food corporation as a lumbering dinosaur on its way to extinction, it is hardly headed toward imminent impotency. Yet these are critical times, and survival in crisis demands not only prudent management but vigorous leadership. Throughout the food industry there are many excellent managers who deliver for their companies the best in quality, service, and most importantly, a respectable bottom line. There are many executives and many styles of managements, but few of these top company officers appear to have the vision, the creativity, or the missionary zeal to assume the long-care concern of their corporation as an institutional form. This situation is further aggravated by the fact that most chief executives have only a 6 to 8 year tenure in which to be judged before passing the baton to another professional manager.

There is a vast difference between pragmatic managerial skills and the aggressive leadership so wanting in today's corporate community. There is a desperate call for leaders who can look beyond the immediacies of today's markets and members, a cry for people of creativity and courage, vision and tenacity as they search for solid answers to new problems.

Leadership presumes the ability to speak out in a powerful and lucid voice to calm the waves of organized discontent. The food industry is only now beginning to respond to the outrages of which they have been accused. For far too long their strange passivity and their disquieting silence have spoken eloquently and disturbingly to a puzzled and fearful public.

The crusade against the food industry has tremendous populist acclaim in today's society with its strong antiauthority attitudes; some psychologists have pointed out that the food processor does represent a father figure. This, coupled with a strong appeal to primitive anxieties, is enough to send even multinational companies into untimely retreat. The total impact is so serious that Robert H. Malott, chairman and chief executive officer of FMC Corporation has been urging corporate managers to become public policy activists. He advocates corporate activism to help shape the political and economic environment that would allow industry to do its job.

The aim of such corporate activist leaders should be to reduce the operational vacuum in which many public officials are comfortably insulated from varying public points of view. Malott also suggests that corporate funds be channelled to those recipients, both individuals and institutions, who would be forthright in supporting strong, objective projects, rather than those who would confuse public protection with political conquest.

It is axiomatic that successful leaders act instead of react; they become the aggressor instead of the victim, the critic instead of the criticized. Almost every food executive in America has smarted under a harsh attack of what he would label misinformation from some prominent spokesman. It has been suggested that the forceful leader make a sharp public rebuttal to challenge the credibility and integrity of the source. The rebuttal would come as paid advertising but not with the purpose of altering public opinion; its goal would call wide attention for more objective journalistic coverage in the future. Admittedly, it would take the strength of industrial magnitude to creep from the shadows of anonymity and meet such a challenge in an open atmosphere; but it could clear the air for a more honest exchange of views in the future.

Perhaps the food corporations have been most lax in the very area where they could readily be most effective - that is in the development of their own primary constituency. The employees, families, and shareholders of the agri-food businesses represent the largest sector of any working group in the United States. Except for an occasional article in their house publication, these are a neglected people.

This group receives information about "their" company from newspapers and media programs; thus they become the echo chamber for the rhetoric of discontent and "progressive reforms."

Under enlightened leadership, this group should stand as the traditional bulwark of loyalty and the first line of defense. It would take creativity, money and patience to accomplish such a goal. But, already, these people have a definite and interested stake in their company, a stake that should be respected and nourished, and one that should stand as a herald to innovative corporate response.

Even within the structure of one individual corporation, there are widely varying goals and interests. Frequently, executives speak in many tongues with different voices on many issues, and these corporate towers of Babel have contributed generously to mass confusion about food safety and nutrition.

The voice of the responsible scientist and the voice of the entire industry should have been stentorian when the industry had the food, the facts and the good will of the public. Through the advertising media, the food industry has enjoyed one of the most powerful pipelines of communication the world has ever known. This communication system has been primarily to promote profit - a totally justified act, but one whose rationale is now deemed insufficient according to current liberal philosophical judgments.

Even today the science of food technology remains a mystery to all too many. On many issues in the past, the industry frequently evaded its responsibility of informing the public; so now the activists have filled the void, and they have skillfully instilled distrust and chemo-phobia into the hearts of most consumers. As yet today, most executives choose to remain silent; and unfortunately many responsible scientists find it exceedingly difficult to present their views to the press, the public, or to political bodies.

Responsible scientists are acutely aware that perfection in science, and especially the biological sciences, is a rarity, if not an impossibility. Realizing this, scientists speak with uncertainty and always indicate the need for more research. In contrast, the ill informed, or the uninformed often testify with a positiveness that leaves no doubt in the mind of the average person.

The safety and quality of food are personal and emotional subjects; consequently, it is particularly important that any information, both by scientists and industry executives, be accurate, balanced and objective. Any spokesman, whether scientist or corporate official, would find it difficult to deliver convincingly such a message in an era when so many people have already made up their minds, and the audience is almost hopelessly polarized.

Even today many corporate managers are totally dependent upon their trade associations or their public relations firms to take their views to the public and to government officials. A low-profile image and safe mediocrity seem to offer less risk to the profit line. Yet at stake is the very operational system that the food industry defends from neither interventionist government, or activist harassment.

The proliferation of self centered organizations has further divided and separated both the business and scientific communities. Here the food industry is guilty of self mutilation. It has ignored the basic principle that in unity there is strength. Suddenly there have appeared countless trade and specialty associations, groups, councils, and committees, each vying to ward off what they see as oppressive government interference - but only because each feels isolated and because nobody else has even voiced a whisper on its behalf. Is there not one gifted leader or one care group strong enough to orchestrate his individual statements into an overall effective message? Obviously there is a need for leaders who can galvanize the strengths of this fragmented food industry.

By their very nature food executives are pragmatists. Too many of the business managers in the industry have responded by exploiting the public outcry and the regulatory policies as those executives press for advantage with the special interest groups. This can be expected when thousands of food companies are committed to a competitive market without any industry wide guidance, or recognized leadership.

Such self serving and single minded policies are exemplified by the sudden saturation of slogans announcing "natural foods" and "no chemical preservatives." This demeaning conduct may provide these companies with some unsound advertising and may satisfy a narrow goal of profitability; but it sets up false standards of identity, and in doing so it exhibits immoral and defeatist behavior on the balance sheet of social responsibility.

To offer guidance in these times of crises, at the close of 1978, The Institute of Food Technologists sent to the presidents and advertising directors of 800 food companies, policy guidelines for advertising (See chapter 10, figure 10.7). It is the hope of the Institute that if the food executives dealt in the whole truth instead of half truth and implied accusations, the public would not only be better informed but better nourished as a result of educated choices.

Today the food executives are an especially vulnerable group. They all too often are judged by their performance in non-profit activities, and their normal profit oriented motives are viewed amid a tidal movement of suspicions. During the last decade, the entire agri-food complex has been the target of harsh and repeated attacks from politicians and activists with evangelical fervor. Few business executives, or even scholars, can articulate simple answers to these accusations, distortions and slander that have become fashionable comments on the American food supply.

The pattern of executive behavior has been one of reaction rather than action; they have yet to gear up their corporate activism to make a positive contribution to the political stage. As both victims and critics of a hostile social environment, most companies do little to alter this climate. Responsible food scientists and especially executives in the industry must take the initiative in anticipating emerging societal needs, and they must establish constructive relationships with the appropriate government institutions. Unfortunately most scientists are not prepared to step forward to present their views with any degree of grace. They normally take refuge in the need to do more research; they should be willing to take the leadership in giving advice based on expert knowledge.

The hesitancy of corporate leaders in defending their stewardship has remained a puzzle. These are men who have demonstrated the ability to achieve a high degree of excellence in performances of managerial efficiency, economic growth and technological innovations. They should also be men of vision who care enough for their institutions to replace short term goals with long term achievements.

The industry needs scientists and leaders who have the quality of leadership combined with a great breadth of thinking and understanding. The call to action is a muted one, and leaders have been slow to emerge. There is a cry for those who are willing to take responsibility, to go to the lonely outposts of thought and action and to persuade others to follow, and to act positively, persuasively, and constructively. Unfortunately, at the moment there are far too few creative geniuses; however, to assure us of our food for the future, leaders with such abilities must emerge.

NOTES

(1) "To the Barricades - Corporate Style." Chemical and Engineering News, February 23, 1978, p. 5.

4 Food Price Inflation— A Heretical View

Dean Peterson

A large (and growing) majority of Americans now regard inflation as our nation's most serious economic problem. The declining value of the dollar, both at home and abroad, is regarded as symptomatic of a national malaise. Arthur Burns, former Chairman of the Federal Reserve Board, has recently labeled "the corrosive influence of inflation" the greatest danger to our free enterprise system. President Carter, in recognition of the seriousness of the problem, has requested that the entire private sector comply with comprehensive "voluntary" wage and price control standards. There is a growing concern within the business community that the current semimandatory standards may be only the first step on the road to a controlled economy.

This analysis is addressed to the causes and effects of inflation in one particular sector of our economy - the United States food system. I shall attempt to identify the specific factors that have contributed to food price inflation in the past and to flag potential sources of future food price inflation.

Food price inflation is a particularly sensitive issue for several reasons. Food continues to be among the largest single category of expenditure for the typical American family. With grocery shopping at least a weekly, and occasionally a daily event, food prices are the most visible symbol of the inflation that pervades the entire economy. Food prices are also typically the most volatile component of the entire price structure, with wide swings in prices reflecting such diverse factors as droughts, floods, and sudden frost in major food producing areas.

THE GENERAL PHENOMENON OF INFLATION

Before considering the specific causes of food price inflation, it is important to distinguish between "absolute" (or "pure") inflation and "relative" inflation, that is between changes in the general price level, and changes in the price of specific items relative to each other. It is widely recognized that pure inflation (i.e., a sustained increase in the general price level) is a monetary phenomenon that can be remedied only be appropriate monetary and fiscal policies. If the prices of all goods and services rose by a uniform percentage, and all forms of income increased by a corresponding amount, inflation would be more of an accounting inconvenience than a serious social or economic problem. Pure (absolute) inflation is simply too much money chasing too few goods and services.

It is relative inflation (e.g., an increase in the price of beef relative to the price of shoes and particularly an increase in prices of all goods and services relative to income) that is the real and legitimate concern for most consumers and economic policymakers. It is an uncomfortable fact of economic life that all prices do not change at the same rate - neither do the wages or incomes of the various groups that comprise our society. It is relative inflation that engenders consumer frustration, price resistance, and even consumer boycotts. Relative inflation (or deflation) reflects real adjustments in the economy, including changes in the supply demand balance for particular commodities, variations in interindustry productivity performance, uneven price or supply effects of government policies and regulations, and/or changes in the international competitive position of particular sectors.

PRICE TRENDS IN THE FOOD SYSTEM

The predominant characteristic of the U. S. food system during the postwar period was declining relative food prices. With the exception of a brief surge during the Korean War (1951-52) followed by three years of absolute declines, food prices declined in real terms for twenty five years. During the twenty year period ending in 1967, food prices rose at an average annual rate of 1.8% per year, or slightly less than the corresponding 2.0% annual increase in the general price level (table 4.1). Larger farms, rising agricultural yields, and more than adequate reserve stocks of basic farm commodities combined to restrain farm prices, while new production technologies, improved distribution systems, and ever larger and more automated supermarkets all served to limit increases in marketing margins. The same pattern continued during 1967-72. With the expansionary guns and butter policies of the late 1960s, the pure inflation rate more than doubled to 4.5% while food prices rose at a slightly lower rate of 4.3% annually (table 4.1).

The relative decline in food prices, accompanied by rising real incomes, contributed to a material improvement in the standard of living of the typical American consumer. From 1947 to 1972, the share of personal income spent on food by the average American consumer declined steadily from 26% in 1947 to 21% in 1957 to 16% in 1972 (table 4.2).

The pattern of declining relative food prices was dramatically reversed after 1972. From 1972 to 1975 the retail price of a market

Table 4.1. Trend of U.S. Consumer Prices for Foods and for all
Items: Selected Years, 1947-77

| | Consumer Price Index for | |
| | Food | All Items |
Year	(1967=100)	(1967=100)
1947	70.6	66.9
1957	84.9	84.3
1967	100.0	100.0
1972	123.5	125.3
1977	192.2	181.5

| | Annual Rate of Change | |
Period	Food	All Items
1947-57	1.86%	2.34%
1957-67	1.65%	1.72%
1967-72	4.31%	4.51%
1972-77	9.25%	7.69%
1967-77	6.75%	6.14%

Source: U.S. Department of Labor, Bureau of Labor Statistics

Table 4.2. Ratio of Personal Consumption Expenditures for Food*
to Disposable Personal Income and Total Personal Consumption
Expenditures: Selected Years 1947-77

Year	Disposable Personal Income (Percent)	Total Personal Consumption Expenditures (Percent)
1947	25.7%	27.2%
1957	20.7%	22.7%
1967	17.4%	19.4%
1972	16.3%	17.8%
1973	16.3%	18.1%
1974	17.0%	18.8%
1975	17.0%	18.9%
1976	16.8%	18.3%
1977	16.8%	18.1%

* Excluding Alcoholic Beverages

Source: U.S. Department of Commerce.

basket of United States farm foods rose by 43%, reflecting a 50% increase in the farm value of the food and a 30% increase in marketing margins (table 4.3).

There is little doubt that the catalyst of sharply accelerating food prices in the 1970's was the surge in export demand that resulted in United States agricultural exports rising from $8.0 billion in 1972 to $12.9 billion in 1973 to $21.3 billion in 1974 - a cumulative increase of 166% over a two year period. The magnitude of the increase was primarily attributable to sharply rising prices for United States farm commodities, but the 38% increase in export volume during the corresponding period was also impressive. From 1972 to 1974, the composite price index (1967=100) for all United States farm crops nearly doubled from 114 to 224.

Detailed exploration of the factors that contributed to the rapid expansion in export demand, and the resulting surge in farm prices, is beyond the scope of this paper. However, the sharp devaluation of the dollar that was occurring during this period, the steady increase in the real standard of living in other industrialized nations (particularly Japan), the dramatic expansion in international purchasing power of the oil exporting countries, and grain production shortfalls in both Eastern Bloc and developing countries all played important roles.

Moreover, it seems highly probable that most of the causal factors cited in the preceding paragraph are likely to be features of the international economic landscape for the foreseeable future. In short, there has been a strong, and probably permanent, upward shift in the demand for United States farm exports that has dramatically reversed the long term trend of declining farm prices. While higher farm exports and increased farm incomes are widely viewed as positive developments, they have unmistakably been a major force behind food price inflation in the 1970s.

IMPORTED FOODS

Sharply higher prices for imported foods (particularly sugar, coffee, cocoa, and fish) have further aggravated inflationary pressures in the United States food sector since 1972. The combination of our devalued dollar, increased purchasing power in other industrial countries, and increasingly successful efforts by primary commodity producers to bolster prices by individually and collectively limiting supplies, resulted in a cumulative 122% increase in the price level of United States imported foods from 1972 to 1977.

Although imports represent only a small proportion (roughly one seventh) of United States food consumption, surging import prices largely negated the effects of falling prices for United States farm foods in 1976 and accounted for the preponderant part (about two-thirds) of the 6% increase in retail food prices in 1977 (see figure 4.1).

Table 4.3.   Market Basket of U.S. Farm Foods:
             Farm Retail Price Spreads, 1967-1978
             (Index 1967=100)

	Retail Price	Farm Value	Farm-Retail Spread	Farmer's Share Of Total Retail Cost
1967	100.0	100.0	100.0	39%
1968	103.5	105.3	102.5	39%
1969	109.1	114.8	105.5	41%
1970	113.7	114.1	113.4	39%
1971	115.7	114.4	116.5	38%
1972	121.3	125.1	119.0	40%
1973	142.3	167.2	126.4	46%
1974	161.9	178.4	150.4	43%
1975	173.6	187.7	165.1	41%
1976	175.4	177.8	174.0	38%
1977	179.2	178.1	180.0	38%
1978*	199	206	195	39%

* Estimated by the U.S.D.A., November 1978

Source: U.S. Department of Agriculture, Agricultural Statistics,
1977; Agricultural Outlook, November 1978; and National Food
Review, December 1978.

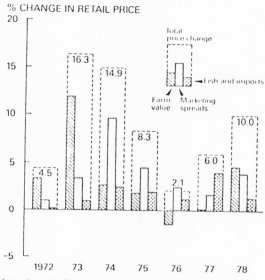

Fig. 4.1. Contributors to increases in food prices

Source: Handbook of Agricultural Charts, U.S. Department of Agriculture, 1978

THE FARM-RETAIL SPREAD: THE MARKETING BILL EXPLORED

There is much public concern, particularly in the political arena, about the shrinking farm share of our food dollar. It was a widely published fact within the agricultural community that the labor bill for marketing farm foods surpassed the farm value of those foods in 1977.

What is not widely recognized, however, is the scope and complexity of the system involved in delivering farm foods to the American consumer and the magnitude of the changes that have occurred in that system over the past decade. Since the marketing bill measures only the direct labor costs of firms engaged solely in food marketing functions, it dramatically understates the true role of labor and labor costs in food marketing. If the labor costs embedded in the goods and services purchased by the food marketing sector (e.g., packaging materials, transportation, and advertising) were included in the published labor cost totals, marketing labor costs would undoubtedly have exceeded farm values in 1967 and probably throughout the entire postwar period. (In 1967, the cost of rail and truck transportation, advertising, and packaging materials totaled $13 billion. Assuming, conservatively, that labor costs were only one-third of this total (i.e., $4.3 billion), the adjusted labor bill would have amounted to $30.2 billion, or $1.4 billion more than the farm value in that year.) If one also takes into account the large "residual" category (12% of the total marketing bill in 1977) which consists largely of food service labor in schools, institutions, etc., it becomes abundantly clear that combined direct and indirect labor costs are by far the dominant component of the United States food marketing bill (table 4.4).

Behind the labor cost bill is a highly intricate network of some 10 million persons directly engaged in processing, distributing, selling, preparing, and serving food to the American public.   Current data suggest that over four fifths of the total man hours required to deliver farm foods to American consumers are expended after the food leaves the farm.   The number of direct man hours used in both the food-at-home and in the food-away-from-home sectors is more than double that required to produce the food at the farm level (table 4.5).

The steady growth in the market share of away-from-home eating (from 27% to total food expenditures in 1967 to 33% in 1977) has further increased the labor component of the food marketing bill. Given the changing character of food marketing and the fact that farmers now expend only an estimated 17% of the 20+ billion hours worked annually in the United States food system, it is hardly surprising that their share of the total food dollar should have declined from 32% to 31% over the past decade. What is surprising is that the decline in their proportionate share has been so small.

The dominant role of labor (some 17 billion direct hours annually) in food marketing is responsible for the sensitivity of the food marketing bill to "pure" inflation. During the decade ending in 1977, hourly labor costs approximately doubled, outpacing the 82% increase in the general price level and leaving food industry workers slightly better off in real terms. However, faltering productivity, primarily in food distribution, led to a sharp excalation in unit labor costs, particularly during the 1972-1977 period. Without productivity gains, increases in the general price level are quickly translated into higher food prices.

While labor costs are clearly the dominant single item of the food marketing bill, they are not the only, nor the most rapidly growing one. The various cost components of the food marketing bill during the 1967-77 period are shown in table 4.4. It is interesting to note that every component except "advertising" and "residual" more than doubled during this period.   The decline in the "residual" catagory probably reflects increased reliance by institutional feeders (such as airlines, hospitals, schools, and in-plant cafeterias) on outside contractors and the consequent allocation of these costs directly to the appropriate functional category. Advertising, which is frequently criticized as an example of the waste and inefficiency of our food marketing system, is the only cost component to decline in real terms over the past decade.

Finally, dramatic increases in the price of energy since 1972, have contributed to higher production costs at both the farm level and in food marketing.   The USDA reports that price of energy purchased directly by food marketing firms rose by 210% during the decade ending

Table 4.4. Cost Components of the Marketing Bill for Farm Foods

	1967	1972	1973	1974	1975	1976	1977(a)	Forecast 1978
Labor (a)	25.9	37.4	40.6	44.2	48.5	54.0	59.8	66
Packaging materials	7.2	10.2	10.9	12.1	13.4	15.0	16.2	17
Rail and truck transportation (c)	4.3	6.1	6.0	7.2	8.3	9.5	10.0	11
Corporate profit before taxes	3.4	4.0	5.4	6.1	7.9	7.9	8.5	--
Business taxes (d)	2.4	3.3	3.5	3.8	4.4	4.8	5.1	--
Depreciation	1.8	2.3	2.5	2.8	3.2	3.5	3.7	--
Rent (net)	1.5	2.0	2.1	2.5	2.8	3.2	3.5	--
Advertising	1.5	1.8	1.8	2.1	2.4	2.7	2.8	--
Repairs, bad debts, contributions	.9	1.3	1.4	1.6	1.8	2.0	2.1	--
Interest (net)	.4	.7	.9	1.2	1.4	1.5	1.6	--
Residual (e)	12.4	10.6	10.3	12.0	15.2	17.1	15.6	46
Total	61.7	79.7	85.4	95.6	109.3	121.2	128.9	140

Note: (a) Preliminary. (b) includes supplements to wages and salaries such as pensions and health insurance premiums. Also includes imputed earnings of proprietors, partners, and family workers not receiving stated remuneration. (c) includes charges for heating and refrigeration. Does not include local hauling charges. (d) includes property, social security, unemployment insurance, State income, and franchise taxes, license fees, and other fees, but does not include Federal income taxes. (e) includes food service in schools, colleges, hospitals, and other institutions, and utilities, fuel, and other costs not shown separately.

Source: U.S. Department of Agriculture, Agricultural Outlook, November 1978.

Table 4.5. Balance Sheet of Total Direct Employment in the United States Food System - 1977

Function	Employ-ment (000)	Average Weekly Hours	Annual Hours (millions) / Estimated Annual Hours	Percent of Total System Hours
Farming:				
Total Hours Used for Farmwork (a)			4,659	-
Less: Hours Attributable to Exports (25%) (b)			1,165	
Equals: Hours Attributable to Producing U.S. Farm Foods			3,494	17%
Food-At-Home Sector:				
Food & Kindered Products-Mfg.	1,637.7	40.4	3,440.5	17%
Food-Wholesaling	593.9	38.6	1,192.1	5%
Retail Food Stores	2,080.8	32.7	3,538.2	17%
	4,312.4		8,170.8	40%
Food-Away-From Home Sector:				
Separate Eating & Drinking Places	3,708.0	28.4	5,475.9	27%
Other Food-Away-From-Home Est. (c)	2,178.0	-	3,216.8	16%
	5,886.0	-	8,692.9	43%
Total Direct Hours in Food Marketing	10,198.4		16,862.7	83%
Total Direct Hours in U.S. Food System			20,357	100%

(a) Includes 350 million hours spent on nonfood crops (cotton & tobacco).
(b) Estimated on the basis of market value of exports to total farm marketing receipts.
(c) Includes food service workers in schools, hotels, motels, hospitals, other institutions, theatres, vending, etc. The USDA estimates that such institutions accounted for 37% of the value of meals and snacks eaten away from home in 1977. This estimate assumes a proportionate input in such operations.

Source: USDA, Changes in Farm Production and Efficiency, 1977; National Food Review December 1978; and U.S. Dept. of Labor, Bureau of Labor Statistics Employment and Earnings.

in 1977. Since energy represents an estimated 12% of the total cost of delivering food from the farm to the table, higher real energy prices have undoubtedly been an important factor in the total inflationary spiral.

To summarize, the cost of marketing farm foods closely mirrors the "pure" inflation in our economy. It is no mere accident that the index (1967=100) for the farm retail price spread in 1977 was 180.0, less than two points below the 181.5 level of the Consumer Price Index for all items (tables 4.1 and 4.3).

There is no hope for relief from escalating food marketing costs (or, consequently, from escalating food prices) unless and until the food marketing sector can reverse the trend of deteriorating productivity. Increased productivity, in turn, will require the understanding and cooperation of all the participants in the food marketing system - farmers, food marketers, the government, and consumers.

ECONOMIC EFFICIENCY IN THE FOOD SYSTEM

The reversal of the long term trend of declining relative food prices, and particularly the deterioration in measured industry wide productivity, raises a serious question concerning the overall efficiency of our food system. An evaluation of efficiency, however, raises further questions concerning what we expect from our food system. Our expectations clearly involve more than simply delivering the maximum quantity of food to the consumer at the lowest possible cost. In other words, we expect our food system to perform a number of non or quasieconomic functions, which are not captured adequately, if at all, by traditional measures of evaluating an industry's economic performance.

What we must expect from our food system is: quality, nutrition, convenience, safety, and variety. There is a growing body of evidence indicating that the food industry has steadily improved its performance on virtually all of these accounts.

While quality is a particularly subjective criteria (and is inextricably linked to such factors as nutrition, safety, and variety), it is clear that American consumers are increasingly demanding and receiving more nutritious, safer, more descriptively labeled foods. The USDA recently reported that, over the past decade, the average per capita consumption of every major nutrient has increased (table 4.6). During the same period, we have reduced our average per capita cholesterol and our saturated fatty acid intake, while increasing our consumption of vegetable fats. We are eating more poultry, fish, and cheese, and less butter, eggs, and pork (table 4.7). In short, we are eating what most nutritionists believe is a better quality diet.

One proxy for the quality delivered by our food system is the premium that consumers are willing to pay for the consistent quality delivery of nationally recognized brands. Three separate studies of the potential savings from buying "generic" merchandise (i.e., merchandise

Table 4.6. Nutrients Available for Consumption, Per Capita Per Day (a)

Nutrient (Unit)	1957-59	1967	1976	1978(b)	1978 (b)	1978 as percentage of:		
						1957-59	1967	1977
Food energy (Cal.)	3,140	3,210	3,390	3,370	3,380	108	105	100
Protein (Gm.)	95	99	104	103	103	109	105	100
Fat (Gm.)	143	150	160	158	159	111	106	101
Carbohydrate (Gm.)	375	374	391	391	392	105	105	100
Calcium (Gm.)	.98	.95	.95	.94	.95	97	100	101
Phosphorus (Gm.)	1.53	1.54	1.59	1.58	1.58	104	103	101
Iron (Mg.)	16.3	17.3	18.8	18.6	18.6	114	107	100
Magnesium (Mg.)	347	343	355	348	351	101	102	101
Vitamin A value (I.U.)	8,100	7,900	8,100	7,900	8,000	99	101	101
Thiamin (Mg.)	1.84	1.91	2.09	2.08	2.09	113	109	100
Riboflavin (Mg.)	2.30	2.36	2.52	2.49	2.50	109	106	100
Niacin (Mg.)	21.1	22.9	26.2	25.9	25.8	123	113	100
Vitamin B_6 (Mg.)	1.99	2.13	2.29	2.31	2.34	110	102	101
Vitamin B_{12} (Mcg.)	8.9	9.6	9.8	9.9	9.8	110	115	99
Ascorbic acid (Mg.)	104	104	116	116	119	115	115	102

Note: (a) Quantities of nutrients computed by Science and Education Administration, Consumer and Food Economics Institute, on the basis of estimates of per capita food consumption (retail weight), including estimates of produce of home gardens, prepared by the Economics, Statistics, and Cooperatives Service. No deduction made in nutrient estimates for loss or waste of food in the home, use of pet food, or for the destruction or loss of nutrients during the preparation of food. Civilian consumption. Data includes iron, thiamin, riboflavin, and niacin added to flour and cereal products; other nutrients added primarily as follows: Vitamin A value to margarine, milk of all types, milk extenders, vitamin B_6 to cereals, meal replacements, infant formulas; vitamin B_{12} to cereals; ascorbic acid to fruit juices and drinks, flavored beverages and dessert powders, milk extenders, and cereals. Quantities of added nutrients for 1960-66 were estimated in part by Consumer and Food Economic Institute. Nutrient data reflect revisions of potato series 1956 to present. (b) Preliminary.

Source: USDA, National Food Review, December 1978.

Table 4.7. Per Capita Food Consumption Indexes (a)

1967=100

	1960	1970	1971	1972	1973	1974	1975	1976	1977 (b)
Meat, poultry, and fish									
Meat	89.4	104.9	107.3	107.2	100.9	106.2	102.8	109.8	109.8
Poultry	91.9	104.0	107.1	105.2	97.8	104.6	101.0	107.6	107.0
Fish	75.3	107.1	107.9	112.8	108.8	110.6	108.2	116.1	119.5
	97.0	110.7	107.9	117.5	121.3	114.7	113.9	121.0	119.7
Eggs	104.2	97.0	98.0	96.1	91.6	89.9	87.0	85.5	84.8
Dairy products (c)	105.4	98.9	99.0	99.5	99.2	97.4	98.3	99.0	98.5
Fats and oils	95.4	106.6	105.2	109.3	109.8	106.9	107.8	112.6	109.6
Animal	119.2	90.4	90.1	83.9	77.8	76.2	72.6	68.0	68.2
Vegetable	82.2	115.5	113.6	123.3	127.5	123.9	127.2	137.2	132.4
Fruits (d)	102.9	102.7	103.0	100.4	102.7	102.3	109.2	111.7	109.8
Fresh	112.0	100.6	99.6	94.4	94.4	97.4	104.3	115.6	106.6
Processed	94.8	104.6	106.1	105.8	110.1	106.6	113.5	115.6	112.7
Vegetables (e)	99.3	101.7	101.7	102.5	105.2	104.2	103.4	107.5	106.5
Fresh	107.6	100.2	100.1	99.9	101.3	101.2	101.5	103.4	102.0
Processed	83.7	104.5	104.8	107.3	112.4	109.8	107.1	115.2	114.9
Potatoes and sweet potatoes	81.8	114.8	115.8	116.0	116.7	117.7	121.3	114.0	117.5
Fresh	133.8	95.0	91.0	91.7	83.6	80.1	90.8	85.6	94.4
Processed	58.2	123.7	127.1	127.0	131.7	134.9	135.2	126.9	128.0
Beans, peas, and nuts	95.6	98.4	100.0	103.8	104.6	100.4	106.6	104.5	103.9
Cereal products	102.0	97.9	98.6	97.6	97.8	96.0	96.5	99.0	96.8
Sugar	98.1	105.9	106.5	108.4	109.2	106.6	102.9	109.4	111.7
Coffee, tea, and cocoa	100.2	93.7	91.6	97.9	96.7	91.8	90.8	93.3	74.5
Total food	96.4	102.7	103.6	104.0	102.2	102.9	102.0	105.7	104.7
Animal products	95.5	102.2	103.8	103.6	99.2	101.8	99.7	104.0	103.7
Crops (f)	97.4	103.2	103.3	104.5	105.9	104.1	104.8	107.8	105.9

Note: (a) Civilian consumption only. Quantities of individual foods are combined in terms of 1957-59 retail prices.
 (b) Preliminary
 (c) Includes butter
 (d) Excludes melons and baby food
 (e) Excludes soup, baby food, dry beans and peas, potatoes, and sweet potatoes
 (f) Includes melons, nuts, soup, and baby food in addition to groups shown separately.

Source: U.S. Department of Agriculture, National Food Review, June 1978.

59

labeled with only its generic description, and the required ingredient list) indicate that consumers can save an average of 15-20% over store brands, and 25-39% over national brands by buying generic merchandise. Despite the potential savings, "generics" have achieved only very limited acceptance. The continued willingness of consumers to pay a substantial premium for store, and particularly for nationally branded products, over generic products which meet USDA specifications with respect to sanitation, wholesomeness, safety, and nutrition is evidence of the quality reserve in our food system

The variety offered by our food system almost defies comprehension. In 1928, food stores handled an average of 867 different items. In 1950, they offered 3,750 items. In 1977, a large supermarket chain carried 51,939 different items, including 29,290 dry grocery items, 5,173 frozen food items, 4,697 refrigerated food items, 4,698 health and beauty aids, and 7,811 nonedible grocery items. In fact, the number of totally new products introduced in grocery stores in 1977 totaled 1,218 - more than the average grocery store's entire merchandise selection in 1928.

Food safety has also been enhanced by more rigorous testing procedures and the elimination of ingredients and additives deemed to be actually or potentially hazardous. Former Food and Drug Commissioner Alexander Schmidt recently concluded that our food supply is safer now than at any time in our nation's history.

Convenience has been the hallmark of our nation's food delivery system. Approximately one food dollar out of every three is now spent in eating fully prepared meals and snacks away from home. Most of the over 5,000 frozen food items stocked by large supermarkets are semi or fully prepared "convenience" foods. Despite the fact that most supermarkets have lengthened their hours (many now offer both Sunday and 24 hour service), an increasing proportion of retail food sales has been through high-margin "convenience" stores. The added convenience of longer store hours is clearly a significant factor in the apparent decline in labor productivity in the food distribution system in the 1970s. Convenience has its price!

In my judgment, the responsiveness of the food system in meeting the quasieconomic needs of its customers has detracted from its measured economic performance. There are obvious costs, as well as benefits, associated with progressive improvements in the variety, safety, quality, nutrition, and accessibility of our food supply. The fact that most consumers have indicated (through their pattern of food purchase decisions) their willingness to pay these costs suggests that the system is meeting their basic needs. That, after all, is the ultimate test of the efficiency of any economic system.

A NOTE ON PROFITABILITY

The food production and marketing process, from the farm through the grocery store or neighborhood restaurant, is both a highly fragmented and a highly competitive business. The basic unit of agricultural production is, and will for the foreseeable future, continue to be, the family farm. Farm incomes, which had lagged behind those of nonfarm residents throughout the twentieth century, rose dramatically in the early 1970s with the surge in farm exports and farm prices. Although farm income has subsequently declined slightly, it is apparent that the financial condition of the family farmer has markedly improved during the 1970s, particularly when farm wealth, as well as current farm incomes, are taken into account. The large family farm in particular, which accounts for the preponderant part of the United States farm production, achieves family incomes well above those of nonfarm residents.

Food marketing, encompassing approximately 22,000 food processors, 40,000 wholesalers, 180,000 supermarkets, and 500,000 food service outlets is also, by its nature, very competitive. The USDA estimates that the pretax profits of food marketing firms average approximately 5% of the food marketing bill. The typical food processing firms achieves after-tax profits of only 2% on sales (table 4.8). In the distribution sector, both grocery wholesalers and grocery retailers typically achieve after-tax profits equivalent to less than one percent of sales.

The narrow profit margin of the average food marketing firm reflects the highly competitive character of virtually every product, and functional sector of the industry. If these margins were completely eliminated, one could achieve a one-time reduction of about 3% in retail food prices. The average margins, however, mask diverse profitability levels among individual firms as evidenced by the wide spread in profit margins of upper- and lower-quartile firms in table 4.8. It is the prospects for improved margins that provides the essential incentive for introducing the new and improved products and processes that provide the only real hope of restraining costs and prices in the food marketing sector.

OUTLOOK FOR THE 1980s
IMPLICATIONS FOR GOVERNMENT POLICY

Most of the factors that contributed to "relative food price inflation in the 1970s were beyond the direct control of individual participants in the food system. Most were also beyond the direct control of government - at least of a government committed to maintaining a market-oriented economy. But government policies, particularly those relating to farm prices, profoundly affected food prices in the 1970s and may play the dominant role in determining whether or not we experience "relative" food price inflation in the 1980s.

A government that is seriously concerned with controlling food price inflation should, at a minimum, avoid pursuing policies that exacerbate inflationary pressures in the food system. Most United States farm

Table 4.8. Food Processing Industry: Ratio of Net Profits to
Net Sales for Upper Quartile, Median, and Lower Quartile Firms
by Major Industry Subgroup, 1977

Industry Subgroup	# of Report- ing- Firms	Ratio of Net Profit to Net Sales		
		Upper Quartile Firms	Median Firms	Lower Quartile Firms
Bakery Products	74	5.53	2.24	.99
Canned & Preserved Fruits & Vegetables	88	4.50	2.66	1.07
Confectionery	39	6.54	2.59	1.59
Dairy Products	112	3.62	1.70	.44
Grain Mill Products	91	3.35	1.83	1.06
Meat Packing Plants	67	2.07	1.12	(0.02)
Soft Drinks, Bottled & Canned	64	10.22	6.48	3.73
Industry Average	535	5.12	2.66	1.27
Net Profit Before Tax to Net Sales		10.24	5.32	2.54
Memo: Industry Average Without Soft Drinks	471	4.27	2.02	.86
Net Profit Before Tax to Net Sales Without Soft Drinks		8.54	4.04	1.72

Source: Dun & Bradstreet, Key Business Ratios, 1977.

Table 4.9.   Comparative Financial Performance
              Food Industry, All Manufacturing, Non-durable
              Goods Industry, 1970-78

	Net Profit After Tax to Assets			Ratio of Food Industry to:	
	All Manuf.	Non-Durable	Food	All Manuf.	Non-Durable
Years 1960-1964-Average	%	%	%		
1965-1969 Average	7.1	7.2	6.0	.85	.83
1970	5.0	5.8	5.5	1.1	.95
1971	5.2	5.6	5.6	1.08	-
1972	5.6	5.8	5.6	1.00	.97
1973	6.7	6.8	6.3	.94	.93
1974	8.0	9.5	6.7	.84	.71
1975	6.2	7.1	7.0	1.13	.99
1976	7.5	7.8	7.5	1.00	.96
1977	7.6	7.5	6.7	.88	.89
1978 (Jan.-June)	7.7	7.2	6.7	.87	.93

Source: Quarterly Finance Report For Manufacturing Corporations,
FTC-SEC.

policies (e.g., grain and dairy price supports, acreage diversion programs, import quotas on beef and dairy products, and high import duties on sugar), however, are directed primarily toward increasing, rather than restraining farm prices. Given the substantial rise in relative farm and food prices over the past decade, a reexamination of the wisdom of such policies seems warranted. In particular, policies which support farm prices at, or near, full "costs of production" (which includes a return to land) eliminate the downside risk in agriculture, encouraging investors to bid up the price of farm land, which increases the cost of production leading to high support prices, ad infinitum. In the past decade the average value of United States farmland has trebled. Unless the land price spiral can be broken, the political and economic pressures for still further increases in relative farm prices will prove irresistible.

Perhaps the time has come to reexamine the basic goals of United States agricultural policy in the context of the global economic environment of the 1980's. If the underlying goal is to provide adequate farm incomes, a strong case can be made that it is more appropriate - whether from the standpoint of equity, or of social or economic policy - to support those with low farm incomes directly, rather than through price support programs which inflate food costs and rebound primarily to the benefit of the large-volume, high-income farmers who now account for most farm sales. Production policies could then focus primarily on encouraging greater yields, higher productivity, and lower costs in a market-oriented environment.

In the food marketing sector, the prerequisite to correcting "relative" inflation is to attain productivity growth that outpaces the national average. Given the fragmentation of our food marketing system, that is a formidable challenge. In the prevailing regulatory environment, it is probably an impossibility. Regulatory initiatives, irrespective of their merits, have unquestionably imposed substantial additional costs on the system. The regulatory environment has not only imposed costs on the food system, it has often prevented the marketing sector from fully implementing innovations (e.g., electronic scanning, mechanical deboning of meat, etc.) which hold the promise of materially increasing productivity. A rigorous application of cost benefit analysis to existing and prospective regulations affecting the food system would be an important step towards restoring healthy productivity trends in the food industry.

SUMMARY AND CONCLUSIONS

The era of declining "relative" food prices ended in 1972. During the 1970's expanded export demand and rising input costs led to large increases in farm prices, which combined with sluggish productivity trends in the food marketing sector to create an unprecedented rate of both absolute and relative food price inflation. Although the measured rate of food price inflation appears to be overstated, because it fails to capture adequately improvements in the convenience and quality delivery of the food system, it nonetheless is, and should be, a source of serious concern, both the government policymakers and to participants at every level of our food system.

The extent to which relative food price inflation will continue into the 1980's will be determined by the priority that consumers, food marketers, and government policymakers attach to controlling it. Government will have to resolve the tradeoffs between supporting farm incomes and restraining farm prices. Food marketing firms will have to resolve the priority they attach to productivity improvements versus other business goals. Finally, consumers will be the ultimate arbiters as to what constitutes an acceptable tradeoff between price and improvements in the quality (comprehensively defined) delivery of the food system.

The most probable outcome, given the structure of the food industry and the range of competing priorities, is that food price trends during the next decade will be neither inflationary nor deflationary but will closely parallel the general price level.

NOTES

(1) Arthur F. Burns, "Burns Weighs the Future of Free Enterprise," The Conference Board Record, January 1979, p. 24.

(2) Agricultural Outlook. U.S. Department of Agriculture, November 1978, p. 13.

(3) National Food Review. U.S. Department of Agriculture, September 1978, p. 18.

(4) Progressive Grocer, October 1978, p. 66

5 Sweden: A Bellwether of Future Policy Trends

Graham T. T. Molitor

CYCLICAL RECURRENCE OF CONSUMERISM

Consumerism, like many public policy issues, recurs in cyclical patterns of activity. A review of the last 100 years reveals several phases or periods, each of 10-20 years duration. New waves of consumer reform emerged slowly and gathered considerable momentum before the Federal government responded.

Each burst of activity in consumer policy making occurred during a period of rapid social change. Often the need for change was prompted by introduction of new technologies.

One reason for such periodic waves, or warps of activity, is that law, itself, is evolutionary. Rules that govern society are ceaselessly in the process of extension, expansion and refinement.

New laws basically reflect society's constant search for perfection. It is an elusive goal, one incapable of ever being fully achieved. Continuous undertakings mean endless tinkering. Mankind's work is never finished. The ongoing nature of this activity involves patterns of adaptation, the evolution of which can be traced and even anticipated.

Consumer laws - and for that matter, laws of any kind - are society's institutional means for continuing the excesses of behavior and constraining social frictions. More laws are inevitable as society becomes larger, more complex and more interrelated. The dynamic nature of this constant change enables one to monitor and forecast the continuum of probable government developments.

Pressures for new laws build up in response to a catalog of social frictions or abuses. Once the body of evidence is compiled and documented, a compelling and sometimes irreversible force for corrective legislation commences.

Swiftness of the public policy process often depends upon dramatic events. "Catalysts" - such as the thalidomide tragedy - greatly speed up the process. Galvanizing events such as this create a sense of outrage that demands immediate corrective action.

The first cycle of consumerism in this century (figure 5.1) began during the Progressive Era and lasted some 20 years - from 1887 to 1907. The second cycle, ushered in by shock of the Great Depression, lasted some 10 years - from 1929 to 1938. The third cycle spanned some 23 years from 1951-1974. It didn't get underway in a serious way until 1958. During that year enactment of the Automobile Disclosure Act, Senator Kefauver's drug investigations/truth in packaging crusade, and President Kennedy's strong commitment set a pace that steadily grew. The fourth cycle, projected for a duration of 20 years, from 1978 to 1998, is just seriously getting underway.

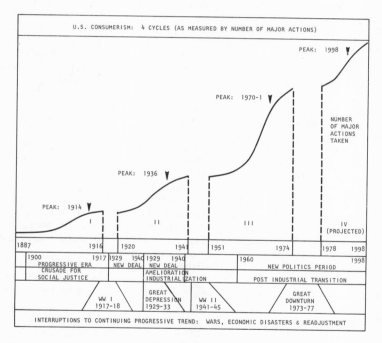

Fig. 5.1. Cyclical recurrence of consumer public policy action - four phases since turn of century

Source: Public Policy Forecasting, Inc.

Each period of social change and consumer activity was cut short by intercession of war and its post war reconversion period. Wartime footing and the aftermath of readjustment substantially alters national priorities. Expendable activities, such as consumerism, are given short shrift. Though pushed into the background, they are not forgotten. As abuses become increasingly difficult to endure, the pressure for change grows.

PRECURSOR JURISDICTIONS - SIGNIFICANCE OF CONSUMER POLICY CHANGES IN SWEDEN

Sweden has been a main focal point for consumer research by this observer. Over the last few decades, time and again new consumer actions have been undertaken first in the Scandinavian countries, and Sweden in particular. Major consumer policies were often established in Sweden from 2 to 20 years prior to being adopted in the United States. The lead lag pattern involved an average of 6-8 years (figure 5.2).

Experience with new reforms in precursor jurisdictions provides a first practical test. Upon implementation of the new law, regulation or voluntary response moves from the realm of ideas to reality. Worthiness is established by the experience of actual practice. Once vindicated or proven, politicians and government officials in other jurisdictions shortly thereafter begin championing implementation in their own area. Among similar nations (or lesser jurisdictions) usually there is little reason why similar solutions to similar problems will not work from one jurisdiction to the other.

Reasons for diffusion of new programs and policies are easily understood. In politics, nothing succeeds like success. Political survival in office depends on success. In turn, success depends upon accomplishment. So, practical minded politicians, if they are intent in holding onto their position, incessantly search for new ways to demonstrate accomplishment. Ideas and theories, once shown to work successfully, provide the grist for demonstrating accomplishment.

The innovator's example establishes a vital juncture. The demarcation is between theory and practice. Once an idea moves out of the realm of mere discussion and is implemented, it ceases to be merely an abstraction.

We can learn much by looking at the "social laboratories" of the world. Their example can be instructive and helpful in considering implementation of similar proposals elsewhere.

ALCOHOL REGULATION: STRINGENT CONTROLS MODERATING USE

"Empty Calorie" Foods - Prime Candidates for Reduced Consumption

With obesity the most widespread public health problem, foods without significant nutritional merit cannot help but be targets for reduced consumption. Foods contributing relatively large amounts of

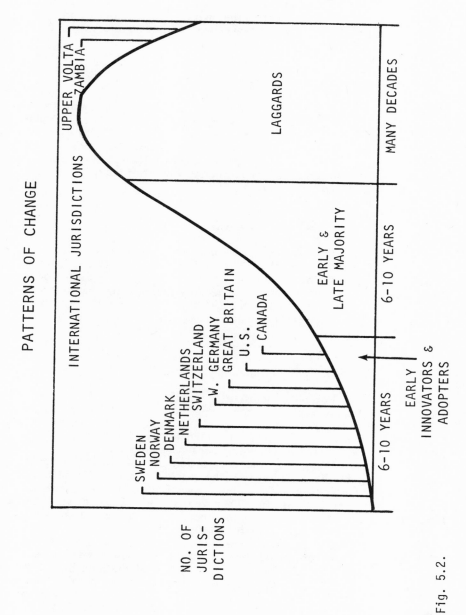

PATTERNS OF CHANGE

Fig. 5.2.

calories but relatively devoid of any meaningful nutrients are prime targets.

Prominent among so called "empty calorie" food components are sucrose and alcohol. Review is limited here to alcohol consumption. There is a tendency to lose sight of the high number of calories provided by popular mixed drinks. Only a few drinks can add significant numbers of calories to the daily intake.

Calories from Alcohol Consumption

Steadily increasing levels of alcohol consumption account for a surprisingly large and growing number of calories in the diet. Alcohol accounted for some seven percent of total calories in the diet - some 225 calories per capita/per day - in recent years. Alcohol has no redeeming virtues from a nutritional standpoint. Though moderate use may be beneficial in some way, from the standpoint of nutrition it has a major negative influence.

Alcohol and Cirrhosis of the Liver

Cirrhosis is a leading killer disease in America today. Ranking ninth as a cause of death among the 10 top killer diseases, its incidence is steadily increasing. For certain age groups the impact is even worse. Cirrhosis as a cause of death was especially high among the following age cohorts (ranking for 1973): third, for persons aged 25 through 34 (surpassed only by cancer and heart disease); and fourth, for persons aged 55 through 64.

Alcohol Consumption and Cirrhosis Mortality

Evidence may not be conclusive as to the precise role increased consumption of alcohol plays in the rising incidence of cirrhosis of the liver. Though some doubts may be raised as to the appropriateness of correlating cirrhosis of the liver with high levels of alcohol consumption, a broad and nearly overwhelming consensus links the two.

Dramatically highlighting the correlation between distilled spirits and cirrhosis of the liver mortality is the graphic display in figure 5.3.

Prohibition at the turn of the century was well underway among the state and local jurisdictions. By 1908 a virtual "tidal wave" of state and local prohibition laws had been enacted. Consumption of alcoholic beverages of all kinds dropped sharply during this period.

The temperance movement, already having succeeded in imposing "dry" laws in a substantial number of states, pressed onward toward national prohibition. Prohibition became the law of the land from 1920 to 1933. Mortality rates for cirrhosis plummeted during this "dry" period. The cirrhosis morbidity rate per 100,000 during Prohibition dropped to one half the rate it had been in 1910. During this brief

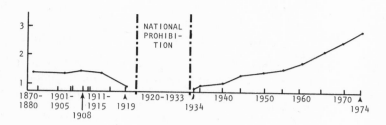

CIRRHOSIS OF LIVER, U.S. DEATH RATE PER 100M

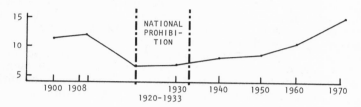

Fig. 5.3. Distilled Spirits Consumption, U.S. Per Capita

Note: "Tidal Wave" of State and Local Prohibition. By 1908
many southern state and local governments had already enacted
prohibition laws, as had Illinois, Michigan, Colorado, Nebras,a
Indiana, Ohio, Wisconsin, Minnesota.

Source: Public Policy Forecasting, Inc.

---

period of forced abstinence cirrhosis reached an all time low for this
Century.

Following repeal of the Prohibition Amendment, the rate of alcohol
consumption began climbing once again. It has been steadily rising ever
since. Closely paralleling increases in per capita consumption of
alcohol has been the rising incidence of cirrhosis of the liver. Currently
this killer disease has reached an all time high for the 20th century.
The rate of morbidity per 100,000 population for cirrhosis of the liver
currently is running in excess of twice the rate during Prohibition.
National health considerations involving excess calories, obesity, nutritional deficiencies and risks provide compelling reason for programs
intended to bring about moderation of alcohol consumption.

Empirical Dimensions of Sweden's Alcohol Problems

Among socially minded Swedish officials there is little reluctance to
intervene and impose new controls to realize social objectives. Such
actions, more likely than not, will be undertaken even though they may

diminish individual freedom. Overwhelmingly the obsession is to establish new social programs to improve society and protect the individuals living in it.

Interventionistic attitudes and a high regard for life extending potentials of new social programs permeate Swedish public policy making. Such attitudes are widely shared by the citizenry, or at least, they are taken for granted.

The typical Swedish bureaucrat is among the most rational, reductionistic, empirical minded, systems oriented, policy planner ever. Swedish officials are "technocrats" in every sense of the word. Swedish government action, in short, is very pragmatic. Invariably policies are based upon quantitative measurements, domestic statistical considerations, and cross cultural statistical comparisons. A driving compassion to be first in all fields of endeavor also plays a significant role in the high standards established in Sweden.

Statistically, the dimensions of the alcohol problem are described by one Swedish alcohol control official as "terrifying." Such language should not be subject to overreaction. Similar, if not worse, conditions are encountered in other nations. Among the many factors compelling intensified activity in alcohol control:

In the prisons, an estimated half of the inmates have problems with alcohol. In the psychiatric service, alcoholics absorb about one third of the work... About one-fifth of the emergency cases admitted to surgery are linked in one way or another to alcoholic abuse. (1)

Sweden has imposed extremely stringent control measures in an attempt to moderate alcohol consumption. Lest one think that alcohol abuse is more widespread and flagrant in Sweden than in other countries, I hasten to underscore that this is not so. Levels of consumption in Sweden rank relatively low compared to other countries. Furthermore, consumption levels in Sweden consistently have remained at relatively low levels for well over one hundred years (see figure 5.4).

Consistently the French have consumed more total alcohol per capita than any other country. Two key measurements of excessive alcohol use are mortality rates for cirrhosis of the liver and alcoholism rates. Compared to other countries of the world, Sweden ranks relatively low (see figure 5.5). Despite this, Sweden has undertaken major efforts to further moderate consumption of alcohol.

"Preventative" Emphasis in Eradicating Social Ills

"Prevention" has become a basic objective in formulating many new Swedish laws and regulations. Official attitudes - indicated time and again through personal interviews, exchanges of correspondence, and careful reading of official Swedish publications - provide convincing evidence of this "preventative" rationale.

Swedish alcohol control policies are motivated by "prevention" to an extreme degree:

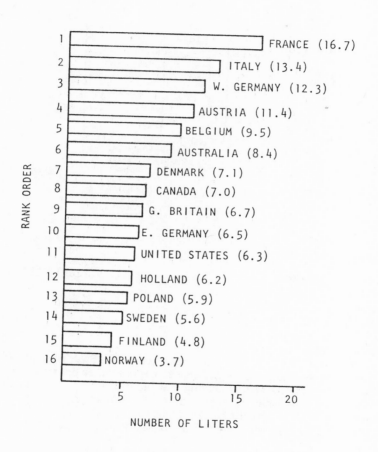

Fig. 5.4. Alcohol - Per Capita Total Consumption (100% Equivalent), 16 Countries, 1971.

Source: Public Policy Forecasting - Based on Swedish Institute
Statistics

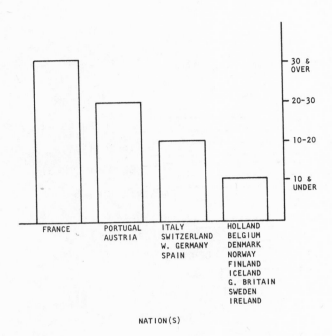

Fig. 5.5. Cirrhosis of the Liver - Mortality (Early 1970s)

Source: Public Policy Forecasting, Inc.

...forestalling and resisting alcohol injuries...in Swedish legislation it is considered a punishable offense to expose other persons to risks of life and limb...the act of driving a vehicle when affected by alcohol is therefore punishable, irrespective of whether any injury has been inflicted or not...drivers have such great responsibility that, from a preventative (emphasis added) point of view, it is necessary to be strict. (2)

The author of a recent book (3) making this same point concerning Swedish alcohol control policy quoted one commentator as follows:

A man can't be allowed to drink as much as he wants. It can hurt him, and hurt society. He's got to be saved from himself.

Quarrelsome as many may be with intervention in all things, effectiveness of results provides demonstrable evidence of success with which it is difficult to argue. Sweden's medical achievements and health successes have become respected the world over. Persons living in Sweden enjoy the longest life expectancy of any country in the world. Death and disease rates in Sweden consistently are among the lowest, if not the lowest, in the world. By many measurements of health care delivery, Sweden heads the list. Yet, Swedish medical care costs are relatively low compared to the United States.

The Swedish must be doing something right. In many different ways these successes can be traced back to the focus on prevention. Sweden is far into implementing social policy goals through eliminating root causes and imposing preventative measures. Most countries still are coping with curative efforts. The basic difference is between curative (after the fact) efforts and preventative (before the fact) undertakings.

Alcohol Taxes and Pricing Policy

Following demise of the monthly liquor ration system in 1955, authorities turned to taxes as a consumption limiting device. Tax rates consciously are tied to alcohol content. The higher the alcoholic content, the higher the tax rate that is levied:

Beverage	Tax as Percentage of Retail Price
Schnapps	90%
Heavy foreign wines	60%
Light foreign wines	50%
Strong beer, Class III	45%
Beer, Class II B	40%
Beer, Class II A	10%

High taxes, of course, are reflected in the pricing policy. The higher the alcohol content, the higher the price of the beverage. At such high prices, many Swedes consider alcoholic beverages almost a luxury. Typically, alcoholic drinks are served sparingly and consumption levels are relatively low.

Government revenues (taxes, tolls and profits) derived from the sale of alcoholic beverages are substantial. Together they accounted for some seven percent of total inland revenues in 1974. Interestingly, approximately ten percent of these revenues are "refunded" for treatment of alcoholics.

Pricing Policy in Establishments Licensed to Serve Alcohol

The prices of alcoholic beverages in Swedish public eating places are virtually cost prohibitive. Each year when visiting Sweden, I search out the most expensive double martini I can find. Last year I paid the equivalent of $12.50, including tip, for a rather modest sized, and not very dry martini! At these rates bar bills can be astronomical. Such high prices, of course, are intended to limit consumption.

Furthermore, licensed restaurants are barred from charging prices which encourage the consumption of high alcohol content beverages. Restaurants licensed to serve alcohol must make satisfactory selection of nonalcoholic beverages available to meet the desires of all categories of patrons.

Restaurants in Sweden do not generally serve as a cultural center for social drinking as they often do in other countries. Many small towns lack public eating places altogether. Taverns and roadside inns are unfamiliar.

Until 1955 restaurants were not allowed to serve alcoholic beverages unless the customer also took a meal at the same time. The maximum amount which could be served was limited to 15 centilitres. For females the level was even lower - 7½ centilitres. During the summer of 1956, throughout Sweden the requirement that alcohol be served only with meals, was suspended as an experiment. As of October 1, 1963, this principle of allowing sales without meals was adopted nationally.

Granting of licenses for on premises sale of liquor is subject to a number of other arbitrary rules. For example, licenses may be restricted on the condition that guests are seated while consuming the beverages, or on the condition that music be played on the premises.

"Cautious liberalization" is an appropriate way of characterizing the Swedish policies toward liberalizing the sale of alcoholic beverages in public places. Opening and closing laws are being liberalized. More places where dancing is carried on are being allowed to operate. All of these laws and customs do delimit alcohol use in public places. In 1973 only 3.7 percent of spirits, 6.7 percent of wine and 31.5 percent of beer were consumed outside the home.

State Alcohol Monopoly

Production and distribution of alcohol in Sweden was nationalized shortly after the turn of the century. Prohibition was rejected by a 1922 national referendum. The vote was fairly close: 924,550 to 888,459.

From 1917 (or possibly as early as 1914) up until October 1955, liquor ration passbooks were used to control the amount of liquor purchases permitted any one person. During that period, ration books were permitted for males over 25 years of age. Married women and abusers were barred altogether. Purchases were recorded in these passbooks. The ration allowed was one to three litres a month. In 1941 the maximum allowance was raised to four litres. Finally it was felt that ration books encouraged individuals to purchase their monthly ration, thereby actually boosting consumption. Accordingly, Swedish liquor ration passbooks ("motboks") were abolished in 1955.

Currently, the sale of all products containing more than 3.6 percent alcohol is monopolized by state owned companies. The marketing environment is neutral. Stores are laid out so they do not induce impulse shopping. State package stores do not encourage purchases. State operated retail package stores numbered about 300 in 1976.

Making Beer Accessible to Discourage
"Hard Liquor" Consumption

By releasing sale of low and medium beer in more accessible outlets - grocery stores - it was hoped the consumption of more potent alcoholic beverages would decline. It didn't work; consumption climbed. Until 1965, grocery stores were permitted to sell only "near beer" (pilsner type). Starting on October 1, 1965, medium strong beer (3.6 percent alcohol content or less) also was released for sale in grocery stores. Low and medium strength beers could be purchased by persons over 18 years of age. "Strong beer" containing not more than 5.6 percent alcohol by volume remained available for sale only in state retail stores or in licensed restaurants.

After intense debate over medium beer sales, it was finally decided to permit only the sale of light beer in grocery stores. A focal point of this controversy was the problem of alcohol abuse among young persons, who, it was feared, were drinking at ever earlier ages, more frequently, in greater quantity, and more often to a state of intoxication. As of July, 1977, only light beer was permitted to be sold in grocery stores, and all stronger beer and alcoholic beverage sales were confined to state controlled sources.

Drunkenness and Driving Privileges

Swedish controls regulating alcohol use and automobile driving may be the strictest in the world. Driving motor vehicles under the influence of alcohol is strictly forbidden by Swedish law. Persons known to be habituates or demonstrating intemperate behavior unconnected to motor vehicular use (e.g., arrest for sidewalk drunkenness) also can have their driver's license suspended. Drinking offenses must be noted by demerit marks in the register of driver's licenses. Persons deprived of their driver's license on the grounds of alcohol abuse are required to wait two years until a new one can be issued.

Swedish police are authorized to stop suspects and subject them to breath-analyzer tests to ascertain sobriety. Police roadblocks checking for drinking drivers frequently are set up on weekends in downtown night club areas. Even Monday morning roadblocks are set up to catch drivers still having excessive alcohol in their blood. When a breath test indicates a state of inebriation, then a blood test must be administered. Blood tests to determine inebriation can be performed at the police station, at a hospital, by a doctor or other specially trained individuals. Levels of concentration of alcohol in the blood are determinative of the penalty imposed. The proceedings are summary in nature and the severity of the punitive action depends upon the concentration of alcohol in the blood:

- 50 mgs. alcohol per 100 mls. blood - "insobriety while driving": person considered "unsober" and risks suspension of license

- 80 mgs. alcohol per 100 mls. blood: suspension of license a near certainty, or "warning notice" may be issued

- 150 mgs. (and higher) alcohol per 100 mls. blood - "drunkenness while driving": suspended license certain, and additional punishment also inflicted

Alcohol concentration of between 50 mgs. and 150 mgs. can result in suspension of a driver's license and a fine, but never imprisonment. Alcohol levels of 150 mgs. and above can result in jail sentences of up to one year; milder offenses can result in not less than a 25 day fine. Such fines are scaled to a person's income level, recognizing the principle of ability to pay as an inherent part of social justice.

Criminal Penalties to Control Alcohol Abuse

The severity and rigorous enforcement of penalties connected with alcohol and automobile use have served to sharply reduce the number of offenses. Drunkenness while driving measured by the number of cases per 1,000 vehicles has been reduced by some 25 percent.

Illicit brewing and distilling may add as much as an additional 25 percent to official sales volume statistics. High prices have resulted in almost a 50 percent increase in offenses involving illegal manufacture and import of alcoholic beverages. However, at the same time, offenses involving illegal sale have declined.

Host guest laws extend criminal liability to hosts. Persons serving alcohol who should have known that their guests would be driving or making a public nuisance of themselves may find themselves criminally responsible. Although the sanction is rarely imposed, the host can receive a fine and even a jail sentence up to a maximum of one half that imposed on the offending party.

Social sanctions play an important part in moderating alcohol consumption in Sweden. Intoxicated persons on the streets and in public places are regarded with great contempt. The deterrent effect of strict criminal and other social sanctions discourages public displays of drunkenness.

Restrictions on the Right to Purchase
Alcoholic Beverages

"Black lists" maintained by state retail stores list persons who are denied the privilege of purchasing alcoholic beverages. Persons whose names appear on "stop lists" include: abusers under treatment, persons who have illegally sold alcohol, persons who within a 12-month period relapse into drunkenness, persons driving under influence of alcohol. At the end of 1973 the black list included 11,641 persons. Swedish population at that time amounted to 8.1 million persons.

Institutional Care and Treatment for Alcoholics

The Temperance Act confers to local government the authority to institutionally commit alcoholic abusers against their will. District Temperance Boards established in each district and overseen by County Temperance Boards possess and exercise this power to commit alcohol abusers to public institutions for care and treatment.

This law encourages informants. The police, doctors, and even neighbors are encouraged, sometimes even duty bound to report offenders. Medical practitioners are required by law to report all cases of alcoholic abuse to Temperance Boards (unless the doctor also is treating the individual for this problem). Every case of drunkenness coming to the attention of the police must be reported to the Temperance Boards. Persons who have not been convicted of drunkenness within a five year period before the offense in question, are designated "persons convicted for drunkenness for the first time"; others with recurrent patterns are designated "recidivists." Notice of conviction is posted in the National Tax Board's special penal register for drunkenness. Such information is available to temperance officials, police and courts.

Alcohol abuse cases referred to local Temperance Boards can be divided into three categories:

1) "Inquiry case" - simple inquiry into living conditions of the abuser;

2) "Remedial measures case" - upon a finding of alcohol abuse remedial, measures must be undertaken (advisory talks of a therapeutic nature, employment assistance, withdrawal of privilege of purchase alcohol, etc.);

3) "Coercive measures case" - detention and supervision in a public institution.

The Temperance Committee may place a person under surveillance, whether the person wants it or not, for one year, if he is: repeatedly arrested (three times for drunkenness during the last two years), posing a safety risk to himself or other people, neglecting to support his family, failing to take proper care of himself, or leading a disturbing life. If these preliminary control measures fail, then the local Temperance Committee can recommend to the County Temperance Committee that the individual be delivered for treatment to an institution. The period of detention varies considerably: one year (usual commitment is for 3 to 4 months, with the balance of the period on probation), two years if the person has been institutionalized once before in the last five years, and four years for recidivists.

On October 8, 1965, a Royal Commission on Alcohol Policy was appointed to consider problems associated with alcohol abuse. The report issued in 1968 proposed a wide range of recommendations. One proposal suggested abolishing punishment for drunkenness and recommended that persons taken in hand by the police be sent to "acute clinics" for care.

Advertising Bans and Restrictions

Advertising alcoholic beverages is severely restricted in Sweden. Under terms of an agreement between the Consumer Ombudsman and the alcohol branch association, extremely stringent advertising and promotion restrictions are imposed on outdoor and movie ads, as well as direct mail. Print ads are required to give a "sober, balanced presentation." Newspaper ads are limited to a maximum of 780 millimeters, and to three fourths of a page in other publications.

Alcohol advertising directed toward youth is strictly forbidden. In a 1973 case referred to the Market Court by the Consumer Ombudsman, a poster advertising medium strong beer directed toward youth, and set up in conjunction with a sports event, was held manifestly improper.

Advertising and promotion statements also are being modified to include warning statements and disclaimers. According to one report the warnings, similar to those for cigarettes, caution that alcohol endangers health. One government newspaper advertisement included a disclaimer that alcohol may improve sexual performance, literally stating: "It's wrong to think that a few drinks will improve your performance in bed."

The Committee on Tobacco and Alcohol Advertising in its June 1973 report considered three basic approaches: 1) total prohibition of all advertising, 2) partial prohibition (e.g., all press advertising), and 3) severe restrictions on content, design, etc. The Commission proposed that tobacco and alcohol advertising and promotion be conducted with particular moderation and restraint. Advertising, moreover, was recommended to be confined to relevant facts about the product, and its quality presented in the most objective manner possible without irrelevant elements. Other proposals included discouraging active marketing and promotion, including outdoor advertising and direct mail.

NEGATIVE MARKETING - NEW CONCEPT WITH PROBABLE APPLICATION TO OTHER ISSUES

Swedish Tobacco Controls - Precedent-Setting "Negative Marketing" Approach

The Swedish Committee on Smoking and Health was not the first such national government committee to respond to health problems connected with smoking. Among the first reports were those emanating from the Royal College of Physicians of London in 1962, and an advisory committee to the U.S. Surgeon General in 1964. The significance of these two early reports was the official government stance and the strident stand taken. They provided a note of finality to long term controversies surrounding smoking and health.

What was precedent setting about the Swedish report was its boldly innovative approach and massive scope. Sweden was the first country to propose a long term, all out coordinated program for combatting smoking, using nearly every technique imaginable.

The remarkable character of these sweeping arrangements merits careful examination. The step by step program aims at all segments of society. It employs all media and information channels.

"Negative marketing" is a newly coined term devised to characterize this massive consumer control effort. The overall objectives are to eliminate, or discourage smoking, to provide as many environments as possible that are free from smoking, and to create a marketing climate as negative towards smoking as can be achieved - short of prohibition.

Many of the concepts, if proven effective, almost certainly will be applied to a considerable range of consumer control policies in other nations. Principles involved are likely to be adopted to control hazardous, harmful or deleterious products (and services). Already under debate for similar treatment are proprietary drugs, sugar, and alcoholic beverages.

Tobacco use is characterized by official Swedish government documents as a "major hazard to public health." Annual per capita consumption of tobacco products in Sweden is almost one third that of the United States. Tobacco use, nonetheless, is considered to be a major health problem. Per capita annual consumption for all tobacco products during 1970 stood at 9.63 pounds in America (for persons 18 years and older). In Sweden, consumption for all tobacco products stood at 3.59 pounds (for persons 15 years and older). Per capita annual consumption of cigarettes during 1970 stood at 3,971 in America (for persons 18 years and older). In Sweden, cigarette consumption stood at 1,620 (for persons 15 years and older) (see figure 5.6)

Self-Regulation Programs

Self-regulation efforts often are voluntarily undertaken by industries facing the prospect of public controversy and impending government regulation. Such responses are a part of a familiar pattern of accommodation in public policy processes (see figure 5.7). In the United States there often is a sequence of events to voluntary industry regulation efforts (see figure 5.8).

Various self imposed restrictions have been undertaken incrementally by the tobacco industry. Recently established agreements restraining promotion of all tobacco products in Sweden go to some extraordinary lengths. Major details provide insight as to the trend and direction of possible future limitations on tobacco products in other countries.

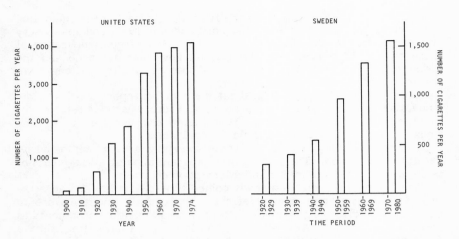

Fig. 5.6.   Cigarette Annual Consumption Per Capita (15 Years & older)

Sources: (a) Public Policy Forecasting, Inc. (1900-1960 data based on USDA-ERS data; 1970 & 1974 data based on USDA data and reflects per capita usage for persons 18 years & older)
          (b) Public Policy Forcasting, Inc. (Based on National Smoking and Health Association data, Sweden, 1973

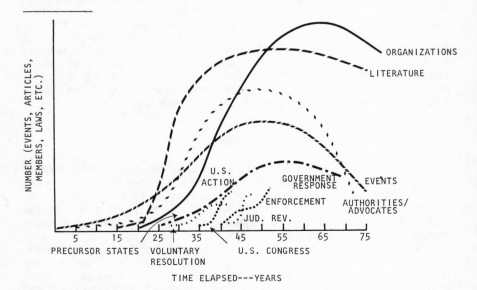

Fig. 5.7. Time Sequences: Typical Convergence of Evolutionary Waves of Change

Source: Public Policy Forecasting, Inc.

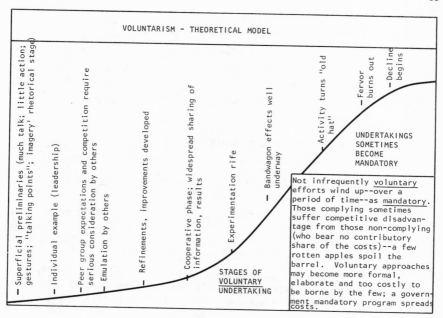

Fig. 5.8. Voluntarism - Theoretical Model

Note: Voluntary efforts at self-regulation can be looked upon as a stop gap, as a natural adjustment mechanism - voluntarism often "buys time" for laggards, smaller units to begin preparing themselves to phase-in to new and usually higher levels of performance.

Source: Public Policy Forecasting, Inc.

The voluntary regulation agreement between the Swedish Tobacco Branch Association and the Consumer Ombudsman became effective in 1975. Voluntary self regulation of tobacco product advertising includes the following principles:

1) Media Limitations

- ban on direct mail advertising addressed to consumers' homes

- ban on cinema advertisements

- prohibition of outdoor (billboard) advertising, except in relation to places of sale

- proscription of ads in magazines directed to persons less than 21 years of age (a listing of affected publication is prepared yearly)

- ban on ads on newspaper sport pages
- ban on ads in sports magazines
- limitation of newspaper ads to a size not exceeding 1520 column millimeters
- restriction of ads in other publications to a size not exceeding one full page.

2) Advertising Content Restraints

- balance and moderation
- disallowance of pictures of humans or nature scenery unless the picture is part of the trademark
- limitation of pictorial displays to a reproduction on the product, its package, trademark or brand name, or usage (e.g., smoking a pipe) - such pictures are to be neutral and not imply messages with persuasive overtones
- insistence on informative headline copy and test results limited to: type of product; contents; method of manufacturing; taste, strength, and other characteristics; usage of the product; raw material origin; disclosure of manufacturer name of location; price; and sales outlets.

3) Additional Promotional Restrictions

- ban on ads in a variety of institutional settings, including schools, health facilities, and places mainly frequented by youth
- limitation of consumer testing (and testimonials) of tobacco products
- ban on distributing any tobacco products to youth.

Labeling Disclosures and Warnings

Stern warning declarations recently were mandated for tobacco packages offered for sale in Sweden. Disclosure was directed by the Swedish Parliament (Riksdag) in 1975. Label designs were completed in May 1976. Implementation commenced January 1, 1977.

Most novel is the requirement for constantly changing the message. This concept has potential application to other consumer products for which cautionary warnings of hazards may be appropriate. (Similar warnings have been suggested or implemented in Western European countries for products other than tobacco - alcohol, sweets, pharmaceuticals.)

Cautionary health warnings and messages for tobacco products are drawn from a repertoire of different texts. There are 16 of them for cigarette packs alone, and special sets of declarations pertain for other tobacco products (see figure 5.9). The current set of declarations is intended to be discarded after two years at which time an entirely different set of declarations will be approved for use. The continual variation in text is intended to draw renewed and maximum attention to the various health hazards posed.

Disclosure of certain "harmful" components of tobacco smoke - not only tar and nicotine, but also carbon monoxide - also is required. Not only must the declaration state tar, nicotine, and carbon monoxide for the brand concerned, but the mean contents of all the brands marketed in Sweden must also be indicated, (a "comparative yardstick" approach), according to a recent report from the Swedish Institute.

Usual format requirements also are imposed for declarations to assure prominence and help put across the intended message. Packaging declarations must appear on the largest surface of the package. In addition, they must be in clear and contrasting color to ensure maximum visibility and impact.

Long Term Tobacco Control Programs and Proposals

Sweden's Parliament (Riksdag) passed legislation in 1968 urging appointment of a smoking and health committee to develop plans for reducing tobacco consumption. The Minister of Finance refused to create such a committee in January, 1971.

Subsequently, the Ministry of Health and Social Affairs was petitioned by the National Smoking and Health Association. The petition resulted in the National Board of Health and Welfare appointing a Smoking and Health Advisory Committee in December, 1971. The Committee's report was submitted in June 1973. Some five years had elapsed from the time of the initial legislative behest.

The Swedish formula starts with the basic premise that society increasingly should undertake programs that are preventative in character. This admonition is part of a general trend toward preventative public policy making. The objective is to eradicate root causes. Such efforts are calculated to eliminate or at least control problems before they pose too great a hazard or burden upon society.

Comprehensive proposals have been developed to ameliorate health hazards associated with tobacco use. Many proposals are still in the discussion stage. More government controls are in the offing.

Product Availability and Pricing Programs and Proposals

Pricing, a traditional regulatory gambit, is heavily relied upon by Swedish government officials to discourage consumption. Comparative prices for a pack of popular cigarettes, in 1976, were almost four times more costly in Stockholm as compared to major cities in the United States.

THE PERSON WHO STOPS SMOKING WILL SOON BE MORE FIT *NATIONAL BOARD OF HEALTH AND WELFARE*	SMOKER'S COUGH IN THE MORNING? *Smoker's cough is a sign of early ill-health. The cough will cease if you stop smoking.* *NATIONAL BOARD OF HEALTH AND WELFARE*
THE MORE YOU SMOKE THE GREATER HEALTH RISKS WILL THERE BE *NATIONAL BOARD OF HEALTH AND WELFARE*	SMOKING DAMAGES THE LUNGS! *It begins with a smoker's cough and it may end up with lung cancer or other lung diseases.* *NATIONAL BOARD OF HEALTH AND WELFARE*
ASBESTOS *is especially dangerous to smokers. If you work in an environment with such pollution you should stop smoking.* *NATIONAL BOARD OF HEALTH AND WELFARE*	THE PERSON WHO STOPS SMOKING INCREASES HIS CHANCES OF REMAINING HEALTHY. *NATIONAL BOARD OF HEALTH AND WELFARE*
YOU WHO HAVE BEEN SMOKING FOR A LONG TIME! *It has been proved that those who stop smoking will decrease the health risks* *NATIONAL BOARD OF HEALTH AND WELFARE*	SMOKERS HAVE MORE SICKNESS THAN NON-SMOKERS *NATIONAL BOARD OF HEALTH AND WELFARE*
WHICH CIGARETTES ARE MOST DANGEROUS? *those yielding most carbon monoxide, tar and nicotine. But it also depends How you smoke.* *NATIONAL BOARD OF HEALTH AND WELFARE*	YOU WHO HAVE BEEN SMOKING FOR A LONG TIME! *Stopping smoking is useful – the risk for disease will decrease and your fitness will improve.* *NATIONAL BOARD OF HEALTH AND WELFARE*
DISEASES OF THE HEART AND ARTERIES *Smokers run an increased risk of heart attacks and certain diseases of the arteries.* *NATIONAL BOARD OF HEALTH AND WELFARE*	IF YOU STILL MUST SMOKE *Avoid inhaling and leave long butts and you will absorb less of dangerous substances.* *NATIONAL BOARD OF HEALTH AND WELFARE*
NON-SMOKERS HAVE LONGER AVERAGE LIFE THAN SMOKERS *NATIONAL BOARD OF HEALTH AND WELFARE*	SMOKING AND AIR POLLUTION *is a bad combination. Smokers are more sensitive to air pollution.* *NATIONAL BOARD OF HEALTH AND WELFARE*
SMOKING DURING PREGNANCY MAY HARM THE CHILD *NATIONAL BOARD OF HEALTH AND WELFARE*	YOU WHO ARE YOUNG! *The earlier you begin smoking the more seriously your health will be affected.* *NATIONAL BOARD OF HEALTH AND WELFARE*

CIGARETTES: 16 ALTERNATIVES TO BE CONTINUOUSLY ROTATED AND REPLACED (SUPPLANTED) EVERY TWO YEARS.

Source: Public Policy Forecasting, Inc. Based on data from National Smoking and Health Association, Stockholm, Sweden.

Fig. 5.9. Tobacco Products: Repertoire of Cautionary Labeling Declarations, Sweden 1977.

Yearly price increases were proposed by Sweden's Smoking and Health Committee. Under the proposal, prices would be increased annually by 10% "in relation to the general price and income level."

In an effort to make tobacco products less available the following proposals were put forward: a ban on coin-operated (vended) sales by 1979, the outlawing of sales or distribution of tobacco to persons under 16 years of age, the termination of tobacco sales in food and other shops not expressly established for the purpose of selling tobacco and the restriction of the maximum amount of tobacco brought into the country by travelers (to the low level now allowed for persons outside the country less than 24 hours).

Reducing cigarette consumption to the low level of the 1920's was an overall goal set by the Committee. Programs also would aim at preventing increased consumption of other alternative tobacco products. However, snuff was recognized for use as a last resort cure.

Not unexpected for any nation with socialized industry segments, government take over of the tobacco industry also was put forward by the Committee. Among the proposals was one reestablishing the state tobacco monopoly. It was contemplated that this would facilitate implementing "negative marketing." Until 1961 all importing and manufacturing of tobacco was handled by a monopoly corporation. Since 1961 there has been a free market. However, the former monopoly corporation, now a state owned company (operating as the Swedish Tobacco Company, Ltd.), dominates tobacco trade with an 85 % market share.

Advertising Programs and Proposals

Tobacco advertising already is severely restricted in Sweden. Sweden's Consumer Ombudsman and the Market Court, two principal and powerful adjuncts of Swedish consumer policy, exercise substantial powers over advertising of tobacco products. Between them they are empowered to intervene and regulate the content and design of advertising. In a 1973 case referred to the Market Court by the Consumer Ombudsman, a Prince cigarette advertisement showing signatures and photographs of well known persons whose attributes were associated with their occupations and an endorsement, "I have gone over to Prince," was deemed improper. Objection was taken to its suggestive design as well as the health risks involved in tobacco smoking.

Outright and total prohibition of all tobacco product advertising has been suggested time and again in Sweden. Freedom of the press and avoidance of censorship have been impelling reasons for the reluctance to impose such additional advertising bans. Most recently a Royal Commission studying advertising policy rejected any such ban. Advertising over state owned radio or television broadcasting channels already is prohibited. Because there is no commercial radio or TV in Sweden, printed advertising is the most widely used medium. Current controversy is pretty much limited to printed advertising.

The Smoking and Health Committee proposals would virtually do away with marketing and promotion of tobacco products. Among their recommendations were the prohibition of all advertising and promotion unless contributing toward developing negative marketing attitudes, a ban on advertising that is "intrusive, outgoing, persuasive (emphasis added) or otherwise more active", a mandate on health warnings in all advertising, the prohibition of scenes in films or television programs that encourage cigarette consumption, the proscription of "obtrusive" marketing and the termination of all commercial marketing promotion.

Restricting Tobacco Usage in Public Spaces - Programs and Proposals

Wide ranging attention was given by the Smoking and Health Committee to suggestions for barring tobacco usage in a variety of different confined public spaces. Objection to smoking in such closed spaces is prompted by "passive smoking" - inhalation of "smoking pollutants" by non smokers. Prominent among the recommendations were the restriction of employers' rights to engage smokers in certain tasks posing adverse synergistic reactions (for example, lung cancer among asbestos workers who smoke is eight times greater than that of non-smokers), the investigation and identification of occupations and environments where other such restrictions should be imposed, the phasing out of smoking privileges in other than working space locations which workers frequent (e.g., recreation areas), the elimination, by steps, of smoking on public premises, the establishment of a non smoking environment status in schools and the creation for children born after 1975 of environments frequented during their formative years that are as free from smoking, and as negative toward smoking as possible.

Anti Smoking Information Programs and Proposals

Experimental anti smoking information programs have been under-taken in preschools, schools, mother care and child care centers, and various places of employment. The Smoking and Health Committee recommendations included expanding information campaigns stage by stage. Anti smoking campaigns, after tried and proven, would be extended to the following areas: maternal and child health centers (by 1975), kindergartens (by 1979), elementary schools (by 1981), and secondary schools (by 1985).

Further dissemination of anti smoking information by the Committee included the following recommendations:

- educate children continually as to harmful effects of tobacco use;

- conduct public information anti smoking campaigns in the mass media;

- promote anti smoking informational programs at courses and conferences held by the National Board of Health and Welfare;

- direct informational programs to the popular movements, youth organizations and other public spirited groups;

- encourage study circle organizers to include smoking health issues in their programming;

- provide government financial support to organizations willing to conduct anti smoking activities;

- distribute anti smoking government publications through chemists' shops (state owned), post offices (also state owned), and tobacconists' shops (Swedish government tobacco companies dominate all trade and command and 85 % share of market, consequently, the pressure on tobacconists to distribute such literature probably is quite strong);

- compel smoking and health education component during compulsory military service.

Health Care Related Programs and Proposals

Emphasizing preventative health measures, the Smoking and Health Committee preferred a number of suggestions aimed at improving health:

- designate the medical care delivery system as an anti smoking channel;

- start with at risk groups (advise all chronic bronchitis patients they ought to stop smoking, etc.);

- provide similar information to all relatives of patients suffering from or susceptible to tobacco smoke;

- provide at smoking withdrawal clinics (established at each of the five regional hospital centers) therapy for high priority persons (e.g., parents of small children, school teachers, etc.);

- provide voluntary access to antidotal clinics;

- rename chronic bronchitis "Cigarettossis" (this is in line with other maladies where the causative agent lends its name to describing the disease, e.g., asbestosis, silicosis);

- discourage smoking which may bring harm to persons other than the smokers themselves: for example unborn children (women smoking during pregnancy may experience unsuccessful outcome); unborn children/youngsters (mothers-to-be and other mothers may contribute to retardation of physical and/or mental development for children up to seven years of age);

- encourage diagnosis, information and treatment in company health services;

- encourage life insurance companies to increase premium rates for smokers;

- extend air pollution standards to include regulation over tobacco generated pollutants (for example, carbon monoxide concentrations in small, poorly ventilated rooms under some circumstances exceed those permitted in working spaces);

- reduce maximum allowable concentration of all constituent substances of tobacco smoke (whenever another country adopts a standard lower than the one pertaining in Sweden, revise the standard to an even lower level);

- commit research to the following areas: antidotal treatment, commencement of smoking habits, recidivism, and influence of smoking.

Significance of Swedish Tobacco Controls

The vast and varied nature of innovative efforts either proposed or actually undertaken in Sweden to control tobacco use are being carefully watched by other governments and the tobacco industry. Positive results, once demonstrated, can unleash a domino-like sequence of similar actions being taken elsewhere in the world.

NOTES

(1) Inger and Bo Lofgren. "Alcohol in Sweden." Swedish Institute, March 1976.

(2) "The Alcohol Question in Sweden." Centralforbundet for alkoholoch narkoti-kaupplysning, circa 1970.

(3) Roland Huntford. The New Totalitarians. (New York: Stein and Day, 1972).

II

The Debate:
A National
Nutrition
Policy?

Introduction

This section looks at the growing interest and controversies concerning nutrition and the changing nature of food and nutrition policies. The authors suggest the role they foresee for nutrition in the 1980s.

Rene Dubos describes how widely persons differ in their nutritional requirements and their capacity to adapt to a diversity of nutritional conditions. He believes that these adaptations make a mockery of attempts to define an optimum diet for the hypothetical average person. Because nutritional requirements of adults seem to be determined by early nutritional conditioning, Dr. Dubos believes that one of the most important problems of nutrition science is to study the effects of early conditioning on nutritional requirements and to determine the later consequences of this. He expects that in the future diets will be designed not only for growth and health, but also for certain psychological functions and cultural values.

Marylin Chou examines how the objectives and constituencies of our food policy have changed, which government agencies are involved in nutrition programs and research, and how much of a nutrition policy we can anticipate in the 1980s. Dr. Robert Olson explains how the current interest in nutrition and hypotheses relating to coronary artery disease evolved. His major objection to the Dietary Goals for the United States, as recommended by the Senate Select Committee is focused on their claim that adherence to the recommended diet will reduce morbidity and mortality. In contrast to the public perception of cholesterol, Dr. Olson describes the essential functions of cholesterol and how the body deals with different ranges of cholesterol intake. As an alternative to diet intervention recommended by Dietary Goals, Dr. Olson suggests effective preventive measures known to decrease mortality from heart disease, namely, exercise programs, avoiding obesity, abandoning cigarette smoking, and controlling high blood pressure and diabetes.

Graham Molitor compares the nutrition goals of selected industrialized countries, giving a historical perspective on changing nutrition concerns. He singles out obesity as the major health problem today. Mr. Molitor discusses the importance and evolution of nutritional labeling, and approaches toward nutrition education.

6 The Intellectual Basis of Nutritional Science and Practice*

René Dubos

Many people of the Western world, especially in the United States, are intensely worried about the quality of their food, and about their nutritional state, but this is chiefly because they constantly read and hear that they have reasons to worry, not necessarily because they are malnourished. Any departure from what is assumed to be the ideal dietary regimen (I use the word "assumed" because convincing evidence is lacking) becomes public event chronicled by the mass media, thus contributing to the now prevalent social neurosis about the general state of the world. In reality, the immense majority of people in the countries of Western civilization now have a diet that is far better balanced, and freer of toxic effects than was the case at almost any time in the past, except perhaps, as far back as the Stone Age. This does not mean that our food and nutritional state are ideal. Their shortcomings, however, do not come from a deterioration of our dietary regimen, but rather from its lack of adaptation to our ways of life. We know a great deal about the production and the characteristics of the various kinds of food, but very little about what should be the diet for a particular person in a particular physiological condition, professional activity or behavioral situation.

In 1946, Oxford University in England was offered large funds to create a new Institute of Human Nutrition. The University refused the funds on the ground that the knowledge of human nutrition was essentially complete and that the proposed Institute would soon run out of meaningful research projects. There were seemingly good reasons for this attitude. Most of the essential growth requirements were then known, and there was an illusion that a consensus would soon be achieved concerning recommended daily allowances (RDA) for each

* This paper was presented at the National Institutes of Health Conference, "The Research Basis of Clinical Nutrition: A Projection for the 1980s," Bethesda, Maryland, June 20, 1978.

dietary item - a consensus also that prevalent methods of food control were sufficient to eliminate most serious dietary accidents because of toxic or other physiological disturbances. The Oxford authorities did not realize at the time that the problems of food production and control differ profoundly from the far more complex physiological problems relating food intake to nutritional state. It is now clear that knowledge is deficient in all the physiological aspects of the nutrition problem. Persons differ widely in their requirements depending upon cultural habits, ways of life, individual genetic differences and last, but perhaps not least, behavioral patterns.   Pathological manifestations have occurred that were completely unanticipated a generation ago and which are still poorly understood today.   Furthermore, and probably most important, human beings are capable of biological and social adaptations to a great diversity of nutritional conditions, and these adaptations make a mockery of attempts to define precisely an optimum diet for the hypothetical average person.

THE NUTRITIONAL ADAPTABILITY OF HUMANKIND

Many people believe that they can function well only when provided with three square meals a day, and certain students of nutrition believe that this formula constitutes, in fact, the surest way to a good nutritional state. But few are the societies in which the practice of three square meals a day is considered desirable for health. Even in Great Britain, the custom of three meals a day became common only in 1890.   In the economically humble French environment from which I emerged, the substantial meal was at noon.   Supper was a desultory affair. As to breakfast, it consisted of bread, with a cup of chocolate for children or of coffee for adults.   Never did a glass of orange or tomato juice reach my lips until ten years after I had settled in the United States. Yet here I am to tell the tale at the age of 78. My sister and brother, who are both in their mid-70s and still living in Paris, are also doing well on the same regimen, as are my French nieces and nephews. There are tribes in which people nibble constantly, and others which partake of only one meal a day. At Harvard University, I knew a famous medical scientist who ate only at dinner time when he could make the meal an elaborate social occasion.

In East Africa, the Kikuyu people are healthy and develop a wonderful physique on a purely vegetarian diet. In contrast, the Masai people who live in the same region derive practically all their nourishment from milk and from the blood of their cattle which they bleed daily; yet, they do as well as the Kikuyu without much intake of the plant fiber which is so much on our mind today.

I could go on and on with examples illustrating that social groups and individual persons have successfully adapted to very different dietary regimens, but I find it more useful to discuss at some length a more drastic phenomenon of nutritional adaptation, namely adaptation to extremely low food intake throughout the life span.

During the 1940s, I participated in the research activities of the Institute of Nutrition for Central America and Panama (INCAP), located in Guatemala City. The average food intake per capita in the villages of Guatemala was then, and still is, extremely low, and deficient in protein. Indeed it would probably be incompatible with the needs of the average European or North American. Many children and young adults died of infection. But the adults who survived, although of very short stature, and seemingly frail, were capable of physical efforts far greater than those expected of vigorous Europeans and North Americans - such as carrying heavy burdens on their back over long distances up and down mountains. Physiologic studies showed that these adult people could maintain themselves in caloric and protein balance on a diet that would have meant starvation for most Europeans, and especially, North Americans. Furthermore, these skinny people, grossly undernourished according to our standards, commonly lived to a good old age. Since Guatemalans of the same ethnic groups, raised in wealthier surroundings and fed a rich and abundant diet, became as large physically as people of Europe and North America and exhibited the high nutritional requirements of these countries; it can be assumed that the anatomical and physiological characteristics of the adult village Guatemalans were not of genetic origin, but resulted from adaptation to low food intake during early life.

Before the war, most adult Japanese men and women were of small size, and this is still true of Japanese persons over forty years of age. In contrast, the average size of Japanese teenagers and young adults is much the same as that of young Caucasians in the prosperous parts of the world. The phenomenal increase of body size in Japan cannot be due to genetic factors since it occurred within one generation. One of its reasons may be the control of childhood diseases, but probably more important are the profound changes in the Japanese diet that occurred during the past few decades. Between 1950 and 1975, for example, the average consumption per capita increased 15 fold (not 15%) in the case of milk, 7.5 fold in the case of meat and eggs, 6 fold in the case of fat, whereas the per capita consumption of rice and potato decreased significantly. The change in stature and physiological characteristics of the Japanese population during the period is illustrated in table 6.1 which presents average values of girls 12 years old.

Table 6.1. Physique of Girls Twelve Years Old

	1950	1960	1970	1974	(U.S. White) 1974
Height (cm)	136.8	143	148	148.5	149.1
Weight (kg)	32.0	36.5	40.3	41.0	40.9
Age of Menses	15 yrs.	14 yrs.	12.5 yrs.	12.2 yrs.	12.5 yrs.

Source: Yasuo Kagawa, "Impact of Westernization on the Nutrition of Japanese: Changes in Physique, Cancer, Longevity, and Centenarians," Preventive Medicine, Vol. 7, June, 1978, p. 211.

Thus it is obvious that the pre-war Japanese people had adapted biologically to a low intake of certain nutritional elements (probably protein and fat) by maintaining a small size during youth and throughout life. This biological adaptive state had such profound effects that adult and old Japanese people grown under such conditions, do not significantly increase in size even when they adopt the much richer and abundant diet of present days. As in the case of behavioral development, there are probably different types of metabolic development pathways which all may be "normal" for different environments.

At the beginning of the present century, American nutritionists had worked out Recommended Daily Allowances for the various essential nutrients, in particular proteins; these values had been established on the basis of studies of nutritional balance carried out on vigorous young adults, chiefly college students from Ivy League Schools. Almost unanimously, however, nutritionists of other countries considered the American RDA far too high. After heated discussions, the commissions on nutrition of World Health Organization and Food and Agriculture Organization decided in the 1970s to scale down the protein requirements of a healthy person by some 30 percent, eliminating thereby, by administrative decision, much of the international "protein gap" which had been postulated in earlier decades! Recent American studies have been interpreted as meaning that the redefined protein standards may be too low because a group of United States university students, fed the lower new "safe" level of protein, developed signs of protein deficiency after two months. The explanation of this finding however, is probably in the fact that at all social levels, American children were (and to a large extent still are) fed diets much richer, and more abundant than European children, let alone children of developing countries. The nutritional requirements of adults thus seem to be determined by early nutritional conditioning. One of the most important problems of nutrition science is thus to study the effects of early conditioning on nutritional requirements, and to determine the late consequences of this early conditioning.

It has long been recognized of course that nutritional requirements change with age and are different for men and women. But the values calculated in the past may have lost much of their validity now that ways of life have changed so profoundly. For example, the amount of physical activity and of exposure to cold are certainly factors of importance in this regard. Furthermore, it is certain that genetic constitution profoundly influences nutritional requirements. Each one of us has a nutritional-metabolic pattern as charcteristic, indeed as unique, as our fingerprints. For this reason, I understand, the minimum requirements of a person of a given age may differ by a factor of three to ten, for any particular item, simply because of genetic differences.

PATHOLOGICAL EFFECTS ASSOCIATED WITH
DIETARY REGIMENS

It might be argued that the easiest way out of these complexities is to provide for each person the maximum practical amount of food. But this is not advisable because there is convincing evidence that any food stuff in excess of the proper amount can become the cause of pathological damage. Classical examples are the claims of association between salt intake and hypertension, and of the correlation between the blood levels of cholesterol and saturated fatty acids with coronary heart disease. At a conference on "Cancer and Diet" held in Seattle, in March, 1977, it was claimed that the change to Western type of nutritional patterns in Japan, mentioned above, has been accompanied by marked increases in the mortality of certain forms of cancer among women 50-54 years of age, as shown in table 6.2.

Table 6.2. Cancer Mortality in Females 50-54

	1950	1960	1970	1974	(U.S. White) 1974
Breast	4	3.7	6.0	7.1	19
Colon	2.7	6.3	7.0	8.1	26
Stomach	72	61.0	54.0	42.0	4.1
Uterus	79	41.0	25.0	21.0	14.0

The increases in mortality from cancer of the breast and of the colon seem the more convincing because they are accompanied by a decrease in cancer of the stomach and of the uterus, thus approaching the patterns common in the United States, and suggesting that Western nutritional habits were really responsible for these dramatic changes.

Correlations derived from epidemiological studies, however, do not constitute evidence of cause effect relationships. A case in point is the current debate over cancers of the bowel (the colon and the rectum). These cancers are common in developed Western nations, but rare in the developing countries. Such difference is certainly due to environmental factors, and not to genetic factors, since Japanese who have settled in the United States succumb to bowel cancer at the high United States rates, rather than at the much lower rates prevailing in Japan. But, whereas the facts concerning incidence seem well established the explanations are highly questionable. Two theories are popular at the present time, one centered on the decrease in dietary fiber intake, the other on the increase in dietary fat wherever people adopt the ways of Western civilization. Either or both of these theories may have some validity, but neither of them has been indisputably established. Any change in dietary regimen involves a multiplicity of other changes in the ways of life and also in chemical intakes, since any item of food contains many substances other than those determined by the analytical processes employed to evaluate their nutritive value.

So called natural foods are no more innocent than processed foods of potential danger. Suffice it to mention, as examples among countless others, that potatoes contain a substance, solanine, which would reach toxic levels if ten times the usual amount of potato were consumed at one sitting. Whole wheat, oatmeal, and other cereal grains contain phytic acid which interferes with the absorption of calcium and iron in unleavened products. Excessive consumption of certain natural plant products can produce goiter. Colza oil (rape seed oil), which is an important item of human nutrition in large parts of Europe, has been shown to produce irreversible lesions of the myocardium in several animal species, even when administered in fairly low doses. And there are many constituents of natural foods that can produce cancers in one animal species or another.

The recognition that potentially dangerous substances are present in practically all "natural" foods puts the problem of food additives in a peculiar light. One can predict that if the standards used to test man made chemicals were applied to "natural" foods, fully half of the human food supply would have to be banned. The Delaney Amendment, which forbids the addition to food of <u>any</u> material shown to produce cancer in animals in <u>any</u> dose, would certainly lead to decisions unacceptable to the public if it were carried out to the letter of the law. The new analytical techniques permit the detection of certain chemicals in such fantastically small amounts, that most items used in the kitchen, including the most favored spices and other adjuvants to food and drink, could almost certainly be shown to contain detectable levels of chemicals having carcinogenic properties in one or the other kind of test system, (the Ames Test). In this regard, it is entertaining to recall that caffein was one of the first substances shown to increase the rate of mutations in bacteria. It will take complex and sophisticated biological and clinical research to develop practical common sense in the evaluation of risk benefit concepts to be used for the definition of sensible threshold levels in food additives and other substances such as pesticides and hormones, which eventually find their way into most articles of food.

FUNCTIONAL ASPECTS OF NUTRITION

As mentioned earlier, the definition of "recommended daily allowance" for the various items of food was derived, at first, from studies made on normal persons, according to age and sex. It is now realized, however, that there are enormous individual differences, some caused by the genetic constitution, and others caused by the past history of the particular person, as well as by the occupation and ways of life of that person. The physiological state of the person at a particular time also influences requirements; this is obvious in the case of pregnancy, or during recovery from some debilitating disease. But there are many other situations in which the nutritional state can influence the response of the person to various forms of stress or treatment. Nutritional science would greatly benefit from the development of functional test designed to measure the ability of the organism to develop scar tissue, and produce antibodies, to generate phagocytic cells, to correct tissue damage, to modify behavior, in brief, to make adequate biological and psychological response, to various life situations. In this regard it is of special interest that at least two news transmitters, produced in the brain, are affected by the nutritional state: Serotonin by tryptophane and acetylcholene by choline or lecithin.

Although there is an enormous scientific literature on the relation between the nutritional state and the susceptibility to infection, only few facts are well established, and the mechanisms involved have rarely been analyzed. Malnutrition increases susceptibility to certain types of infective agents, but not to others. In fact, paradoxically, malnutrition increases resistance to a few pathogens, at least in experimental infections. For example, animals fed a diet somewhat low in paraaminobenzoic acid have been shown to be extremely resistant to experimental malaria, probably because plasmodia have high requirements for this vitamin.

I shall end with another kind of functional response to infection which seems to be profoundly affected by the nutritional state. A few decades ago, numerous tests were carried out by very competent groups of epidemiologists and statisticians to evaluate the protective efficacy of BCG vaccination against tuberculosis in children, but the results differed from one part of the world to another. For example, all the tests carried out by English and Scandinavian teams in England and in Scandinavia showed that BCG induced a high level of protection. In contrast, tests carried out by American teams in Indian tribes of the South west, in the deep South, and in Jamaica, gave little, if any, evidence of antituberculous protection. It is possible of course that the samples of BCG vaccine used by the various teams differed somewhat in immunizing potency, but it is certain on the other hand that there were great differences between the populations tested. One can take it for granted that most English and Scandinavian children were in a good state of nutrition, whereas malnutrition was prevalent in all the ethnic groups studied by the American teams. Experiments in mice have revealed that BCG vaccination has very little protective value against intravenous injection with virulent tubercle bacilli, when used in animals fed a deficient diet. Although these experiments were not sufficiently developed to reveal the cellular nor humoral mechanisms responsible for the failure of BCG vaccination in malnourished animals, they point to the importance of the nutritional state in resistance to mycobacteria.

CONCLUSIONS

During its first phase, nutritional science was focused on the identification of essential food factors, the definition of their chemical structure, the determination of minimum requirements according to age and sex, and to some extent, the study of their metabolic role. During the past two decades, emphasis has shifted to the recognition and study of pathological effects produced, not only by undernutrition, but also, and even more, by overnutrition.

In my judgment, we are now about to enter a different phase of nutritional sciences. One based on functional tests determining the role of food not only in growth and disease, but in the various functions which enable the body and the mind to respond effectively to challenges and stresses in the various manifestations of life. This new phase will require not only physiological studies, but also a behavioral approach. It will inevitably bring to light that the human species is as adaptable with regard to nutritional requirements, as it is with regard to other aspects of its life. There are, of course, biological invariants in the need for food. But to a large extent human beings determine what they become, and what they are able to do, by what they elect or can afford to eat, and vice versa, what they eat influences what they become, and are able to do. This will inevitably raise questions of value which are parascientific. The post war Japanese are taller than their parents, but this does not mean that they will live longer, will be happier, or will become more productive in the arts and sciences.

It seems reasonable to envisage a time when dietary regimens can be designed not only for growth and health, but for certain physiological functions and cultural values. When, and if, we can reach the proper level of knowledge, nutrition will become a part of a new science, as yet undeveloped, human ecology.

7 Changing Food Policies

Marylin Chou

BACKGROUND

Since World War II, American agriculture has undergone major changes. The Second Agricultural Revolution took place in the 1950s, with the shift from animal to mechanical power. Farm production per hour of farm labor increased almost three fold between 1950 and 1973, while labor used in farming decreased by more than 50 percent. The increased productivity was brought about by advances in plant and animal research and by the use of agricultural chemicals. The incentive to adopt these technologies came from the increased demands of a steadily growing urban population and rapidly increasing land prices.

Until this time, American farmers, like farmers throughout the world, were at the mercy of nature's whims. Droughts, floods and plagues could destroy crops and wipe out their annual income in one night. Therefore, many farmers, especially those who had marginal farms, moved into urban areas or sought income from nonfarm activities. With fewer people farming and a growing population to feed, government policy tried to encourage farmers to increase production by guaranteeing farm prices. This incentive along with the application of scientific farming methods, was sufficient to create farm surpluses.

Concurrently, food processors improved food processing and packaging techniques, enabling food to stay fresher longer, and to be transported longer distances. With improved technologies came greater varieties of food. An abundant supply of low cost food, as well as a sense of complacency regarding our ability to feed ourselves, and a growing market abroad, was abruptly shaken in 1972 with the extraordinary grain purchases by the Soviet Union, combined with poor harvests abroad. Suddenly our grain reserves were depleted, and domestic food prices reflected the shortage. The energy crisis in 1973 further underlined our sense of insecurity and made us recognize that our economic well being could be affected by conditions abroad. Soviet

103

and Chinese food policy decisions were raising the cost of the bread and meat we ate, while providing our farmers with record incomes.

THE EXPANDED CONSTITUENCY AND COMPONENTS
OF FOOD POLICIES

These events brought home how economically interdependent the domestic economy was to events and policies abroad. Farm policy could no longer be restricted to the interests of the farmers. Moreover, the shrinking farm population gave farmers fewer votes. Many new interest groups became concerned about how food prices would affect them, so that policies had to meet the demands of a much broader constituency. Consumers also became more vocal. Although difficult to describe as a movement in terms of a unified force, their goals have sought to provide the following: stability of food prices and supplies, adequate nutritional supplies to low-income consumers, programs such as zero tolerance regulations, unit pricing, and nutritional labeling, humanitarian food aid abroad, and equitable incomes for farmers and fair prices for consumers.

Surprisingly, both farmers and consumer groups have shared an alliance over varying issues with organized labor. (2) When expedient, rural forces have regrouped with urban interests. This new complexion of the constituency, concerned with multiple objectives, has widened the scope of policies to include more than the traditional interests of farmers and producers.

Farm policy can no longer be considered in isolation. It must be treated as a component of domestic, as well as foreign economic policies. For example, the United States sells one third of its agricultural production abroad, which has paid for two-thirds of its oil imports since 1974. (3) Farm policy must ensure that the agriculture and food system contributes to national economic growth, internal stability and external payments balance, thus expanding the range of competitive objectives between which tradeoffs must be made. (4) Food and agriculture's component parts include balance of payments, establishment of food reserves, inflation, unemployment, income supplements, and government program costs. Changes in policy in these areas can also affect the nutritional status of the population. Food policies, therefore, must be concerned with balancing the interests of different groups in society so that food prices are consistent with a stabilized economy while also providing returns to farmers that will ensure a steady expansion of their output. This new multidimensional nature of food policy has also increased the number of government agencies at the executive and legislative levels that participate in the food policy making process. Of the 38 federal agencies involved in some aspect of food, at least 24 have been created since 1970. (5)

INTEREST IN NUTRITION

Concurrent with the growing public awareness of food as it affects domestic and foreign policy has been a growing interest in nutrition. In 1967 the United Senate Subcommittee on Employment, Manpower and Poverty shocked the American public with their reports regarding evidence of malnutrition in Mississippi. The irony of a nation with overflowing agricultural reserves being capable of feeding the poor raised many questions of responsibility and policies. As a result, in 1968 the Senate Select Committee on Nutrition and Human Needs began investigating the issue of hunger and malnutrition among America's poor and recommending solutions to the problem.

The following year the White House Conference on Food and Nutrition and Health with 3,000 delegates representing academic, medical, industrial and agricultural interests met with approximately 400 poor people to discuss their nutritional problems. The White House Conference marked the beginning of the growth of public and congressional interest in nutrition. (6)   Prior to this, government involvement in nutrition was limited to laws governing fortification and efforts at nutrition education during World War II. (7)   The Senate Select Committee's first report, The National Nutrition Survey, found that among 12,000 individuals living in low income areas in Texas, Louisiana, New York and Kentucky, the most widespread nutritional problem was one of "multiple nutrient deficiency of a combination of one or more nutrients such as protein, vitamins, minerals, and calories." (8)

Within eight years, the Federal government's commitment to nutrition programs has increased from less than $500 million to over $8.5 billion annually. The coverage has been extended to more than 15 percent of the population via programs of assistance to low income families, and in particular, those most vulnerable to nutrition problems such as pregnant and nursing women, infants, young children and the elderly. These programs have been based on the assumption that under nutrition is a result of low income and that the way to alleviate poverty is through nutrition programs. Critics of this approach believe that "nutrition" has become a euphemism for "social welfare" and has been used as a convenient vehicle to try to alleviate poverty, when in actuality the programs have done very little to alter poverty or effect a better social welfare system. (9)   Furthermore, the Food Stamp and food distribution programs have served as income supplements rather than nutrition programs.

Ten years after the release of the first Senate Select Committee's report describing the nutritional deficiencies of those low income families surveyed, the Senate Select Committee changed its focus. The major public health problem perceived shifted from undereating to overeating, from the poor minority to the middle class or affluent majority. Their thesis was that our diet has changed so much over the past 50 years that it is now a threat to public health and may be responsible for heart disease, cancer, obesity and stroke, among other "killer diseases." Fat, sugar and salt were singled out as the sources of the problems.

As the quotes in figures 7.1 and 7.2 indicate, the subject of dietary guidelines is fraught with controversy. Those recommending more specific dietary guidelines believe that our present diet is responsible for the "killer diseases," whereas the opponents claim that diet may be only one factor among many, and the role it plays is still scientifically unproven. Due to these uncertainties, they feel the public should not be led to think dietary guidelines will prevent chronic diseases. Senator McGovern and Dr. Hegsted argue that, even without scientific proof, there is more risk invovled to the American people if they continue their present pattern of overeating than that which would result from some dietary modifications. The report from the Office of Technology Assessment takes the pragmatic position that since diets can be altered more easily than some of the other factors influencing diseases, the role of nutrition deserves greater attention. By contrast, Professor A.E. Harper of Wisconsin University believes that misdirected attention is being given to nutrition as a low cost substitute for comprehensive health care.

As indicated by the opinions expressed, there is no consensus among scientists that dietary guidelines as proposed by the Senate Select Committee are appropriate for the population at large. The only areas of agreement are obesity, tobacco, and alcohol as links to certain chronic diseases.

The emphasis on disease prevention, however, is a tribute to our medical achievements in overcoming most of the deficiency and infectious diseases responsible for early deaths. Our concern now is how to delay the onset of the chronic diseases. Our standard of living and affluence have enabled us to give priority to quality of life considerations which transcend the capabilities of nutrition. We are not dying of chronic diseases in epidemic proportions. While the total number of deaths from cardiovascular disease and cancer has increased over the last several decades, the mortality rate for cardiovascular disease has shown a significant reduction and, for all cancers, except lung cancer, has declined or remained stationary (see table 2.2).

If one assumes that diets may be partly responsible for disease, then food becomes a suspicious target. Because most foods are processed outside the home, there is a growing uneasiness about the ingredients included and excluded from such food. The food industry has had to assume the responsibility for either too much fat, sugar and salt or for refining some of the essential minerals or fibers from traditional staples. As a result, processed foods have inherited a negative connotation. As our improved standards demand higher standards of quality and safety, and as we become aware of more finite nutritional requirements, it would be logical, although overwhelming, to exercise the same analytical concern over "natural" foods as we do over processed foods. If we are concerned about the health effect of chemicals, we should not assume that what is old and familiar is necessarily safer. We should remember that even water can be dangerous if too much is consumed at one time.

THE CONTROVERSY OVER DIETARY GUIDELINES

Senator George McGovern:

...our diets have changed radially within the last 50 years, and great and often very harmful effects on our health. These dietary changes represent as great a threat to public health as smoking. Too much fat, too much sugar or salt, can be and are linked directly to heart disease, cancer, obesity, and stroke, among other killer diseases. In all, six of the ten leading causes of death in the United States have been linked to our diet.

...I think it is very difficult to prove many of these things in an absolute scientific sense. But where you have an overwhelming body of opinion beginning to build, it seems to me as public policymakers, we under a somewhat different criteria in terms of what we recommend to the public in contrast to a scientist who is working and looking for absolute proof. We are not recommending that laws be passed, and say people can't eat fat. We are simply saying this report indicates there is a consensus building on the part of the medical profession that the American people in many cases are eating too much, in other cases they are eating too much fat, too much sugar, too much salt, and we think those things ought to be reduced.

Is there more risk involved to the American people in making the moderate dietary changes...than there is not making those changes?

Sources: Dietary Goals in the United States, Select Committee on Nutrition and Human Needs, U.S. Senate, Washington, D.C., December 1977, p. XIII.

Diet Related Killer Diseases, III, Hearings before the Select Committee on Nutrition and Human Needs of the United States Senate, March 24, 1977, pp. 18-19.

D. Mark Hegsted, U.S. Department of Agriculture:

...the major health problems of the United States and other affluent countries are coronary artery disease, stroke, cancer, diabetes, hypertension and obesity... All of these diseases are clearly associated with the diet we eat... Some people have argued...that we do not know enough to recommend a change in the American diet. I believe that we know so much that we cannot afford to ignore what we do know.... The issue is not have we proven that a change in diet will be beneficial or can we predict the results of a moderation in the diet...we can, however, ask what are the proven benefits of the American diet. There are no positive arguments for a diet which is high in fat, sugar and cholesterol and there are a host of arguments against it. The real issue is how soon, by what mechanisms, and hos rapidly we move to encourage consumption of a more moderate diet.

...We do not need consensus; what we need is leadership.

Source: "U.S. Dietary Goals." Talk presented at the 1978 Food and Agricultural Outlook Conference, Washington, D.C., November 17, 1977, pp. 1, 4-5.

Office of Technology Assessment:

...the Federal government has failed to adjust the emphasis of its human nutrition research activities to deal with the changing health problems of the United States. The consequences of continuing to pursue the present preoccupation with nutritional deficiency diseases will seriously affect the quality of life of present and future generations into the 21st century.

...The role of nutrition must be given priority in the prevention and improved management of today's major health problems. Nutritional factors deserve particular attention for two reasons. First, it is possible to change diets while some of the other factors that influence disease development cannot be altered. Second, nutrition is basic to health and deserves attention as one of many factors that influence health and disease...

Source: "The Role of Diet in the Prevention of Chronic Disease and Obesity," Nutrition Research Alternatives, Office of Technology Assessment, OTA-D-74, U.S. Congress, Washington, D.C., September 1978.

Edward H. Ahrens, The Rockefeller University:

The committee has made a prejudgment on the outcome. To imply that achievement of six goals will lead to reduction in new events of coronary disease is misleading and counter-productive.

The committee should emphasize uncertainties still exist...recommendations should not imply that by needing recommendations, the public will reduce its risk of suffering the diseases identified with the McGovern report... We simply don't know enough about nutrition today in relation to coronary disease, cancer, diabetes, etc.

Source: Diet Related Killer Diseases, III. Hearings before the Select Committee on Nutrition and Human Needs of the United States Senate, March 24, 1977.

Fig. 7.1.

Gilbert A. Leveille, Chairman, Department of
Food Science and Human Nutrition, Michigan
State University:

...The American diet has been referred to as
"pathogenic" by some and as "disastrous" by others,
implying that our diet has "deteriorated" in the
past 50 to 75 years....The American diet today is
better than ever before and is one of the best, if
not the best, in the world today...any dietary
guideline must have, as a fundamental basis, the
objective of meeting essential nutrient needs, and,
secondarily, must deal with other recommendations
that would contribute to ensuring the public
health....The Dietary Goals, published by the
Senate Select Committee, assume 1) that the diseases of primary concern, namely cardiovascular
disease and cancer, are of epidemic proportions
in the U.S. And 2) that appropriate dietary modifications can delay or prevent these diseases....
The concept that dietary modification will prevent or delay artherosclerosic heart disease
remains a hypothetical and not a demonstrated
fact...On the basis of the totality of available
evidence, it seems highly premature to make any
major recommendations for the prevention of
cardiovascular disease. Rather, it would seem
far wiser to recommend the establishment of a
system for the evaluation of individuals to
establish that segment of the population at
risk and to make appropriate dietary and other
recommendations for these individuals....The
report of the Senate Select Committee proposes
that a relationship exists between diet and the
incidence of cancer. Evidence for such a
relationship is extremely meager. The recommendation...that a shift from foods of animal
origin to those of plant origin would protect
the population from cancer is unfounded and
is not supported by available evidence.
Health problems which exist in this country
and which should receive attention are dental
caries, obesity and iron deficiency anemia.

Source: "Establishing and Implementing Dietary
Goals," talk presented at the 1978 Food and
Agricultural Outlook Conference, Washington,
D.C., November 17, 1977, pp. 1-4.

Council for Agricultural Science and Technology:

Although the health problems the Goals address
are real, the problems are highly complex,
multifactorial in nature, and inadequately understood. In addition to nutrition, the causative
factors of the degenerative diseases the Goals
are designed to alleviate include genetics,
smoking, overeating, inadequate exercise, alcohol
consumption, and other life habits.
...To control obesity, the appropriate emphasis is on a generation reduction of fat, refined
sugar, and alcohol because these substances supply
energy but lack other nutrients....Associated
with the Goal should be more exercise to assist
in avoiding and controlling obesity.
...The recommended replacement of a large dose
of meat in the average diet with carbohydrate
should be approached with caution because of the
probability that this would increase iron-
deficiency anemia.

Source: "Dietary Goals for the United States: A
commentary." Council for Agricultural Science
and Technology, Report No. 71, November 30, 1977.

Fig. 7.2.

A.E. Harper, Professor, Departments of Biochemistry
and Nutritional Sciences, University of Wisconsin:

Evidence that the incidence of heart disease and
cancer can be reduced by modification of the diet
is highly speculative...

What we need, rather than general guidelines
aimed at disease prevention, is more emphasis on
providing the knowledge that we have about nutrition
and maintenance of health for the public, to ensure
that,...the ability of people to achieve their
full genetic potential will not be impaired by
nutritional inadequacies, excesses or imbalan
and their bodies will not be limited in their
ability to respond to diseases, stresses or
other environmental insults...

...We have become preoccupied with chron
degenerative diseases and the major causes
in the U.S.... This has general appeal--bot
rich and the poor age and die; it is a commo
problem of concern to everyone. In most coun
with a high standard of living, comprehensive
care programs for the entire propulation have b
developed.... There is great resistance to expe
ing tax funds in the amount required for the
development of a comprehensive health-care prog
... However, with an acceptable euphemism, a le
expensive alternative is possible...the euphemis
is "nutrition,"...a substitute for health care.

Source: "What are Appropriate Guidelines?" Food
Technology, September 1978, p. 53, 48.

Drs. Franz Ashley and William Kannel:

Data from the Framingham study examined by Ashley
and Kannel in 1973 indicate that each 10 percent
reduction in weight in men 35-55 years old would
result in about a 20 percent decrease in the
incidence of coronary disease.

Conversely, each 10 percent increase in weight
would result in a 30 percent increase in coronary
disease.

The clinical and preventive implications seem
clear. Weight gain is accompanied by atherogenic
alterations in the blood, lipids, blood pressure,
uric acid and carbohydrate tolerance. It is uncertain whether the nutrient composition of excess
calories, derived largely from saturated calories
accompanied by cholesterol and simple carbohydrates,
or the positive energy balance per se, is important. But whatever the cause, development of
ordinary obesity encountered in the general population is associated with excess development of
coronary heart disease.

Source: "Dietary Goals for the United States,"
Senate Select Committee on Nutrition and Human
Needs, February 1977, p. 33.

PROSPECTS FOR A NATIONAL NUTRITION POLICY

Considering the lack of consensus regarding dietary intervention among scientists and affected interests in the food industry, what can we expect in terms of a national nutrition policy in the 1980s? The experiences of other countries that have instituted national nutrition policies indicate that three basic elements are required for successful implementation: 1) government commitment 2) a policy and coordinated program, and 3) the administrative machinery to implement the program. (10)

In terms of governmental commitment, the interest in nutrition is at an all time high. At the Federal level, seven departments operating through 14 agencies, as well as 14 congressional committees and 20 subcommittees, are concerned with nutrition. Secretary of Agriculture Robert Bergland reflects the traditional concerns of the Democratic Party in trying to formulate the Department policy responsive to the consumer which aims to protect the broad public interest, in contrast to the interests of one sector, such as the producers. He has stated:

The nation needs a nutrition policy from which we can build a food policy. These must serve the framework for farm policy...a national food policy should recognize the linkage between nutrition, food consumption, food processing and agricultural production...policy should concern itself with every step in the national food system, from farmer to consumer. The nation, its people, demands that the whole food industry be pre-eminently responsible to the consumer. (11)

Carol T. Foreman, Assistant Secretary of the United States Department of Agriculture, has stated the USDA position as follows:

The USDA seeks the development of policies that provide an adequate supply of safe, high quality and nutritional food at reasonable prices, while providing a reasonable return on investment to those who produce and distribute food, and assuring some assistance to those at home and abroad who cannot afford an adequate diet even at reasonable prices. (12)

The USDA has undergone major reorganization over the past two years. The 1977 Farm Bill directed the Secretary to establish human nutrition research as a separate and distinct mission of the Department. In response to this directive, the Department established the Human Nutrition Center in 1978 and appointed Dr. D. Mark Hegsted as the Administrator. The choice of Dr. Hegsted is indicative of the direction the USDA is taking (see figure 7.1 for Dr. Hegsted's views on dietary intervention). The Center conducts basic research on nutritional needs and composition of specific foods. The USDA budget for human nutrition research has risen from $25.1 million in fiscal year 1977 to $47 million in 1979, of which $23.4 million is allocated to the Human Nutrition Center. (13)

Judging from the number of departments, agencies and legislative committees concerned with nutrition, one can assume a sufficient commitment exists at the executive and legislative level for formulating a national nutrition policy. The policy enunciated by the USDA has set the tone. A major problem, however, is that to fulfill the goals of a national nutrition policy requires long term research in human nutrition because the science of nutrition is still in its infancy. Such research requires substantial funding. As table 7.1 describing the nutrition research priorities and food and nutrition programs of federal government agencies indicates, the Department of Health, Education and Welfare and the United States Department of Agriculture are responsible for most of the federally supported human nutrition research. In the past, HEW emphasized research relating to specific diseases or curative oriented research; whereas the USDA has been primarily concerned with nutrition and food in relation to maintenance of health. The USDA is now aiming to have a more preventive focus that also integrates the role of food production and marketing.

The priorities in human nutrition research for the 1980s are ambitious and laudable, but they require a high level of funding and the appropriate scientists to carry out the research. According to a study by the Office of Technology Assessment, Nutrition Research Alternatives, and a report by the General Accounting Office, Federal Human Nutrition Research - Need for a Coordinated Approach to Advance our Knowledge, there is a shortage of nutrition research scientists, and no accurate figures exist on how many scientists are currently engaged in human nutrition research. (14)

Moreover, the reports criticize the unstructured, diverse and piecemeal approach to nutrition research as presently exists among the 14 federal agencies which lack coordination, focus and direction. (15) Associated with this criticism is that one of the major obstacles in the implementation of a national nutrition policy is the lack of a clear locus of responsibility within government for that subject. (16) Neither a new agency nor the USDA or FDA has been designated as the lead agency. Whichever group or agency is given the responsibility to formulate and carry out a food and nutrition policy will require a substantial budget as well as adequate authority to be effective in harmonizing the many interests. In the coming decade Congress will have to resolve the leadership dilemma for the implementation of an effective policy.

Even the definition of what constitutes human nutrition research differs from one agency to another, so that expenditures for human nutrition research in fiscal year 1977 were estimated at between $50 million and $117 million, depending on how "nutrition research" was defined. (17) These amounts seem relatively low when compared to the General Accounting Office estimate that federal programs associated with assuring good nutrition cost an estimated $40 billion annually. (18) George Briggs of the University of California at Berkeley has estimated that one third of these costs might be saved through good nutrition. (19) Because many of the links between diet and health are still hypothetical, and because diet may only be one of many factors causing

Table 7.1. Federal Government Agencies Active in Food and Nutrition Programs and Their Nutrition Research Priorities

Department	Agency	Food and nutrition programs	Research priorities
Health, Education, & Welfare	National Institutes of Health		*National Institute of Arthritis, Metabolism, and Digestive Diseases (NIAMDD).* Basic physiological studies of nutrients; basic metabolism studies; obesity; trace elements nutrition support of patients; fiber; anemias.
			National Institute of Child Health and Human Development (NICHHD). Nutrition and fetal development; metabolic capacities of normal, low-birthweight, and premature infants; diet modification for low-birth-weight and premature infants; optimum nutrition in developmental years; nutrition and reproductive potential; genetic variability—nutritional interaction; prevention—metabolic antecedents of adult disease.
			National Cancer Institute (NCI). Nutrition support of cancer patient; nutrition in cancer etiology; host-tumor interactions and competition for nutrients; prevention strategies based on nutrition; diet and nutrition in the rehabilitation of cancer patients.
			National Heart, Lung, and Blood Institute (NHLBI). Nutrition in etiology of arteriosclerosis and hypertension; achieving and maintaining dietary change; development of food composition tables; methodology—collecting, recording, and evaluating dietary data.
			National Institute of General Medical Sciences (NIGMS). Traumatized/burned patients and nutrition.
			National Institute of Environmental Health Sciences (NIEHS). Neurotoxicity; mutagenesis; teratology; environmental contaminants in food.
			National Institute of Neurological and Communicative Disorders and Stroke (NINCDS). Protein-calorie malnutrition, B-vitamin deficiencies and the nervous system; genetic disorders and the nervous system; specific nutritional problems in the central nervous system; stroke.
			National Institute of Dental Research (NIDR). Sucrose and caries; poor nutrition and periodontal disease; poor nutrition and oral mucus membranes; nutrition in craniofacial malformations and oral-facial structures; nutrition and salivary gland development.
			National Institute of Allergy and Infectious Disease (NIAID). Interrelated factors hearing on malnutrition, infection, and the immune system.
			National Eye Institute (NEI). Vitamins A, B-12, and other nutrients in visual processes; diseases of visual system, e.g., keratomalacia; metabolism of visual cells; protein changes in the lens.
			National Institute on Aging (NIA). Nutritional status of the elderly; aspects of increase in life span including dietary manipulations; vitamin supplementation in elderly; nutrient intake as a consequence of economic status in elderly; relationship among nutrition, cellular structure, and function in elderly.
			Division of Research Resources (DRR). Nutrient requirements for growth, gestation, lactation in primates and laboratory rodents; standard diets for specific objectives; interaction of various nutrients on physiological function in laboratory animals; differences in nutrient requirements among strains of animals within a species.
	Food & Drug Administration	Regulatory activities related to: nutrition labeling, ingredient labeling, food for special dietary use, food advertising, nutrition quality of foods	Nutrient efficacy and safety; nutrient interrelationships as concerned with disease prevention; nutrient bioavailability for food fortification purposes; nutrient quality assessment of processed foods; medical food assessment; food composition and nutrient analysis as related to FDA mission; and consumer studies of perceptions about food values and nutritional quality and educational models to help correct misconceptions about them.
	Health Resources Administration	Health and Nutrition Examination Survey	Assessment of the nutritional status of the American people.
	Center for Disease Control		Epidemiological surveillance studies in cooperation with State agencies assistance to AID in similar international areas.
	Health Services Administration		Collaborative research and screening program for phenylketonuria.
	Alcohol, Drug Abuse, & Mental Health Administration		Effects of alcohol consumption on nutrient metabolism and nutritional deficiencies; study of food additive consumption and hyperactivity in children.

Department	Agency	Food and nutrition programs	Research priorities
Agriculture	Agricultural Research Service*		**Human Requirements for Nutrients** Determine the requirements for lipid intake and identification of the forms of these nutrients in foods that may be useful in meeting these requirements.
			Determine the requirements for mineral intake by humans and identification of the forms of these nutrients in foods that may be useful in meeting these requirements.
			Determine the requirements for vitamin intake by humans and identification of the forms of these nutrients in foods that may be useful in meeting these requirements.
			Determine the requirements for protein and amino acid intake by humans and identification of the forms of these nutrients in foods that may be useful in meeting these requirements.
			Determine the requirements for carbohydrate and energy intake by humans and identification of the forms of these nutrients in foods that may be useful in meeting these requirements.
			Food Composition and Improvement To provide accurate, up-to-date, and comprehensive information in a readily usable form on the composition of all important foods for those nutrients required by and biologically useful to man.
			To provide the technology for the nutritional improvement of foods when enhanced levels of certain nutrients in the diet are needed to correct possible dietary faults.
			Food Consumption and Use To provide accurate, up-to-date, and comprehensive information in a readily usable form on food consumption and dietary levels.
			To provide consultative assistance on food and nutrition problems and provide sound guidance materials on nutrition for the consumer and for nutrition educators, program leaders, and food program managers; to identify techniques which will assist people in selecting nutritionally adequate diets within different budget limitations; to identify means to modify undesirable food habits; to strengthen nutritionally desirable food choice.
			To identify and develop suitable and safe procedures for food management and preparation for home and institutional consumers, for best retention of both nutritional and eating qualities and to avoid food-borne illness.
	Cooperative State Research Service**		Nutrient requirements; nutritional status of special population groups including children, low income, and aging; metabolic function of nutrients in the diet and their interactions; nutrient content of foods; effects of processing on nutrients; food delivery systems; food habits and use); dietary patterns.
	Economic Research Service***		Economic and social research relating to domestic food programs; nutrition policy in LDCs; food choices (demand); nutritional programs for the elderly.
Defense			Determination of nutritional and dietary standards for Armed Forces personnel subsisted under normal and special operating conditions; evaluation of nutritional adequacy of food as consumed; evaluation of the nutritional status of Armed Forces personnel; establishment of sanitary and food hygiene standards for all food program activities; food aspects of preventive medicine.
National Aeronautics & Space Administration			Nutritional control of neurotransmitters; role of dietary protein and specific amino acids in optimizing human performance under stress.
Veterans Administration	Department of Medicine & Surgery		Research in disease and diet: nutrition and disease or clinical nutrition, dietary therapy; effect of disease on nutrition; environmental toxicants, alcohol, and nutrition; nutrition and cancer; nutrition and vision research; nutrition-related therapy.
			Metabolic effects: Investigations on or related to malabsorption syndromes, inborn errors of metabolism, and familial or inherited nutritional defects.
			Nutrition requirements: Studies of nutrient metabolism, malnutrition, neuroendocrine nutrient interactions, fundamental intermediary metabolism involving the role of one or more nutrients.
State	Agency for International Development		Development of new low-cost nutritious foods; development and dissemination of new appropriate technologies; understanding nutritional needs and requirements; testing and evaluation of nutrition program alternatives; research on methodologies for improving national nutrition planning and programing.
National Science Foundation			Basic research in the behavioral, education, and social sciences in areas applicable to foods and nutrition.

*Under USDA's recent reorganization, ARS is now called Federal Research, and is housed within the Science and Education Administration.
**Under USDA's recent reorganization, CRS is called Cooperative Research and is housed within the Science and Education Administration.
***Under USDA's recent reorganization, ERS is called Economics and is housed within the Economics, Statistics, and Cooperatives Service.
****Under USDA's recent reorganization, ES is called Extension and is housed within the Science and Education Administration.

Source: Nutrition Research Alternatives, Office of Technology Assessment, U.S. Congress, Washington, D.C., pp. 18-20.

certain chronic diseases, such estimates must be regarded as speculation. The prospect of such savings, however, has served as an impetus towards forming a national nutrition policy, particularly to those considering the cost of a national health plan.

Areas which the Office of Technology Assessment report identified as most in need of increased funding are the role of diet in the prevention of chronic disease and obesity; nutrition education and consumer information; monitoring nutritional status; and nutritional policy and management. The General Accounting Office report also cites "instability of federally funded extramural research" as a barrier to progress in nutrition research. (20)

The most likely scenario for the 1980s is that the momentum towards formulating a national nutrition policy will gradually bring together pieces of the policy for which a consensus can be reached. The subject of nutrition is almost as popular as taxes and inflation, so that party politics will not alter the course. With Senators such as McGovern and Dole agreeing on the importance of a nutrition policy, the question is not whether we will have a nutrition policy, but when we will have it. Because of the many competing priorities and special interests now involved in food policy, the time required for these many interests to iron out their differences and reach agreement remains a question.

The consensus is mounting that overnutrition, rather than malnutrition, is more of a health problem in the United States. Overnutrition leads to obesity that results in increased susceptibility to disease. (21) In our concern to avoid obesity, however, it will be important to maintain adequate nutrient intake, so that what we do eat must be more nutritious. As we consume less, consumption of iron, calcium and other minerals will have to be carefully monitored.

As more information becomes available on the relationship between diet and disease, dietary guidelines will be tailored according to the needs of the particular age, sex, activities and other determinants. General recommendations for a healthful diet and the prevention of obesity will be carefully distinguished from specific dietary recommendations for the management of chronic diseases that have to be made on an individual basis. (22)

In the near term, recommendations for a healthful diet will be acceptable in only the most general terms and will concentrate on moderation and variety, such as eating a variety of nutritionally complementary foods to achieve a balanced diet and reducing energy (caloric) intake to control obesity. (23) Exercise will be recommended as frequently as weight control. Overconsumption of fats, sugar and alcohol will be the major concerns. Dietary guidelines cannot spell out what each person or group should consume in actual amounts of protein, carbohydrates, fats, sugar and salt until more conclusive evidence is available. We are capable of recognizing the risks of "too much," but exactly "how much" is still not known. Policies directed towards tobacco consumption and production should be monitored as precursors of policies and alternatives which may affect the producers of food ingredients linked with chronic diseases.

It will be necessary to evaluate and modify guidelines and policies as new information is revealed or conditions change. The results of tomorrow's efforts in human nutrition research will help to develop more of a consensus among scientists, and thereby fill in the missing links. Since 1960, there has been a 20 percent reduction in coronary disease mortality. As Dr. Robert Olson, Chairman of the Department of Biochemistry at the St. Louis University, observed, "We are in a dynamic state and should observe what is happening under our present dietary conditions." (24)

The commitment and momentum towards developing a national nutrition policy exists among the public and government sector. The private sector - members of the food industry - will follow suit once policy is settled. In the interim, conflicting interests are vying for survival. Once the rules are clear and food producers and processors are convinced that consumers want and are willing to pay for quality and nutrition, they will respond. But more will be required; and the food industry could provide the leadership. Consumers need to be educated on the nutritional properties and contributions of foods, including the pros and cons of processed foods. Those formulating new regulations affecting food need sound information and guidance to insure that new regulations are realistic and can be implemented. The food industry should take a leadership role in anticipating what the issues will be, so they can provide assistance rather than reaction. A less adversarial relationship between the food industry and public, and food industry and government, would be beneficial to long range food technology and food science. For this to occur will require greater understanding by the public of the scientific process, a directed sense of responsibility by industry and constructive encouragement by government.

While there was lack of recognition of the breadth of nutrition in the 1960s, nutrition has become such a popular subject today that there now is lack of recognition of its limits. (25) In the 1970s nutrition has been used as a vehicle to alleviate poverty and prevent chronic disease and death. In the 1980s, one hopes the results of the research in human nutrition presently underway will provide us with realistic parameters of the benefits and limitations of good nutritional practices. The overall objective of a nutrition policy is to promote optimum health and performance. (26)

In addition to government departments and legislative committees recognizing the need for a national nutrition policy, nongovernmental organizations such as the Food and Nutrition Board of the National Academy of Sciences, the Council on Agricultural Science and Technology, and the National Nutrition Consortium have been interested in the formulation of a nutrition policy. The goals of a national nutrition policy as defined by the National Nutrition Consortium, are unequivocal (see table 7.2). Implementing the policies and programs of these goals however, requires a high level of consensus and effective administrative machinery.

Table 7.2.   Goals of a National Nutrition Policy
             (Proposed by the National Nutrition Consortium)*

1.   Assure an adequate wholesale food supply at reasonable costs
     to meet the needs of all segments of the population, this
     supply being available at a level consistent with the afford-
     able life style of the era.

2.   Maintain food resources sufficient to meet emergency needs
     and to fulfill a responsible role as a nation in meeting
     world food needs.

3.   Develop a level of sound public knowledge and responsible
     understanding of nutrition and foods that will promite maxi-
     mal nutritional health.

4.   Maintain a system of quality and safety control that justi-
     fies public confidence in its food supply.

5.   Support research and education in foods and nutrition with
     adequate resources and reasoned priorities to solve impor-
     tant current problems and to permit exploratory basic re-
     search.

Source: Nutrition Review, Vol. 32, No. 5, May 1974.

* The Consortium is comprised of the American Institute of
Nutrition, The American Society for Clinical Nutrition, the
American Dietetic Association, and the Institute of Food Technol-
ogy.

With other countries leading the way in developing nutrition policies, we will be able to learn from their experiences. These countries are mostly those in which the government has assumed the cost for national health care and are therefore most aggressive about trying to change their population's eating habits. Increases in cardiovascular disease, largely responsible for a 25 percent increase in medical expenditures over a 10 year period, was one of the principal reasons why Sweden developed a national nutrition policy. Norway's similar concern, as well as her desire to reduce her dependence on food imports, have resulted in one of the most comprehensive nutrition and food policies where agricultural policies have been adjusted to achieve optimum nutritional standards. The plan encompasses food pricing and production policies to encourage Norwegians to adopt healthier eating habits: A diet composed of more vegetables, cereals, fish, and poultry, and less red meat, saturated fat and sugar. Even the French Health Ministry is trying to urge its citizens to cut down on fatty meat, pastries and alcoholic beverages. Instead, it is promoting milk and starchy foods, particularly bread. Similar efforts are underway in Canada and the United Kingdom.

Furthermore, the beneficial or negative effects of specific nutritional and food safety actions abroad can be monitored and adapted if applicable. For example, Norway has recently forbidden the use of all food coloring additives, while the Netherlands has outlawed food fortification. In the United States, cereal enrichment has been a major factor contributing to the virtual elimination of vitamin deficiency diseases that killed thousands of Americans annually fifty years ago. (27) If future diets are to emphasize less meat and more vegetables and cereals, it seems essential that cereals continue to be enriched with those nutrients formerly obtained through meat.

In the developing countries, where there is litttle choice between a meat or vegetarian diet, the cereal enrichment and fortification process has provided a low cost, effective solution, which has had more effect on human health than comparable investments in medical care. For example, the alternative to fulfilling the Vitamin A requirements of India's population is a two fold increase in fruit production and a three fold increase in vegetable production. (28) In fact, India has done more research than the United States on fortification of salt with iron and how nutrition affects resistance to diseases, so we may learn as much from developing countries as industrialized ones. (29)

A component of a national nutrition policy also includes our role and responsibility in relation to the nutritional needs of developing countries. In the last ten years we have recognized that the key factors in improving nutritional status are increased agricultural productivity and more equitable income distribution. With these achievements come better living standards, better education and improved diets and health. Understanding these factors, we can best help developing countries improve their nutritional status by helping them develop the institutional infrastructure necessary for increased food production as well as helping them apply technologies which enhance the quality and safety of their respective diets.

Since 1975, many recommendations to improve the knowledge base and the organization necessary to evolve a national nutrition policy have been made by nongovernmental and governmental agencies. (30) In the efforts to strengthen and coordinate the administrative procedures and the various related programs should begin to take shape. Further coordination and leadership will be needed, but the momentum is building consensus, to start working towards piecing together the components required for formulating a national nutrition policy.

NOTES

(1) R. D. Knutson; J. B. Penn; and T. A. Stucker "Agricultural Food Policymaking: Process and Participants." Agricultural-Food Policy Review. U.S. Department of Agriculture, ERS AFPR-1, Washington, D. C., January 1977, p. 4.

(2) Ibid. , p. 4.

(3) Projections through 1985 indicate that the United States will continue to produce at least one fifth of the world's grain, over one third of the world's commercial output of meat, and about half the world's commercial production of oil meal. (From talk by Secretary of Agriculture Bob Bergland before Foreign Agricultural Attaches' Luncheon, Washington, D. C., December 5, 1978.)

(4) T. K. Warley, Agriculture in an Interdependent World; U.S. Canadian Perspectives. National Planning Association, Washington, D. C., 1977, p. 8.

(5) Emil Mrak. Paper presented before the California Agricultural Leadership Program, Sacramento, Ca., November 2, 1978, p. 2.

(6) Nutrition Research Alternatives. Office of Technology Assessment, Congress of the U.S., Washington, D. C., September 1978, p. 74.

(7) Kenneth Schlossberg. "Nutrition and Government Policy in the United States." Nutrition and National Policy. Beverly Winikoff, editor. Cambridge, Mass.: MIT Press, 1978, p. 350.

(8) Ibid. p. 338.

(9) A. E. Harper. What are Appropriate Dietary Guidelines? Food Technology, September 1978, p. 48.

(10) Schlossberg, Nutrition and National Policy, p. 326.

(11) Robert Bergland. Remarks before the Conference on Nutrition and the American Food System, #6269, USDA 1579-78, Washington, D. C., June 2, 1978, p. 5.

(12) Carol Foreman. "Consumer and Food Policy in North America." Remarks before the Conference of American Agricultural Economics Association, #6489, USDA 2304-78, Blacksburg, Va., August 9, 1978, p. 3.

(13) Rupert Cutler. Testimony before the Nutrition Subcommittee of the Committee on Agriculture, Nutrition and Forestry, U.S. Senate, Washington, D. C., #5114, USDA 553-78, February 22, 1978, pp. 5, 29, 33.

(14) Nutrition Research Alternatives, p. 23.

(15) Ibid. p. 15.

(16) Schlossberg. p. 333.

(17) Nutrition Research Alternatives, p. 20.

(18) Future of the National Nutrition Intelligence System. U.S. General Accounting Office, Washington, D. C., November 7, 1978, p. 36.

(19) Ibid. p. 1.

(20) Nutrition Research Alternatives, p. 22.

(21) A. E. Harper. National Nutrition Policy, April 20, 1977, p. 15. Unpublished paper.

(22) Ibid.

(23) Dietary Goals for the United States: A Commentary. Council for Agricultural Science and Technology, Report #71, November 30, 1977.

(24) Robert Olson. Private communications, August 11, 1978.

(25) A. E. Harper. National Nutrition Policy. Unpublished paper.

(26) Ibid. p. 9.

(27) Donald F. Miller. "Cereal Enrichment/Pellagra-USA...In Perspective 1977." Paper presented before the American Association of Cereal Chemists, San Francisco, October 24, 1977.

(28) Alan Berg. The Nutrition Factor - Its Role in National Development. Washington, D. C.: The Brookings Institution, 1973, p. 108.

(29) World Food and Nutrition Studies, Volume IV, National Academy of Sciences, Washington, D. C., 1977, p. 21.

(30) These include: Senate Select Committee on Nutrition and Human Needs, Towards a National Nutrition Policy, 1975; Congressional Research Service, The Role of the Federal Government in Human Nutrition Research, 1976; National Academy of Sciences, World Food and Nutrition Study, 1977; Congressional Research Service, The Role of the Federal Government in Nutrition Education, 1977; Office of Science and Technology Policy, New Directions in Federally Supported Human Nutrition Research, 1977; General Account Office, Federal Human Nutrition Research - Need for a Coordinated Approach to Advance our Knowledge, 1978; Office of Technology Assessment, Nutrition Research Alternatives, 1978; General Accounting Office, Future of the National Nutrition Intelligence System, 1978. Nutrition Research Alternatives, p. 74.

8 The U.S. Quandary: Can We Formulate a Rational Nutrition Policy?

Robert E. Olson

At the present time there is unprecedented interest in the subject of nutrition in this country by our people, by consumer advocate groups, by health food interests, by voluntary health agencies, and by the United States government through its National Institutes of Health and the various Congressional committees. This interest provides unprecedented opportunities for health education in the field of nutrition and it behooves all of us who are professionals in this field to take advantage of this receptive market, but not to abuse it by promising a health panacea through diet intervention. It is obvious that a receptive audience also provides opportunities for quacks and charlatans to sell their ideas on the values of health foods, nostrums and even dangerous drugs like laetrile. In a way, the American public has become a battle ground for the selling of nutritional ideas based on both fact and fraud. Scientific bodies are shouting that more research is needed to develop a base of scientific knowledge to make better dietary recommendations, whereas the health quacks are promising cures for all chronic diseases through nuts, fruits, fad diets, and attractively packaged powders. One might ask, "Why has this interest in nutrition mushroomed to such a high level?"

CONSCIOUSNESS III

Charles Reich's book on the Greening of America (1) may provide a clue. It was an account of the evolution of attitudes among college students in the 1960s. Between 1945 and 1960 a generation of young people grew up with seemingly unlimited promises of a marvelous future. They came out of increasingly affluent homes. They were respectful of science because of the important contributions of the physicists to the development of the atomic bomb and of atomic energy, and the important contributions of medical scientists to the

119

development of antibiotics capable of conquering most infectious diseases. Great sums of money were voted by the Congress for development of scientific training and research in all fields, particularly in the biomedical field. But then in the 1960s several catastrophes took shape. One was the assassination of President Kennedy who, to many young people, was a heroic president. Second, the conflict of Vietnam with all its questionable goals and methods began the process of disillusionment and raised the serious questions about the justifiability of that war.

In 1962, Rachel Carson published <u>Silent Spring</u> (2) which attacked the use of pesticides in enhancing agricultural production on the grounds that it was contaminating the environment and causing untold damage to other forms of life including man. The environmentalist movement began to form with the stated objective of attempting to preserve the native land against the onslaughts of modern science and technology. With these developments the young people in the 1960s developed sort of an Hegelian conflict. The thesis was the promise of unlimited opportunities, security, success and freedom, and the antithesis was the threat of the A-bomb, the horrors of Vietnam, regimentation of individuals in industrial, military, and government establishments and even the capitulation of universities to what they deemed a lock step educational experience. Protests erupted on campuses with students rebelling against essentially all of our institutions. Out of this revolt, according to Reich, came what he called consciousness-III. Consciousness III had five precepts. Preserve idealism by emphasizing self. Feel good at any cost. Reject grades, and ratings of excellence as being superfluous. Reject the hierarchy, oppose establishments, and foster reform. Finally to engage, if necessary, in civil disobedience. The fulfillment of these precepts was expressed by greater emphasis on self, back to nature with health foods, devotion to rock music and casual dress, participation in the sensuous life including drugs, and insistence on "entitlement" to certain benefits particularly related to health and economic security regardless of work expended.

Yankelovich in a recent survey found that consciousness-III traits are visible in our middle age population, i.e., that which represents the mature Vietnam demonstrators, in that there is a great stress on: Focus on self, a new naturalism, and rejection of the various industrial and technical processes that have made our civilization rich in goods, and distrust of institutions generally, including government, industry, medicine and the scientific establishment, increased devotion to the psychology of entitlement which has to do with entitlement to health, entitlement to information as expressed by the "Sunshine Laws", and increased requirement for public disclosure and demands for labeling.

MYTHOLOGY OF FOODS

How does all this pertain to the present craze about nutrition? In my opinion it fits very well into the psychology of the Vietnam alumni in that they are concentrating on one aspect of self preservation. One very important avenue to self preservation is good health and good health care. Since there is in general, distrust of scientific institutions, and disenchantment with professional approaches to these problems, mythology has been substituted for science. The mythology of food is an extremely ancient and recognized pheonomenon. The idea that foods have emotional and cultural value as well as nutritional value, even superior powers for producing "good vibrations" for healing, and for preventing disease beyond their actual nutritional value, is the basis for the health food industry. Some emotional contrasts that have arisen from this view are the following: Meat and animal products are bad, but cereals are good; food additives are bad, but vitamins are very good. We are in the midst of a megavitamin period now, in which not only bonafide vitamins are recommended in large amounts, but phony vitamins such as vitamin B-15 (pangamic acid), and vitamin B-17 (laetrile) are advertised as vitamins, when in fact, they have no biological value as vitamins.

The interesting thing about the etiology of the chronic degenerative diseases is that there are dietary determinants that contribute to the progression or retardation of these diseases. It is very easy for the "believer" to take this basic concept of dietary determinants in chronic diseases and fuse it with the "mythology of foods" to arrive at conclusions beyond the proper scientific limits. Their conclusion is that because there are some dietary determinants of coronary disease, of hypertension, of diabetes and cirrhosis of the liver, that by manipulation of the ratios of macronutrients, it is now possible to prevent these diseases.

This hypothesis has been applied most intensely to the problem of coronary artery disease, and its underlying atherosclerosis. Atherosclerosis is a disease of unknown etiology for which there are three current hypotheses that are under investigation to define this etiology. At the present time, approximately 600,000 persons die annually from coronary heart disease and an additional 200,000 from strokes and other complications of atherosclerosis in our country. We should not forget that atherosclerosis and its complications are among the leading public health problems in this country.

THE LIPID HYPOTHESIS FOR ATHEROSCLEROSIS

The Lipid Hypothesis is only one of three current hypotheses put forward to explain the etiology of coronary artery disease. It states the lipids in the diet, chiefly saturated fats and cholesterol, are the principal determinants of serum cholesterol. Serum cholesterol in one of its lipoprotein forms (LDL) is, in turn, responsible for the initiation of, and progression of, atheromas which are the lesions of the arterial wall which cause heart attacks and strokes. A corollary to this hypothesis is that lowering of serum cholesterol by dietary change should reduce the mortality from atherosclerosis. This hypothesis has

its origin in the observations of a Russian physiologist, namely
Anitschkow, who, in 1913, (3)   fed rabbits diets containing cholesterol,
and observed that these rabbits developed hypercholesteremia, and
subsequently atheromas of the aorta which, although not identical with
human lesions, had a superficial resemblance to them.   At that time,
many investigators took issue with his hypothesis because the "cholesterol effect" which was demonstrated in rats and dogs which were much
more resistant to cholesterol feeding.   The question was raised whether
or not the rabbit was a proper model for the study of this disease in
man, a question which remains with us to this very day.

The next development came with reports from "China watchers".
Dr. Snapper, an American pathologist, spent a decade or so in China in
the 1930s and studied disease patterns in that country.   He reported (4)
that the prevalence of myocardial infarction and atheromatosis in
persons autopsied in China was markedly less than that in the United
States.   This led to the conclusion that environmental factors played a
role in the disease and Snapper suggested that the Chinese diet
composed principally of rice, fish and vegatables, might be protective.

The   marked   difference   in   geographical   distribution   of
atherosclerosis and its complications were studied intensively in various
populations in the 1930s and early 1940s, and in general, showed a high
prevalence of the disease in Western Europe, the United States,
Australia, and relatively low rates in the Third World, in developing
countries including Asia, India, and Africa.   Ancel Keys and his
colleagues (5)   from the University of Minnesota, began a systematic
epidemiologic study in seven countries to test the lipid hypothesis;
that is, to detemine on epidemiologic grounds whether the association
between dietary fat, serum cholesterol and coronary heart disease was
valid.   He and his colleagues studied populations in Greece, the
Netherlands, Yugoslavia, Italy, Japan, United States, and Finland. (6)
As a result of this international study of 12,770 men, 49-59 years of
age, Keyes and coworkers concluded that, in general, there was a
correlation between the total fat content of the diet, the serum
cholesterol value, and the appearance of heart attacks.   What was not
demonstrated, however, is that altering the diet had a beneficial effect
on mortality in any of these populations.

A prospective study of factors relating to coronary heart disease
was undertaken in 1950 in 5000 inhabitants, 30-59 years of age in
Framingham by the United States Public Health Service.   After eight
years of follow up (7)   it was observed that coronary heart disease was
associated with age, maleness, serum cholesterol levels above 239 mg%,
systolic blood pressure about 150 mm mercury, and smoking cigarettes.
Because of these associations these variables were classified as "risk
factors", (see table 8.1) and physicians were admonished to attempt to
modify these factors in patients at risk for coronary disease as part of
general preventive medicine.   Although Cornfield (8)   pointed out that
the Framingham data in 1960 supported the assumption that risk
increases steadily as a power fraction of rise in cholesterol levels
beyond 200 mg%, the National Cooperative Pooling Project shows no
effect of serum cholesterol below 249 mg% upon mortality rate from

Table 8.1.   Risk Factors for Coronary Artery Disease

   1.   Family history of heart disease
   2.   Hypertension
   3.   High blood cholesterol
   4.   Cigarette smoking
   5.   Obesity
   6.   Diabetes

Table 8.2.   Revised U.S. Dietary Goals (1978)

1. To avoid overweight, consume only as much energy (calories) as is expended; if overweight, decrease energy intake and increase energy expenditure.

2. Increase the consumption of complex carbohydrates and energy intake to about 48 percent of energy intake.

3. Reduce the consumption of refined and processed sugars by about 45 percent to account for about 10 percent of total energy intake.

4. Reduce overall fat consumption from approximately 40 percent to about 30 percent of energy intake.

5. Reduce saturated fat consumption to account for about 10 percent of total energy intake; and balance that with poly-unsaturated and mono-unsaturated fats, which should account for about 10 percent of energy intake each.

6. Reduce cholesterol consumption to about 300 mg. a day.

7. Limit the intake of sodium by reducing the intake of salt to about 5 gram per day.

Source: "Dietary Goals for the United States," Select Committee on Nutrition and Human Needs, U.S. Senate; U.S. Government Printing Office, 1977, p. 4.

coronary heart disease. (9)

In any event, on the basis of this epidemiological data in 1961, the American Heart Association, through its Nutrition Committee, first made a recommendation to the general public to modify their usual diet by eating foods which contained less saturated fatty acids, cholesterol, and increasing the intake of vegatable oil, rich in polyunsaturated fatty acids as a preventive measure against coronary heart disease. The American Medical Association Council of Food and Nutrition, the Food and Nutrition Board of the National Academy of Sciences -National Research Council, in a combined policy statement ten years later (1972) supported the role of diet in the prevention of heart disease, but only recommended that physicians consider this evidence in prescribing preventive measures for their patients. The AMA's recommendation fell short of urging dietary modification to the general public.

THE McGOVERN REPORT

The American Heart Association has been the most militant of all the agencies in insisting that its dietary program will reduce the morbidity and mortality from coronary heart disease in this country. In fact members of the Council on Atherosclerosis of the American Heart Association were the star witnesses before the Select Committee on Nutrition and Human Needs of the United States Senate, chaired by Senator McGovern in urging the adoption of the American Heart Association program of dietary prevention by this Committee, not only for atherosclerosis and its complications (atherosclerosis, heart attacks and strokes) but also cancer, diabetes and cirrhosis of the liver. These "Dietary Goals for the United States", published in February 1977, (10) and revised in December 1977 (11) are presented in table 8.2 and figure 8.1. To reach these goals, the United States population would have to increase consumption of fruits, vegetables and cereals, decrease consumption of red meat, eggs, and whole milk, increase the consumption of vegetable oils, decrease the consumption of table sugar, and eliminate the use of table salt. What is most objectionable about these "Dietary Goals" is that the claim is made that adherence to the diet changes recommended will reduce morbidity and mortality from the six killer diseases cited earlier. The evidence to support this claim is totally lacking at this time.

The McGovern report was a political document written by lawyers which, in my opinion, was motivated by two considerations. The first was that if chronic disease mortality and morbidity could truly be reduced by dietary intervention, it would make the cost of national health insurance considerably less. Since both Senators Kennedy and McGovern are strong supporters of national health insurance, this would aid and abet their legislative program. Secondly, the McGovern Committee perceived correctly that there was a market for nutritional recommendations in the country based on the receptivity of the population to nutritional advice already mentioned, and they felt that

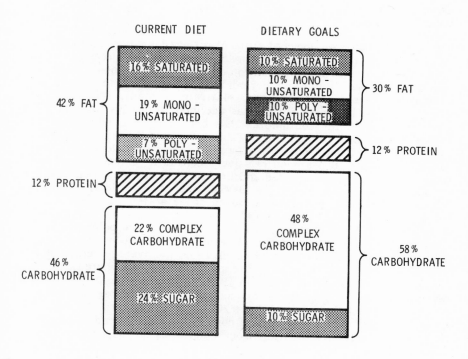

Fig. 8.1. The Distribution of Macronutrients in the Current American Diet, with Recommended Changes

Source: "Dietary Goals for the United States," 2nd ed., Select Committee on Nutrition and Human Needs, U.S. Senate; U.S. Government Printing Office, 1977, p. 5.

this diet would "sell", and in fact, might even get some votes.

Much is made in the McGovern report about the changing patterns of nutrient consumption in the United States since 1900 featuring an increase in fat and sugar consumption, and a decrease in consumption of cereals and complex carbohydrates. These changes, it is argued, are related to the rising incidence of coronary heart disease. Table 8.3 presents the food energy available per capita per day, and percent furnished by protein, fat, carbohydrate, calorie between 1900 and 1970. Calorie availability has declined slightly from about 3500 to 3200 calories. Total fat intake has increased from 32% in 1900 to 41% in 1965-1970. Carbohydrate, on the other hand, has declined from 56% to 47%. If one, however, looks at nutrient fat available per capita per day in terms of contributions from animal and vegetable sources (see table 8.4), it is clear that the contribution of fat from meat, poultry and fish has declined over the same period from 37 percent to 34 percent. Contribution from eggs has been relatively constant, and that from dairy products, including butter, has declined from 42% to 29%. The large increase in fat consumption has been due to a tripling of the intake of vegetable fats and oils. Table 8.5 shows the fatty acid intake over the period from 1900-1970. One sees that the intake of saturated fat over this period has been relatively constant. On the other hand, oleic acid intake has increased and linoleic acid has increased from 10 to approximately 20 grams per day at the present time. This has increased the ratio of polyunsaturated to saturated fatty acids (P/S ratio) from 0.2 in 1900 to 0.4 in 1970.

With regard to cholesterol intake, it has been pointed out by Gortner (12) (2) that the intake of serum cholesterol has not changed significantly in the USA since 1900. In 1909, the average person in the United States consumed 509 mg of cholesterol per day, whereas, in 1950 the intake was 577 per day, and in 1970, 556 mg per day. At present, per capita egg consumption in this country is less than one egg per day per capita, which contributes about 200 mg of cholesterol per day. To imply that reduction in egg or beef consumption would lead to a further reduction of coronary disease in our country is not supported by any tangible evidence. The vegetable oil manufacturers in this country are advertising their products as "cholesterol free", as if that were tantamount to "germ free", "poison free", and "coronary artery disease free". Cholesterol has become the nutritional bogeyman of the times, and to be avoided as if it were a carcinogen. Actually cholesterol is an essential metabolite, and if it were not synthesized in the human body at the rate of 1.0 gram per day, it would be a nutritional essential as, in fact, it is for certain insects. With an intake of 500 mg per day, and an absorption rate in man of 40%, only 200 milligrams enters the body and mixes with the endogenous pool. Sensitive feedback mechanisms in the liver retard the endogenous synthesis rate so that the body pool of cholesterol remains constant. In most individuals cholesterol intake in the range of 300-800 mg per day has no effect on the serum cholesterol. The Framingham Study (13) showed no relationship between dietary fat and cholesterol intake and serum cholesterol levels in 1000 persons. Nichols et. al. (14) observed the same lack of correlation between

Table 8.3.   Food Energy Available Per Capita Per Day, and Percent Furnished by Protein, Fat, and Carbohydrate

Year	Food Energy KCAL	Percent of Calories from		
		Protein	Fat	Carbo-hydrate
1909-1913	3,490	11.7	32.1	56.2
1925-1929	3,470	10.9	34.7	54.4
1935-1939	3,270	10.9	36.3	52.8
1947-1949	3,230	11.7	38.9	49.4
1957-1959	3,140	12.0	40.7	47.3
1965-1970	3,160	12.1	41.0	47.0

Note: Components may not add up to 100% due to rounding

Source: Consumer and Food Economic Research Division, Agricultural Research Service, Dept. of Agriculture, Hyattsville, Md.

Table 8.4.   Nutrient Fat Available Per Capita Per Day

Year	Fat, g	% Meat, poultry, fish	% eggs	% dairy products incl. butter	% Total	Fats & Oils	% Total
1909-1913	125	37.4	3.8	41.9	83.1	9.8	16.9
1925-1929	135	32.9	3.8	41.5	78.2	14.0	21.8
1935-1939	133	29.9	3.5	39.9	73.3	18.4	26.8
1947-1949	141	33.5	4.3	36.8	74.6	17.8	25.6
1957-1959	143	33.0	4.0	33.6	70.6	22.3	29.3
1965-1970	145	33.6	3.4	29.0	66.0	26.7	34.1

Table 8.5.   Fatty Acids Available, Per Capita Per Day, and Percent of Total Calories

Year	Fatty Acids			Calories Furnished by Fatty Acids		
	satu-rated, g	Oleic acid, g	Lin oleic, acid, g	% total satu-rated	% Oleic acid	% Lin-oleic acid
1909-1913	50.3	51.5	10.7	12.9	13.3	2.7
1925-1929	53.3	55.2	12.5	13.7	14.2	3.2
1935-1939	52.9	54.5	12.7	14.4	14.8	3.5
1947-1949	54.4	58.0	14.8	15.0	16.0	4.1
1957-1959	54.7	58.2	16.6	15.6	16.6	4.7
1965	53.9	58.8	19.1	15.2	16.6	5.4

Source: Consumer and Food Economics Research Division, Agricultural Research Service, Dept. of Agriculture, Hyattsville, Md.

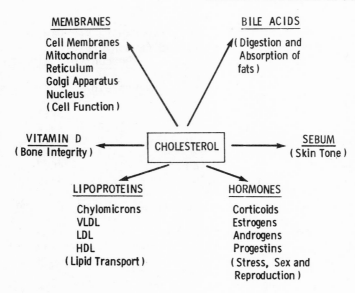

Fig. 8.2.   The Essential Functions of Cholesterol

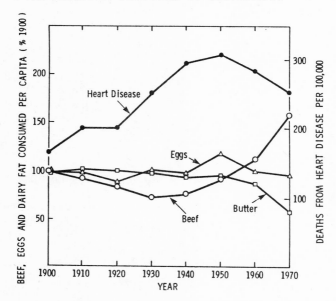

Fig. 8.3.   The Relationship between the Mortality Rate from Heart Disease and the Consumption of Beef, Eggs, and Butter by the U.S. Population from 1900-1970.

Source: Author's own chart adapted from data from Bureau of Health Statistics.

dietary habits and serum cholesterol levels in a population of 2000 persons studied in Tecumseh, Michigan. Some of the essential functions of cholesterol are shown in figure 8.2.

Three foods would be greatly reduced under the program of "Dietary Goals", namely, eggs, butter and beef. Figure 8.3 shows the relationship between mortality due to coronary heart disease and the intake of these three foods by the United States population between 1900 and 1970. No relationship between the intake of these foods and the changes in coronary disease mortality are apparent except that beef consumption changes reciprocally with the coronary artery disease mortality rate. Truswell (15) has recently reviewed the data relating given foods to serum lipid levels. He concludes by saying: "We should think in terms of whole foods and try not to generalize physiological effects from partial knowledge of their biochemical composition".

Needless to say these "Dietary Goals" have been the center of intense controversy as chronicled in the several volumes of testimony given to the McGovern Committee (16) and in the nutrition litera-ture. (17) In my own testimony before the McGovern Committee on July 26, 1977, I advance six arguments against the adoption of the "Dietary Goals" in their present form.

1.   Epidemiological data represents the association of variables related to a disease without proof of cause and effect.   Such associations represent the beginnings of a hypothesis, in this case the Lipid Hypothesis, not its establishment as fact. 2.   In the multiple etiology of chronic diseases, there are many factors besides diet which determine the progression of disease, and these vary widely from individual to individual. It cannot be stated with certaintly that diet is the most important or even an important variable in the causation or prevention of the six killer diseases cited in this Report. 3.   There is no evidence that adoption of the "Dietary Goals" will alter the morbidity and mortality from the six killer diseases. Eleven intervention studies by diet and drugs in five countries successful in altering serum cholesterol levels by 5-16% have not altered the mortality rate from coronary and other diseases in the experimental group. 4.   Changing the diet pattern of the United States in the direction of "Dietary Goals" with the specified reduction in protective foods such as meat, eggs, and whole milk would almost certainly increase malnutrition in the vulnerable groups studied in the Ten State Nutrition Survey. 5.   No role is contemplated for the physician and other allied health professionals in the "Dietary Goals". It is my opinion that any public health education program that does not have the support and involvement of the health professional worker is doomed to failure. The AMA is on record with Senator McGovern to the effect that it deems these goals "inap-propriate at this time". 6.   There are always harmful effects from premature health education programs. In general, the evidence must be very convincing, and the degree of controversy minimal, if advice on health is to be given successfully to the public through ordinary communication channels. "Dietary Goals" meet neither of these basic criteria.

Perhaps the most cogent argument against the adoption of these

"Dietary Goals" in the hope of preventing the chronic degenerative diseases is that no efficacy of this regimen has been shown in extensive clinical testing. Even Dr. Mark Hegsted of Harvard University, a strong proponent of the "Dietary Goals" admitted in his introduction to the report that "we have not demonstrated that the dietary modifications we recommend will yield the dividends expected...but...we cannot afford to temporize".

Many of us, on the other hand, feel that a properly conducted and positive clinical intervention trial of the effect of diet (and/or drugs) on morbidity and mortality from coronary artery disease, as well as mortality from all causes, is necessary before one can advice physicians and the public at large to adopt a regimen designed to prevent this disease. For example, clinical trials of the value of small pox and polio vaccination were strikingly positive, and only after they were completed was public health action initiated with essential eradication of these two diseases. We have no such similar data on the effect of diet upon mortality in patients with coronary artery diseases. Dr. Ahrens of Rockefeller University (18) has recently summarized the eleven intervention trials in five countries in which diet or drug therapy aimed at lowering serum cholesterol was studied for an effect on heart attacks and overall mortality. These clinical investigations shown in table   8.6 involved about 5000 men studied for 40,000 man years and accomplished a 5-16% decrease in serum cholesterol without affecting overall mortality. Some of these were secondary preventive studies involving persons with a prior heart attack and some were primary, using subjects free of known previous disease. The age range of these subjects was 30-59 years of age, and if diet were an important variable in our culture, some effect would be anticipated. Additional primary intervention studies initiated by the World Health Organization and the National Heart and Lung Institute of DHEW are still in progress, and there is no evidence as to whether they will be positive or not.

WHAT IS SOUND PREVENTIVE MEDICINE FOR CORONARY DISEASE?

Is there anything we can do to stem the epidemic of coronary heart disease? One of the factors not emphasized in the original McGovern Report but mentioned as a goal in the revised edition is weight control. Obesity, or overweight due to increased fatness, is a risk factor for coronary heart disease. The obese person has an increased probability of developing hypertension, coronary heart disease, gall bladder disease and diabetes, and his risk of dying prematurely from any of these diseases is now documented. The prevalence of obesity in the United States in 1960 rose from about 3% in the second decade in which most people are within 10% of their desired weight, to about 30% in the sixth decade and then declined somewhat in the seventh and eight decades, due to the premature death of obese individuals but also to weight reduction in old age. Obesity constitutes an internal indicator that

Table 8.6. Large-scale Trials of the Lipid Hypothesis in Five Countries

	Primary or Secondary	Volunteers Mean Age (Years)	Volunteers Number of	Duration (Years)	Cholesterol Levels (% Diff. T-C)*
DIET TRIALS					
Rose (London)	S	56	80	2	- 7
Christakis (New York City)	P	? (40 to 59)	814	5	-10
Laren (Oslo)	S	56	412	5	-14
Bierenbaum (New Jersey)	S	? (20 to 50)	100	10	-10
Medical Research Council (27) (London – soya oil)	S	? (<60)	393	2 to 7	- 9
Turpeinen (Helsinki)	P	50	406	6	-16
Dayton (Los Angeles)	P/S	66	846	8	-13
DRUG TRIALS					
Dewar (Newcastle upon Tyne)	S	52	400	5	- 8
Oliver (Edinburgh)	S	52	426	5	- 5
Coronary Drug Project (NIH, USA)					
Clofibrate	S	44	1103	5	- 6
Niacin	S	44	1119	5	-10

* T = trial value. C = control value

Source: Ahrens, E.H. "The Management of Hyperlipidemias: Whether, Rather Than How," Ann. Int. Med. 85, 87, 1976.

caloric intake has exceeded caloric need at some time in the past and that current caloric intake is too high to maintain desired weight. Vigorous effects should be directed to the prevention and treatment of obesity in order to promote the health of our middle aged population. This requires diet modification to provide diets containing fewer calories but all the protective nutrients plus moderate exercise programs in order to increase energy expenditure. Such a program does not require a major revision in the proportion of fat and carbohydrates in our diet, but limitation in the amounts to achieve weight control in those persons who need it. Exercise may play a key role in heart disease prevention. In fact, our sedentary habits, dependence on the automobile, addiction to TV viewing, and spectator sports instead of participant games, may be more critical than our intake of meat, whole milk and eggs. Diabetes mellitus is another risk factor for coronary heart disease which should be under a physician's surveillance and carefully regulated. Finally, cigarette smoking should be avoided, and high belood pressure controlled by psychological or pharmacological means. Abandonment of smoking and reduction of blood pressure in hypertensive persons, in contract to diet intervention, have been demonstrated to decrease mortality in other preventative studies.

Thus, there are several measures that we can recommend to persons at risk for coronary heart disease that have been validated as positive factors for survival. It seems wiser to me to give advice about those changes in life style which are known to alter mortality from heart disease, and avoid giving advice about those questionable others.

NOTES

(1) C. Reich. The Greening of America, Westminster, Md: Random House, 1970.

(2) R. Carson, Silent Spring, Boston: Houghton Mifflin, 1962.

(3) N. Anitschkow, and S. Chalatow, Uber Experimentelle Cholesterinsteatose und ihre Bedeutung fur die Enstehung Eigen. Pathologischen Prozesse. Centralblatt f. allg. Path. U. Path Anat. 24, 1, 1913.

(4) I. Snapper, Chinese Lessons to Western Medicine, New York: Interscience Publishers, 1941.

(5) A. Keys, Ed. Coronary Disease in Seven Countries, American Heart Association, New York: Monograph 29, 1970.

(6) Ibid.

(7) T.R. Dawber, A. Kagan, W.B. Kannel, and N. Revotskie, The Framingham Study: A Prospective Study of Coronary Disease, Fed. Proc. 21, (Suppl. III, Part II) 62, 1962.

(8) J. Cornfield, Joint Dependence of Risk of Coronary Heart Disease in Serum Cholesterol and Systolic Blood Pressure; A Discriminant Function Analysis. Fed. Proc. 21 (Suppl. II, Part II) 58, 1962.

(9) R. R. Beard, W. E. Conner, T. R. Dawber, V. G. de Wolfe, J. T. Doyle, F. H. Epstein, L. H. Kullner, A. M. Lilienfield, J. Stamler, J. Stokes III, P. W. Willis III, and W. Winkelstein Jr., Primary Prevention of the Atherosclerotic Diseases. Circulation XLII, A-55 to A-95, 1970.

(10) Select Committee on Nutritional and Human Needs, U.S. Senate, Dietary Goals for the United States, U.S. Govt. Printing Office, Washington, D. C., 1977.

(11) Select Committee on Nutritional and Human Needs, U.S. Senate, Dietary Goals for the United States, U.S. Govt. Printing Office, Washington, D. C., 2nd edition, 1977.

(12) W. A. Gortner, Nutrition in the U.S. 1900-1974), Can. Res. 35 3246, 1975.

(13) T. Gordon and W. B. Kannel, The Framingham Diet Study: Diet and the Regulation of Serum Cholesterol. DHEW Report, Section 24, Washington, D. C., 1970.

(14) D. E. Lanphier, A. B. Nichols, L. D. Ostrander and C. Ravenscroft, Daily Nutritional Intake and Serum Lipid Levels. The Tecumseh Study. Am. J. Clin. Nutr. 29, 1384, 1976.

(15) A. S. Truswell, Diet and Plasma Lipids - a Reappraisal. Am. J. Clin. Nutr. 311, 977, 1978.

(16) Diet Related to Killer Diseases, Vols. III-VI and Supplementary. Hearing before the Select Committee on Nutrition and Human Needs of the U.S. Senate, 95th Congress, First Session, U.S. Govt. Printing Office, Washington, D.C., 1977.

(17) Dietary Goals for the United States; A Commentary, Council for Agricultural Science and Technology, 1977. A. E. Harper, Dietary Goals - a Skeptical View. Am J. Clin. Nutr. 1978: 310. "Twenty Commentaries: The McGovern Dietary Goals for the U.S. are Examined by Twenty Correspondents," Nutrition Today vol. 12(6), 10, November/December, 1977.

(18) E. H. Ahrens, The Management of Hyperlipidemias: Whether, Rather than How. Annals of Internal Medicine, 85 1976: 87.

9 National Nutrition Goals— How Far Have We Come?

Graham T. T. Molitor

Nutrition issues and physical exercise programs periodically have received attention, particularly in the advanced affluent nations. Diet and health issues currently capturing attention in these countries involve setting national nutrition goals. There is a common pattern among these goals - reduce fat, cholesterol and salt intake, moderate consumption of sugar and alcohol, increase carbohydrates and fiber, and engage in regular physical exercise (see figure 9.1 and 8.1).

Sweden was the first nation to actually implement such a program. Sweden embarked on its ten year diet and exercise program in 1971. The Senate Select Committee on Nutrition and Human Needs, chaired by Senator McGovern, put forward its recommendations on national nutrition goals in 1977 (see chapter 8 p. 194). The controversy has not yet subsided. Considerable time doubtlessly will elapse before actual steps toward implementation of those goals are realized.

Time elapsed between the Swedish implementation and mere publication of the McGovern Committee recommendations was six years. Once again, this lead lag pattern - an average of six to eight years as between Sweden and the United States - follows, and reaffirms, the time lapse noted for other consumer issues (see chapter 5). Though United States implementation is not yet to be realized, implementation of at least some measures aimed toward the stated goals has already begun. More will be undertaken over the next several years.

OBESITY: THE NUMBER ONE NUTRITION PROBLEM

Obesity is probably the most widespread public health problem today. Estimates of the number of overweight Americans vary tremendously. Low estimates of 20% have been put forward. Other estimates go as high as 60% of the population.

Americans simply eat too much. Calorie consumption is excessive

1. Sweden - Ten-Year Diet and Exercise Program, 1971

Reduce calories to avoid overweight.

Reduce fat (from 42% calories in 1972 down to 35% calories by 1981).

Replace saturated fat with polyunsaturated fats.

Control cholesterol intake.

Reduce sugar by at least 25%.

Increase iron (especially among women of child-bearing ages).

Control alcohol beverage intake.

Increase regular exercise.

2. Norway: Nutrition Goals (Recommendations to the Storting by Royal Norwegian Ministry of Agriculture Report, 1975)

Reduce fat from 1973 level to 42% down to 35% of energy intake.

Increase starchy foods.

Reduce sugar.

Substitute polyunsaturated fats for saturated fats.

3. Canada: Quebec's Nutritional Goals (Key points according to Dr. Jean Mayer)

Cut sugar in half.

Reduce fats by 25%; eat less meat, fried foods; use low fat milk, yogurt and cheeses.

Control alcoholic intake.

Increase starch and fiber.

Conserve nutritive values - use proper refrigerated storage, avoid overcooking.

Eat a wide variety of foods to ensure a well balanced diet.

Exercise regularly.

Fig. 9.1. National Nutrition Goals

Source: Public Policy Forecasting, Inc. Data Bank.

to needs. From another perspective, excessive calorie intake is related to reduced activity levels and lack of proper exercise. Today, more than ever before, overeating and lack of proper exercise threatens not only health, but life itself.

The solution to this most serious diet and health problem is simple to formulate: Reduce the quantity of calories consumed, and increase regular physical exercise. The obvious is easier said than done.

Obesity is the principal object of concern. Correcting the situation is within each person's grasp. However, convincing the American public to undertake the effort, encounters enormous obstacles. Lack of understanding and lethargy are prominent among the major barriers.

Great debates without apparent resolution engulf certain diet and health controversies. Divided opinion casts uncertainty on diet needs and excesses associated with cholesterol, saturated fat, sugar and salt. Moderation doubtless is an appropriate answer.

CONQUERING NUTRITION DEFICIENCY DISEASES

It wasn't until the 1920s that the vitamins were actually discovered, and still later until many were isolated. Minute quantities of these key nutrients and their widespread availability at low cost resulted in a virtual disappearance of nutrition deficiency disease and related deaths in many advanced countries.

The first introduction of essential vitamins and minerals to overcome nutrition deficiency diseases began in the 1920s. Iodization of table salt was begun in the year 1924 in the state of Michigan. As new knowledge became available over the next several decades, one after another of the life saving nutrients was quickly introduced into the food system.

Today, thanks to the widespread fortification of certain basic foods, and thanks to the widespread education efforts that constantly remind consumers of the need to daily obtain a balanced nutrient intake, the plight of age old deficiency diseases has virtually passed from the scene. Nutrition deficiency diseases have become virtual laboratory curiosities (figure 9.2).

NUTRITION TRENDS: PAST, PRESENT, AND FUTURE

Nutrition concerns previously centered mainly on simply getting enough calories to avoid hunger or starvation, and on nutritonal deficiency diseases, the impacts of which were clearly visible.

Present concerns are focused on both micro- and macro-nutrient needs. Current national nutrition goals focus on macro-nutrient intake levels - optimum amounts of carbohydrate, protein, and fat (and selected foods) and micro-nutrient deficiencies. New needs and uses of vitamins and minerals are continually being determined. Subclinical maladies due to micro-nutrient deficiencies are just beginning to be recognized as national health problems. Ever more complex nutrition concerns loom on the horizon (figure 9.3). These matters are highly technical and increasingly beyond present levels of public understanding. Nutrition needs subsequently will belong to scientific specialists to whom we must look for the best available scientific guidance.

NUTRITION LABELING: TECHNICAL DISCLOSURE TO EDUCATE CONSUMERS

Initially published in August of 1973, the current nutrition labeling regulations went into effect for the most part, July 1, 1975. The regulations provide that when nutrients are added to any product or when a nutritional claim is made (either in labeling or in advertising), then the label must bear all of the nutrition information specified in the regulations. The development of a uniform nutrition labeling system is one of the most important information developments affecting nutrition education.

Nutrition labeling is important because it provides a continuing base of highly prominent information. Over the years constant exposure of consumers to nutrition information will provide widespread understanding about nutrition needs. Beneficial effects will not occur overnight. Understanding will occur incrementally, developing over long periods of time.

NUTRIENT COMPOSITION DISCLOSURE: HOW MUCH INFORMATION IS ENOUGH?

Minimum nutritonal labeling disclosure requires listing only eight to ten nutrients. In point of fact, however, recommended daily dietary allowances have been established in this country for twenty-two essential nutrients. Beyond this, as many as sixty-three nutrients are recognized as essential for human health and well being. Still further beyond this there are some one hundred to two hundred fifteeen nutrients, related components, and component constituents.

In other words, only minimal nutrition information is included in everyday nutrition labeling. What should we make of ignoring some forty three or even hundreds of components? Just how much further must consumer information programs go? So far, they touch only the "tip of the iceberg."

Medical Curiosities
(U.S. morbidity—or mortality—per 100,000 population)

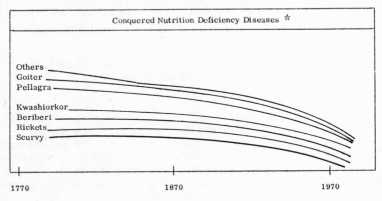

Medical Crusades
(U.S. morbidity per 100,000 population)

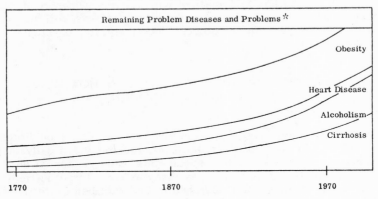

Fig. 9.2. Conquered and Extant Dietary Diseases

---

* Schematics are symbolic, not factual, and generally pertain
to advanced, affluent nations.

Source: Public Policy Forecasting, Inc.

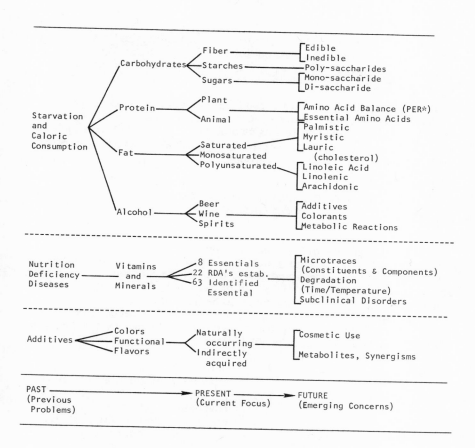

Fig. 9.3. Dietary Concerns - Increasingly Particularistic

 * PER: protein efficiency ration

** Isoleucine, Leucine, Lysine, Methionine, Phenylalanine,
Threonine, Tryptophan, Valine.

Source: Public Policy Forecasting, Inc.

NUTRIENT FOOD GROUPS:
COMMODITY PROMOTION TO EDUCATE CONSUMERS

The Food and Drug Administration pursues technical disclosure of nutrient components. The United States Department of Agriculture, on the other hand, seeks to popularize understanding, and encourage use by promoting commodities high in certain key nutrients - the "Basic Four" food groups.

During wartime, a seven food group plan was conceived and implemented in 1943. Many other food guides have been suggested. Some of them included as few as two or three groups. Others included as many as ten to eighteen specific groups. One approach even breaks out as many as twenty-one food groups.

DIFFICULTY OF SPECIFYING NUTRIENT USAGE OR
FOOD GROUP NEEDS

Assuming agreement can be reached on the number of specific nutrients and/or food groups which should provide the starting point, the questions of appropriate usage levels must be considered. Is disclosure by a "standard reference male and/or female" (middle age, medium height, weight, etc.) specific enough to be helpful?

Nutrition needs are highly individualized and dependent on a wide range of variables. A representative list of some factors varying nutritional need include, but is not limited to:

age	hormones
sex	enzymes (deficiencies, efficiencies,
height	etc.)
weight	psychology (stress, etc.)
activity	diet (individual, family, ethnic,
occupation (longshoreman vs.	neighborhood, region, etc.)
80-year old grandmother)	pregnancy
lifestyle	lactation
income	post operative condition
culture	disposition to disease
clothing	disease condition
climate	physiological adaptations
metabolism	enzyme deficiencies/
	efficiencies

Translating the scientific facts of nutrition into practical nutrition knowledge is not as easy an undertaking as it may appear. Nor is effectiveness of any nutrition education effort improved by putting forward several differing basic approaches. The United States Department of Agriculture's "Basic Four" food groups approach, on top of the Food and Drug Administration's more technical prescription of a minimum of eight essential vitamins and minerals in label disclosure, actually may create confusion; hinder, rather than help. Two nutrition disclosure approaches instead of a single nutrition education theme limits effectiveness of nutrition communications, and may generate unnecessary consumer bewilderment.

Public information campaigns, if they are to successfully reach the general public, must be keyed to a few simple propositions. Too simplistic an approach may not provide enough information and be self defeating. Too complex and detailed an approach encounters the resistance of consumers who simply lack the interest, skill or time to translate complex nutrition and scientific data into practical and useful knowledge. Unfortunately, nutrition information is anything but a simple proposition.

III

Agrifood Technology: Resources, Attitudes, and Regulation

Introduction

AGRIFOOD TECHNOLOGY: RESOURCES, ATTITUDES, AND REGULATION

Of the critical issues facing the 1980s, none is perhaps more important than the role that government regulation will play in our lives. The agrifood area will be increasingly subject to (or to some, beset by) regulation. Fortunately, voices of reason are making themselves heard from many quarters - consumers, the food industry, academia, and the government. Consumers have started to learn that life's many "environments" are not free of risk, that there is a need to balance risks, and to stress that hidden risks are not acceptable. Both the food industry, and the government are beginning to recognize that reasonable regulation has very important indirect benefits, as it has substantial indirect costs. The estimate of total costs of all regulation has been widely publicized - set at $102 billion for 1978 and projected to go much higher in the 1980s. The indirect benefits of regulation, however, have not been spelled out as clearly. A cleaner, healthier environment translates into many benefits ranging from higher work force productivity to increased public confidence in the products of industry. Judicious, economic use of agricultural chemicals not only results in a healthier, less damaged environment, but also in increased farm incomes as operating costs drop.

Increasingly, cost/benefit or risk/benefit analyses are being called for in an effort to insure that regulation's social benefits exceed its costs. Two additional commonsense steps are required in agrifood regulation. This section of the book addresses them. The first is the need for more information - ranging from the education of farmers about the cost, yield, and environmental benefits of integrated pest management techniques, to including sufficient information on food containers so that Americans who are highly allergic to certain foods and food components may avoid illness.

Increased food product information will become more important as consumers become more knowledgeable and demand that the government make the food industry provide that information. Equally important is that technological advanced in food formulation have made early food regulations inapplicable. Furthermore, advances in analytical chemistry allow us to detect infinitesimal traces of substances in our food, but do not yet enable us to determine if such traces are harmful. The pressures of consumers and demands of consumer activists, as well as increased suspicion of technology, will likely be translated into more regulation in the 1980s unless more information (including communication between affected parties) is made available. In fact, one contributor to this section points out that new, more rigorous production and marketing standards could be avoided by the simple expedient of fuller product disclosure.

The second step is to employ technology to meet society's requirements for a safer and healthier agrifood environment. Rather than regarding technology (and science) as something occult, to be feared, would it not be better to use technology to its fullest? After all, it has given us the most varied, least costly, safest food supply of all history. It can surely give us even safer food. Technology, however, must be allowed to continue to flourish if society is to realize its objectives. Kenneth Schlossberg, in the September 1978 issue of Food Technology, pointed out that industry, in particular the food industry, cannot afford to ignore public concerns nor avoid participating in what Irving Kristol has called competition for the public trust. This participation or, more accurately, industry leadership, is critical to America's political health.

Marylin Chou introduces this section with an overview of the socioeconomic and cultural factors that are likely to affect eating habits and trends in food technology in the 1980s. Some of these factors give rise to increasing public demand for government regulation of the food processing sector - a topic which is discussed from both government and industry perspectives by Robert Schaffner and Steven Goldby.

Dr. Schaffner chides the food industry for its short sightedness in espousing the "only natural ingredients" approach, stating that this only serves to undermine public confidence in safe food additives. Restoration of public confidence calls for a positive industry government approach to allay the fears of consumers that all food additives are unsafe.

Mr. Goldby, from his perspective as president of a firm at the leading edge of food additive technology, fears that the current regulatory environment is stifling technological advance. This comes just at a time when advance is absolutely crucial in meeting world demand for food, and in employing nutrition as a preventive medicine.

Wayne Henry takes the regulatory-technology question one step further in his discussion of two extremely successful engineered foods, whose potential is limited only by our imagination. Consumers are wary, however, of engineered foods, and in Dr. Henry's view, this is caused in part by a lack of consumer and regulator education.

Marketing services, as an element in the food chain, take an extraordinarily large share of total food expenditures. The Office of Technology Assessment, recognizing the need to decrease these costs, examines and assigns priorities for assessment to new food marketing technologies which are likely to be adopted and to raise major policy issues over the next decade.

Turning to the resource area, Don Price addresses the near term question of diminishing conventional energy resources and the consequent need to be conserving in the agriculture and food sector. He points out that the rapid increases in agricultural productivity that we have enjoyed over the past four decades were due to heavy use of fossil fuels, and that these productivity increases have reached their plateau in recent years. Food certainly uses and is dependent on fuel, but there is now another side to this relationship - the dependence of fuel on food, specifically food exports.

William Burrows and Norman Sauter examine the demand for and supplies of <u>portable</u> fuels in the new framework of supply dominated energy decisions. On the demand side, alternative engines are examined to determine which best provides for mobile applications in agriculture.

On the supply side, three scenarios of future consumption of petroleum are given with various projections of crude oil reserves. Alternative sources of protable fuels are examined, including that area of special interest to many, biomass.

In the following paper, Don Paarlberg outlines Brazil's efforts to obtain energy from biomass. He reports on the findings of a recent United States visiting team of economists and agricultural scientists who studied Brazil's work in converting sugarcane into alcohol. He discusses the factors and aspirations that led Brazil to undertake an ambitious program of converting sugarcane and cassava into ethyl alcohol. His conclusions will interest those who feel biomass conversion is a viable alternative for the United States.

The section concludes with two papers in the agricultural area. David Harmon addresses the principal issues in the use of agricultural chemicals in an attempt to determine how government policy might be used to mold a regulatory business environment that fulfills two seemingly incompatible goals: Those of encouraging innovation so that sustainable yield increases are possible, and those of minimizing ecological stress so that high but realistic levels of protection are afforded. Consonant with these goals, Mr. Harmon explores various paths to more reasonable and effective regulation.

Sylvan Wittwer then turns down the microscope and examines specific yield increasing and loss decreasing technologies that could be "on the shelf" in the 1980s. He examines them from the standpoint of whether they will lessen or increase the need for regulation. What should be of great interest to government decision makers here and abroad, as well as to the public, is that these technologies are cost effective, environmentally benign, sparing of scarce resources, and both scale and politically neutral.

10 Changing Attitudes and Lifestyles Shaping Food Technology in the 1980s

Marylin Chou

The foods we consume in the next decade will be determined largely by the interaction of socioeconomic conditions and food technology. Within the next ten years we anticipate changes in foods and eating habits which will reflect nutritional, cultural, and socioeconomic needs. This paper discusses some of the conditions and concerns in the coming years as well as certain trends in food technology which are likely to be strengthened in response to such conditions.

QUALITY OF LIFE

One of the major concerns of the seventies has been the so-called "quality of life" issues, which encompass health, safety, protection of the environment, and conservation. The issues relating to the environment were magnified by the energy shortage. Suddenly we became aware of living in a finite world with limited resources as well as limited capabilities to absorb waste. We moved from a "psychology of abundance" to a new concern for quality, conservation, and ecology. For example, we are now so sensitive to waste that "recycling" has become a word with moral as well as economic inferences. Our values shifted from mastery over nature toward living in harmony with it. (1)

Unlike the sixties, when growth and technology were pursued as desirable goals, the benefits of technology were questioned in the seventies. Technology is being blamed for introducing so many hazardous substances into our environment and food chains ... that some fear we are polluting ourselves to death. (2) No longer is there automatic acceptance of technological innovation. The consequences of technological growth are assessed in terms of social justice and equity. (3) What we appear to be seeking now is "ecologically compatible growth," growth which is compatible with the carrying capacity of the earth's biosphere and resources.

Many observers believe that nations, institutions, and individuals are becoming increasingly interdependent.   The energy crisis in 1973 followed by the shortfall in world food grains supply underlined the interdependence of nations.   International boundaries to commerce are being obscured as we see raw materials shipped to one country for processing and then reshipped or returned for consumption.

WASTE RECOVERY

These new attitudes, coupled with recognition that in the United States as much as 25 percent of the food that is produced and enters the food distribution system never reaches the consumer,are placing greater emphasis on the development of waste reduction technologies.   Moreover, the economic burden of regulations pertaining to processing waste provides the incentive for industry to find profitable uses for recovery of waste by-products.   Food losses in the distribution system could be reduced by 30 to 50 percent by making better use of readily available techniques which would result in a 10 to 15 percent increase in our food supply. (5)   The concern about waste involves many interests.   Nutritionists are concerned about lost nutrients; environmentalists are disturbed about the waste food that compounds pollution and disposal problems; conservationists point to the large amount of nonrenewable resources used but not consumed; consumer groups blame waste for contributing to spiraling food costs, and the food industry is recognizing that waste represents lost profits. (6)

Bread provides an example of the extent to which losses cause waste.   Bread constitutes a significant part of diets throughout the world.   In some countries bread supplies as much as 75 percent of the total calorie intake.   The staling of bread represents a critical economic and technical problem in the bread industry.   Under optimum conditions, most white bread produced in the United States has a commercial shelf life of two days.   Staled bread results in the return to the bakery of an average of 8 percent of the bread produced in the United States.   In 1969 this loss represented over 110 million pounds or, on a worldwide basis, one billion bushels of wheat. (7)   For other parts of the world where baking technology and use of additives are not as advanced as in the United States, bread products have a shelf life of only a day.   This is unfortunate in light of the limited food supplies in certain of these countries and ironic in terms of our current interest in breads "free of artificial preservatives."

Most waste reduction technologies examined and developed during the past decade have focused on reducing pollution caused by food processing waste and using the waste for human food, animal feed, energy, or landfill.   Sweet potato peels, citrus sludge, municipal sewage, animal manure, beef slaughtering by-products, seafood waste, and dairy waste are among the many sources being examined as new food, feed, or high protein concentrates. (8)   For example, approximately one-third of today's harvested seafood is discarded and could be used as human food. (9)

Use of these new technologies will be based on economic considerations as well as nutritional and safety factors. Single Cell Protein (SCP) is one of the best examples of the constraints involved in the use of a waste reduction technology. SCP is a complete protein grown indoors on a variety of substrates, including organic waste products and municipal trash. SCP requires no fertilizer. It doubles its mass in two hours compared to grasses which take one to two weeks. Waste disposal is not a problem since nearly all its constituents are used. Production of SCP, a fermentation process, is highly efficient since it does not depend on weather and requires very little space. Limitations to its use, however, are its cost of production because of the substantial quantities of water, minerals, and power it requires, and human safety questions regarding its high nucleic acid content. At the present time, SCP is mainly used as an ingredient in livestock feed. Production of SCP is currently taking place in some countries that have to import feed or protein supplements for livestock, such as the Soviet Union, France, Taiwan, Czechoslovakia, and India. For human consumption, SCP has been primarily limited to the form of torula yeast which is used more for its functional rather than nutritional qualities in salad dressings, pastas, spreads, soups, and confections. In the future, however, with more favorable economics and with solution of the nucleic acid problem, SCP could fulfill much of the world's human protein requirements.

As we become more capable of detecting toxicities at the molecular level, and as we recycle more of our resources within food chains, a question we may face in the eighties will relate to the potential dangers of toxic concentrations. (10) It may also become more difficult to track down food borne infections in the future as more components of foods are manufactured, transported, stored, prepared, and consumed in a variety of places and conditions.

In the decade ahead we anticipate that continuing emphasis will be focused on identifying the causes of food, and nutrient loss at each stage from harvest to consumption in order to develop new techniques for preventing and controlling food losses, and to upgrade wastes into edible products. The largest potential new sources of food are the upgrading of waste products from grain and oil seeds to directly consumable human foods, and the development of food ingredients using fermentation techniques. (11)

DIET AND HEALTH

Poll after poll indicate that Americans are becoming more concerned about health and nutrition, and the relationship between diet and health. Thirty years ago we were concerned about minimum daily requirements to prevent dietary deficiency diseases. We are now concerned about maximum levels, as illustrated in Dietary Goals of the

Senate Select Committee on Nutrition and Human Needs. (12)

Initially when Pasteur discovered that disease was caused by infectious organisms, scientists assumed a causal effect for all diseases. They resisted the possibility that diseases were caused by a deficiency or lack of something in the diet. With the discovery of vitamins about 75 years ago and the recognition that dietary deficiency diseases could be eliminated by an adequate intake of essential nutrients, nutritional strategy in the United States has been focused on prevention of nutritional deficiency. The message has been to eat more meat, more milk, more eggs, more fruits and vegetables, and more cereal products to obtain enough protein, vitamins, and minerals. The message was developed when we had no ideas about the ultimate effects of such a diet, and little understanding of the relationship between diet and the chronic diseases facing affluent societies. (13)

Dietary deficiency diseases, prevalent at the turn of the century, have been eliminated due to accessibility to a greater variety of foods, as well as by enriched and fortified foods. The addition of B vitamins to cereal products has eliminated beriberi, pellagra, and ariboflavinosis; adding iodine to salt has eradicated goiter; fortifying milk with vitamin D has decreased the incidence of rickets. An example of how effectively fortification has eliminated deficiency diseases is illustrated in the following example. In 1938, pellagra was the leading cause of death in eight Southwestern states. After two years of fortifying the traditional cornmeal with niacin, all incidences of this dietary deficiency disease were eliminated. Pellagra caused the deaths of 7,000 people in the United States in 1938, compared to less than 100 deaths from pellagra over the last 10 years. Today the average doctor would not even be able to recognize a patient suffering from pellagra.

Now that we have eliminated the most serious dietary deficiency diseases, we are refocusing our nutritional strategy. We have devoted our past efforts to assuring an adequate diet - one with sufficient proteins, vitamins, and minerals. Concern over diet related "killer diseases," however, is based on the proposition that much of our ill health is due to overnutrition - not simply eating too much, but eating too much of specific nutrients, such as salt, sugar, and fat. Some have interpreted this new emphasis to mean that today's foods are the cause of diet related diseases. These people tend to believe that the diet of their ancestors was healthier. Figure 10.1 illustrates the divergence in viewpoints regarding the benefits of processed foods.

Most of today's nutritional problems in the United States arise not from inadequacy of the food supply but from inappropriate use of the available food, and from socioeconomic complications such as poverty, disruption within families, and alcoholism. (14) Educating the public on the varieties of foods they need for optimum growth, functional performance and well-being is the key to nutritional improvement. To blame "variety" or "processing" as the cause of poor health is almost like blaming the automobile for accidents. In both cases, education is essential.

Consumption of highly refined foods, such as certain snack foods and soft drinks, may lead to nutritional deficiencies if these foods are

Table 10.1. The Pros and Cons of Processed Foods

DR. ALEXANDER M. SCHMIDT, FORMER U.S. COMMIS-
SIONER OF FOODS AND DRUGS

FDA'S RANKING OF MAJOR HAZARDS
ASSOCIATED WITH FOOD

FOOD BORNE INFECTION RANKS WHERE IT DOES BECAUSE
OF ITS CONTINUING WIDESPREAD INCIDENCE, AND BECAUSE
OF THE HIGH RISK IN SOME INSTANCES, SUCH AS BOTULISM.
WE EVEN PREDICT THE HAZARDS OF FOOD BORNW INFECTION
WILL INCREASE AS FOODS ARE SYNTHESIZED, AS THEY ARE
MANUFACTURED IN ONE PLACE, CONSUMED IN OTHERS, AND
STORED AND MOVED REPEATEDLY.

MALNUTRITION AT PRESENTLY IS POORLY MEASURED AND
POORLY UNDERSTOOD. BIOCHEMICALLY PROVABLE NUTRI-
TIONAL DEFICIENCIES DO OCCUR IN NUMBERS SUFFICIENT
TO BE OF CONCERN NOW, AND WHEN A LARGER PART OF OUR
FOOD SUPPLY IS MANUFACTURED, THE PROBLEMS MAY
INCREASE. IT IS OFTEN NOT READILY APPRECIATED THAT
WE REALLY DO NOT KNOW EVERYTHING THAT SHOULD BE
INCLUDED IN ARTIFICIALLY CONSTITUTED FOODS, AND IN
WHAT AMOUNTS, IF THE ANALOGS ARE TO BE NUTRITION-
ALLY EQUAL TO TRADITIONAL FOODS. WE WILL NEED TO
KNOW MUCH MORE ABOUT TRACE MINERALS, TO GIVE ONE
EXAMPLE, BEFORE WE CAN WISELY TELL SOMEONE HOW
MUCH OF EACH HE HAS TO PUT INTO HIS ARTIFICIAL
MEAT...

FOOD ADDITIVES ARE LAST BECAUSE SO MUCH IS KNOWN
ABOUT MANY OF THEM, AND ALL ARE NOW, AND SURELY
WILL CONTINUE TO BE, WELL REGULATED.

SOURCE: "FOOD AND DRUG LAW: A 200-YEAR PER-
SPECTIVE," NUTRITION TODAY, VOLUME 10, NO. 4,
1975, P. 32.

GILBERT A. LEVEILLE, CHAIRMAN, DEPARTMENT OF
FOOD SCIENCE AND HUMAN NUTRITION, MICHIGAN STATE
UNIVERSITY.

WE HAVE SEEN MANY IMPROVEMENTS IN THE QUALITY OF
OUR FOOD SUPPLY AS MEASURED BY ITS SAFETY,
WHOLESOMENESS AND VARIETY, IT IS UNPARALLELED IN
THE WORLD TODAY.... ANY NOTION THAT A RETURN TO
THE DIET OF THE PAST WOULD IMPROVE THE WELL-
BEING OF AMERICANS IS NOSTALGIC NONSENSE.

SOURCE: "ESTABLISHING AND IMPLEMENTING DIETARY
GOALS," PRESENTED AT THE 1978 FOOD AND AGRICUL-
TURAL OUTLOOK CONFERENCE, WASHINGTON, D.C.,
NOVEMBER 17, 1977, P. 2

DR. WALTER MERTZ, CHAIRMAN OF THE NUTRITION INSTITUTE
OF THE U.S. DEPARTMENT OF AGRICULTURE

...WHY ARE WE CONCERNED WITH TRACE ELEMENT RESEARCH?
THIS CENTURY HAS SEEN VERY PRONOUNCED CHANGES OF
DIETARY HABITS IN THE U.S... FOR WHICH WE HAVE NO
HISTORICAL PRECEDENT AND, THEREFORE, NO ASSURANCE THAT
THEY ARE COMPTIBLE WITH GOOD HEALTH.

--...THE FIRST RESULTS FROM OUR ABILITY TO PARTITION
FOODS...PARTITIONING ALWAYS AFFECTS IMPORTANT NUTRITIENTS
...PARTITIONING OF BUTTER FROM MILK REMOVES THE IMPOR-
TANT MINERAL ELEMENT, CALCIUM, WHICH MANY BELIEVE COUNTER-
BALANCES THE POTENTIALLY HARMFUL EFFECTS OF FATS IN
MILK....

--THE SECOND PROFOUND CHANGE OF OUR DIETARY HABITS IS
RELATED TO FABRICATED FOODS...REGARDLESS OF WHETHER
THESE ARE MADE FOR ACCEPTABLE REASONS, THEY ALL HAVE IN
COMMON THAT THEY REPLACE PRODUCTS FOR WHICH MANKIND HAS
HAD THOUSANDS OF YEARS OF EXPERIENCE.

--...A CONTINUATION OF THE PRESENT TREND TOWARD CONSUMP-
TION OF MORE PARTITIONED, REFINED AND FABRICATED FOODS
MUST EVENTUALLY LEAD TO A POINT WHERE THE REST OF THE
DIET CANNOT MEET THE REQUIREMENTS OF ALL ESSENTIAL
NUTRIENTS ANY MORE....

SOURCE: "STATE OF KNOWLEDGE OF NUTRIENT DATA: TRACE
MINERALS," STATEMENT BEFORE THE SUBCOMMITTEE ON DOMES-
TIC AND INTERNATIONAL SCIENTIFIC PLANNING, ANALYSIS AND
COOPERATION, COMMITTEE ON SCIENCE AND TECHNOLOGY, HOUSE
OF REPRESENTATIVES, WASHINGTON, D.C., JULY 12, 1978.

THEODORE LABUZA, PROFESSOR, FOOD SCIENCE AND TECHNOLOGY,
UNIVERSITY OF MINNESOTA

FRESH VS. FROZEN VEGETABLES

ALL FOODS DETERIORATE IN QUALITY DURING STORAGE: FRESH
FOODS HAVE THE SHORTEST SHELF-LIFE DUE TO MICROBIAL
DECAY AND CHEMICAL AND PHYSICAL CHANGES WHICH REDUCE
QUALITY AND NUTRIENT VALUE....DURING STORAGE FRESH
GREEN BEANS CAN LOSE 50 PERCENT OF THE VITAMIN C IN
TWO DAYS AT 48°F WHEREAS, IT TAKES FROZEN BEANS ONE
YEAR AT 0° F FOR THE SAME LOSS TO OCCUR.

SOURCE: FOOD AND YOUR WELL-BEING, AVI PRESS, WESTPORT,
1977, P. 288.

consumed in excess and in place of conventional foods. Nutrition education will have to emphasize that nutritional adequacy be attained through the use of a wide variety of foods having complementary patterns of nutrients. Moreover, as the diet conscious public reduces their caloric intake, the few foods they consume must become more nutritious.

In the United States, those who have nutritional problems are not suffering from nutritional deficiency diseases, but rather have indications of borderline malnutrition. These people are found among such groups as the urban poor, the elderly, migrant workers, and pregnant and lactating mothers. (15)

The incidence of death in the United States, from 10 of the 15 leading causes of death has decreased in the past twelve years. Within the last 50 years, average life expectancy has increased by 20 years. Infant mortality has dropped 38 percent in the past fifteen years, from 26 to 16 for each 1,000 patients; while material deaths have decreased from 37 to 11 per 100,000 (see table 2.2, p. 31).

Now that we are living longer, we are encountering diseases of aging, and we have the luxury to consider how to improve the quality of that life. Medical science cannot eliminate heart attacks to achieve immortality, but it can aim to delay heart attacks, cancer, stroke, diabetes, and hypertension so that they are not the prominent causes of death or disability before age 65.

As a country becomes more affluent, concern for diseases related to overconsumption causes a decline in the amount of food consumed and a change in the quality of the diet, a trend taking place in several Western industrialized countries. Total energy requirements have declined as improved transportation and mechanization have reduced the physical work required for many occupations, and leisure activities have become less physically taxing. Between 1955 and 1973, per capita calorie consumption declined in a number of industrialized countries, among them Denmark, Norway, Sweden, and Great Britain. (16)

By contrast, per capita calorie consumption has remained relatively stable during the past 65 years in the United States. Because of more sedentary life-styles, the excess caloric intake is resulting in obesity becoming one of the major health concerns. In the United States protein consumption was estimated to be at its highest at the beginning of the twentieth century, when consumption of meat and grain products was very high, and protein came from animal and vegetable sources in roughly equal proportions. Animal sources now account for about 67 percent of the total supply, and thus the shift to animal sources of protein has been at the expense of carbohydrates and vegetable protein contained in foods such as flour, cereal, and potatoes.

Total fat consumption has increased since 1910, but consumption of animal fat has decreased while consumption of vegetable fat has increased. Concern over the dietary link between animal fats and cardiovascular diseases has evidently played a role in the decline of per capita egg consumption from 42.4 pounds in 1960 to 34.6 pounds in 1978; of milk from 321 pounds to 288.9 pounds; and of butter from 7.5 to 4.6. (see table 10.1). (17)

Table 10.1. Trends in U.S. Per Capita Consumption

	1960 (pounds)	1978 (pounds)
EGGS	42.4	34.6
MILK	321.0	288.9
BUTTER	7.5	4.6
MARGARINE	9.4	11.9
MEATS	134.1	149.6
CHICKEN	27.8	47.5
SUGAR (SUCROSE)	97.4	93.2
FRUITS	90.0	80.3
VEGETABLES	96.0	95.2
FISH	10.3	12.9

Source: National Food Review, USDA Economic Statistics and Co-operative Service, December 1978.

While 1976 vegetable consumption figures are slightly lower than 1960, compared to 1970, there has been an increase in consumption of fresh vegetable products. Sweet corn has increased 12 percent, lettuce 6 percent, tomatoes 4 percent, carrots 2 percent, and cabbage 1 percent. (18) The change in eating habits can be partially attributed to health consciousness and concern over excess calorie consumption.

Americans have become so health and diet conscious that over the last 10 years our concept of a square meal has gone from "meat and potatoes" to "meat and vegetables." The concern for the relationship between health and overconsumption is evident in the 1975 Food and Drug Administration Consumer Nutrition Knowledge Survey, which indicated that 6 out of 10 shoppers said someone in their household was dieting. (19) Besides "thinking thin," physical fitness has become a major preoccupation. This preoccupation will continue into the next decade even though the forms of exercise may change.

Coronary heart diseases and cancer are two of the major health concerns of affluent industrialized countries. Both of these diseases are linked with diet and an aging population. These chronic diseases appear more prevalent in developed countries because in developing countries death registration is not compulsory, not all cases are diagnosed, and many more die of infections at younger ages than those at which most people get cancer or heart disease.

An example of this is shown in figure 10.2 comparing the mortality data from various diseases in India vs. the United States in 1965. The overall death rate for the United States was about 700 per 100,000 per year, whereas in India, it was more than twice that. United States life expectancy at birth was 70 years, compared to 40 years in India. For this reason, heart disease in the United States was the chief cause of death. In India the infectious diseases of tuberculosis, pneumonia, dysentery, and small pox were responsible for causing the early deaths so that the citizenry never attained the age to die from chronic diseases of the aging. (20)

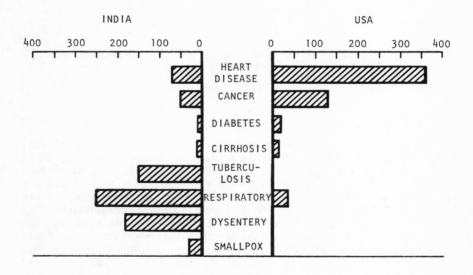

Fig. 10.2. Comparative Death Rates from Selected Causes in India
_____ and the U.S.A., 1965 (Deaths per 100,000 Population)

Source: World Health Statistics Annual, 1965; World Health Organization, Geneva 1968; Demographic Year Book, 1966; United Nations, N.Y., 1967.

Critics of the American diet might misinterpret this chart to mean that Americans would be healthier consuming an Indian diet, when in fact most Americans are dying of diseases associated with the aging. This chart also shows the danger of drawing conclusions from epidemiological data which correlates variables of a disease without respect to cause and effect.

At the present time there is substantial controversy over the causes of coronary heart disease. As figure 10.3 indicates, there is considerable question regarding the relationship of dietary cholesterol and heart disease. Many scientists question whether the whole population should be told to reduce their cholesterol intake, because as many people died of heart disease with low blood cholesterol as did those with high blood cholesterol. Based on the lack of evidence, they believe that dietary intervention should be recommended to only those individuals, between 5 and 20 percent of the population, who have elevated blood lipid problems.

At this point it is impossible to conclude that reduced cholesterol consumption has any effect on reducing coronary heart disease. In fact, deaths from heart disease in the United States have actually declined during the period beef consumption has increased. (21) If it is concluded in the next few years that dietary cholesterol does not affect coronary heart diseases, the public reaction will be one of further confusion and resistance to accept both the medical profession's and industry's credibility.

Interest in diet related health problems will continue to mount as the nation tries to formulate appropriate dietary guidelines. To avoid further loss of credibility, the appropriate government agencies and scientists should explain to the public the current state of knowledge about the potential benefits of modifying dietary habits, without overstating the benefits that could possibly result.

Dietary guidelines suggest that we should consume less fatty red meat and more poultry, fish, lean meat, bread, rice, and potatoes. Meat, however, provides the best source of iron and zinc, essential nutrients which are less available in vegetarian diets. Moreover, consumption of cereal grains increase the phytic acid which tends to bind zinc, calcium, and iron, and reduce their absorption into the system. Interactions between nutrients in the diet require further understanding.

During the past century our interest in food has traveled from obtaining enough food to survive to determining how much of a micro trace element is too much. Once our food supply became dependable, we divided the components of food into calories, proteins, fat, vitamins and minerals, and attempted to relate the effect of these components to human functions. Within the past 50 years, we have come to recognize the constitutents comprising each of the components. We are now refocusing the microscope to explore the role of trace elements and microtrace constituents. We are seeking to determine which micronutrientss are essential under differing conditions, how they react with one another and on other nutrients, how much is beneficial, and how much more is toxic.

The growing interest in nutrition requires research to determine more precise knowledge of nutrient requirements of individuals through various stages of growth and the development of foods capable of providing the required nutrients. (22) Meaningful results from human nutrition research, however, are limited by high costs, multiple

THEODORE P. LABUZA

CONTROVERSY OVER CAUSES OF CORONARY HEART
DISEASE

THE FOLLOWING LIST GIVES THE VARIOUS FACTORS THAT EPI-
DEMIOLOGISTS, SCIENTISTS, AND PHYSICIANS HAVE CONNEC-
TED WITH HEART DISEASE. A VALUE OF ONE WOULD BE THE
ABSOLUTE CAUSE OF HEART DISEASE AND ZERO MEANS NO
EFFECT.

CAUSE	CREDITABILITY FACTOR
CHOLESTEROL IN DIET	0.5
SATURATED FATTY ACIDS	0.8
REFINED SUGAR	0.5
HYPERTENSION	0.8
HYDROGENATED FATS	0.5
HOMOGENIZED MILK	0.2
LACK OF FIBER	0.7
ZINC/COPPER RATIO IN DIET	0.6
DEGREE OF WATER HARDNESS	0.5
OBESITY	0.7
LACK OF EXERCISE	0.7
HEREDITARY FACTORS	1.0
CIGARETTE SMOKING	0.8
STRESS OF SOCIETY	0.9

SOURCE: FOOD AND YOUR WELL-BEING, (WESTPORT, CONN.:
AVI PUBLISHING CO., 1977), P. 175.

SIR JOHN McMICHAEL, M.D.

SEVEN-COUNTRY STUDY

1970--SEVEN-COUNTRY STUDY CONCERNED WITH CORONARY
THROMBOSIS INVOLVING 10,000 PEOPLE IN U.S. AND
EUROPE REVEALED:

--MOST CORONARIES OCCURRED AROUND MID-AVERAGE
  LEVEL OF BLOOD CHOLESTEROL (WHEN EASTERN FINNS
  NOT INCLUDED)
--CORRELATION OF CORONARY DISEASE (CD) WITH FAT
  INTAKE IS NOT SIGNIFICANT
--DIDN'T MAKE SLIGHTEST DIFFERENCE TO DEATH RATE
  OR RECURRENCE WHETHER PATIENTS ATE SATURATED
  OR POLYUNSATURATED FATS
--IT IS THE QUANTITY OF FAT AND NOT THE NATURE
  OF THE FAT WE EAT.

SOURCE: DIET RELATED TO KILLER DISEASES, III,
HEARINGS BEFORE THE SELECT COMMITTEE ON NUTRITION
AND HUMAN NEEDS OF THE UNITED STATES SENATE,
MARCH 24, 1977, P. 13.

Fig. 10.3. The Question of Diet and Heart Disease

DR. D. MARK HEGSTED

HARVARD SCHOOL OF PUBLIC HEALTH

THE DIET OF THE AMERICAN PEOPLE IS BECOMING INCREAS-
INGLY RICH IN MEAT AND OTHER SOURCES OF SATURATED
FATS AND CHOLESTEROL. AND THIS DIET WHICH AFFLUENT
PEOPLE GENERALLY CONSUME, EVERYWHERE, IS ASSOCIATED
WITH SIMILAR DISEASE PATTERNS, HIGH RATES OF HEART
DISEASE, CERTAIN FORMS OF CANCER, DIABETES, OBESITY,
AND THESE ARE THE MAJOR CAUSES OF DEATH AND DIS-
ABILITY IN THE UNITED STATES. ALTHOUGH WE RECOG-
NIZE THESE DEGENERATIVE DISEASES UNDOUBTEDLY HAVE
A COMPLEX ETIOLOGY, IT APPEARS AN INAPPROPRIATE
DIET CONTRIBUTES TO THEIR PREVALANCE.

SOURCE: DIET RELATED TO KILLER DISEASES, III,
HEARINGS BEFORE THE SELECT COMMITTEE ON NUTRITION
AND HUMAN NEEDS OF THE UNITED STATES SENATE,
MARCH 24, 1977.

EDWARD H. AHRENS, JR.

ROCKEFELLER UNIVERSITY

IS IT PROPER TO ANTICIPATE WHAT WE HOPE THE RE-
SULTS WILL BE IN A TRULY DEFINITIVE TEST OF THE
LIPID HYPOTHESES, AND MAKE BROADSCALE RECOMMEN-
DATIONS ON DIETS AND DRUGS TO THE GENERAL PUBLIC
NOW? I SINCERELY BELIEVE WE SHOULD NOT DO SO,
PARTLY BECAUSE ANY SUCH ADVICE IS PREMATURE IN
TERMS OF OUR KNOWLEDGE OF EFFICACY AND OF NON-
TOXICITY, AND ALSO BECAUSE THE EFFECTIVENESS
OF A PUBLIC HEALTH APPROACH DEPENDS SO CRITI-
CALLY ON HAVING A CONVINCED BODY OF MEDICAL
OPINION TO SUPPORT SUCH MEASURES. THE MEDICAL
BODY POLITIC IS NOT CONVINCED TODAY THAT LIPID-
LOWERING IN THE GENERAL PUBLIC IS EITHER
FEASIBLE OR EFFECTIVE IN REDUCING THE INCIDENCE
OF CORONARY HEART DISEASE. NOR AM I, ALTHOUGH
I SUSPECT WE ALL HAVE HIGH HOPES.

SOURCE: DIET RELATED TO KILLER DISEASES, III,
HEARINGS BEFORE THE SELECT COMMITTEE ON NUTRITION
AND HUMAN NEEDS OF THE UNITED STATES SENATE,
MARCH 24, 1977, P. 11.

DR. WILLIAM KANNEL

FRAMINGHAM STUDY

...UNCONVINCED THAT THERE WAS ANY PROOF AT ALL THAT
THE INTERFERENCE WITH THE DIET ON A LARGE SCALE
WOULD IMPROVE THE INCIDENCE AND MORTALITY OF CORO-
NARY ARTERY DISEASE...

THERE ARE FEW PROPHYLACTIC MEASURES OF PROVED
EFFICACY IN CORONARY HEART DISEASE. THIS APPLIES
TO PRIMARY AND SECONDARY PREVENTION.

JUST AS MANY PEOPLE DIED OF HEART DISEASE WITH LOW
BLOOD CHOLESTEROL AS DID PEOPLE WITH HIGH BLOOD
CHOLESTEROL.

SOURCE: DIET RELATED TO KILLER DISEASES, III,
HEARINGS BEFORE THE SELECT COMMITTEE ON NUTRITION
AND HUMAN NEEDS OF THE UNITED STATES SENATE,
MARCH 24, 1977, PP. 15, 100, 348.

Fig. 10.3. The Question of Diet and Heart Disease

variabilities, and ethical constraints.   Complications involve interactions among specific nutrients and variability in requirements among
different individuals, and variability in requirements, over time, for
individuals. Moreover, ethical considerations have restricted the use of
human volunteers in biological research. (23) Lifetime animal-feeding
studies are also costly, and we are still unsure of the relationship
between the results of animal experiments and human behavior.

As obesity becomes the major concern in diet related illnesses, it is
important, although ironic, to remember that "the less we eat, the more
important it is to eat the right things." While attempting to reduce
calorie consumption, it may be necessary to increase the nutrient
density of those foods which are consumed. (24) This requires an even
more careful selection of foods to comprise a complete diet, a difficult
task for some nutrients such as iron, zinc, and copper, at very low
calorie intakes. (25)

The development of responsible fortification procedures will become
a major consideration in the 1980s. With increased ability to engineer
foods, and increased understanding of the role of trace elements to
destroy or enhance other elements beneficial or harmful to human
health, food processors will be confronted with new product decisions
similar to those in the past decades involving the addition of RDA
vitamins and minerals. (26)   (RDAs are defined as "levels of intake
essential nutrients considered adequate to meet known nutritional needs
of practically all healthy persons.") Responsible fortification policies
will favor fortification of certain staples and basic grain products and
restoration of nutrients in conventional and formulated foods. Fortification of "fun foods" should be discouraged to prevent excessive
nutrient consumption, added cost, and misleading the consumer to think
that three candy bars claiming one third of the Recommended Daily
Allowances fulfills their day's nutritional requirements.

Engineered Foods

New food products are already incorporating, the public's concern
over excess calorie and cholesterol consumption. The interest in foods
fortified with proteins and vitamins will be replaced by concern over
fat, sugar, salt, and minerals such as calcium, zinc, and iron. 1976 was
dubbed the "Year of Special Dietary Interest Products" with the
introduction of acidophilus milk, high fiber and/or low calorie bread,
low cholesterol, poultry based frankfurters and other meat substitutes,
light beer (low calorie), and low cholesterol cheese. (27)

As Americans become more weight and health conscious, we
anticipate a trend towards more foods engineered for specific nutritional, dietetic, and functional purposes. Considering the popularity of
diet soft drinks, it is conceivable that certain beverages will eventually
be engineered to be almost complete foods, on the basis of their caloric
and nutrient intake, or engineered to contain no calories for those who
are dieting. Foods may also be formulated for specific functions such
as to provide quick energy or to avoid anxiety or irritation. If foods can
be used to modify moods, we should consider the possible abuses before
they occur in the future.

Medical Foods

In the coming decade, as we increasingly understand how diets affect our physiological functions, we should see more medical foods formulated for management of specific diet related diseases such as metabolic defects and allergies, anemias, malabsorption problems, gastrointestinal diseases, diabetes, renal malfunctions, and high cholesterol. According to one set of figures developed by the United States Department of Agriculture, better diets might reduce the following health problems (see table 10.2).

Table 10.2.   Reducing Diseases through Improved Diets*

DISEASES	% REDUCTION	DISEASES	% REDUCTION
DIABETES	50	ARTHRITIS	50
HEART AND VASCULATORY	25	DENTAL HEALTH	50
		ANEMIA	33
OBESITY	80	EYESIGHT	20
ALCOHOLISM	33	ALLERGIES	40-60
INTESTINAL CANCER	20	DIGESTIVE	25
RESPIRATORY AND INFECTION	20	KIDNEY	20
MENTAL HEALTH	10	MUSCULAR DISORDERS	10
INFANT MORTALITY AND REPRODUCTION	50		

* E. Edith Weir, "Benefits From Human Nutrition Research," ARS, USDA, August 1971, Washington, D.C.

There is a growing recognition of the importance of nutrition in alleviating certain medical, surgical, and traumatic conditions. In the United States there are over 100 commercially available items identified as medical foods, and it is anticipated that the number and variety will increase as their functional design improves and their therapeutic advantages become more widely recognized. (28)

Encouraged by the needs of the aerospace program for easily consumable, low residue, and high calorie dietary products, there has been a steady increase over the past 20 years in the development and commercial availability of specially formulated preparations that are useful in the dietary management of patients. It is generally assumed that the nutritional needs of an individual with a disease, disorder, or other medical condition are either greater than those of a normal healthy person or are unique because of the medical condition. (29) Traumatized patients often have increased nutrient requirements that are related to increased energy and caloric needs. Caloric requirements could increase up to 200 percent, and protein catabolic responses might increase protein requirements from 60 percent to 500 percent. (30)

For patients incapable of swallowing food through the mouth, it is now possible to sustain life totally through intravenous feedings. Unlike the traditional intravenous feeding of sugar water which supplies 500 to 600 calories a day, intravenous hyperalimentation (IVH), or parenteral nutrition, is capable of supplying an adult with 3,000 calories of dextrose, amino acids, electrolytes, vitamins, minerals, and essential fats. The solutions can be tailored to the needs of the individual patients. This feeding system has been developed by Dr. Stanley J. Dudrick, Chairman of the Department of Surgery of the University of Texas Medical Center, over the last decade. Dr. Dudrick and others estimate that in at least 10 percent, and perhaps as much as 30 percent of the deaths which occur in hospitals, malnutrition is the direct or an important contributing cause. (31) Many patients die because they are unable to eat or absorb enough nutrients to sustain life - not because their illness is incurable. By preventative malnourishment, parenteral nutrition has enabled cancer patients to withstand higher doses of anticancer drugs, thus increasing their chances for cure. This total feeding system has also eliminated the need for surgery for some patients suffering from inflammatory bowel disease. The disease is cured through intravenous nutritional therapy without drugs or surgery.

In the future, Dr. Dudrick hopes to use IVH to starve cancer cells, or enhance their susceptibility to therapy, and to isolate the precise dietary components that promote clogging of the arteries and heart disease. More research needs to be directed toward special nutrient and drug interactions that may occur in the intravenous feeding of patients when the body's normal absorptive mechanisms are bypassed.

Due to changing patterns of health care delivery and long term management of patients with certain nutritional disorders such as cancer, the market for parenteral and enteral nutritional products will expand. It has been estimated that the market for intravenous products in 1980 would be two to three times its 1975 sales volume, while the market for medical foods would grow even more rapidly. (32) Palatability and taste fatigue have been identified as two important factors affecting the prolonged use of medical foods.

ENERGY AND LABOR

1985 has been targeted as the year in which an energy shortage will once again reach crisis dimensions in the United States. When and whether this occurs is open to question. Less questionable, however, is the assumption that the price of energy and the cost of labor will continue to increase during this period. How will the higher costs of energy and labor affect consumers and producers in the coming decade?

Although United States consumers spend less of their disposable income on food than other industrialized countries, they will undoubtedly resent seeing their staples and processed foods rise in price (see figure 10.4.)

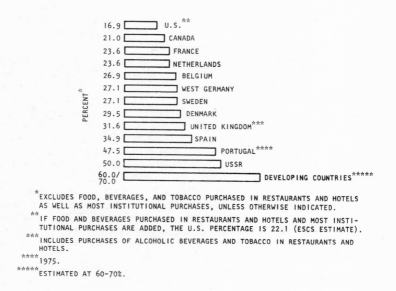

PERCENT*

16.9 ⬜ U.S.**
21.0 ⬜ CANADA
23.6 ⬜ FRANCE
23.6 ⬜ NETHERLANDS
26.9 ⬜ BELGIUM
27.1 ⬜ WEST GERMANY
27.1 ⬜ SWEDEN
29.5 ⬜ DENMARK
31.6 ⬜ UNITED KINGDOM***
34.9 ⬜ SPAIN
47.5 ⬜ PORTUGAL****
50.0 ⬜ USSR
60.0/
70.0 ⬜ DEVELOPING COUNTRIES*****

* EXCLUDES FOOD, BEVERAGES, AND TOBACCO PURCHASED IN RESTAURANTS AND HOTELS
AS WELL AS MOST INSTITUTIONAL PURCHASES, UNLESS OTHERWISE INDICATED.
** IF FOOD AND BEVERAGES PURCHASED IN RESTAURANTS AND HOTELS AND MOST INSTI-
TUTIONAL PURCHASES ARE ADDED, THE U.S. PERCENTAGE IS 22.1 (ESCS ESTIMATE).
*** INCLUDES PURCHASES OF ALCOHOLIC BEVERAGES AND TOBACCO IN RESTAURANTS AND
HOTELS.
**** 1975.
***** ESTIMATED AT 60-70%.

Fig. 10.4. Share of Total Private Consumption Expenditures of
Food, Beverages, and Tobacco, 1976.

Source: Organization for Economic Cooperation and Development -
except USSR and Developing Countries which are ESCS Estimates)

Marketing costs now comprise 60 percent of the total food bill.
Labor is the major contributor to food marketing costs, accounting for
45 to 48 percent, followed by packaging costs which range between 12
and 13 percent, transportation 7 to 8 percent, profits 7 percent,
advertising 2 to 3 percent. (33) (see Chapter 4, Food Price Inflation - A
Heretical View.) Labor is becoming an increasingly large component of
the price of food since price is affected by rising wages at each level of
production from the farmgate to the table. From 1970 to 1978, the
labor portion of the food dollar rose 49 percent. In 1977, for the first
time in history, the cost of wages and salaries in the food dollar was
more than the farm share. (34) In 1978, two thirds of every dollar spent
for United States farm raised foods went to pay the bill for getting the
food from the farm to the supermarket. (35)

While labor costs have increased, productivity has not, an important
factor responsible for higher food prices. Traditionally improved
productivity is the result of developing labor saving technologies to
enable greater mechanization per worker. With greater allocation of

research funds directed to complying with new regulations, the pace of research and development has been slowed and capital investments discouraged. Moreover, changes in lifestyle brought about by more women working, more single households and greater affluence have increased the demand for convenience built into foods and more meals consumed away from home. These changes translate into more labor required to produce the foods consumed. Higher labor costs have served to decrease productivity while increasing the price of food. With innovative technology lagging, one alternative for obtaining cost reductions will be through product differentiation to increase market shares.

Increased marketing costs will continue to account for most of the rise in consumer food expenditures, particularly because increases in the cost of labor affect so many. The food industry, employing 25 million people, is the largest enterprise in America. (36)

While higher energy costs and the general inflationary trend are major contributors to increased marketing costs, increased costs resulting from inadequate competition, excessive advertising, and packaging will be monitored closely by consumer groups and regulatory agencies.

Will concern over future energy scarcities and increased energy cost cause consumers to make more efficient use of appliances? Will consumers demand foods which require less energy to prepare at home? Will shelfstable foods become more popular as more become available? The answers will most likely be based on cost and taste considerations.

Sterile Milk

Sterile fluid milk is an example of a food product which, while energy conserving, has not yet been widely adopted in the United States. Sterile milk differs from pasteurized milk in its ability to be stored unopened at room temperature for up to six months. Sterile milk is heated to 280°, which kills the microorganisms that cause spoilage, as compared to pasteurized milk heated to 160°, which does not kill all the bacteria. At the present time the cost of producing sterile milk is approximately one-third of a cent per quart higher than pasteurized milk. The savings to the consumer would be in the cost of refrigeration energy and the cost of driving to the supermarket to pick up milk. The savings to producers and distributors would be in the energy and labor costs of transporting and refrigerating products. Since 1940 the number of milk processing plants has declined from 8,500 to 1,500 in 1974. (37) Fewer processing plants mean increased distances that refrigerated trucks must travel to deliver milk products. As the cost of distribution and marketing rises, it may become more economical for supermarkets to start carrying sterile milk. Consumers may have to adapt to a slightly cooked flavor, although a process developed and patented by the DASI Industries, Inc. of Maryland claims that most people cannot tell the difference. (38) Sterile milk will probably gain a foothold in institutional use and in other milk products such as ice cream mix before it is widely accepted by consumers. There are some who believe that the need for energy conservation in the United States will dictate the adoption of aseptically packaged milk so that it will become a standard supermarket item during the 1980s. (39) At present, sterile milk is useful for campers, second home owners, small users, and the elderly for reserve supplies where accessibility to markets may be inconvenient.

Europe started to use sterile milk around 1963, and the volume has been growing steadily. Some estimate that by 1980 sterile milk will capture 65 percent of the milk market in continental Europe. (40)

Current food processing operations evolved in an era of cheap energy, raw material, and labor. It is estimated that the food system involving processing, distribution, and preparation uses about 17 percent of total energy consumption. Energy in processing food accounts for about 30 percent of the total in the food system and is the largest user sector.

It has been estimated that major changes in processing methods can reduce energy use by 35 percent, waste and effluent by 80 percent, and increase processing yields by 5 to 20 percent. (41) Energy-saving technologies should be focused on those areas of food processing where the greatest losses are occurring (see Appendix A).

Food Preservation

In the years ahead, major improvements in processing efficiency and major reductions in process energy requirements will come only through new knowledge of the mechanisms causing food loss. The five pathways for food loss are microbes, enzymes, chemical, animal/insect, and mechanical; while the five methods for food preservation are heat, refrigeration, drying, chemical, and mechanical. Current successful processing methods use combinations of preservation methods to achieve a desired shelf life. Chemical preservation methods continue to be attractive from an energy and capital investment viewpoint, but work on new chemical preservations has been hindered by the extensive toxicity testing requirements for all new additives. (42) Until recently funding for research in support of food preservation and processing was minimal. Greater support was given to production related work.

Many new techniques in food preservation, however, are based on ancient practices. For instance, dehydration using the sun as the source of energy for drying was employed before Biblical times. Over the centuries, dehydration has been improved by mechanical devices and methods. Since 1976, the United States Department of Agriculture and the Department of Energy have been funding research directed towards using solar energy in food processing. Researchers are trying to determine the potential energy savings of developing solar collectors to provide hot air for the various dehydration procedures in drying seafood, vegetables, fruits, and other food materials. At present, the major problem in using solar energy for the drying process is the enormous capital expense required for the equipment. Experiments to date indicate that the most feasible use of solar energy is in dairy operations where solar water heating is physically and economically practical. Experiments at Michigan State University conclude that the current economics of solar water heating limits potential saving in food processing plants to 20 to 50 percent. Geographical location has a significant effect upon solar water heating feasibility, with southern states showing an advantage over northern. (43)

Another method of dehydration is freeze-drying. Among the most successful products using this technology is freeze-dried coffee. Freeze-drying is one of the most effective means of preserving taste, quality, and appearance. Unfortunately, it is also the most expensive dehydration method since it is capital and energy intensive.

The United States Army Natick Research and Development Command, which pioneered the freeze-drying technology, is also responsible for developing dehydrated, reversible compressed foods. Upon rehydration, compressed foods make a complete recovery to round, plump, fully shaped vegetables, fruit, or meat with normal textural and taste properties. The major advantages of compressed foods are significant reduction in volume which reduces storage and transportation space as well as packaging materials; increase in stability and shelf life; and less packaging waste. These advantages have made compressed foods useful for the armed services, astronauts, food service industry, and campers. The volume reduction of compressed foods range from 75 percent for peas to 90 percent for beans, enabling one case of compressed green beans to equal nine cases of the canned product.

Where cost of drying had once been the major disadvantage of compressed food, new processing techniques using microwave heating, vacuum drying, or air drying for part of the process, are lowering the cost of the process and making certain compressed foods competitive or potentially cheaper than canned or frozen foods. (44) Studies comparing the cost of shipping compressed, frozen, and canned green beans to Europe have shown how compressed foods can be competitive when the costs of storage, distribution, handling, and preparation are included. (45)

Food Packaging

Food packaging costs are likely to increase 7 percent a year through 1980 due to the cost of materials and increased use. Packaging costs now account for 13 percent of the food marketing bill. Packaging space limitations will favor compact, stackable packaging. Since packaging now accounts for 30 to 40 percent of municipal waste, packaging in the 1980s will be designed to be less wasteful of raw materials and energy, and be more easily disposable. There will be new methods of wrapping and coating for protective purposes. Consideration will be given to reusable containers, as well as packaging which can be used as a source of fuel. Retort pouches are energy conserving in production, use of materials, and in food preparation. Less heat is needed to penetrate the center of the food compared to thermal processing. Retort pouches were developed by the United States Army Natick Research and Development Command in the 1960s for a wide range of space foods. The pouches did not gain approval from the Food and Drug Administration for use in the United States until 1977, although they have been widely used in Japan and Europe. (46)   The main disadvantage of retortable pouches is that it takes over three times as long to fill and seal compared to using metal containers.   With a number of United States companies working on producing foods in retory packages, a solution to this problem will undoubtedly be found, and we can expect to see more foods packaged in retort pouches in the 1980s. (47)   (see chapter 14, pp. 231-232).

REGULATIONS AND CONSUMER CONCERNS

Is it possible to determine who represents the consumer?   With a nation of over 200 million people from different regions, different ethnic backgrounds, and varying ages, it is obviously a difficult if not impossible task to define who the consumer is and what his interests are.   According to one view, consumers are a heterogeneous collection of men, women, and children...all of whom have as a common denominator only the desire and need for safety and wholesomeness in what they eat, use, and serve to their families. (48) Beyond that, those who argue for what the American consumer wants, prefers, needs, and should be required to accept may well be expressing merely their individual preferences or their own dietary foibles.

According to a survey ("Consumerism at the Crossroads") conducted by Marketing Sciences Institute, food manufacturers are heading the list of those industries picked by consumers and activists for future consumer action. (49)   While the consumer activists want more regulation and businessmen want less, the report indicates that the public is fairly evenly divided on the issue of how much regulation, not wanting either more or less.   According to the study, each group of consumer activists has its own characteristics and its own point of view, depending on the issue.   The differences, however, between the consumer activists and the consumer, according to the study, are only a matter of degree.   The gulf between perception and attitude of senior business executives and those of the public is greater and more serious. (50)

Opinion surveys conducted by federal agencies and private organizations substantiate the growing public interest in food, diet, and health. (51) According to a 1978 survey conducted by Yankelovich, the information that consumers want above all is information on diet and health. (52) There is growing public concern for nutritional adequacy and safety of food. The problem, however, is that the concept of "good nutrition" is poorly understood. Polls reveal that the public is anxious for more information, but whom to believe and what to believe are major problems.   The consumer finds both government and industry suspect.

According to a sample of 1,000 households polled in 1976 by the A.C. Nielsen Company, the public is more aware of the negative implications of certain foods from a nutritional point of view than the positive benefits derived from eating so-called "proper foods" (53). Principal reasons given for avoiding certain foods are directly related to health and nutritional questions:

"Too much fat
I'm weight conscious
Too many calories
No nutritional value
Not healthy or good for you."

Nielsen contends, however, that to be effective, nutrition must be placed in the context of taste and price, which are more important considerations than nutrition within a family's preference.

According to the 1975 FDA survey of 1664 women, the younger consumers, between 18 and 34, are likely to be better informed about food and nutrition than older women. (54) There is also a marked difference in understanding between those in the upper socioeconomic strata and those in the lower. Significantly, it is the more informed who indicate a willingness to change their shopping, cooking, and serving behaviors.

For example, the word "processing" tends to evoke a conditioned negative response because it is associated with the introduction of contaminants, poisons, impurities, and artificialities. Words like additives and chemical also tend to carry the same negative connotation and require clarification.

The low profile assumed by most of the food industry has not been in its own best interest. The public has been given only one side of the story. While the consumer activists have pleaded their case, the food industry has hoped that ignoring the issues of health and safety would cause them to disappear. No information has not been a substitute for misinformation. Moreover, those food companies which have promoted "natural" foods "free of artificial preservatives and flavors" have helped to lower public confidence in processed foods. In their effort to provide consumers with choice in order to increase this year's profits, they have told the public that "natural" foods are better than processed foods. Some companies have further lessened their credibility by promising or implying nutritive attributes which lack scientific data. It is not surprising, therefore, that the public tends to feel that the messages coming from the food industry are basically self-serving.

The public, industry, and government are all handicapped now by insufficient information and an inability to apply what data is available to long-run effects. For example, our ability to find toxicities is far greater than our ability to comprehend how much toxicity is harmful to human health. In recent years more sophisticated techniques have enabled us to detect minute toxic substances. When the Delaney Amendment was introduced twenty years ago, we were able to detect no more than 50 parts per million; we can now detect parts per trillion. This ability has raised the standards of safety at a time when demands brought on by urbanization and the desire for variety, convenience, and foods tailored to lower calories and fat content have caused greater use of additives to fulfill these requirements. In some instances, knowledge of the presence of traces of impurities has given the impression that danger pervades the entire food supply. In most instances this has caused needless anxiety since our bodies have the ability to deal with certain levels of toxicity.

Food Labeling

Nutrition labeling was established in 1973 for protein and 19 vitamins and minerals as a percent of United States Recommended Dietary Allowances in a specified serving of food. Although many consumers may not know how to translate the RDA's, labeling has raised their interest in the nutritional content of foods to the degree that food items have become conspicuous by the absence of labeling. Labeling has also stimulated the "nutrition conscience" of the food industry. (55) Those who favor labeling all ingredients look upon food labeling as a key element in preventive health programs. Others question the value of labeling only processed foods since chemicals are the sole constituents of all foods. Questions exist today over which foods should be nutrition labeled; how the information should be expressed; whether certain constituents should be prominently displayed particularly for special diets; and how far the Food and Drug Administration should go in defining the terms "Low," "Reduced," "Free" and "High" for constituents such as cholesterol, calories, sodium, and fiber. The format for effectively presenting so much information is a consideration which will have to be resolved in the 1980s.

Food Safety

Concern over food safety during the last quarter of the century results from a combination of factors (see chapter 2). The abundance of our food supply permits the luxury of trying to avoid any and all risk. Whereas in the past, new food-processing techniques and additives took centuries to introduce, the time scale of interduction has been reduced to decades or less. (56) The time to judge exposure to these new additives has simultaneously been shortened. The rise in numbers of new additives has also caused concern, although in recent years the rate has been declining. Between 1958 and 1967 about 30 new additives were approved each year. Today, due to stringent regulations, the number is closer to ten a year. (57) Urbanization has also caused the consumer to depend so heavily on the food industry that a sense of resentment has accompanied this dependency.

The scientific lag between our ability to detect toxicity and our ability to comprehend how much toxicity is harmful to human health has caused our attention to focus on unknown risks such as the question of whether two or more components interact synergistically to create greater hazard, and what the long-term effect over 20 to 30 years of exposure to low levels of known carcinogens might be. To date, no practical hazard based on this situation is known to exist. (58)

Chemical additives comprise a small fraction of our total food consumption. The concentration of any single toxic substance in any commonly accepted food is usually very low. Individual toxicants of different chemicals ingested cannot be added up to a total toxicity for that day. It is possible, however, to have antagonistic interactions between chemical substances in food so that the toxicity of one element is offset by the presence of an adequate amount of another element, e.g., iodine inhibits the action of some goiter-causing agents. (see figure 2.1, "The preoccupation with food safety," p. 22.) (59)

Intentional additives, such as flavoring, coloring, emulsifiers, etc., account for less than one percent of our annual food consumption and are tested. Most natural products, however, are not tested, and some contain harmful or toxic elements. Due to FDA regulations regarding new additives, we know more about the safety of additives than the safety of natural foods. Additives cannot be used unless proven safe under toxicological examination. Since 1958, the FDA requires that any new additive must be proven safe at levels of intended use. Through a series of prescribed tests on laboratory animals, the manufacturer who wishes to use an additive must establish the safety of its use, obtain a regulation from the FDA permitting that use, and must prove to the FDA that the additive will perform the function claimed.

To determine the safety of our foods in the coming decade, it is necessary to identify, quantitate, and evaluate the hazards associated with foods. These hazards have been classified by the FDA in order of seriousness as follows: Food borne diseases of microbial origin; environmental contaminants; natural toxicants; pesticide residues; food additives. (60)

Food safety research needs to be directed toward developing rapid procedures for detecting and quantifying food poisoning organisms and their toxins. Analytical methods need to determine the effect of these hazards on man so there are some scientifically based acceptable levels of contaminants. (61)

As understanding of foods and their effects on health increases, foods will increasingly be assessed on the basis of their individual benefits, safety, acceptability, toxicity, and relationship to chronic disease. Moreover, as this understanding is shared with the public, perhaps the existing adversary climate of mistrust can be changed to one in which confidence in technology is restored. Government should provide a regulatory environment that protects the public but does not stifle the development of improved foods.

Regulations aimed at banning the "unknown" and concentrating only on risks may affect the development of improvement in future food quality and quantity, an important consideration in terms of feeding an increasing world population with limited resources.

Irradiated Foods

The irradiation process presents an interesting example of how new food safety regulations can impede as well as promote technological innovation. The irradiation process is a technology which complies with many of the concerns of the 1980s. It is energy conserving in using less energy than other food processing/preservation systems and in producing foods which can be stored at room temperature for several years. Because of the reduction of refrigeration and freezer requirements, irradiated food products are capable of energy savings in excess of 50 percent. (62) Moreover, irradiated foods are "ready to eat," so that the energy used in the preparation and serving of these foods is minimized. Because irradiated foods are not subjected to the high temperatures of thermally processed foods, the packaging requirements for irradiated food items are less energy consuming and less costly.

It is estimated that the world's food supply could be increased by 30 percent if postharvest losses could be avoided. The irridiation process can prevent food losses incurred through microbial spoilage, sprouting, or insect infestation by treating poultry, meat, fish, fruits, vegetables, and grains with relatively low doses of radiation. The ability of irradiation to reduce or eliminate certain pathogenic microorganisms, such as C. bottulinum, trichinae, and salmonellae, is also beneficial to public health and productivity. It is estimated that as much as 50 percent of the fresh poultry sold in the United States is contaminated with salmonellae, and that 2,000,000 cases of salmonellosis are contracted annually. (63) Salmonellosis alone resulted in medical costs of about $1.2 billion annually, which does not include losses incurred by absenteeism. (64)

Another benefit of the irradiation process is that vitamin and amino acid retention is higher than in thermally processed foods because less chemical changes occur. Irradiated foods closely resemble the foods prepared from fresh items in terms of taste, appearance, and texture. The process sterilizes food by sending gamma rays or high electron rays through the food. Radiation is used to destroy microorganisms in the food.

During the 1970s concern over the formation of carcinogenic nitrosamines and the possible carcinogenicity of nitrates and nitrites in cured meats has challenged food scientists to find other preservation technologies to prevent botulism. Radiation sterilization has proved to be an alternative since it makes possible the reduction of the nitrite used by over 80 percent without significantly affecting the taste, color, texture, and overall acceptance of the product. In addition, many processed meat, poultry, and fish products which are presently preserved by adding nitrites can be preserved by irradiation without nitrite for nonrefrigerated storage. The technology of irradiation, therefore, is capable of reducing and eliminating certain chemicals in foods used for preserving or disinfesting which are suspected of being carcinogenic.

In the United States, determination of the safety and wholesomeness of the irradiation process has been based on regulations governing additives, so that testing procedures must be run for every food intended for irradiation. The U.S. Army Natick Laboratories has spent over $50 million on its irradiated foods project since its inception in 1953, and claims to have conducted more animal feeding studies to test the safety of irradiated foods than any country for any food preservation process. (65) Animal tests for poultry should be completed by 1981, at which time the Natick Labs will submit a petition to the FDA. Assuming the petition takes a year to process, and the irradiation process is adopted commercially, irradiated chickens could be on sale in the United States by 1983.

The concept of wholesomeness generally implies nutritional adequacy; microbiological safety; zero induced radioactivity; organoleptic and esthetic characteristics; and absence of toxic, carcinogenic, mutagenic, and teratogenic effects. (66) One reason why it has taken so long for irradiated foods to gain the approval of the FDA is that the concept of wholesomeness is more inclusive today than in the 1960s because of the increased ability to detect toxicities and higher standards for nutritional adequacy.

There appears to be three major disadvantages in the irradiation process. First, meat irradiation is not economically adaptable to small scale operations. The same disadvantage applies to heat sterilization and freeze drying. The estimated cost for irradiating meat is from 3 to 20 cents per kilogram, depending on factors such as dose of irradiation, temperature of the food during irradiation, irradiation source, throughput per hour, and processing hours per year. The second disadvantage is that the processed and hermetically packed meats to be stored without refrigeration after irradiation have to be irradiated while frozen to preserve high organoleptic quality and high nutritional value. Fresh meats, poultry, and fish distributed under refrigeration, however, have to be frozen while irradiated with low doses. The major problem to overcome before irradiated foods gain public acceptance is that the public must understand that irradiated foods are safe. Many people still associate anything related to atomic radiation with the horrors of fallout from nuclear weapons. Public education efforts must explain that irradiation does not cause foods to be radioactive and that those irradiated foods available for consumption have been tested and proven to be safe toxicilogically, microbiologically, nutritionally, and chemically.

Presently Japan has the world's largest food irradiation operation, processing 10,000 tons of potatoes per month. Dutch health authorities have allowed the use of irradiated fish, poultry, and other foods. As of 1975, more than 50 countries had some form of food irradiation research and application. (67) In 1976 the Food and Agriculture Organization, International Atomic Energy Agency, and World Health Organization approved the wholesomeness of eight irradiated foods and recommended them to all member nations. The foods were potatoes, wheat, chicken, papaya, strawberries, rice, fish, and onions.

SOCIAL AND ECONOMIC TRENDS

Key social trends in the coming decade will include an increased number of households, smaller family units, more working women, and a population whose composite age will steadily grow older. The income trends for 1975 through 1985 (see figure 10.5) suggest the following:

1) An increasingly large number of families will shift into upper income brackets.

2) There will be substantial expansion in disposable income (if one assumes a real annual growth rate in incomes of 2 to 3 percent).

3) The real income gap between affluent and poor families may increase.

4) The multiearner families will become even more prevalent than at present.

5) Families with incomes over $25,000 (in 1975 dollars) will account for approximately one-half of family income. (68)

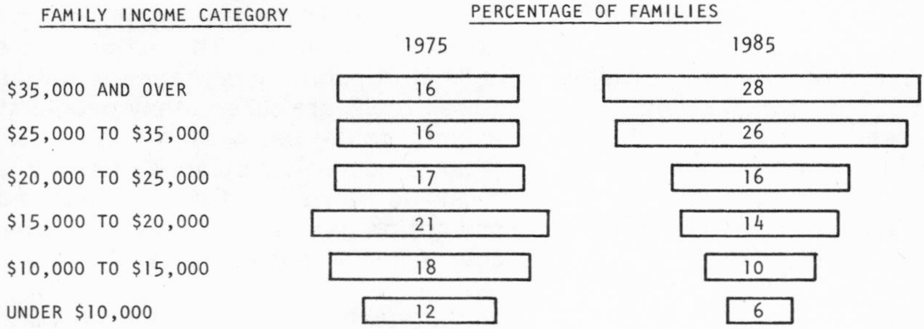

FAMILY INCOME CATEGORY	PERCENTAGE OF FAMILIES	
	1975	1985
$35,000 AND OVER	16	28
$25,000 TO $35,000	16	26
$20,000 TO $25,000	17	16
$15,000 TO $20,000	21	14
$10,000 TO $15,000	18	10
UNDER $10,000	12	6

Fig. 10.5. Changing Distribution of Family Income (1975 dollars)

Source: Fabian Linden, "Age and Income--1985," Conference Board Record, 13, June 1976.

To satisfy the needs of the large proportion of affluent and cosmopolitan 25 to 44 year olds in the 1980s, partially prepared convenience foods, rather than complete meals such as TV dinners should be popular. (69) Women are buying fewer frozen prepared main dishes because of a desire to personalize their own meals. Increased leisure time affords individuals with time on weekends for creative gourmet endeavors, but these efforts should be distinguished from weekday meals where time is a major consideration.

The 25 to 34 year old age group, which will account for almost one-third of all households, represents the generation raised in relative affluence, not limited by a sense of "deferred gratification." They are the best educated segment of the population, with 24 percent of family heads having college degrees. In 1975, 75 percent of them were married and over 50 percent of the families owned their own homes.

As polls reveal, it is also this age group which is best informed on nutrition, health, and safety and most willing to change their shopping, cooking, and eating habits. (70) They are also demanding in terms of value and quality. One can only assume a continuation of these characteristics in perhaps more sophisticated terms.

In the coming decade we will continue to see smaller family units but an increasing number of households. In 1977, 66 percent of the adult population (14 years and older) were either childless couples or singles, a 50 percent increase since 1960. (71) Of these adults living without children in their households, approximately 28 percent were married persons and 28 percent were singles. (see figure 2.1, p. 22).

Those living in nontraditional households are not so apt to be tied to schedules or routines. Meals will be more spontaneous, not necessarily nutritionally balanced on each occasion. Smaller size packages of food will be more attractive to this group to avoid waste and temptation. Storage space will be at a premium in housing for singles. "More" is not a better value if it deteriorates in storage or adds to body weight. This group may also be more self-indulgent and interested in disposable products. Because of their flexible eating habits, the concept of "super meals" which provide one day's nutrition in one meal might become popular, just as the multipurpose vitamin pill is presently used to "play it safe" rather than for dietary needs.

The spontaneous charcteristic will not only affect what they eat but where they eat. If eating out does not cost much more than eating at home, they may prefer to eat out more frequently. Cooking appliances such as the microwave oven, which allow them to decide what and where they eat at the spur of the moment, will be increasingly attractive. The idea of "planning" may become "inconvenient."

Microwave Ovens

The microwave oven meets the needs of many of the changing lifestyles of today's household. The reduced preparation and clean up time enables family members to eat at different times more easily and eliminates the need for planning ahead. The working woman can decide after she gets home whether to eat out or pull something out of the freezer. A hostess can serve gourmet dishes with minimum effort. In a survey of microwave users designed to determine what microwave foods they would like to see available or improved for home consumption the responses in order of greatest frequency mentioned included: 1) hors d'oeuvres, particularly egg rolls; 2) frozen ethnic foods, with Mexican most popular, followed by Italian, Chinese, and Kosher; 3) pizza; 4) pot pies; and 5) low-calorie foods. (72)

Ten percent of America's 80 million homes now own microwave ovens. (73) In 1975 microwave oven sales exceeded those of gas ranges. By 1985, some project that 50 percent of American homes will have microwave ovens. (74)   Although the growth of microwave oven sales during the first half of 1978 appeared to be flattening out, ownership of microwave ovens has reached the level where food processors and packaging producers are designing foods and packaging for microwave use. (75)   This trend toward specially formulating foods and packages for microwave use is certain to encourage microwave oven sales.

Microwave oven use and microwave foods for the institutional market are also expanding. Projections of commercial microwave oven use are that the number of units in use will double to 487,000 by the end of 1981. (76) Although hospitals have been the largest market to date, an increasingly greater use by the food service industry is foreseen.

A survey of leaders in the food industry indicated that 53.7 percent of those surveyed think that the use of the microwave oven will grow by anywhere from 50 to 100 percent within the next seven years. (77) One major reason for growth is the built-in convenience of microwave oven foods. Almost 40 percent of the employees in the food service industry are full or part-time students who lack culinary skills. As the cost of labor increases, convenience foods requiring a minimum of skilled labor to prepare will become increasingly attractive.

New uses of microwave oven foods in the 1980s might serve the needs of a growing proportion of our population - the elderly and single households. The idea of "meals on wheels" could be implemented by trucks outfitted with microwave ovens. (78).

Owning a microwave oven today is a luxury, and those who can afford one are in the upper income level. In fact, top line models are the best sellers. (79) The microwave oven may well follow the pattern of the food processor where the lowering of prices opened a surge of sales, but the most expensive food processor continued to maintain its position.

A few years ago only 114 of the products in stores were suitable for microwave use. Other foods would lose their flavor. Flavors were rebalanced and strengthened. Now up to 95 percent of all foods can go into microwave ovens. (80)

Built-In Services

In the coming decade an increasing number of foods will have more services built in. Convenience and variety will characterize the coming generation of foods, not only for the United States consumers, but also for those in developing countries where work occupies longer hours and cooking facilities are limited.

There will be a growing demand for foods which are nutritious, quick to prepare, and easy to clean up. Technological advances will be linked to time and effort reduction. (Examples are the popularity of food processors and microwave ovens.) New smaller appliances which perform the function of the oven and broiler but use less energy will become increasingly popular. Range-top cooking utensils which provide new approaches to cooking will also gain interest, if they save time and energy or provide nutritional benefits. One pot meals may also gain popularity.

The attitude toward convenience foods and services has also changed. Advances in food technology are quickly adopted and taken for granted. There is no longer a sense of guilt associated with using convenience foods. They are chosen for use based on their results, taste, ingredients, and size. Frozen concentrated orange juice is more popular than freshly squeezed or canned orange juice because we have grown accustomed to its taste, it is more convenient than freshly squeezed, and it's cheaper than fresh or canned orange juice.

There is increasing demand for convenience built into foods due to a number of life-style changes. Although many women revere the "good old ways" of grandmother, they are reluctant to return to them. Family life-styles have changed from a communal focus to a more individual one. Women today do not consider their role as mothers to be limited to cooking, sewing, and housework. More outside involvements are beginning to replace the home centered interests. The family may eat together a few times a week or on special occasions only. A survey found that various family members now eat at different times of the day 41 percent of the time and prepare their own meals 30 percent of the time. (81)

With more meals consumed away from home and more snack-type meals consumed on the run and at different times of the day replacing the traditional three "square meals," the goal of providing a well-balanced meal will become more of a challenge. Concern is often voiced over whether increased consumption of fabricated foods will mean a decreased intake of vitamins and minerals. To address the concern, one must focus on the specific foods and the intended use, and how they are formulated. (82) For example, coffee whiteners constitute only a small part of the total food intake. Therefore they are of less concern than most meat analogs which could substitute for a major part of our protein intake. Soy protein extenders for meat would not raise the same nutritional issues as soy analogs, because the extender would substitute for part, not all, of the meat. (83) It is therefore important that alternate or imitation foods contain equivalent nutritive content to the comparable food they replace.

In the coming decade we can also expect food processors to respond to consumer concern over nutrition and quality by upgrading food processing methods with the aim of retaining or restoring nutrients and quality. Recognizing the vitamin C loss which occurs in potatoes during storage and processing, several potato processors have been fortifying dehydrated potato flakes and frozen potato products. (84) This ability to compensate for vitamin C loss during storage and processing enables processed potatoes to provide more vitamin C than fresh potatoes. Vitamin C is one of the most perishable vitamins and deteriorates when storage temperatures are above 45 farenheit.

FOOD SERVICE OUTLOOK

Based on demographic and social patterns which have been described earlier, there should be an increase in the "away from home" eating markets. By 1980 it is estimated that half the meals consumed will be prepared by the food service industry. In 1978, 27 percent of the food dollar was spent on meals away from home, compared to 20 percent in 1963. (86)

According to a study on eating out, the main reason that people eat out is for a change, to have something different. (87) This reason was apparently more important than the convenience of not having to cook and clean up. When asked about cost and nutrition of food eaten out compared with food at home, two-thirds of the persons interviewed said that food purchased at a fast food restaurant would be the same, or less costly, than the same food prepared at home. Yet it is the same fast food type of restaurant which is regarded by some as providing food which is less nutritious than can be obtained at home. In this situation, cost and convenience was more important than nutrition.

In a nutritional study of hamburgers, cheeseburgers, french fries, vanilla shakes, and specialty items purchased from Burger King, McDonalds, and Burger Chef in Gainesville, Florida, the nutritional content was compared to the recommended dietary allowances for grade school and high school children. Assuming the intake of three meals a day, a fast food meal appeared to provide at least one-third of the RDA considered adequate, with the exception of iron. (88)

With the increasing proportion of meals eaten outside the home, the food service industry is capable of providing strong leadership in food processing as well as in changing food habits. Institutional feeding has the unique ability to prepare meals with ingredient formulation, nutritional fortification, and menu portion control. Fabricated and fortified foods lend themselves to such preparation, which accounts for the greater use of analogs and extenders in institutional feeding than in home cooked meals.

With 485,000 food service establishments serving over 40 billion meals yearly, the food service industry has already had a significant impact on changing food habits. Diets can be changed more easily than generally assumed. An example of this is the current interest in ethnic foods. This interest is evident in both increased numbers of ethnic meals served at home as well as ethnic meals eaten out. The desire to duplicate at home foods eaten away from home is evident in the popularity of cooking equipment such as the individual hamburger grill, the pizza baker, the doughnut maker, the Chinese wok, and the crepe pan as well as prepared foods purchased in supermarkets which emulate those eaten at fast food establishments, such as fried chicken, french fries, fish sticks, pizza, and egg rolls.

Another possible influence the food service industry may have on changing eating habits may reflect a change in attitude towards waste and overindulgence. Fewer restaurants are serving formal fivecourse meals. Dessert has become an extra and costs a substantial proportion of the cost of the entree. A number of restaurants are experimenting with offering smaller portions of the entree at lower prices and have found the public receptive, both for waste and waist reasons. Since the shift in attitude is from quantity to quality, consumers seem less influenced by pocketbook factors, since very often they spend as much by ordering a salad or other item which brings the bill up to the same total. One can speculate on whether the effect of eating and seeing less on one's plate in restaurants and institution cafeterias might influence the size of portions served at home.

There are many who believe the food service industry will grow at twice the rate of the retail food business during the next 10 years. Estimates of the public and "captive" segments totaled $102 billion in 1978, (captive establishments include hospitals, schools, universities, plants, airlines, and the military), with the public sector comprising $61 billion and enjoying a real growth rate of twice as much as the captive. The highest growth rates in the public sector are found in the limited menu restaurants - fast food establishments and recreation and sports centers. They have shown a 13 percent to 14 percent compound annual growth rate from 1975 to 1978. (89)

OUTLOOK

Just as the decade of the seventies witnessed a growing public interest in nutrition, the decade of the eighties will see a continuation of this concern. Nutrition has become everyone's concern. The value of the controversial Dietary Goals proposed by the Senate Select Committee on Nutrition and Human Needs was in bringing to the public's attention the question of nutrition and diet-related diseases.

Nutrition, as the science of food and its relationship to health, is still in its infancy. Jean Mayer, former chairman of the White House Conference on Food Nutrition and Health, has described nutrition as "an agenda of problems," the solution of which requires the application of all man's knowledge and technology. (90) As a result, hypotheses abound and nutrition is credited or blamed for unrelated cures and sicknesses. Only a decade ago nutrition evoked little interest. Today it is used as a solution for social, economic, and health problems. In the coming decade, the public will see nutritional theories come and go. Popular books and foods will promise that special diets will provide improved health, sex, longer life, and whatever else is desirable.

What must be done to decrease the level of confusion and improve credibility? First, the public must be considered as reasoning adults. They must be told what the major issues are, what is known scientifically, what is not known, and what research is seeking to determine. Conflicting scientific views should be discussed. Responsible scientists need to come forth to provide information to the public which is accurate, balanced, and objective. The benefits as well as the risks of advances in food technology should be explained. Where risks are involved, scientists should indicate the probability of these risks rather than assume the public is not capable of understanding them. They should also provide perspective on the risks to avoid creating a sense of alarm if none is warranted. The public needs to recognize the incremental process involved in scientific development. Where misinformation has been given, scientists should be willing to refute it publicly. Food scientists in the future must assume the leadership in answering problems of food safety as well as in solving the problems of quantity and quality. (91)

Some of the credibility problems which the food industry presently faces are a result of past and present marketing and advertising claims. These claims have been promoted by the marketing divisions of some food companies which have been preoccupied with short-term profits and performance rather than the credibility and long-term economic health of their company. In an effort to start building consumer credibility, the Institute of Food Technologists has produced guidelines for marketing executives in the food industry and advertising agencies which deal with technical issues regarding food safety and nutrition. The guidelines are addressed to claims which imply a superiority of natural over processed foods, claims which disparage food additives, claims which highlight unproven health benefits, and dubious nutritional claims or comparisons (see figure 10.6 for full text). (92)

Appropriate policies or approaches need to be adopted at different levels. Of foremost importance, the food industry should join forces and recognize its common interests. Rebuilding credibility requires a community of interests. The saccharin issue, for example, was a question of "whose ox was being gored." It is time that the food industry recognizes its common concerns and devotes some of its money and energy for its common good.

The food industry can provide leadership by addressing the public's concerns relating to food quality and safety. It should supply consumers with facts. Where factual answers are not yet available, it should explain the current lack of knowledge so that the public can appreciate the way in which scientific knowledge changes and develops. What more convincing way to build credibility than to tell the public its limitations so that the facts it does provide are not considered self-serving. This approach would certainly be more useful than ignoring the issues and reacting defensively with too little too late only when an answer is required because the issue has become emotionally charged.

The communications branch of the food industry should transfer its knowledge of what factors influence consumer food choices to help consumers select diets that promote good health. Food companies would be well advised to make certain that their advertising does not misrepresent the nutritional value of foods they sell. Promises of the beneficial results of eating certain foods should be responsible if credibility is to be restored. Consumers need to be educated on their own nutritional needs and the nutritional value of different foods.

Much of today's cost of regulations are directed toward compliance with practices which promote safety and quality of food products. In general, the food industry has accepted the responsibility of safety and quality assurance. If greater emphasis is placed on quality and nutritional value, the pressure to produce more new products could be

Advertising Guidelines for Dealing with Technical Issues Regarding Food Safety and Nutrition

Issued by the Institute of Food Technologists

MUCH of today's food advertising and promotion material, in print and on the air, deals with aspects of food quality, especially food safety and nutrition, either directly or by implication. Most of this copy speaks to legitimate consumer concerns, and describes ways in which a client's product or service can fill a consumer need or expressed desire.

Some, however, exploits ill-defined public fears or even ignorance, in ways which the Institute of Food Technologists feels are contrary to the long-term best interests of both the consumers and producers of food products. We feel that where these claims involve technical or scientific facts or judgments, IFT has an obligation to speak out against them.

We feel that marketing executives and top management in the food industry should carefully consider each promotional claim and implication made for their food products or services. Immediate marketing gain, essential as that may be, is only one factor in the long-range economic health of companies and of the entire field of food processing and preservation as a whole.

CHIEF among our concerns are:

● *Claims which state or imply that "natural" foods are superior to processed foods.*

While statements such as "100% natural" or "No chemicals added" may provide legitimate consumer information (to the extent they are factual), to imply that "natural" foods are intrinsically safer or nutritionally superior to processed foods is simply not true—the human body does not "recognize" the source of the molecules it receives, whether from raw foodstuffs or from added ingredients. For everything we ingest, natural or man-made, there are safety limits beyond which we should not go.

As for nutritional value, nutrient losses in processed foods are often less than in those intended for sale raw or "natural." Processing or fortification, in fact, often leaves a foodstuff a better source of specific nutrients than it was in its natural state.

● *Claims which disparage "food additives."*

Additives are used for specific purposes, such as improved safety, nutrition, function, or economics. To be allowed in food, additives must have a long history of safe use or have passed stringent government-prescribed safety testing. Implying that "additives" as a group are bad, or that their use may lead to harm, is irresponsible and only adds to the public's nervousness and fear. "Food additives" should not be thought of as a group of chemicals, but rather as functions filled by the individual compounds, whose benefits and risks in use should be evaluated individually.

● *Claims which highlight unproven health benefits.*

As new findings emerge from scientific studies on the role of specific nutrients or food components, promotional statements often follow quickly, such as "The wonder ingredient you've heard so much about." Such comments tend to confirm in the public's mind what may be only a passing fad. The same can be said for claims which arise from strictly epidemiological studies attempting to relate diseases or cures with public activities or habits. "Seventy percent of drivers involved in auto fatalities had eaten carrots within 24 hours of the accident"—but so what?

● *Claims which make emphatic nutritional claims about foods with dubious nutrient content, or which unfairly compare nutritional benefits of different foods.*

Such claims border on the illegal now, and will undoubtedly be more strictly regulated in the future. All emphatic statements as to nutrient value, and all claims which compare the nutritional value of different foods, should be defensible scientifically and quantitatively.

AS MEMBERS of a scientific society, we are concerned that the misuse of technical information in promotional efforts by food companies can only lead to negative consumer reaction and increased governmental control. Therefore, we urge that you examine the marketing practices in your own organization, with the aim of maintaining an environment within which the consumer can continue to make his/her own choices, and to enjoy the benefits of all that modern food technology can provide.

Fig. 10.6.

Source: George F. Stewart and Howard W. Mattson, "Food Advertising and Promotion - A Plea for Change," Food Technology, November 1978, p. 32.

translated into new products with higher nutritional value. More research could be directed toward identifying nutritional properties of foods and understanding the short-and long-term effects of food ingredients on health and physiological functions. The USDA is allocating $25 million in 1979 to identify and appraise the nutritional properties and contributions of foods, including the study of fresh and processed foods; to assess bioavailability and chemically useful forms of nutrients in foods; and to determine and evaluate nutritional antagonists in food.

A number of large food companies have recently adopted corporate nutrition policies which recognize the need to improve communications and quality. G. Robert DiMarco, Group Director of General Foods, has summarized the policy statements that were common to a number of such policies. (93)

1. Research departments were given the responsibility of maintaining an adequate staff of professional nutritionists and consultants to conduct nutritional research, to review nutritional claims on labels and in advertisements, and to support nutritional labeling.

2. Education to promote nutritional understanding for consumers, and in a few cases for management, is also seen as a responsibility in most policies.

3. A statement that food products will be safe, wholesome, and appropriate for their use and will comply with existing government standards and regulations was common to all policies.

4. Nutritional equivalency in foods designed to replace basic and/or natural foods was common to all policies.

5. Most advertising and promotional policies prohibit the use of nutritional claims or allusions there to unless the product makes a significant nutritional contribution to the diet.

6. Some policies recognized the need for foods which have no primary nutritional value and which are often referred to as "fun foods."

The emphasis on quality rather than quantity has already been reflected in a number of food companies' policies on new products. New dessert and snack products are planned to have a market life of more than two or three years rather than the usual one year. Although the product development budget may not be reduced, companies are becoming more selective about which new products are being intro-duced. Some are keeping products in test markets six times longer than in the past. (94)

Due to a larger proportion of research and development budgets allocated to defensive research complying with regulatory measures, less long-range industrial research is directed toward new processes, products, and services. (95) Twenty years ago, business did 38 percent of all the basic research in America, compared to 16 percent in 1978. (96) The United States has already lost its technological lead in a number of areas. For example, the equipment for thermal processing for both rigid containers and flexible pouches are being supplied to us by European companies. (97) Japan has the world's largest food irradiation plant and has been consuming irradiated food for three years. Although irradiated foods were considered safe enough to feed our astronauts in space in the 1960s, regulatory hurdles have continued to block its usage.

According to Dr. Bruce Hannay, Vice President of Research and Patents at Bell Laboratories and President of the Industrial Research Institute, "We see increasing concentration of effort in cost reduction, and product differentiation designed to increase market share, but requiring no significant innovation. The U.S. productivity growth rate is lagging." (98)

It has been suggested by Donald P. Kelly of Esmark that the costs of energy and pollution control will substantially increase capital requirements for food processors and will make entry into the market place much more difficult. This might result in industry showing increasing signs of concentration with fewer small firms. (99) During the past 30 years the number of food manufacturers decreased from 44,000 to 22,000.

In addition to responsible scientists and corporate policies, the media must also exercise responsiblity in reporting facts. News stories are generally only newsworthy when they contain extraordinary and unusual slants. If the public is to become educated, it must be given the spectrum of opinions - the benefits, risks, probabilities, and the uncertainties. Only when the public understands the issues and stakes involved in technological growth, can legislators and regulators reflect reasonable policies appropriate for the technological needs of the coming decade.

As a result of technological advances in food production and processing over the past 25 years, we have much greater flexibility in the choice of techniques to produce food as well as the choice of raw materials to fabricate food. The technological ability to synthesize flavors and nutrients has freed us from depending on nature to provide the conventional sources of food. The synthesized substitutes have not only provided more food but also provided cheaper alternatives. Mass use of synthesized nutrients, as well as improved technology, have driven down costs dramatically. A good example of how increased efficiency has affected cost is in the cost of enrichment. To enrich 100 pounds of flour cost $.17 in 1941, $.02 in 1967, and $.0004 in 1978.

Not only are synthesized nutrients often cheaper as a source of nutrition than the nutrients derived directly from food, but they can also be more efficient in value, such as sweetness or protein quality, as well as more efficient in use of resources such as land and water. In developing countries effective nutrition interventions, such as fortification of bread, salt, or cereals, are likely to have more effect on human health than comparable investments in medical care.

These technological advances have provided benefits which most of us now take for granted. In 1930 the average grocery offered 900 food items compared to today's estimates of from 11,000 to 39,000 depending on the store or supermarket chain's size (see chapter 4, p. 60). Improved processing techniques have not only improved year round quality but have also shortened the time and effort required for preparing food, and have decreased the cost of food. In 1978 Americans spent 17 percent of the their disposable income on food; in 1950 22 percent; and in 1776 more than 70 percent.

Because we in the United States have an abundant supply of food at a reasonable cost, we tend to forget that this situation is unique and does not prevail in the majority of countries abroad. In recent years the United States has been exporting over 50 percent of its wheat, rice, and soybeans. Not only are many countries in the world depending on the United States for food, but our national economy has also become dependent on food exports. Food exports have become our major source of foreign exchange and have paid for two-thirds of our oil imports.

In the decade of the seventies we were jolted into recognizing that we are living in an interdependent world of limited resources and ever-growing demands. In the coming decade, food science and agricultural technology must focus on technologies which are more efficient in conserving nonrenewable resources and more capable of converting underutilized ingredients into food. If we consider that more than 80 percent of the foods presently consumed in the United States are processed, improvements in processing technologies could result in returns far outweighing costs. (100) Food science and food technology research related to processing, packaging, storage, distribution, safety, and nutrition deserve support and encouragement by the public and private sector.

Concerns over quality of life and the relationship of diet to health will strengthen in the 1980s and encourage the development of nutritious foods engineered for functional purposes. People will expect foods to provide special benefits. The increase in the number of smaller family units and double income households will provide a market for more expensive convenience foods, ranging from minimal preparation to gourmet facsimiles.

At the same time regulatory restraints engendered by concern over food safety and nutritional adequacy will continue to impede development of new foods and technologies in the United States. The cost and time involved will discourage innovative research in all but the largest food companies. Research and Development funds will be allocated to regulatory compliance, quality assurance, cost reduction, and product differentiation. In the coming decade, the United States will continue to find itself in the unfortunate position of watching technologies it originated adopted abroad before gaining approval at home. The best example is irradiated foods which addresses the concerns of the 1980s in its energy and waste conserving benefits as well as in its capacity to alleviate the major United States food safety problem, namely food borne diseases. Until the FDA approves of each irradiated food, we will continue to lose a substantial proportion of our food supply through spoilage and infestation while we continue to instead use certain chemicals suspected of being carcinogenic.

It is important for the economic health of the food industry as well as for the development of new foods and technologies which meet the demands of the future that members of the food industry jointly apply their abilities in anticipating public policy issues so they can adopt reasonable approaches to set their own priorities and provide guidance to those who are creating or revising regulations or laws affecting food. Anticipating public policy issues involves responding to legitimate consumer concerns. No information is not a substitute for misinformation. Ignoring the issues will result in government filling the vacuum with more protective legislation. Historically this has led to reduced competition, higher prices and lower consumer satisfaction. It is time the food industry recognize that a more responsive policy will promote its own best interests.

APPENDIX A

Losses in the Food Processing Pipeline

The food processing operation can be pictured as a pipeline connecting the grower with the consumer. Leaks occurring in each of the five areas of processing include raw material handling, preprocessing and storage (such as in cleaning for bulk grain or potato storage), final processing and packaging, distribution, and consumption.

Losses which reduce efficiency can be cataloged by processing area. Some representative examples are:

A. Raw Material Handling
   1. Nonoptimum picking dates
   2. Mechanical damage
   3. Incomplete harvest
   4. Excessive respiration or physiological stress
   5. Insect and microbial damage
   6. Incorrect irrigation spray or fertilizer application
   7. Poor plant location (excessive shipping)

B. Preprocessing and Storage
   1. Mechanical damage
   2. Microbial and insect invasion
   3. Insufficient storage life
   4. Inefficient raw product grading
   5. Physiological breakdown
   6. Incorrect storage conditions

C. Final Processing

1. Excessive trimming, peeling, cutting, washing
2. Inefficient use of byproducts and waste
3. Excessive water use
4. Excessive heat inputs
5. Inefficient separation, mixing, etc.
6. Excessive delays in processing
7. Overpackaging

D. Distribution

1. Loss of quality during storage (i.e., staling)
2. Packaging failure
3. Improper storage conditions
4. Excessive storage and handling
5. Insufficient preservation
6. Improper product style
7. Improper inventory management
8. Inefficient shipping

E. Final Use

1. Improper storage
2. Improper menu planning
3. Improper trimming
4. Improper serving times
5. Handling losses and bruising

As foods move from the field to the consumer their value is increased by labor inputs, changes in location, and through the concentration of edible portions in a more useful form. Seasonal foods also increase in value through storage.

Food losses at the consumer level are the most wasteful. Current processing methods which create such losses include packaging systems requiring liquid packing media to fill the void space in rigid containers. Up to 30 percent of the weight of a consumer size can of vegetables can be poured away as waste upon use.

Other examples of inefficient processing and preservation include unwanted fat and bone present in wrapped meat; the limited shelf life of dairy products, fresh produce, and processed meats; and the absence of fully ripe fruits and vegetables at retail. Staling of bakery items represents a significant loss of nutritionally adequate food at retail.

Source: Robert C. Baker and Willard B. Robinson, Potential Increases in the Food Supply Through Research in Agriculture, PB 257-359, prepared for National Science Foundation, NTIS/PS-75/403, Virginia, 1975, pp. 49-50.

NOTES

(1) Ian Wilson, Planning for Social and Political Change over the Next Decade. Paper presented to the Seventh World Planning Congress, London, September 27, 1978, p. 7.

(2) Duane S. Elgin and Arnold Mitchell, "Voluntary Simplicity, Life Style of the Future?" The Futurist, August 1977, p. 206.

(3) Wilson, Planning for Social and Political Change over the Next Decade, p. 7.

(4) Ibid. p. 11.

(5) Guy Miles, Alternative Food Delivery Systems: An Exploratory Assessment. Report prepared for the National Science Foundation, September 1977, p. 35. (See appendix for where losses occur.)

(6) Ibid.

(7) Robert C. Baker and Williard B. Robinson, Potential Increases in Food Supply Through Research in Agriculture, PB-257 359. Prepared for National Science Foundation, July 1975, pp. 23-25.

(8) Edward J. Lehmann, Synthetic Foods. Prepared in cooperation with the National Science Foundation, National Technical Information Service, NTIS/PS-75/403, Virginia, 1975.

(9) Baker and Robinson, Potential Increases in Food Supply through Research in Agriculture, p. 32.

(10) Alexander M. Schmidt, "Food and Drug Law: A 200-Year Perspective," Nutrition Today 10, no. 4, (1975): 32.

(11) Baker and Robinson, Potential Increases in Food Supply through Research in Agriculture, p. i, d.

(12) Dietary Goals for the United States, Select Committee on Nutrition and Human Needs, U.S. Senate, Government Printing Office, Washington, D. C., December 1977.

(13) D. Mark Hegsted, U.S. Dietary Goal. Paper Presented at 1978 Food and Agricultural Outlook Conference, Washington, D. C., November 17, 1977, p. 3.

(14) A.E. Harper, National Nutrition Policy. Uncirculated Paper, April 20, 1977, pp. 8-9.

(15) Ten State Nutrition Survey, 1968-1970. Department of Health, Education and Welfare, Center for Disease Control, Atlanta, Georgia, DHEW Publication No. (HSH) 72-8134.

(16) Food Consumption Statistics, 1955-1973. Paris: OECD, 1975, pp. 67, 204, 245, 273.

(17) National Food Review. USDA Economic Statistics and Cooperative Service, December 1978.

(18) "Uprooting an Eating Habit," Food Processing, September 1978, p. 82.

(19) FDA Consumer Nutrition Knowledge Survey, Report 11. Division of Consumer Studies, Bureau of Foods, DHEW Publication No. (FDA) 76-2059, 1975, p. 77.

(20) Robert E. Olson, "Clinical Nutrition, An Interface between Human Ecoology and Internal Medicine," Nutritional Reviews 36, no. 6, (June 1978): 174.

(21) See chart comparing heart disease and beef, eggs, and dairy fat consumed per capita in chapter 8 "The U.S. Quandary: Can We Formulate a Rational Nutrition Policy?"

(22) New Directions in Federally Supported Human Research. Prepared by Nutrition Research Interagency Working Group, Office of Science and Technology Policy, Executive Office of the President, Washington, D. C., December 1977, p. 8.

(23) Gilbert A. Leville, Establishing and Implementing Dietary Goals. Paper presented at the 1978 Food and Agricultural Ourlook conference, Washington, D. C., November 17, 1977, p. 5.

(24) Ibid.

(25) Baker and Robinson, Potential Increases in Food Supply through Research in Agriculture, p. 45.

(26) Ellen Haas, Statement before the House Science and Technology Subcommittee on Domestic and International Scientific Planning, Analysis and Cooperation Regarding Recommended Dietary Allowances, Washington, D.C., July 12, 1978.

(27) James J. Albrecht, New Foods and Ingredients. Paper presented at The American Chemical Society, Williamsburg, Virginia, August 2, 1977.

(28) A Review of Foods for Medical Purposes: Specially Formulated Products for Nutritional Management of Medical Conditions. Federation of American Societies for Experimental Biology, prepared for IDA, June 1977, p. v.

(29) Ibid., p. 15.

(30) Ibid.

(31) Jane E. Brody, "Hospital Deaths Being Cut by Use of Intravenous Feeding Technique," New York Times, November 25, 1977.

(32) A Review of Foods for Medical Purposes: Specially Formulated Products for Nutritional Management of Medical Conditons, pp. 44-45.

(33) Howard W. Hjort, Food Prices and Inflation: Perspectives and Prospects. Paper presented before the Federal Statistics Users Conference, Arlington, October 12, 1978, pp. 6-7.

(34) James C. Webster, Statement presented before the Missouri-Kansas AP Editors and Publishers in Kansas City, Missouri, November 19, 1978, USDA 3177-78, p. 9.

(35) Carol Tucker Foreman, Remarks prepared for Food and Consumer Services at the George D. Aikem Lecture Series, University of Vermont, Burlington, March 26, 1979, p. 8.

(36) Baker and Robinson, Potential Increases in Food Supply through Research in Agriculture, p. 1.

(37) Patricia Wells, "A Milk Whose Future is Now," New York Times, January 1, 1978.

(38) Energy-Saving Sterile Fluid Milk. Department of Energy Information, Office of Public Affairs, December 13, 1977.

(39) "Energy-Saving Possiblities Spark Interest in Non-Refrigerated Milk," Super Marketing, January 1978.

(40) Wells, Patricia, A Milk Whose Future is Now.

(41) Baker and Robinson, Potential Increases in Food Supply through Research in Agriculture, pp. id-ie.

(42) Ibid., p. 57.

(43) Robert E. Berry, Solar Food Processing - 1977. Submitted to Office of Conservation and Solar Applications, Department of Energy, May 12, 1978, pp. 2-4.

(44) "Microwave/Freeze-Dried Compressed Foods," Food Processing 39 (July 1978): 44-46.

(45) H.A. Hollender, Private communication, November 29, 1978.

(46) "Update-Natick R & D 'Foods of Tomorrow'," Food Processing 39 (July 1978): 44.

(47) For further details on the retortable pouch, in "Emerging Food Marketing Technologies: Priorities for Assessment," pp. 364-365.

(48) H.T. Austern, The Flavor of Industry. November 1972, p. 549.

(49) Consumerism at the Crossroads. Marketing Sciences Institute, 1977.

(50) Ibid. , p. 28.

(51) Luise Light, "Nutrition Education: Policies and Programs," Nutrition Program News, U.S. Department of Agriculture, Washington, D.C., January-April, 1978, p. 1.

(52) Yankelovich, Skelly and White, Inc. Presentation on tables: "Nutrition: A Study of Consumers' Attitudes and Behavior." A National Probability Study for Woman's Day, April 1, 1978.

(53) Eugene Telser and John Stermer, Nutrition: Consumer Beliefs and Actions. A.C. Nielsen Company, presented at the 1977 Institute of Food Technologies, June 7, 1977.

(54) Consumer Nutrition Knowledge Survey, Report 11, p. 29.

(55) J. Michael McGinnis, Statement before the Subcommittee on Domestic and International Scientific Planning, Analysis and Cooperation, Committee on Science and Tehcnology, House of representatives, Washington, D. C., July 12, 1978, p. 8.

(56) Sanford A. Miller Additives in Our Food Supply. Hearings before the Senate Select Committee on Small Business, January 13-14, 1977, Washington, D. C., pp. 538-546.

(57) Sherwin Gardner, Statement before Senate Select Committee on Small Business, January 13, 1977, Washington, D. C., p. 130.

(58) Naturally Occurring Toxicants in Foods. Report by the Institute of Food Technologists, March 1975.

(59) Ibid. See also Table 2.1.

(60) Alexander Schmidt, "Food and Drug Law: A 200-Year Perspective," p. 32.

(61) James R. Kirk, "Research Priorities in Food Science," Food Technology, July 1977, pp. 68-70.

(62) Ari Brynjolfsson and Eugen Wierbicki, "Irradiation Update," Food Processing, May 1977, p. 97.

(63) Ibid. (And private communications with Eugen Wierbicki, November 29, 1978.)

(64) E.J. Gangarosa, History of Surveillance Programs for Salmonellosis Seminar. U.S. Department of Agriculture, Washington, D. C., January 10-11. 1978.

(65) "Radiation Petition Readied by Natick," Food Engineering, August 1977, p. 34.

(66) Eugen Wierbicki, Ari Brynjolfsson, Howard Johnson, and Durwood B. Rowley. Preservation of Meats by Ionizing Radiation. Paper #14 presented before the 21st European Meeting of Meat Research Workers, Berne, Switzerland, 31 August-5 September, 1975, p. 11.

(67) Ibid.

(68) William Lazer, "The 1980s and Beyond: A Perspective." Michigan State University Business Topics, Spring 1977, pp. 28-29.

(69) Donald P. Kelly, "Outlook 1980," Food Processing January 1977, p. 5.

(70) James H. Fouss, "The Consumers' Understanding of Nutritional Needs," Food Processing, January 1978, pp. 40-41.

(71) Census Bureau, Department of Commerce, Current Population Report, Series P20, #326.

(72) Cal Andres, "Food Service Market: 'Microwave Foods'," Food Processing, August 1978.

(73) "Microwave Oven Sales Lose Some Speed," Business Week, July 31, 1978, p. 99.

(74) Cal Andres, "Food Service Market: 'Microwave Foods'," p. 30.

(75) Business Week, July 31, 1978, p. 100.

(76) Cal Andres, "Food Service Market: 'Microwave Foods'," p. 30.

(77) Ibid. p. 32.

(78) Ibid. p. 30.

(79) Business Week, July 31, 1978, p. 99.

(80) D. Richard Ensor, "Flavor Makers: Adding spice to Life?" N.Y. Times Magazine, November 11, 1978.

(81) Kelly, "Outlook 1980," p. 8.

(82) Michael J. Phillips, "The Future," Food Engineering, July 1978, pp. 105-106.

(83) Ibid.

(84) Cal Andres, "Consumer Nutrition awareness is Changing Processing/ Marketing of Foods for Home and Away," Food Processing, August 1978.

(85) John M. Bryan, "New Foods Will be Keyed to Dieting, Nutrition, and Naturalness," Food Processing, May 1977.

(86) "Meals Out Found to Eat into Food Budgets More," Wall Street Journal, October 25, 1978.

(87) Eugen Telser, "The Future...: 15 Experts Analyze Events" Food Engineering, June 1978, p. 105.

(88) Howard Appledorf, "Nutritional Analysis of Foods from Fast Food Chains," Food Technology, 28, no. 4, 1974.

(89) Roy G. Hlavacek, "Processing/Packaging for the Growing Food Service Industry," Food Processing, August 1978, p. 26.

(90) Sanford A. Miller, The FDA Program in Nutrition. Paper presented at the NIH Conference, "The Biomedical and Behavioral Basis of clinical Nutrition - A Projection for the 1980s," June 20, 1978, p. 10.

(91) Emil Mrak, "Food Science and Science and Technology: Past, Present, and Future," Nutrition Reviews 34, no. 7 (July 1976): 200.

(92) George T. Stewart and Howard W. Mattson, "Food Advertising and Promotion - A Plea for Change." Food Technology, November 1978, pp. 30-33.

(93) G. Robert DiMarco, "The Food Industry and Nutrition, Opportunities and Responsibilities." Food Technology, December 1977, p. 31.

(94) Albrecht, <u>New Foods and Ingredients</u>, pp. 1-2.

(95) Albrecht, <u>New Foods and Ingredients</u>, p. 7.

(96) Jesse Warner, "Why More Regulation Means Less Innovation," <u>Chief Executive</u> 6, (Autumn 1978).

(97) Baker and Robinson, <u>Potential Increase in Food Supply through Research in Agriculture</u>, p. 63.

(98) Albrecht, <u>New Food and Ingredients</u>, pp. 7-8.

(99) Donald Kelly "Outlook 1980s," <u>Food Processing</u>, January 1977, p. 5.

(100) Kirk, "Research Priorities in Food Science," p. 66.

11 The Effect of Government Policies on Technological Innovation in the Food Industry: A Government Perspective*

Robert M. Schaffner

What are the various questions that the consumers and the general public have regarding government policies, rules, and regulations, and how they affect technological trends and innovations in the food industry? Probably the latest government action that may affect consumers was the recent defeat in Congress of the bill to create an Office for Consumer Advocacy.

On February 26, 1978 Mark Green, the Director of the Public Citizens Congress Watch Organization, writing in the Washington Post, described the antigovernment mood in an article explaining why the House voted down the Consumer bill. He stated:

> Business efforts successfully capitalized on a current fad, which one could call "the new anarchism." It holds that all regulation is bad and indeed that all government is bad. From Wallace to Reagan, to Ford, or even Carter the sense that government is the problem, not the solution, has spread from the ultra-right to infect some moderate members of Congress as well.

I cite this quotation not to start a discussion on whether or not the defeat of the bill was good or bad, but merely to show that the antigovernment mood is still alive and healthy and it may be growing.

We in the Food and Drug Administration are constantly being criticized by the industry for overregulating it and, on the other hand, consumers are telling us that we are not doing all we should to protect their interests, health, and well-being

So that everyone is treated fairly and equally, we believe that regulations available to all are the best method of informing industry

---

* Remarks presented at the Food, Agriculture, and Society Research Program Meeting, Washington, D.C., March 29, 1978.

and consumers of our ground rules. They are necessary to properly administer the laws that we are charged by Congress to enforce. Certainly our regulations have significant impact on food technology and affect food formulations, processing, packaging, labeling, and marketing. For example, the requirement that food ingredients are safe does inhibit the food processor when formulating new foods from using ingredients solely for their functional effect without considering their safety. Food processing techniques are also affected by our Good Manufacturing Practices Regulations because they may increase the expenditure of money, time, and effort for some manufacturers by requiring them to use more adequate quality control procedures and manufacturing practices than they would without the use of GMPs. Frequently labeling regulations inhibit the so-called "free and easy labeling and advertising." To focus on specifics rather than generalities, I would like to raise issues on food standards, food safety, and food labeling.

FOOD STANDARDS

The 1938 Federal Food, Drug, and Cosmetic Act provides for the establishment of standards of identity, quality, and fill-of-container for foods. The Commissioner of Food and Drugs, in order to promote honesty and fair dealing in the interest of consumers, is authorized to establish food standards. Since that time more than 400 standards have been promulgated by the Food and Drug Administration.

It has often claimed that standards stifle food industry progress. The standards and the rules by which they are established or amended support consumer protection and fair competition. Frequently only those who find themselves unable to "get the jump" on their competition are distressed that their progress will be stifled.

Our older standards were of the recipe type and required an amendment each time a new ingredient or change in process was desired. Starting in 1965 with the Breaded Shrimp Standard, most new and revised standards provide for the "safe and suitable" approach toward ingredients. The phrase "safe and suitable" was adopted to establish a mechanism to allow flexibility in selecting ingredients for food products. It was necessary to provide this flexibility in selecting ingredients for food products. It was necessary to provide this flexibility in order to take advantage of changing technology and economic conditions which would benefit the consumer. Alternative approaches were found impractical because changes of food standards often require a minimum of two or more years.

At the present time there are over 100 standards containing the concept of "safe and suitable." There are approximately 20 published proposals also containing this feature. Until recently this matter of "safe and suitable" had been widely accepted by food component suppliers, food processors, and consumers. However, this past summer following FDA publication of the final regulation amending the standard for ice cream to include this concept, a controversy arose. The milk producers took strong exception; they argued for retention of the existing recipe type standard.

Since the early 1960s, the recipe type standard for ice cream set out minimum composition requirements as to milkfat and milk solids-not-fat. The new standard retained the existing minimum composition requirements of milkfat, but the minimum milk solids-not-fat was replaced by a corresponding minimum requirement expressed as protein quantity and quality. Because of the improved manufacturing practices for whey and its improved quality, the limitation on the kind and amount of cheese whey was removed. We also removed the limitation on casein, and caseinates.

The opponents of our proposed changes argued that the physical and nutritional attributes of ice cream will be eroded. They further argued that there will be an increased cost to the taxpayer because the government would be required to purchase the unsold nonfat milk, which would be displaced by the other dairy ingredients which could be used.

Various Congressional groups also got into the act, and the upshot of all of this was that in December we withdrew the new proposal and announced that we will not make a new proposal until after we hold a series of public hearings on the whole question of "safe and suitable." On January 11, 1978 we had the first pilot hearing with our Consumer Ad Hoc Group in Washington, and many of us were rather surprised at the views expressed by these consumer advocates. For example, many thought that the manufacturer would determine for himself that a food additive was "safe and suitable." These consumers did not realize that since 1958 all new food additives have to be approved by the FDA. Some consumers believe that the recipe type standard instills a measure of safety as well as discretion. Products containing "S and S" alternate ingredients are confusing to consumers - it becomes a subtle altering of traditionally understood and accepted foods. Consumers fear "S and S" will become so flexible that dangerous (long-term before discovery) and economically deceptive substances will be allowed in standardized foods. Consumer representatives feel that industry is already allowed broad enough discretionary powers and that more definite boundaries need to be provided for these substances. These comments certainly indicate that neither the government nor industry has done an adequate job in informing consumers what the "safe and suitable" approach means. If further hearings bring out similar consumer responses, the Agency may have to seriously consider the desirability of either reverting to the recipe type standard or to at least require nutritional profile standards on certain ingredients that are used in standardized food. Is there anything that industry can or should be doing to help solve this problem?

FOOD SAFETY

For some time now there has been increasing insistence for assuring greater safety for added components of foods regulated by the FDA.

This evolutionary development has occurred because of greater consumer expectations, increasing communication of information to consumers, and increasing analytical capabilities which have defined problems unrecognized in the past. By Congressional request, the FDA is in the early stages of a new program with the goal of assuring a higher level of safety for all food additives to be evaluated on the basis of modern scientific standards.

I need not remind you that many consumers are of the firm belief that food additives are unsafe. This belief is reinforced by the ranks of antiadditive consumer activists as well as by a barrage of information and misinformation from the media.

I believe that a positive approach to allay the fears of consumers is an absolute necessity. This must be carried out not only by industry but by government as well.

What are we at the FDA doing concerning this matter of food additives? Our new program basically involves updating the toxicology profile of all food additives in order to provide specific assurance that food additives do not induce cancer, other chronic diseases, reproductive effects, or mutagenic changes in future generations. We are not saying that currently regulated additives are known to produce harmful effects in our population, but rather that there is a need to produce additional information to assure safe continued use of these ingredients by applying modern test methods.

The FDA in this new program attempts to act rather than react on the basis of each additive as it comes into question. What is industry doing to allay the public's fears about these chemicals?

One industry solution is, in my opinion, not a solution. For example, lately we have been seeing many so-called new products on the market that have been labeled and advertised as containing only natural ingredients with no food additives or preservatives. In many instances, these same companies continue to be rather extensive users of food additives in other products that they have been manufacturing and selling to the public. It seems likely that this trend of stressing "only natural ingredients" could further undermine the public's confidence in food products that contain safe food additives. If the top management of these companies looked at this trend very seriously, they might wonder if it is really "good business." Manufacturing operations and distribution systems might have to be drastically changed if food additives are eliminated by "popular demand." The safe food additive ingredients which ease production problems, increase shelf life, and generally improve acceptability would cease to be used. How would the convenience foods fare if, for example, they had to exclude ingredients that extend shelf life and it became necessary to manufacture and distribute foods on an every day or every week basis?

When questioned about the possible incongruity of their labeling and advertising programs for these different types of products, the company officials say that they want to offer the consumers a choice of either additive-containing foods or natural foods. They do not admit that they want to "work both sides of the street."

It would seem to me that a much sounder position would be for the executives to have their food development technologists investigate the real need for the specific additives that are now in their existing foods and to eliminate the unnecessary ones.

LABELING

Now let us look at labeling. We believe that informed consumers are essential to the fair and efficient functioning of a free market economy. For that matter, this is a policy mandated by Congress in both the Federal Food, Drug, and Cosmetic Act and the Fair Packaging and Labeling Act.

During the past few years a large number of labeling regulations were promulgated by the FDA. Ground rules in the interest of both the consumer and industry were established. These include nutritional labeling, common or usual names, valuable or characterizing ingredient percentage labeling, declaration of what components are not in foods, definition of frozen heat-and-serve dinners, and imitation and substitute foods.

At the Consumers Ad Hoc meeting held January 11, 1978 the consumers also discussed the total label. They appeared to like some of the regulations that we have issued regarding labeling, but they felt that generally we have not gone far enough. They, as you all know, keep stressing the consumers' right-to-know. There was some discussion on our labeling requirements of imitation and substitute foods. Some of you know that our Food, Drug, and Cosmetic Act states in part that "a food shall be deemed to be misbranded if it is an imitation of another food unless the label bears the word 'imitation'." For many years we received complaints from industry that progress in the food industry was being inhibited by having the use the term imitation. This subject was discussed at great length at the 1969 White House Conference on Food, Nutrition, and Health. In the early seventies there was considerable discussion on this subject at the Food and Drug Administration.

It was finally decided that the term imitation need not be applied to the name of a food it simulates and for which it substitutes if it is not nutritionally inferior and if the food is labeled with a common or usual name which is not false or misleading.

One woman, who is a consumer liaison to the Food and Nutrition Board of the National Academy of Science, expressed her concern over this when she stated, "Fake foods are replacing the basic four."

A great deal of stress was given to percentage ingredient labeling. Some time ago the FDA had proposed percentage ingredient labeling for infant foods, and we had suggested that all ingredients present at five percent or more in the formula be shown by percentage on the label. Many of the consumer advocates, however, think that percentage labeling should apply to all foods and they believe that all food ingredients that have as little as two percent of some substance in the formula should show the percentage on the label. Some also said that sugar, salt, fat, and cholesterol information should be displayed in bold face on the label, and that open dating should be mandatory.

Some people, both in and out of government, feel that if complete labeling were made mandatory, there would not be the need for many other regulations. It seems to me that complete labeling might be a substitute for some government regulations, and I believe this group should discuss this possibility.

Let us also discuss the "safe and suitable" concept for food ingredients in standardized foods. The examples of regulations that I presented are instances where the Food and Drug Administration has attempted to allow for greater flexibility in our rules in order to encourage technological development and still have safety. However, I have pointed out that there is apparent consumer distrust of regulations that allow for flexibility. I think, therefore, we should all address ourselves to finding out if there are ways to restore the confidence of the consumer and still have flexible regulations.

12 The Effect of Government Policies on Technological Innovation in the Food Industry: An Industry Perspective
Steven Goldby

INTRODUCTION

The technology of raising, processing, preparing, and distributing foods is the nation's most important single industry because it affects every other industry in the country.

An overstatement? Food technology impacts the ability of the working population. For example, millions of American women have been freed from kitchen drudgery by technological advances and thus they have been able to enter the work force at levels unthought of in other countries. Moreover, there are six key political trends that will affect income between 1975 and 1985 for the average American home. Four of those six factors were related to the increasingly important role of women in the American work force.

Most significant are the facts that multiearner families will become more prevalent; families with incomes over $25,000 will account for approximately half of the population, and almost twice as many families will have income of more than $35,000 as measured in 1975 dollar. (1)

Not only does this affect every industry in the nation, but it is also a trend that could not exist were it not for dramatic changes in food technology and distribution patterns in the three decades after World War II.

What are the most important changes that have occurred?

1. Packaging techniques have extended the shelf life of commodities in the United States 200 to 300 percent when compared with other "industrialized nations" such as France, Spain, and the Soviet Union. A very small portion of the products in an American supermarket are perishable in the sense that they must be disposed of in three or four days. Retortable pouches, which enable foods to be preserved without canning or freezing, have enormous potential for the future.

2. Frozen foods have added a dimension of convenience to the farmer, processor, retailer, housewife, and restaurant.

3. Freeze drying, a technology whose impact has been felt largely in the beverage area (instant coffee), carries great impact for the future if costs can be reduced.

4. Mass food preservation techniques, such as cryogenics and the design of special environments, have reduced food spoilage in the United States to an infinitesimal level compared to other countries.

5. Quality control and analytical techniques, employed in food processing and food handling, have made outbreaks of food poisoning and spoilage rare.

6. The microwave oven has almost revolutionized the fast food industry and large commercial restaurants. It has been estimated that a fifty percent increase in "away from home eating" should be anticipated by 1985. Currently, Americans spend $50 billion on meals eaten away from home. Furthermore, microwave ovens for individual residential use surpassed the sales of conventional ovens in 1975.

7. Process technologies, such as the refining of oils and the manufacture of dairy products and margarines, are totally different from what they were at the end of World War II.

8. Adaptation of analogs, specifically the ability to synthesize food and to remove man's dependency on nature, grows in importance each year. Synthesized substitutes provide more food at a cheaper price. "Meatless meat" such as vegetable proteins can be produced at less cost than real meat, and is more adaptable to large scale food preparation methods because it is less susceptible to deterioration when stored. If the prices of commodities continue to rise, the development and use of new analogs will continue at an accelerating pace.

9. Nutritional fortification of standard foods may be the most important advancement. There is a direct correlation between the enrichment of grains, breads, and cereals and the virtual disappearance of vitamin deficiency diseases (pellagra, goiter, beri-beri, rickets, and others) in the United States. Figure 12.1, which was developed by Donald Miller (Food and Drug Administration nutritionist) shows that there were approximately 6,000 deaths from pellagra in the United States in 1938 when bakers began to enrich bread with high vitamin yeast. By 1943, when an estimated 75 to 80 percent of all family flour and baker's white bread was enriched, the number of pellagra deaths dropped to about 2,000. With standards and requirements established for rolls, rice, and most pasta products during the last 25 years, the disease has become virtually nonexistent.

10. Color, flavoring, and texturizing agents - critical to the food industry's growth - have been improved. Many of the food products which exist in the United States today could not be formulated economically without the use of many of the 3,000 ingredients which the chemical specialty industry provides to food processors.

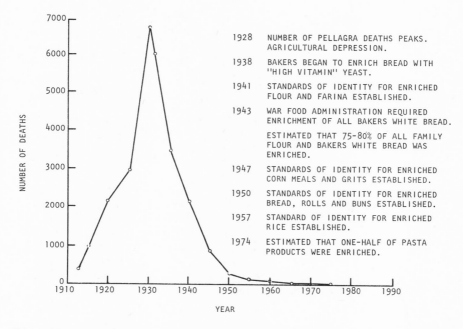

1928	NUMBER OF PELLAGRA DEATHS PEAKS. AGRICULTURAL DEPRESSION.
1938	BAKERS BEGAN TO ENRICH BREAD WITH "HIGH VITAMIN" YEAST.
1941	STANDARDS OF IDENTITY FOR ENRICHED FLOUR AND FARINA ESTABLISHED.
1943	WAR FOOD ADMINISTRATION REQUIRED ENRICHMENT OF ALL BAKERS WHITE BREAD.
	ESTIMATED THAT 75-80% OF ALL FAMILY FLOUR AND BAKERS WHITE BREAD WAS ENRICHED.
1947	STANDARDS OF IDENTITY FOR ENRICHED CORN MEALS AND GRITS ESTABLISHED.
1950	STANDARDS OF IDENTITY FOR ENRICHED BREAD, ROLLS AND BUNS ESTABLISHED.
1957	STANDARD OF IDENTITY FOR ENRICHED RICE ESTABLISHED.
1974	ESTIMATED THAT ONE-HALF OF PASTA PRODUCTS WERE ENRICHED.

Fig. 12.1. Number of Reported Deaths from Pellagra in the United States.

Source: Miller, Donald F. "Cereal Enrichman/Pellagra - USA... In Perspective 1977." Paper presented before the American Association of Cereal Chemists, San Francisco, October 24, 1977.

All of this has led, in turn, to greater economies in the production of finished food products and a nation that devotes less of its disposable income to food than any other country in the world. The average family in the United States allots less than 20 percent of disposable income for food as compared to 43 percent in France, 40 percent in Italy, and 32 percent in England.

Thus, every industry is impacted by food dollar expenditures. Every industry must depend upon the remaining dollars after food expenses.

Despite these contributions by food technology and the critical future need for still further innovation, we have an environment in the United States that discourages research investment in this field. Consumer activists, the media, certain members of Congress, and government regulators have erected almost unscalable barriers to the realization of new concepts in food technology. Unless national leaders hear from the public, which has benefited so handsomely from past investments in improving the way that things are done, the prospects for the future will be gloomy.

CURRENT PROBLEMS AND CONCERNS

Food Additives

No area of food technology has received as much negative attention as has food additives. For example, the Department of Consumer Affairs of New York City published a "Consumer's Guide to Food Additives" in mid-1977. It is totally negative, condemning each and every additive that is used in food processing with a significant amount of editorializing regarding "what might be discovered if extensive tests were conducted." The author, Elinor Guggenheimer, states in her introduction:

> I hope you will refer to this booklet while shopping and avoid buying foods that contain chemical additives, which may be dangerous to your health.

> Also, join with us in letting food manufacturers and the FDA know how you feel about food additives. Without chemicals oranges may not be so orange, tomatoes may not be so red, butter and cheese may not be so yellow, and corn flakes may no longer have a shelf life of one year, but we may live longer, healthier lives.

She goes on to state:

> Although consumers have been conditioned to expect perfection of color and texture, a new level of awareness calls for safety and nutrition above aesthetics.

The following is a representative description of an additive as presented in the City of New York booklet:

> Glycerides - mono and di-glycerides. Available fats and oils are used as emulsifying and defoaming agents. They are used in bakery products to maintain softness, in beverages, ice cream, ice milk, lard, chewing gum base, shortening, oleomargarine, sweet chocolate, whip toppings. They are suspected of causing reproductive problems and malformations. Glycerides are on the list called 'Generally Recognized as Safe'; however, di-glycerides are on the FDA list of food additives to be studied for harmful effects.

Nowhere in this booklet does the Consumer Affairs Department of the nation's largest city offer a positive word for additives. The bibliography which is recommended for consumer readership includes "The Chemicals We Eat," "Caveat Emptor," and "Poisons in Your Food."

In contrast, Dr. Richard Hall, an industry food scientist, pointed out that "the chief fact is that additives, being more tested than the ingredients that nature puts in our food supply, are much safer and in a remotely normal diet, have never hurt anybody." (2)

Furthermore, he has written that "the attitude of concern is extraordinary in that the real dangers the consumer must face, and the only ones that have caused harm, are those which arise from food contamination or spoilage, or from poor food choices."

The importance of food flavor cannot be overestimated. If it lacks good flavor, food often will go uneaten, regardless of the other excellent qualities it might possess. Many foods would not exist without flavoring agents. For example, there would be no spicecake, gingerbread, or sausage. Poppy, caraway, and sesame seed rolls all take their characteristic flavors and names from substances commonly labeled as additives. Many flavoring agents are well known such as spices and essential oils including cloves, ginger, pepper, and citrus oils. Less familiar to the public, but equally important, are the aromatic chemicals which must be used to impart such flavors as pineapple, cherry, walnut, and wintergreen. A vast number of these aromatic chemicals are "nature identical," - they have been identified as the active flavor components in spices, fruits, meat, etc. The flavor of vanilla bean extract is due to the chemical vanillin, and it is of no consequence whether this stems from extraction from the bean or synthesis in the laboratory. Still other flavoring agents are flavor enhancers. These substances do not add flavor themselves, but bring out the natural flavor of the food to which they are added.

Because many of the natural flavors are in short supply, or are only available during certain times of the year, synthetic flavors have an important place in the food supply. For example, the consumption of synthesized strawberry flavor, converted to its equivalent in fruit, approximates twice the United States production of strawberries for all purposes. And the consumption of synthesized grape flavor (almost all of the Concord type), converted to its equivalent in food, approximates five times the United States production of Concord grapes for all purposes.

Without food additives the appearance, palatability, and wholesomeness of many foods could not be maintained. The taste and quality of perishable items are at a peak at harvest. Many other foods are at their best when they come from the production line of the food processing plant. In a short period of time fresh fruits and vegetables begin to change color, flavor, texture, and appetite appeal. Processed foods also go through similar changes. Hence the food processor uses certain ingredients to delay the undesirable changes in food. For example, before antioxidants were developed and before their safety and usefulness were established oxidative degradation presented severe problems to the food industry and the consumer.

Mold and bacteria cause food spoilage. These microorganisms not only spoil the palatability of foods, but some are also capable of creating serious illnesses in man. Salmonella and Clostridium botulinum (botulism) are examples of food borne microorganisms that are known to be toxic to man. Before the advent of substances effective in controlling microorganisms were available, some foods such as bread became visibly moldy and inedible very quickly while others, not so readily detectable by the consumer, became the vectors of disease and death.

Interestingly, some of the substances used to prevent food spoilage due to mold and bacteria have been used for centuries. Good examples are common table salt, sugar, and various spices. For ages sugar has been used by homemakers, as well as industry, in making jams and jellies and in helping to preserve many canned and frozen foods. The salting and spicing of meats to prevent spoilage is also of ancient origin.

Additives are also used to impart and to maintain a desirable texture in food. Such agents fall under the categories of emulsifiers, stabilizers, and thickeners. Without emulsifiers the main ingredients of a dressing would separate. In baked goods such characteristics as volume, uniformity, and fineness of grain would be lost without such ingredients. Chocolate candy would change surface color when exposed to temperature change. The oils in pickled products would not be soluble in water. Without stabilizers and thickeners we would not have chocolate milk as we know it; the particles of cocoa powder would settle to the bottom. Commercial ice cream and other frozen desserts would lose their viscosity and coarse crystals would form. Again, such agents have been used for centuries. Pectin and gelatin are two such examples.

Such examples could be listed for every processed food product. So we must ask what the risks are and what the rewards are that modern man faces in modifying his food supply.

Benefits and Issues in Modifying Foods

The World Health Organization has estimated that 20 percent of the world food supply is lost through spoilage. Each time an additive is banned we take an unknown step toward limiting food availability and the consumer's range of free choice.

Furthermore, and of relatively little discussion in the press, there is the fact that all foods are composed of chemical substances, regardless of whether they are grown in a field or produced in a factory. Potatoes contain over 150 different chemicals and milk some 95. Those chemical names listed on containers of processed foods may appear frightening and unappetizing, but if potatoes carried their nutritional content on their skins, the chemical names would be equally strange. Furthermore, the fact that one of the chemical constituents, solanine, is a toxic substance if consumed in sufficiently large doses would certainly not entice one to eat it.

What also fails to be articulated in general discussions about additives is the body's natural ability to detoxify and excrete most chemicals. The cyanide found in apricot pits and lima beans and the nitrates in spinach, beets, lettuce, eggplant, cereal, and turnip greens question the assumption held by many that natural foods are safer than processed foods. There is no scientific reason to believe that naturally grown foods are composed of chemicals that are safer and nutritionally more beneficial than man-made substances.

Excluding sugar, salt, corn syrup, and dextrose, the average American adult consumes a total of one pound of 1,800 other additives

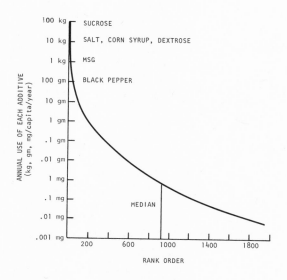

Fig. 12.2. Per Capita AnnualUse of Food Additives Ranked in
Decreasing Order.

Source: Hall, Richard. "Food Additives," _Nutrition Today_ 8,
July/August 1973, p. 21.

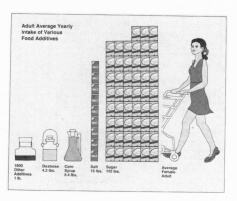

Fig. 12.3. Adult Average Yearly Intake of Various Food Additives

Source: Hall, Richard. "Food Additives," _Nutrition Today_ 8,
July/August, 1973, p. 21.

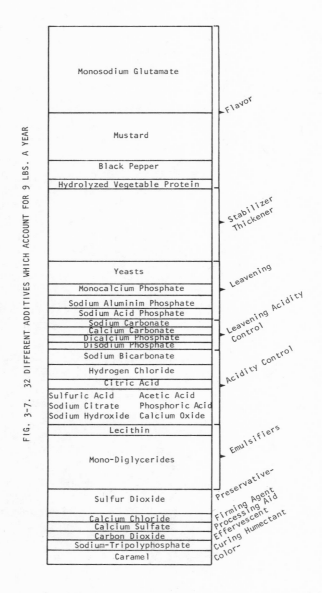

Fig. 12.4.   32 Different Additives that Account for 9 lbs. a year.

Source: Hall, Richard. "Food Additives." *Nutrition Today*, 8, July/August, 1973, p. 22.

each year, according to a study by <u>Nutrition Today</u> magazine. Half of these 1,800 additives are consumed in quantities of less than one-half a milligram per capita. In addition, there are 32 other additives, many of them regarded as natural ingredients, of which the average person consumes another nine pounds. These include such items as mustard, black pepper, yeast, citric acid, caramel, sodium bicarbonate, etc. Figures 12.2 through 12.4 show the approximate consumption of all additives by the adult population in the United States.

Thus the question of additive use is, to a large measure, an emotional one as portrayed by the media with input from a variety of sources, many of them uninformed. And the primary concern that is voiced is the risk of illness, in particular cancer, from food additive ingestion.

But the factual evidence does not support claims that the United States population is suffering from an increase in cancer from food sources. If we use the turn of the century as a time against which to compare today's cancer problem, there has indeed been an increase in the incidence of cancer, but the increase is predominately attributable to cigarette smoking, and greater longevity. Cancer is predominately a disease which emerges with increasing age.

For men, the cancer death rate per 100,000 population has increased over 50 percent since 1950 for blacks, and 20 percent for whites. The increased death rate is mainly the result of lung cancer, which rose from 18 deaths per 100,000 in 1950 to 52 deaths per 100,000 in 1974. For women, since 1950 the death rate has declined five percent for blacks, and ten percent for whites. This is mainly due to a sharp reduction in deaths caused by cancer of the uterine cervix, attributed to the increased use of Pap tests and regular checkups. The lung cancer rate has tripled from 4 per 100,000 in 1950 to 12.3 in 1974, while deaths from cancer of the stomach have declined among the United States males and females since 1930 (see fig. 2.1, describing cancer death rates by site, p. 22). There is no evidence that links food additives with lung cancers.

It is not wise, however, to ignore the concern of the general public and that of congressional and regulatory leaders, whether or not those concerns are valid or emotional. Rather, it is incumbent upon industry to perform tests, research, and development toward producing additives that minimize actual risk and perceived risk. And this is being done.

Many additives by nature are of extremely low potential toxicity. It is therefore difficult to determine their possible hazards to man, even after exhaustive testing. It is probably true to say that there will always be an area of doubt concerning the possible effects of ingesting small amounts of additives over the course of a lifetime. One cannot be fully sure of the safety of any additive until it has been consumed by people of all ages in specified amounts over a long period of time, and has been shown conclusively, by careful toxicological examination, to have no harmful effects.

Since humans cannot be used for testing by exposure to unknown chemicals for substantial periods of time, tests are conducted on rats and other animals such as mice and dogs. Test animals are fed quantities of an additive that far exceeds the amount likely to be found in food.   Tests are conducted for both short periods and over the animals' lifetime, and are even continued into succeeding generations. Any change in growth, body function, tissue, and reproduction is reported, as is the incidence of tumors.

The largest dose that appears to produce no effects in animals is taken, and a safety factor reducing that dose by a factor of 100 is applied to arrive at an "acceptable daily intake" for humans. (Under United States law an agent shown by appropriate tests to cause cancer in animals at any dose cannot be used as a food additive.)   The acceptable daily intake calculated in this fashion is the daily intake that, for an entire llifetime, appears to be without appreciable risk. It is expressed in terms of milligrams of the additive per kilogram of body weight.   One must then calculate how much of the additive a person might be expected to ingest in a day from all dietary sources.   This quantity is then compared with the acceptable daily intake in order to decide whether the use of the additive should be permitted, and whether the specific tolerances for maximum limits required for it by good manufacturing practices in individual foods are safe to the health of the consumer. However, the margins of safety afforded by these scientific guidelines are often disregarded by the body politic and the media.

The Regulatory Environment

The February 1978 issue of Food Technology is dedicated to the question "How Well Is Congress Informed?" The article begins with the following editor's declaration: "Not only is Congress fully imbued with the conviction that science and technology are now very major forces which determine the shape and future of our national life, but it is equally determined to define its own role and to develop its own initiatives in meeting the challenges which these forces produce." (3)

The most telling article is one authored by William Wampler, ranking Republican minority member of the House Committee on Agriculture. The following six paragraphs reflect his views:

The question raised by this symposium - how well is Congress informed regarding food science? - is timely and important to the food industry and to the public. A quick answer is: Not nearly well enough.

The problem - as I see it - is not what people are telling Congress but rather what knowledgeable professionals are not telling Congress. Too often, the men and women who can provide answers or at least point Congress in the right direction don't want to get involved. When they do, their voices are often drowned out by the chorus of pseudotechnologists - the adversary angels of a thousand causes, some meaningful and momentous but most manufactured and mischievous. So the people who should be heard aren't.

Recently, the Washington Post carried a story based on a National Science Foundation study which held that "After three decades of robust growth and high productivity, scientific research at American universities is showing signs of marked deterioration."

What's behind this deterioration? The Post story said, "High quality research is continuing in many fields, but at many universities, laboratories are becoming outdated, support money is growing scarce, and scientists are shifting to less imaginative but "safe" lines of inquiry in order to get government grants."

My own personal interest in agricultural research stemmed from a similar concern. For example, I found it hard to comprehend how a nation which had devoted 38 percent of its federal research and development budget to the food and agricultural sciences in 1940 could allow that research to deteriorate to only 1.8 percent last year.

Imagine that agriculture, our country's largest single industry - with assets totaling nearly $600 billion...employing either directly or indirectly 14 to 17 million workers...providing enough food and fiber to feed and clothe 215 million Americans and millions overseas - received less than one-third as much in federal research funding last year as was spent on the space shuttle. (4)

Another author, who presented a paper during the same symposium on Food, Science and Public Policy, said:

Politically, I think there is not a predisposition in Congress that makes life difficult for you in the food field. There has been a lot of controversy and bad news about foods over the past four to six years. It doesn't take too many cases like saccharin, MSG, and Red No. 2 to make the public very, very skeptical and suspicious of the food industry and food technology and wonder whether the government is adequately protecting them.

It is my opinion that there is, and will continue to be for some time, a very critical and skeptical attitude toward the food industry on the part of key members of Congress and the staff people and on the part of new members and new appointees to be regulatory agencies and the executive branch of the government. And if they are to err from now on on the question of food safety and food quality, they are going to err on the side of "when in doubt, don't." (5)

That attitude has already dramatically changed the food industry and its research over the past decade.

Today food companies devote most of their technology budget on quality control and label it "research." These are the millions that are spent to maintain products and processes in line with an ever growing list of Food and Drug Administration and Congressional requirements. In a large typical food processing plant everything is analyzed, verified, sampled, and reported to an extent that is uncommon in other industries.

Take, for example, the manufacture of a can of vegetable soup. Every incoming ingredient must be inspected and reported upon. Standards have been established for packaging, process machinery, and the product at various stages of "cooking." Sampling and testing procedures that are required in common in the food industry account for hundreds of millions of dollars. Whether or not the industry is justified in labeling these procedures, and techniques to improve them, as "research and technology" could be considered a matter of opinion. Nonetheless, that is the direction the government has established and that the industry chooses to follow.

To reduce costs, the industry devotes another 30 to 40 percent of its efforts, again labeled "research", to redesigning plants and equipment to be more efficient. Still further "research" monies are spent on the periodic retesting, by newer and more exacting procedures, of currently used food ingredients.

And that leaves little to be spent in the area of new food additives. Hence, additive research has fallen largely to the chemical specialty companies - some 250 pharmaceutical and other specialty houses that include some food ingredients as part of their total product mix.

Before one cent can be expended on research to develop a new food ingredient at a chemical specialty company, that product must be sold to management against all of the other potential products that might bring a faster, surer yield. Today it costs several million dollars and takes at least five years to develop a new food ingredient, put it through the safety testing and regulatory cycles, and introduce it to a market. Is there any question why the chemical companies are scarecly willing to undertake such research?

Further, and finally, the rules by which regulatory agencies operate are subject to changes. For example, in May 1977, Dr. Robert Schaffner, the FDA's Associate Director of Technology, cautioned at the American Chemical Society national meeting that new colors produced from natural products will require a Color Additive Petition. Dr. Schaffner said the agency was being asked by ingredient suppliers whether the regulations pertaining to natural colors were the same as synthetics. "They are," he said. The Petition should include feeding studies, chemical specifications, and details of the manufacturing process. Explaining that natural ingredients change substantially after processing, Dr. Schaffner commented, "Even though dehydrated beets, for example, were admitted more or less routinely without animal testing as a color additive in 1967, in 1977 certain minimal animal testing would be required before similar substances would be permitted."

Furthermore, all of the products that are now approved as ingredients were subject to reevaluation. Hence, those considered "safe" because of long history of use are hardly "safe" to manufacture or to count upon for future sales and profits.

Food ingredient specialties comprise a very small portion of the chemical specialty industry's sales volume. And, for the most part, chemical companies in recent years have been unwilling to spend millions of dollars to defend their position in this field. Hence regulatory attitudes have been allowed to stifle the development of food ingredient technology.

One exception (the company that the author is associated with) is attempting a breakthrough. Dynapol is involved in new areas of polymer chemistry for both the food industry and others. It is striving to develop additives that, like fiber in food, will pass through the gastrointestinal tract and, rather than be absorbed, will be eliminated unchanged. Such an achievement will settle, once and for all, the primary safety concern for additives in processed foods.

The Dynapol concept is based upon the physiological fact that digestion is largely a process where food is separated into its molecular components which are then enzymatically reduced to molecules small enough to pass through the gut wall. Molecular size is, generally speaking, the barrier to intestinal absorption. Most vitamins and minerals, being small molecules, are rapidly absorbed from the gastrointestinal tract. Significantly, the same can be said at present for most food additives, such as colorants, antioxidants, leavening agents, thickeners, and flavors. Not all of these are small molecules originally, but the digestive process renders them so. Thus these substances also pass through the wall and eventually get into the bloodstream which quickly transports them to the liver and other organs and tissues. It is at the passage of substances through the gut wall that the question of safety begins. And this is where Dynapol scientists intervene. They have conceived the idea of attaching functional food additives to large molecules of inert polymers so they will stop at the wall and thus be harmlessly excreted without ever entering the body itself.

The mission of a food additive, as Dynapol sees it, is to exert a certain technical effect on the food to which it is added. Once the food is swallowed its mission is fulfilled.

Dynapol, as a young research company, has confined its research to those areas where clear industry need and technical feasibility coincide. The company's work to date has been in the areas of food colorants, antioxidants, and nonnutritive sweetners. To an extent the company has been supported by funds made available under research contracts with larger food companies. The company is now in the stage where its initial products have established their performance in foods and are undergoing the long-term safety studies needed for FDA approval.

The biggest hurdles we still face are in the areas of FDA clearance and pricing that will appeal to the food industry. Because of the millions of dollars that must be spent on finding substitutes for existing but threatened food additives, and the greater expense of their manufacture, the costs of polymer linked ingredients will need to be higher.

ASSESSMENT OF TECHNOLOGICAL ADVANCES IN FOOD
PROCESSING, PACKAGING, NUTRITION, ETC.

How Technological Advances Could Affect Changes in
Properties Sought in Food Products

Perhaps the most dominant force behind food technology
achievements for the future will result from the world's population
growth. Expanding at about 2 percent per year, world population will
double in little more than a generation. Merely maintaining current per
capita consumption levels will therefore require a doubling of food
production over the next generation. And fully 80 percent of the annual
increment in world population growth occurs in the poorest countries.
The Philippines adds more people each year than does Japan; Brazil adds
2.6 million people in a year; while the Soviet Union adds only 2.4
million.

What this points to is: Greater food yields from the richer countries
flowing to the poorer ones; new ways of processing and preserving foods
for shipment and distribution to the underdeveloped countries; and
technological advances that will enable the world to eat products that
are now ignored, discarded, or utilized only in rare instances.

For example, technology for the substitution of vegetable for animal
proteins has made considerable progress, mainly in the area of soy based
meat substitutes. The development of a technique for spinning soy
protein into fibers, duplicating the spinning of synthetic textile fibers,
permits the close emulation of the fibrous qualities of meat. Food
technologists can now compress soy fibers into meat form and with the
appropriate flavoring and coloring come up with reasonable substitutes
for beef, pork, and poultry. With livestock protein (particularly beef)
becoming more costly, this technique is likely to gain a strong
commercial foothold in the future.

The first meat product for which substitution is succeeding
commercially is bacon. The soy base substitute looks and tastes like
bacon, and while the extent of substitution is still small, it is growing.
The substitute product has the advantage of being high in protein, low in
fat, and storable without refrigeration.

The greatest near term area of protein substitution promises to be
the use of vegetable protein to augment meat proteins in ground meats.
Soy protein "extenders," as they are known, are being added to a variety
of processed and ground meat products, frequently improving flavor,
cooking qualities, and nutrition as well as reducing prices. Soy protein
extenders are already widely used in food service institutions throughout the United States and limited supermarket sales to the public have
also begun.

Although the average American already consumes nearly one ton of
grain per year, both directly and indirectly, indications are that this
could climb even higher in the years ahead. Projections by the United
States Department of Agriculture show per capita beef consumption
reaching 140 pounds by 1985, but a continuing rise in the cost of beef

could alter this trend downward as consumers seek more economic substitutes.   As the substitution of high quality vegatable protein becomes as wide spread as that of vegatable oils for animal fat, it is conceivable that, in the United States, per capita claims on agricultural resources could eventually begin to decline.   A combination of convergent economic anc ecological forces and health considerations could lead in this direction.

Another promising technology is the preservation of foods by irradiation. As feeding studies throughout the world are moving toward completion, the vast potential of irradiation as a food preservation technique is growing. while early studies show that irradiation also degraded food quality, recent research results have shown that lowering the temperature of foods to -30 before irradiation treatment will produce sterilized, shelf stable products with materially improved flavors.   Other quality factors benefited by irradiation at low temperatures are better color, reduction in off odors, and improved texture.   Low dose irradiation techniques have been developed for meats, vegetables, fruits, grains, and spices for extending storage life, ripening control, insect disinfestation, prevention of sprouting, and control of mold growth.

The entire process basically involves treatment with heat to inactivate enzymes, packaging in a sealed container under vacuum, bringing the food package to the temperature at which it will be irridiated, and exposing the food package to ionizing radiation until the required absorbed dose is obtained.

Although studies of irradiation have been conducted by the United States government since the early 1970s, much of the advanced work is being conducted in India, the Netherlands, Germany, Hungary, and Japan. With the high cost of research and the minimal payout that can be expected from exporting foods to poorer nations, it is not clear whether the United States food industry will assume a leadership role in the development of this technology.

The Future for "Engineered" Foods

As long ago as 1970, a restaurant in New York began to serve "BLT" sandwiches, "scallops," Virginia "Wham," starchless spaghetti with meat sauce, hot "turkey," "tuna" salad, chili burgers - all based on vegetable protein - as well as nondairy milkshakes, and the food was rated "good" in an issue of New York magazine. One restaurant does not set a trend. Nor do a dozen. But it illustrated the point that engineered food can be made tasteful and appealing.

Actually, many of the engineered protein ingredients which are already on the market, or under development, are not designed for direct human consumption. They are formulated to be used by food processors and food manufacturers. Fish protein concentrate and eviscerated fish protein are typical ingredients with a variety of uses -

one of them as a possible raw material for new engineered protein foods. Some engineered foods have made it into the end product category. Egg replacers and egg extenders made from water soluble proteins in whey are one such example.

Although there is no real protein shortage in the United States, increased cost of protein and some shortages have been a force in spurring this research.

Protein ingredients of all types, added to foods for humans and pets, were estimated at about 970 million pounds in 1972. Engineered textured vegetable protein consumption was estimated at 52 million pounds. By 1980, protein ingredients are expected to reach a 2,046 million pound level - a 9.8 percent average annual growth rate - and textured vegetable proteins are expected to be consumed at a 358 million pound rate - a 28 percent annual average growth rate.

Textured vegetable proteins now are being used most extensively in the school lunch program. About 56 percent, mostly in the form of extruded products, are mixed into chopped meat. By 1980, it is estimated that 57 percent will be sold to the public eating establishment and other institutional categories, while school lunches will constitute 25 percent. Commercial and other large categories will take 15 percent.

What is the actual world situation regarding protein and what will it become? In 1968, the world's total protein requirements were 139 billion pounds. And there were 355 billion pounds available. That is based on a 40-pound per year protein requirement. Factoring in a very conservative one percent growth of food production per year we will find that the year 2000 requirements will reach 263 billion pounds, and that there will be availability of 480 billion pounds.

The problem lies with the distribution. Countries in South American and Africa have already run into trouble, and that will become worse if present trends continue. There are underdeveloped areas in Asia which also reflect a deficiency in protein. In these countries, animal protein constitutes only a small portion of the diets and most of their food protein comes from cereals and starchy roots which do not contain the necessary amino acids. The solution, according to some sources, is the full development of engineered food technology.

Even for public establishments and institutions textured (or engineered) food products faces regulatory restrictions. Before a new product may be marketed, it must gain acceptance of the United States government. In February 1967 the Federal Food and Drug Administration recognized the use of fish protein concentrate made from hake for human consumption. Then in July 1970 the FDA amended the ruling and also approved the use of fish protein concentrated made from herring processed by solvent extraction of fat and moisture with isopropyl alcohol. The FDA bans other types of fish at present because of their high viscera, bone, and fat.

The FDA regulators are concerned about the psychological reaction of the consumer to eating a product containing an ingredient made from whole fish. They know that the consumer often does not read the list of ingredients on a package prior to purchasing it, but is more likely to read the list just before using it. Thus the government is concerned that a product that is safe for human consumption may cause a new wave of consumerism.

Most of the engineered foods use soy protein source because the soybean is valuable for its nutritional and functional properties. And its cost is low. Furthermore, many soybean products are used as ingredients.

Soybeans contain nearly twice the protein content of cheese, twice the protein of bread and meat, and ten times the protein of milk. Secondly, the yield per acre of edible protein is very high. For example, a grazed acre of land produces about forty-three pounds of animal protein, while the same acre - planted with soybeans - yields nearly 450 pounds of vegetable protein. When a 60-pound bushel of soybeans is processed, it yields 11 pounds of edible oil and 47 pounds of meal containing 44 percent protein.

Overall world demand for soybeans is increasing at an average rate of eight percent per year with the United States now producing about 86 percent of the total world supply. The majority of textured vegetable proteins are used in meat analogs because they resemble meat. Analogs of dessert and dessert toppings and vegetables have been tested, and in some cases are being marketed.

But the possibilities of utilizing textured vegetable protein is only limited by human imagination. A new kind of food could be created which does not resemble any of the natural foods. However, to make such items palatable will probably involve the use of food colorings, flavors, and other additives, which brings us back to the previous problem of regulatory control of such items.

Finally, while the United States Department of Agriculture created the market for the textured vegetable protein products, the FDA can be expected to regulate quality control and formulation of vegetable protein products to a greater extent over the next several years.

Engineered foods, given the previous constraints, do represent a future potential. Sales in 1972 were estimated at only $24 million, but by 1975 they had risen to $45 million; and 1980 is forecasted at $161 million - all based on present manufacturers' prices. Then, from 1980 through 2000, the average rate of growth is projected at 12 percent per year. Certainly this field of engineered products contains the potential to solve much of the world's protein and food shortages.

NUTRITION AS A PREVENTATIVE MEDICINE

Malnutrition is an illness which frequently shortens life expectancy. In the United States it can, and frequently does, exist in obese people. And this is an area which must be dealt with through education of the population. In the female after age 40, 42 percent were considered obese based on skin fold assessment. Relatively speaking, people in the United States are at least 20 percent overweight for their ideal height, bone structure, and other physical characteristics. In the male, this is about 1 out of 4.

A recently conducted study further indicated that 20 percent of the United States population suffers from anemia. Such levels are consistent in surveys in such states as Texas, Louisiana, South Carolina, West Virginia, and Kentucky. In Washington, California, Michigan, Massachusetts, and New York the percentage is less, but still in the range of around 10 percent. But the large nutritional problem lies in Latin America, South Africa, and India where studies have shown that 20 to 30 percent of the time that a young child experiences acute infection it is probably related to malnutrition. The United Nations World Health Organization states that, on the average, 3 percent of the children under 5 in low income countries suffer from severe protein/calorie malnutrition. According to Alan Berg, a visiting professor of nutrition at Massachusetts Institute of Technology, the scope of malnutrition, when adults are included, is something on the order of 1½ billion persons worldwide. In his book, The Nutrition Factor, he states:

> Malnutrition today affects vastly more people than malaria ever did.

> But hope today lies with food technologies that a decade ago would have been dismissed as fanciful. Perhaps more important, new proved concepts have evolved that may lead to substantial advances. Many can now sprinkle synthetic micronutrients for milling flour. The child fed a few slices of bread baked from that flour has the vitamin, mineral, and protein equivalent of a diet studded with fruits, vegetables and milk. Or, man can produce a whole range of palatable new foods, bolstered by nutritious oil seed products that, until a few years ago, were considered unsuitable for human consumption. (6)

CONCLUSION

What will be required to meet the increasing challenges of providing wholesome, nutritious, reasonably priced food to feed a growing population? How will we offset the cost increases attributable to higher labor and energy costs? To begin with, there will need to be a joint effort of many disciplines to develop improved foods and technologies and to reeducate the public and its leaders.

Advances in food technology historically have provided substantial benefits to the public. These include better nutrition, more variety, enhanced taste and eye appeal, greater safety, and lower cost. To have an environment that encourages the innovation needed in the years ahead, these benefits must be well understood by the public now. The regulatory environment will not become receptive to the new and different until our national leaders know that the public sees the need for it.

In addition, it must be recognized that the regulatory environment has an impact on the investment in innovation. The past decade has seen a shifting, more stringent process for regulatory approval of new food technology. Some of this results from new scientific knowledge, but most derives from policy decisions based on skepticism and fear of the new.

Development of new food technology is a long, costly, and risky endeavor. Uncertainty of the regulatory policies that will exist upon program completion is an additional risk that can tip the balance against such investments. Industrial research must have the prospect of financial return to be justified. Government leaders must recognize that unpredictable regulations stifle needed research. With such recognition, establishment of a dependable regulatory environment would be major encouragement to investment in meeting future world needs for better less expensive foods.

NOTES

(1) William Lazer, "The 1980's and Beyond: A Perspective," Michigan State University Business Topics, Spring 1977, pp. 28-29.

(2) Richard Hall, "Food Additives," Nutrition Today, July/August 1973, p. 20.

(3) Max Milner and Ogden C. Johnson, "The Reason for This Symposium," Food Technology 32, no. 2 (February 1978): 75.

(4) William C. Wanpler, "What the People are Telling Congress," Food Technology 32, no. 2, (February 1978): 760.

(5) Kenneth Schlossberg, "The Congressional Hearings Mechanism," Food Technology 32, no. 2, (February 1978): 78.

(6) Alan Berg, The Nutrition Factor (Washington: The Brookings Institution, 1973), p. 107.

13 Future of Engineered Foods

Wayne Henry

To ask 100 food scientists the definition of an "engineered food" would more than likely bring 100 different answers. By my definition, formulated, fabricated, or engineered are synonymous. A loaf of bread is a simple example of an engineered food. In fact, any food short of a natural food has to some degree been modified or "engineered." A progressive modern food scientist should look at natural food sources such as wheat, soybeans, corn, pineapple, mushrooms, milk, eggs, and all natural agricultural products as a source of raw material for which he can improve existing foods or engineer new foods.

One of the most classic if not the classic example of engineered food is margarine. Reportedly invented in 1869, the original formula used beef fat to replace milk fat. As the concept and acceptance of margarine grew, and with aggressive research, the beef fat was gradually replaced by vegetable fat. Margarine is an excellent example of progressive thinking scientists finding a more efficient use of raw ingredients. When we examine the cow as a factory for manufacturing butter, we find she is very inefficient. In the 1940s butter was consumed in the United States at a per capita ratio of approximately 9:1 over margarine. Presently, that ratio is 3:1 margarine over butter. Economic health and consumer education have accounted for this tremendous gain in margarine consumption.

Engineered food connotes the efficient use of all food products providing the consumer with alternatives to more expensive original food products. There are by my definition many engineered foods that could be discussed in detail; however, for this position paper I shall center my remarks around edible soy protein and instant breakfast.

In the last 10 to 15 years considerable research has been spent on engineered foods and more recently the nutrition of our foodstuffs has been placed under the research microscope. Vegetable proteins in general, and soy proteins specifically, have played and continue to play a major role in processed foods.

The foresight of the soybean industry has put the soybean far ahead

216

of other cereal grains as a source of raw material for engineered foods. It has taken 40 years of research, education, advanced technology, and marketing efforts to bring the edible soy protein industry where it is today. Soy proteins are a natural additive to various food systems but specifically are additives to meat products for several reasons:

1) Soy proteins are nutritious. They provide nutrition similar to meat protein.

2) Soy proteins are functional. Certain soy proteins are good for their emulsifying and binding properties and aid in the retention of meat juice and fat. This function results in less cooking loss and a finished meat product that is more flavorful and juicy.

3) Soy protein products are economical. When compared to other proteins of comparable nutritional value, they provide one of the best proteins that money can buy.

In general, the industry offers the following basic protein products: Soy flour, soy grits, soy protein concentrate, isolated soy protein, and textured soy protein (the baby of the family).

Each one of these products will be briefly reviewed along with a more in-depth discussion on the role of textured soy protein in meat systems.

SOY FLOUR

Soy flour has been used as an additive for many years especially in cooked sausage and non specific meatloaf. It was used to extend meat because it was inexpensive. As a result it was, and in certain cases still is, misused. It was recognized many years ago that soy flour would retain meat juice and fat under processing conditions. Its main disadvantage is mouth feel and taste. Obviously, these two factors limit its use.

There are basically three types of soy flour produced: White flour, cooked flour, and toasted flour. Toasted flour has far more usage in meat systems than the other two. In fact, white flour (particularly enzyme active) will have a detrimental effect on a finished product. White flour and cooked flour are more commonly used in the baking industry and other food systems such as baby formulations, production of hydrolyzed vegetable protein, and so forth.

SOY GRITS

Soy grits are normally manufactured with at least two different heat treatments and two mesh sizes. Soy grits are identical in composition to soy flour. As the name implies, the only difference would be particle size.   Like soy flour, toasted soy grits are preferred in meat applications over untoasted grits. Soy grits have more utility in coarse ground meat products such as patties, meatloaf, etc., than emulsified items. Grits will provide a small texture improvement over flour.

SOY PROTEIN CONCENTRATE

Soy protein concentrate is manufactured from the flour simply by removing soluble carbohydrates. The resulting product is a 70 percent protein. Soy protein concentrate has undoubtedly been one of the finest products offered to the food industry for many years. It has proven to be a sound investment for the producer and processor, and it provides the public with an excellent functional and nutritional food. Soy protein concentrate is used in meat systems for its emulsifying, binding, and nutritional properties. It is used in baby foods, dietary foods, and geriatric formulations. Production of breakfast cereals is a great use for soy protein concentrate. It is very versatile in its functional and nutritional properties. Following the introduction of soy protein concentrate came soy protein isolate.

SOY PROTEIN ISOLATE

Isolated soy protein is a 90 percent protein product produced primarily from the white flake which is still enzyme active, and in which the protein has not been denatured. The product is rather expensive to manufacture and the capital cost is high, yet the product has found a permanent home in food and non food applications. It functions as an emulsifier, binds fat and water, has certain gelforming properties, adhesive properties, and much more. It is used in sausage, canned goods, gravies, imitation dairy products, and specialty foods.

TEXTURED SOY PROTEIN

The products that I have mentioned so far have been around the industry for some time and have found a definite place as an ingredient for engineered foods. The latest member of the edible soy protein family is textured vegetable protein and the potential of this member is limited only by man's imagination. This product can be engineered to look and taste like bacon, ham, poultry, shrimp, crab, coconut, various nuts, beef, pork, carrots, mushrooms, and so forth.

Basically, textured soy protein is made by one of two methods, thermoplastic extrusion or the spinning of protein fibers similar to the spinning of nylon. The spinning technique involves the use of isolated soy protein. The protein is chemically treated and a very unique engineering development spins the protein into bundles of fibers. Flavor, color, and binding materials such as starch and gum are incorporated, and we have the production of a complete meat analog. The spinning method is considered the Cadillac of the industry for producing a total meat analog. Many meat experts cannot detect a difference between the real meat and the soy protein meat analog. The one major problem and it is a big one, is cost. It costs as much or more to produce the simulated meat than the cost of meat itself. For this reason the first method I mentioned, thermoplastic extrusion, is the more popular and most economical means for producing excellent textured protein. Consequently, thermoplastic extrusion is the method which is playing the major role with the last member of the soy protein family, textured vegetable protein.

Soy flour, which contains a minimum of 50 percent protein, is the prinicipal raw product used for thermoplastic extrusion; however, concentrates and isolates can also be extruded. The flour is subjected to high temperatures, pressures, and various levels of moisture. The resulting product takes on a fibrous network similar to meat protein. The size and shape of the product is controlled by various dies, cutting knives, and classification of the finished product. Flavors and colors may be added prior to or after extrusion. The textured protein is dried to approximately 6 to 8 percent moisture, and packaged.

Relative to the other edible soy proteins, textured protein is unique in that, (as the name implies) it offers texture to the finished product. No matter how nutritious a food may be, if it doesn't taste good or bite right people won't eat it. Textured protein has the "bite" built in and, along with the blandness of the product, it assumes the flavor of the surrounding media. Thus it is an ideal ingredient for engineered foods.

Excellent food products can be engineered by combining various percentages of meat and/or fish protein with textured vegetable protein. The specific driving force that has brought about the use of textured protein in meat systems has been economics. At today's prices, one pound of protein extracted from textured soy protein would cost approximately 54¢, whereas one pound of protein extracted from lean ground beef would cost approximately $5.45. Thus, there is and will continue to be a strong incentive to replace meat protein with soy protein.

The growth of engineered foods using soy protein as a replacement or complement to the staples, i.e., milk, meat, eggs, has been significant. However the "forecasters" projected far greater gains than have been realized. The impact of convenience foods and meals eaten away from home, together with the economic advantages, should have contributed to those forecasts being easily exceeded. Probably the greatest factor that has held the growth down is that the food processor has sacrificed quality by adding too much soy protein. If the manufacturer of engineered foods would contain his greed, i.e., hold down the percentage of soy protein added so as to produce a good tasting, nutritious quality product, the potential demand for textured soy protein would be unlimited.

Another engineered food with a great success story is Carnation

Instant Breakfast. Carnation developed and produced Instant Breakfast in the early 1960s. A consumer research study indicated that over 50 percent of the people in the United States were not eating a nutritional breakfast, and approximately 27 million were not even eating breakfast. This study exposed a need and opportunity to formulate (engineer) a convenient, good tasting, nutritional product. In the past very few formulated foods have been researched and produced with such a wide scope of objectives as Instant Breakfast. In the developmental stage there were three objectives that had to be fulfilled. The product had to be nutritionally adequate, palatable, and convenient. Actually, there must have been four objectives because regardless of the above, if the product was not produced at a cost that the consumer would pay, it wouldn't be successful.

When the product was being developed, minimum daily requirements (MDR) and recommended dietary allowance (RDA) were used as a basis to formulate. The product was designed to provide a minimum of 25 percent of the MDR for both vitamins and minerals. In addition, the product was designed to provide a minimum of 25 percent of the RDA for protein.

Although Instant Breakfast is in both the liquid and powder state, the original product was a powder designed to be reconstituted in a glass (8 oz.) of whole milk. With the use of several acceptable flavors, the combination with milk made the product very acceptable and palatable. The powdered product is considered very convenient particularly when compared to a so-called conventional breakfast (eggs, toast, bacon). However, to make the product even more convenient, Instant Breakfast was liquified and canned and thus all the consumer has to do is to open the can and drink it. The consumer acceptance for both the powdered and liquid form has been extremely favorable.

The following is a list of the various ingredients, with a brief description, that goes into the engineering (formulating) of Instant Breakfast.

Instant Breakfast

Corn syrup solids and hydrolyzed cereal solids are made by converting cornstarch·to simple sugars, chiefly glucose - similar to Karo syrup.

Sodium caseinate is a derivative of casein (milk protein). The sodium in this compound increases the solubility (dispersion) of the protein to provide a smooth mixture. Sodium and protein are essential nutrients.

Isolated soy protein (protein which has been isolated from soybeans).

Lecithin is a derivative of soybean oil and is used to enhance the mixing properties of the powder in milk.

Lactose is the natural sugar (carbohydrate) of milk.

Ammonium carrageenan is a compound extracted from seaweed and is used as a thickening agent, giving body to a milk beverage.

Sodium silicoaluminate is a mineral compound containing sodium, silicon, and aluminum. It is an inert substance which serves to prevent caking of the powder and aids its flowability.

Sodium ascorbate (vitamin C), vitamin E, vitamin A, niacinamide (niacin), calcium pantothenate (pantothenic acid), thiamine mononitrate (vitamin B_1), pyridoxine hydrochloride (vitamin B_6), and folic acid are all forms of vitamins which are required in human nutrition.

Magnesium hydroxide (magnesium), ferric orthophosphate (iron), basic copper carbonate (copper), and zinc oxide (zinc) are sources of minerals which are required in human nutrition.

Sodium citrate is composed of sodium and citric acid, the primary acid in citrus fruits. It is used to provide a degree of tartness to Strawberry Instant Breakfast.

It is interesting to note that Carnation Instant Breakfast and 8 oz. of milk compares favorably with the so-called conventional breakfast consisting of poached egg on toast, two strips of bacon, and a glass (6 oz.) of tomato juice.

The increased use of new and unfamiliar ingredients along with the lack of consumer and regulatory education has brought about an era of wariness to many fabricated foods. Politicians with little or no technical knowledge have sought to "protect" their constituents and seek regulations restricting new ingredients. Also the virtues of natural food are vocalized more and more by consumers interested in health foods. This along with the private interest groups of dairy and meat industries, etc. has brought pressure on the state and federal regulatory agencies to restrict the use of new ingredients. In spite of the problems associated with engineered, fabricated and/or formulated foods, we have seen and will continue to see a tremendous growth. Nutrition is very high on the priorities of most consumers, and they are becoming more aware of the source of their food. However, economics and palatability have and will continue to have a major role in the consumers' choice of new fabricated foods. Simply stated, if food does not taste good and does not provide the acceptable economics, it simply won't be purchased. The new food must provide one or more of the following factors to be successful: A lower cost, more convenience, be more functional, and be of high and consistent quality.

The success of engineered foods such as those engineered with vegetable protein, and Instant Breakfast, are good examples of why formulated foods will continue to grow and benefit the consumer. However, to achieve the success warranted, we must have a better balance than the current constraint imposed by the regulatory agencies. Product safety, nutrition, label, and standard of identity cannot be ignored; however, the limination of politics from regulations can gain new vistas for engineered foods. By having the freedom of choice, it is the consumer who will benefit in the end.

14 Emerging Food Marketing Technologies: Priorities for Assessment

Michael J. Phillips
William W. Gallimore
J.B. Cordaro

Speculation on the future is as old as man. Serious attempts to determine the consequences of technology to society are relatively recent, however. It was not until the mid nineteenth century that formalized speculation about the direction and destination of progress found its way into the literature and scientific thought of that time.

In 1852 Hans Christian Andersen wrote about tourists of the future traveling in steam powered airships from America to Europe. The most famous nineteenth century "futurist," the French writer Jules Verne, used science as material for fiction. Verne projected the science of his day into the future, but he envisaged that this science would have effected little or no change on the people of that future. Edward Bellamy's Looking Backward (1888) was one of the first efforts to reach a worldwide audience. It described whole societies 200 years in the future and the changes caused by the introduction of certain imagined technologies. (1)

All futurists have the same problem - describing something that does not exist. There is no "average" futurist; they are all products of different nations, different languages, and different training. Thus each writer's perception of the future is influenced by background as well as by beliefs.

Not surprisingly, therefore, there is a wide variety of views, from the Club of Rome's rather somber outlook of the world's ability to sustain present growth and prevent a global catastrophe within the next century, to Herman Kahn's more optimistic outlook that technology will be able to supply needed solutions to the world's problems.

There are two futurists' ideas that have particular relevance. The first is that the future should be viewed not as a single future, but many possible ones, and that if enough people agree on a desirable future and work toward that end, this will essentially be the future that will unfold. The second idea is from the French futurist Bertrand de Jouvenel, who stated that to preserve the ability to make choices and not become victims of necessity, public policy leaders should identify

222

emerging situations while they are still manageable and not yet at the crisis stage.

Although there are many differing conceptions of what the world or the United States may be like in the year 2000, the outlook is in general more optimistic than pessimistic. One accepted method of predicting and understanding possible changes in the world's future is to identify present trends. The following are some of these trends that certain futurists believe will, if they continue, make the world different in the future:

- Increasing world political unification and cultural standardization

- Growing affluence, with resulting increase in leisure time

- Decreasing importance of the family as a social unit

- Less industry orientation of developing countries

- Increasing longevity and personal mobility

- Rising educational levels

- Greater emphasis on religion

That these trends, if continued into the future, will affect all segments of our lives is not in question; and since the importance of food in our lives cannot be questioned either, it is essential that we be aware of changing conditions that will affect the food sector. It is important to note that American consumers spent an estimated $180 billion (2) for domestically produced food in 1977, approximately two-thirds of which ($123.5 billion) was for marketing services. Because food expenditures have been increasing and marketing services take such a large share of these expenditures, there is the incentive by industry to develop and adopt technologies that will help lower marketing costs. The development of new products, the need to reduce energy consumption, and concerns over the food supply are other reasons for developing new food marketing technologies. On the other hand, the emergence of change in certain socioeconomic factors may create a climate that forces or encourages the industry to change, economic incentives to the contrary. An understanding of the issues involved and their expected impacts on society is therefore an important consideration to policy leaders in legislative and policy deliberations.

Policy issues arise from either perceived or expected impacts resulting from the adoption of technologies. Impacts may be positive, negative, or a combination of the two; and not all impacts create policy issues. That is, negative impacts that are not severe or widespread may not brought to the attention of policymakers, while technologies with primarily favorable impacts may create issues only about whether policies should encourage their development and adoption.

This paper reports the results of a completed preliminary analysis by the Office of Technology Assessment. The purpose was to identify and rank by priority emerging food marketing technologies likely to raise major policy and legislative issues, and to indicate areas where assessments might be conducted. Also included as part of the report is a discussion of social and economic factors that should be expected to interact with those technologies. These factors are equally as important to the execution of assessments in this area as are the technologies themselves.

Four types of technologies are discussed: 1) available technologies in food marketing that will be more widely adopted; 2) technologies in the development phase; 3) technologies that will be developed and possibly adopted by the year 2000; 4) technological gaps.

PRIORITIES FOR TECHNOLOGY ASSESSMENT

Technology assessment is the systematic identification, analysis, and evaluation of the potential impacts of technology on social, economic, environmental, and political systems, institutions, and processes. It is concerned particularly with second and third order impacts of technological developments and with the unplanned or unintended consequences, whether beneficial, detrimental, or indeterminate, which may result from the introduction of new technology or from significant changes in the application or level of utilization of existing technologies.

Food marketing comprises the activities that take place within the food system from the farm gate to the consumer. These include processing, wholesaling, retailing, food service, and transportation.

An effective food marketing system should provide an adequate and continuous supply and variety of wholesome, nutritious foods to all consumers at reasonable prices and provide reasonable returns to producers and sellers. While simple to state, assessing performance is complex because cost efficiency is a major governing factor, and yet fulfilling other requirements may increase costs. For example, seeing that food meets safety standards may add to its cost. In the short run, a technology may increase efficiency and lower cost to the consumer, while in the longer run it could result in structural changes to the industry that could impede competition and result in less-than-reasonable prices for consumers. Any technology that would require a large outlay of capital and therefore drive out smaller firms could lessen competition and increase prices. Likewise, returns to the various segments of the system must be sufficient to attract needed capital and make changes necessary to meet performance standards.

The marketing system breaks down logically into two major segments: Processing and distribution. Processing technologies are classified in this report under five headings: 1) Preservation, 2) new and improved equipment and processing techniques, 3) new and modified food products, 4) new sources of food ingredients, and 5) packaging. Distribution technologies are classified under four headings: 1) Wholesaling, 2) transportation, 3) retailing and food service, and 4) those technologies that cross over the above three in their application and effects.

This paper synthesizes the priorities and cuts across both processing and distribution and considers the total marketing system. It identifies the seven technologies that emerged as highest priority for future assessment (see table 14.1, which lists the major technologies or technological areas and the areas on which these technologies may be expected to impact). The criteria for setting priorities within this listing include how each technology affects, or might affect, the total marketing system, the probability for the development or adoption of that technology, and its expected impacts in relation to the food system and the social and economic climate.

Table 14.1. Issue Areas of Food Marketing Technologies with High Priority of Assessment

IMPACT AREAS	1 Engineered Foods	2 Sanitation in Distribution	3 Retort Pouch	4 Electronic Checkout	5 Technologies to Prevent Food Loss	6 Electronic Food Shopping	7 Recyclable Returnable Containers
Marketing Functions							
Processing	X	X	X		X		X
Packaging	X		X	X	X	X	X
Wholesaling		X	X	X	X	X	X
Retailing		X	X	X	X	X	X
Food Service	X	X	X	X	X		X
Transportation	X	X	X		X		X
Nutrition	X				X	X	X
Food Safety	X	X	X		X		X
Industry Structure		X		X		X	X
Employment			X	X	X	X	X
Energy	X	X	X		X	X	X
Other Resources	X			X	X		X

Several technologies discussed in the report represent technological gaps rather than developed technologies. Those technologies needing further research and development are identified at the end of this paper.

Cross impacts occur, and no one impact can be singled out as the most important or far reaching. In many cases, the adoption of Technology A will impact on Area A while the adoption of Technology B will impact on Areas A and B, and in turn affect the adoption or limit the impact of Technology A. This interrelation and interaction of technologies and impacts is, in the end, the most important consideration of a technology assessment.

Nutrition and food safety are affected by processing and packaging technologies but may also be affected by technologies in food distribution (wholesaling, retailing, transportation, food service) such as those in sanitation and loss prevention. Many of the distribution technologies are expected to affect industry structure, and in some instances this may affect how firms interact with each other, with other marketing segments, and with consumers. Capital requirements for many technologies are the prime cause for many of the structural changes that take place. Many technologies are adopted to improve productivity and substitute for labor (employment), and these generally will give rise to issues of job loss or labor relocation. The prospects for future increases in energy costs encourage development of energy-saving technologies, so the energy-producing industries will be affected.

Many of these high priority technologies are directly concerned with preventing losses in our food system, either through more efficient processing methods or waste reduction in the delivery system, and with producing new foods to substitute for traditional foods. This reflects the concern that between now and the year 2000 our food supply will have to be better managed and more effeciently utilized if the United States is to supply food needed in the rest of the world and keep domestic prices at reasonable levels.

A comprehensive summary of the seven highest priority technologies follows.

Fabricated Foods

The technologies that are used to produce fabricated or engineered foods are considered high priority candidates for assessment because they are already in use, their impacts have already been felt to a certain degree, and it is highly probable that their development and use will continue in years ahead. Sales of fabricated foods were more than $6 billion in 1972 and are expected to exceed $11 billion by 1980.

Fabricated foods may be divided into two types - ingredients (extenders, fillers, emulsifiers) and analogs (substitutes).

The extender used most widely in meat products today is vegetable protein, usually from soy, in hamburger or meat loaf. Analogs are substitutes fabricated to resemble a specific traditional food, such as breakfast sausage from vegetable protein or non dairy coffee whitener, cheese, whipped toppings, or egg substitutes from vegetable oils.

Several advantages have been cited for these products: Lower cost, extended food supply in times of shortages, reduction in energy use, better control of nutrient content, and more efficient utilization of resources. The issues that surface from these foods, however, are already of serious concern to producers, consumers, and nutritionists, among others.

Because fabricated foods make use of a number of additives and unconventional ingredients, about which official standards and regulations are frequently incomplete or in disagreement, many persons worry that those who consume these products are not being adequately protected. Others, however, believe that these regulations overly restrict the development and acceptance of what may be a viable solution to the problem of maintaining an adequate, dependable, and nutritious food supply.

Nutritionists and others are concerned about the effect consumption of fabricated foods may have on overall nutrient intake. While the use of vegetable protein as a meat extender or analog may be one way of providing an inexpensive source of protein, the overall consequences of ingesting vegetable, rather than animal, protein (either in part or whole) have not been satisfactorily determined. On the other hand, these technologies afford the opportunity to supply specially formulated foods that will meet the dietary needs or improve the nutrient intake of selected target populations.

The other issues that should be considered are adequate labeling and resource use. How should these foods be labeled to properly identify ingredients and yet not present barriers to consumer acceptance? If the use of these foods becomes even more widespread, how will this affect the agricultural production sector, particularly the meat, poultry, and dairy producers?

An assessment of these technologies must study the issues that will arise in the areas of food safety, nutrition, regulations, labeling, and resource use.

Food Sanitation in Distribution

Preventing the adulteration and spoilage of food is of concern throughout the food system. Since the problem of maintaining adequate sanitation is a serious one in the distribution system, particularly with the railroads, this area emerges as a high priority for assessment. Technologies and systems exist that could be used to solve this problem, although development of additional technologies is needed.

Contamination of food and food products in rail cars has two major causes: Cars are not cleaned adequately and may be infested with pests, chemicals, or microorganisms, or cars used to transport food may have previously transported toxic substances, residues of which remain.

Several solutions to this problem are possible. Railroads need an efficient tracking system to monitor cars used to carry toxicants, so they will not subsequently carry food or food products. Also, a method for detecting contamination in cars is needed. More thorough cleaning techniques must be developed for the rail system to have quality assurance in its freight car fleet.

Examples of possible technologies that have been suggested and should be considered for assessment are:

1. Freight cars designed specifically for food products that will be more resistant to contamination and infestation.

2. Equipment and procedures for decontaminating freight cars. This would include trained inspectors operating with specific guidelines relative to food safety.

3. Freight cars specifically designed for food use and a system that will keep track of this "dedicated" fleet and schedule the cars efficiently. This must include and effective means of enforcement to maintain the integrity of the system

A major policy issue in this area is funding the development of these technologies. At present, the railroads appear unable to secure the capital needed to initiate and maintain such a system. Serious attention should be given to the desirability of policies that would help railroads finance these needed improvements.

An assessment in this area should also determine if this system is needed and feasible, whether it should be encouraged through regulation, voluntary cooperation, or some type of incentive arrangement.

Retortable Pouch

The technology that produces the retortable pouch, while still being developed, has current applications; the pouch has received limited approval for use from relevant regulatory agencies (FDA and USDA). Further adoption and use of this technology can be expected to have strong impacts and far-reaching consequences throughout the marketing system, particularly in the areas of energy, food storage, transportation, and the environment. Owing to these expected impacts, retortable pouch technology ranks high on the priority list for assessment.

The pouch is a multilayer, adhesively bonded package that will withstand thermoprocessing temperatures and that combines many advantages of the metal can and the plastic boil-in-the-bag. The quality of foods processed by this method is said to be superior to that of foods retorted in conventional cans, and taste tests indicate that it may approach that of frozen foods.

Energy savings are possible in processing because of shorter cooking times at lower temperatures. However, while the pouch itself would appear to offer savings in energy use, these savings can only be confirmed by a thorough analysis of different systems that are or might be used commercially.

Savings of as much as 50 percent (pouch vs. can) may be projected in the area of transportation owing to improved product-to-package weight ratio. One question that must be answered, however, is the relative durability of the pouch for transportation purposes. Retortable pouches now in use are protected by an outer protective package, which limits the potential savings.

If the technology becomes widespread and inroads into the $17 billion frozen food and $20 billion canned food markets are as significant as expected, issues to be addressed include loss of revenue to producers of metal cans, and industries producing raw materials, displacement and relocation of large segments of the labor force, and possibly considerable loss of jobs.

Environmental impacts of this technology may be considerable, in both a positive and a negative sense. The pouches are not recyclable, as compared to cans and most bottles, which would negate some of the initial energy and raw materials savings. However, retortable pouches can be used as fuel; therefore, even without recycling, most of the energy initially expended in their manufacture could be reclaimed, while at the same time minimizing solid waste problems. It is essential that these problems be recognized, and that expected negative consequences be thoroughly assessed as industry adopts these new food packaging technologies.

Electronic Checkout

Electronic checkout systems are already in use in about 300 stores, or less than 1 percent of all food stores, in the United States as of the end of 1977. There is every indication, however, that the development and use of these technologies will continue to expand, with economic and social consequences for retailers, consumers, labor, and the telecommunications sector. Because of these impacts and the emotions they have aroused, electronic checkout technologies must be among those areas considered high priority for assessment.

At present, two electronic checkout systems have been developed. The first is an electronic cash register, which may be self-contained or tied to a central store computer. It relies on individually price marked items and manual entry into the register. The second system, which has received the most publicity and generated the most opposition from consumers, is tied to a central computer and uses a scanner that reads the Universal Product Code (UPC) currently printed on a number of food packages. This system, like the first, has the potential to improve merchandising decisions resulting from better inventory control, improved labor scheduling, less need for storage space, more thorough analysis of sales, increased product movement, and better use of shelf space.

In addition, the UPC scanner system eliminated the need to mark prices on individual packages, since this information would be stored in the central computer and transmitted to the terminal when the UPC is read. It is this elimination of pricing that has created most of the public opposition to this system. Bills have been introduced in more than 30 state legislatures and in the United States Congress to require that prices be marked on every item.

Opponents claim that lack of pricing deprives consumers of information they need to make rational purchase decisions and to assure proper charges. Proponents believe that this is outweighed by the many economic benefits that may accrue from the use of this system, stressing that this would probably result in lower food prices.

An assessment should consider impacts of many elements of this technology. What particular components of the system generate savings, and how much of the savings are cash savings due to increased productivity of labor versus secondary savings from better management of inventory, pricing policies, etc.? How much of these savings would be passed on to the consumer? How, in fact, would this technology affect consumer purchase decisions if products were not marked with individual prices? If this is indeed a problem, are there alternative solutions? How would widespread implementation of this system affect industry structure and competition, given the high initial capital required for installation (about $200,000 per store)? If individual prices were required by law, would this deter the growth of high volume, low price discount stores that might offer substantial savings to consumers?

The adoption of this technology would cause a reallocation of labor. How would this affect the 1.7 million food store employees and labor in related industries? Increased use of the electronic checkout may involve increased use of electronic funds transfer. What will be the impact on individual privacy and liability for losses and errors in the system?

Technologies to Reduce Food Losses

Approximately one-fifth of all food produced for human consumption is lost annually in the United States. Technologies that reduce the extent of these losses can help in substantially increasing the food supply available from existing resources and will become increasingly important as worldwide pressure increases for more food. Such technologies include those that reduce waste in packaging and transportation throughout the marketing system and reduce losses that occur from pilferage and general lack of security control.

Waste resulting from mechanical harvesting might be reduced by improved harvesting technologies or by gleaning the produce left by mechanical harvesting. Waste resulting from spoilage and bruising in transportation might be reduced by using such alternatives as bulk packing at the field for short distance delivery to stores or by educating consumers to the benefits of damaged, but equally nutritious, produce. In addition, technologies are needed that will reduce the amount of food lost at the retail level to both damage in handling and pilferage.

The first part of an assessment of loss prevention technologies should determine the extent of loss in the marketing chain, when it occurs, and what technologies are available to reduce this loss. Another area that should be considered is the potential for utilizing produce that does not now meet grade standards because of size or blemished, what consumer objections would have to be overcome to accomplish this, and whether it would be economically feasible. Technologies to reduce losses at retail, such as the electronic checkout for better inventory control, should be considered, as should better designed locking systems for rail cars and trucks to reduce losses during transportation.

Electronic Food Shopping

These technologies are not as likely to be widely adopted within the next ten years as are the electronic checkout systems, but their gradual evolution would have very significant impacts on the marketing system; hence the high priority accorded them for assessment.

Three electronic food shopping systems are considered: Warehouse-to-door systems, automated mini markets, and mobile markets. These technologies apply primarily to large metropolitan areas and the special distribution needs of rural areas.

Possible advantages of ordering and delivery directly from warehouses to the consumer include savings in time to the consumer and savings in transportation costs, fuel use, and convenience, and possibly safety, to the consumer (particularly the elderly). An assessment should analyze these technologies to determine whether they can indeed provide the same services as retail stores at less cost. Automated mini markets, a convenience store where most items are dispensed automatically, as well as the warehouse-to-door system, are dependent to a certain extent on some type of credit, probably electronic funds transfer which would be card activated. Both systems are dependent, therefore, on the development and use of electronic funds transfer technology. Mobile markets would move products into certain areas on a scheduled basis. Tests indicate that this is a high cost operation, but this cost may decrease if the operation were to become widespread.

The main advantage of all three systems is that they would make food available in inner city and rural areas, where such services may be at a minimum. The most apparent disadvantage is that with remote ordering or with a smaller amount of food from which to choose, the consumer would be faced with a limited selection and in some instances would not be able to examine certain foods, particularly fresh produce, before purchase.

All of these technologies should be examined in relation to alternative systems such as industry cooperative programs for improving stores in the inner city, consumer cooperatives, and direct marketing by farmers in rural areas. Providing all types of food delivery services in all locations may be too costly. However, an assessment should consider providing as much choice as possible to consumers regardless of location.

Returnable and Recyclable Containers

Technologies for recyclable containers, returnable cans and bottles, and other refillable containers have a high probability of being an important part of our future, and the impacts of adoption will be widespread. These technologies have developed because of socio-economic pressure, and the pressure will in all events continue to build for new solutions through technology to the problems of conserving natural resources and reducing the expense of keeping our environment free of pollution from discarded containers. This is an instance of social and economic pressure creating demand that established the high priority given to these technologies for assessment.

Returnable and recyclable containers are being produced today, and many communities have set up collection points for cans, bottles, and other recyclable products. The public definitely seems interested in the concept of recycling, even if the specific technologies or systems to date may not have met with their approval.

These technologies fall into three categories: Recyclable beverage containers, returnable and recyclable food containers, and the general concept of recycling applied to all food products. The issues, however, are generally the same for all and fall into the areas of economics and the most efficient resource utilization.

In some instances returnables may add to the cost of distribution and handling of products (one study estimates it would cost 2 cents more per quart to deliver milk in returnable bottles), but whether this cost would be passed on to the consumer has not been determined, although it seems a reasonable assumption. Included in this issue is the high initial capital cost of converting production lines in bottling plants to handle returnables. An assessment should evaluate policies for overcoming such capital problems.

Delivery problems may also result from a widespread conversion to returnable bottles, since by law they cannot be transported in the same vehicle as new food products. This may give rise to new products that do not depend on bottles (such as powders to be mixed with carbonated water in the home.)

Recovery and recycling of the materials from food containers may be one method of extending our natural resources. Various technologies for collection and processing of these materials have been initiated - for instance, large, central, high technology plants for separating recyclable metal, glass and other materials from refuse relative to separation by consumers of these materials before the refuse enters the recycling system. There may be no one system applicable for every situation, but people may have to make a choice of whether they wish to participate by paying for a centrally located or industry based system with taxes or fees, or whether they would prefer to lower the cost by participating directly.

TECHNOLOGIES NEEDING MORE RESEARCH

Research is needed to further develop many technologies identified in this paper that are not now in an adoptable state. The list below is not in priority order and does not include those technologies selected for high priority assessment that would more clearly specify needs for more research.

The listing of these technologies should not imply that they are being advocated but rather that they are currently not developed to the point of adoption, or that not enough research has been conducted to be able to assess their potential.

The processing and distribution technologies needing further research are:

1. More efficient utilization of water in processing

2. Development of containers or rail cars for better quality preservation

3. Central cutting and packing of meat

4. Solar energy technology in processing

5. Meals-on-wheels and other delivery of complete meals to the home

6. New analytical instrumentation and processes for detecting ingredients in foods

7. Intermodal terminals constructed in main food distribution centers

8. Moisture reduction processes.

There is a high possibility that these technologies will play an extensive role in revolutionizing our food marketing system over the next ten years. This early warning information provides signals for decision makers to allow them to plan for the long term consequences of these technological applications. Decision makers now have an advanced opportunity to examine the many ways in which these technologies will affect agricultural production, food manufacturers and processors, food retailers, and peoples' lives. Further analysis that would help to balance judgments about the positive and negative consequences of these technologies should explore the physical, biological, economic, social, and political impacts and the parties that will be affected when these technologies are applied on a national scale.

NOTES

(1) Edward Cornish, The Study of the Future (Washington, D. C.: World Future Society, 1977).

(2) This represents 25 percent of total consumer expenditures of $730 billion excluding energy and services. Stated another way, Americans spent $2.50 of every $10 at food stores and away-from-home eating places. Survey of Consumer Buying Power, Sales and Marketing Management, New York, 1977.

15 Fuel, Food, and the Future

Donald R. Price

The future always has locked within it some unknowns and surprises. We can predict with great accuracy that greater quantities of food are going to be absolutely essential throughout the world. If the population explodes to the extent predicted, we have one tremendous challenge before us if great starvation is to be avoided. If the population is contained at 50 percent of that predicted, or somewhere below 5 billion by the year 2000, the challenge is still a major one.

One's prediction with regard to fuel availability for the future to produce the food needed must contain far more uncertainty. The reserves of oil and gas are at best poor estimations; however, if the world continues on the same course, the finite reserves available must surely be on the downhill side of depletion within the next decade.

At this moment we do not have a substitute fuel source to power the heavy duty mobile work vehicles on the farm. We can, of course, hope for and work toward a suitable substitute, but none are now in sight. As oil supplies grow shorter, we can expect localized shortages to begin to surface similar to those that developed during the embargo of 1973. We simply must see to it that these shortages do not hamper or reduce the capacity to produce food. To avoid catastrophe, a carefully developed energy policy for the United States food system is needed today that anticipates the situations of the future.

AGRICULTURE PRODUCTION

In the January 27, 1978 issue of Science, (1) Dr. S.H. Wittwer of Michigan State University gives his views on the productivity of agriculture. He reports that the major productivity of major food crops has plateaued. Yields of wheat, maize, sorghum, soybeans, and potatoes in the United States have not increased since 1970. World grain yields have declined. Increased production has been achieved largely by cropping more land.

After World War II, farm yields rose rapidly with advances in the use of fertilizer, pesticides, irrigation, mechanization, and new varieties of seeds providing the ingredients that made it possible. Major increases in production efficiency were attained, and the result was plenty of food, in fact large surpluses, at low cost. All of the ingredients, with the possible exception of new seeds required greater inputs of energy. Agricultural production doubled from 1950 to 1970 while labor requirements were reduced by nearly one-half. The end result is both good and bad - good because the capacity to produce quality food in adequate quantities has prevailed, but bad because the production system has become heavily dependent of fossil fuels that are becoming short in supply.

It is probably a fair conclusion to state that we are also on the downhill side of improvements in productivity. New developments will continue to flow from scientists, but not of the nature that revolutionized the production system in the late forties and fifties. In fact it appears that we must expend a great deal of effort going back and adjusting some of the developments of earlier years to protect the health of the public and improve the efficiency of energy use. One fact seems to be certain. We must make adjustments to the existing practices and still gear up for increased production.

FOOD AND FUEL INTERDEPENDENCY

From the above discussion it should be clear that food is dependent on fuel. It may be less clear that fuel, to a certain degree, is now dependent on food. In 1976 we exported approximately $23 billion worth of agricultural products. (2) In the foreign exchange, those exports paid in effect for 68 percent of the total oil imports of $34 billion. The food producing capability in the United States, which uses only 3 percent of the total United States energy consumed, returned energy in the amount of 68 percent. In addition there is the energy available from the food in terms of calories consumed by humans and animals. With current prices and technology, agricultural production still produces about $3 worth of exportable food for every dollar spent for energy.

In the food production process, a greater utilization of solar energy takes place than in all other solar applications combined. The plants, through photosynthesis, capture solar radiation and use it in combination with carbon dioxide from the air and water and plant nutrients from the soil to produce grains, vegetables, fruits, fiber and other products that contain energy.

WHAT DOTH THE FUTURE HOLD?

From all indications and projections, the future may look rather bleak. However, I believe that we can expect all kinds of unpredictable, dynamic developments in the next 25 years and beyond. It may seem that we have reached some peak of human development, and that all new ideas, invention, and developments that are worthwhile have already surfaced or are right now within our grasp. I suppose it is possible, but history should make us rather skeptical that such is the case.

We have been crisis oriented in the United States since its inception, and our best efforts always seem to come forth in such times. We are certainly nearing a crisis in oil and natural gas supplies and world food shortages may not be that far away. Economic and social ills could result from either of these shortages. That should be all the incentive needed to plunge headlong into finding our way out of the dilemma. The wheels of motion are turning, perhaps not yet fast enough, within the Federal, state, and local arenas. The new United States Department of Energy is well into research, development, demonstration, and even commercialization of energy conservation technologies and the use of alternative sources. The research and development needs in energy and food production will keep a generation of scientists busy and hopefully productive.

The future holds some things that are clearly visible in both the food and energy area. We know with reasonable accuracy our current rate of use of scarce fuels and the rate of use by most other countries. The accelerated rate of use is clearly not possible many years into the future. The current population and worldwide increases are reasonably well defined, and again we can clearly see that the future food requirements are going to increase drastically. We have a fairly good data base that tells us how much energy we use to produce food, and again it is clear that some major adjustments must be made in the next decade.

The bottom line now becomes one of identifying the shape, form, and costs of these adjustments. They fall within the broad categories of conservation, substitution, and use of alternative and renewable energy sources. Food production is affected by, and participates extensively in, all categories.

Conservation

Not one single segment of our society is exempt from the requirement to conserve energy wherever possible. All of us can and should participate in the goals to use less and use it more efficiently. This is the only hope for the near term future (next 10 years). In a recent unpublished survey when individuals were asked to respond to the question, "Do you agree or disagree that conservation is a good idea, but there is not much I can do personally about it," 44 percent agreed. True there are some major areas where large quantities of energy can be saved, transportation for instance, but the real savings will come from the accumulation of small savings from each individual.

Agricultural production falls into the category of small users because only three percent of the total is consumed in the farming operation. Yet there are ways to save, and the active participation of workers in all segments of agricultural production is needed. It is true that a spirit of efficiency has been an active ingredient into the production system in the period of the "green revolution." Yet there is room for improvement, and let us look at some of the areas where potential savings are possible.

One misconception needs to be considered here as we begin. A change in life-style or farming practice does not mean a reverting back to primitive conditions. Gavett (3) estimated that to produce United States crops grown in 1974 with the animal power and technology used in the "good old days" in 1918 would require 61 million horses and mules. To produce this number from the 3 million now in existence would require 20 years. Just to feed the animals, once we had them, would require the total production from over 180 million acres of cropland, which is about half the current cropland in the United States.

The food available for humans would obviously be greatly reduced, and certainly food prices would rise and agricultural exports would cease. In addition to the horses and mules, some 30 million farm laborers would be needed (about one-third of the current work force). Factory wages are at least double those paid to farm workers; therefore, this would cause an additional major increase in the cost of food. From the biological, social, and economic standpoint, we cannot go back to animal and human power in agriculture in the United States. We are beyond the point of no return and can only pick and choose from those items in the past that fit into the scheme today and help to make the total operation more efficient.

Now that some of the extremes have been forfeited, what is left to do? In order of intensity, we need to look at conservation in use of fertilizers, irrigation, harvesting, preplant, on-the-road vehicles, crop drying, and pesticide use.

Fertilizers

The use of nitrogen fertilizers is credited with providing one-third the productive capacity of crops according to USDA reports. (4) Work by Taylor, et al. (5) indicates that if nitrogen fertilizers were to be limited to 50 pounds per acre, an additional 18 million acres of cropland would be required to maintain current production levels. Fertilizers are big energy consumers with an estimated 33 percent of the total energy input to crop production consumed by the use of fertilizers. (6) Most of the inherent energy contained in fertilizers is the natural gas required to produce the nitrogen fertilizers. Crops vary in their demand for nitrogen partly due to the natural capability some legumes, such as soybeans, have for fixing their own nitrogen. Corn is a major grain crop that does not have this natural capability, although scientists are researching the plant breeding characteristics to determine if it may be possible to develop this capability in a new variety of corn. Applications of supplemental quantities of nitrogen to corn can result in a net return of six units of energy for every unit expended in fertilizer production. (7) This helps to allow plants to transform more solar energy into usable and storable plant products.

Since fertilizer is a big energy user and its use is essential, what can and is being done to conserve? First, the energy efficiency in the fertilizer production process can be greatly improved. The Department of Energy is funding research at the Tennessee Valley Authority that has brought to the demonstration phase new technology that reduces energy input significantly. The process makes use of natural chemical reactions that take place in the production cycle to generate heat used in the drying process. Other improvements and some substitution, to be discussed later, are expected to improve the efficiency and reduce the use of scarce fuels.

Another obvious conservation practice is to apply only as much fertilizer as can be used effectively by the plants. Plant scientists have identified these optimum levels for most plants, and farmers have followed these recommendations and reduced their fertilizer applications in many situations. A companion to this practice is one of applying the fertilizers at a time when the plant can use it before it volatilizes or leaches away.

Using legumes as a source of nitrogen was a common practice of the fifties. Legume crops such as clover were rotated with the corn crop. The legumes were plowed under, and the nitrogen captured in the soil for later use by the corn. This can be used today; however, the net result is lower production capacity for corn. The legumes will provide significant nitrogen, but supplemental nitrogen would be required to prevent nitrogen deficiency. If legume nitrogen is used to replace commercial fertilizers by crop rotation, the corn crop in the corn belt would essentially be reduced by one-third over a period of three years. Some alternatives that are under study include growing a legume winter crop to be plowed down in the spring, and this could supply nearly one-half of the corn crop requirement. The legume crop has the additional advantage of reducing soil erosion. This practice will likely increase as the cost of nitrogen fertilizers increase. A similar practice is to grow a legume between the rows of corn. These legumes fix nitrogen and supply some to the corn crop. Studies by Kurtz, et al. (8) showed that the yields varied from 80 percent to about the same as the yields obtained from nonintercrop. The reductions are largely due to competition between the legumes and the corn plant for water. Further research could help bring this practice up to greater potential.

Another fertilizer substitution potential is the use of animal manure as a source of fertilizer. One common mistake that some advocates of more use of manure make is that the manure is not now being utilized. With very few exceptions the animal manures being produced in the United States are all being applied back to the land. Some large beef feed lots are among the exceptions. The use of manure is an old practice, and one that can and should be used to the maximum extent possible.

What is the potential? Heichel (9) estimates that domestic animals in the United States produce about 300 million tons of dry manure annually, of which 50 percent is collectable in a controlled system. The nutrients in this quantity of manure could fertilize about 70 million acres of cropland, or about 18 percent of the cropland of the United States in 1975. It is a good substitute and obviously should be used to the maximum, and my opinion is that, for the most part, it already is being used. What we need is to develop ways to store and apply the manure at the optimum time for best use by the plant. Much of the manure now leaches away, is carried off the field in surface water, or volatilizes away while in storage or lying on the field.

Irrigation

Irrigation uses about 13 percent of the energy used in production agriculture in the United States. It is a valuable use because crops are now being grown on land that before irrigation was not able to support production. There are a number of ways to reduce the energy use in irrigation. Some are similar to fertilizer use. By carefully scheduling the application of water, both energy and water can be conserved. As we learn more about plant-water relationships, improved scheduling can have even greater effects. The use of trickle irrigation with vegetable crops reduces energy used to move the water, and less water is required because less is wasted.

Improvements in pump design and operation can reduce energy requirements for pumping. Time of day operation can be helpful by operating the pumps during off peak power use times.

Planting, Tending, and Harvesting

Experiments show that under some conditions one or more of the unit tillage operations can be eliminated without reducing yields. There continues to be a considerable amount of research work to determine the energy savings through reduced tillage practices. Work by Wittmus, et al. (10) provided data on conventional no-till in Nebraska. Table 15.5 illustrates some results from this study. From this table one can see that the energy use was reduced, but to a relatively small degree compared to the total energy use. The tillage operation accounts for a small proportion of the total energy requirements.

The yields from reduced tillage studies vary considerably with type of soils, water availability, and type of crop. Some soils where reduced tillage is used still produce about the same yields while other soil types may produce appreciably less with reduced tillage.

Table 15.1. No-till Versus Conventional Tillage in Nebraska

| Operation | Gallons of diesel fuel equivalent required per acre | |
	Conventional	No-till
Tillage and Seeding	4.1	1.0
Fertilizer	30.2	30.2
Herbicide and Insecticide	1.1	1.4
Irrigation	30.9	30.9
Harvest	1.1	1.1
Drying	13.7	13.7
Transportation	3.0	3.0
	84.1	81.4

Source: Wittmus

Crop Drying

The drying of crops has become an energy intensive operation using primarily liquid propane gas. Corn is by far the single largest use (approximately 600 million gallons of liquid propane gas equivalent annually), while tobacco ranks second (350 million gallons). Soybeans, rice, peanuts, and sorghum each use less than 20 million gallons.

The shift to heated-air drying of farm crops, especially corn and tobacco, has been rapid and dramatic. The rapid change from natural air drying of ear corn to at least 70 percent field shelling is questioned because of the increased requirements of fossil fuel. Several key factors brought about these changes. This practice allows more control over time of harvest and less exposure of the crop to bad weather. Shelling of ear corn reduces the volume to be handled by about half and converts the product to free flowing form. Shelled corn that is dried is easily handled and stored in a high quality condition. The storage structure may be made bird and rodent tight, and the grain is harvested and placed in storage virtually untouched by human hands.

Now that a case has been made for continuing the practice of drying the grain, the next requirement is to determine how to do it with a minimum amount of energy. Studies are in progress to find ways to improve the efficiency of the energy used in drying. A process called dryeration, developed several years ago, potentially reduces the fuel use by 20 to 30 percent of conventional high speed-high temperature drying. Work is continuing in this area to determine a combination of high temperature-low temperature and natural air drying to obtain maximum efficiency.

One could continue consideration of many other potential energy conservation practices in agricultural production; however, this sampling should be sufficient to verify that there is room to save. For a more complete look at potential conservation, consider reviewing CAST Report No. 40 (1975). (11)

Substitution

If a substitute fuel, such as coal, can be used in place of oil or natural gas, this is also a desirable conservation of scarce fuels. The use of alternative sources of energy is also a substitution practice and will be discussed later.

One of the first areas we considered, fertilizer, offers considerable potential for substitution. Nitrogen fertilizers are mostly made from natural gas as the hydrogen is extracted and combined with nitrogen in the air to form anhydrous ammonia, and can be used directly as a fertilizer or converted to nitrogenous compounds. The source of hydrogen could be coal instead of gas, and the technology is already available. Another source of hydrogen is from electrolysis of water. A nuclear plant located in a remote area could produce the electricity needed for the electrolysis.

The electric heat pump is being studied as a source of heat for drying grain. Electricity produced by coal, hydro, or nuclear could be replacing Liquid Propane gas or fuel oil.

Research is underway to develop biological controls for plant pests to reduce the need for pesticides. Despite the effort in this area, there are few effective biological means for controlling the attack of insects on plants. The development of plant varieties that have improved resistance to disease and insects is a similar substitution for pesticides. Part of the problem here is that plant varieties that are resistant in one year may lose their resistancy in a few years due to mutation of the pathogen. Therefore a continuing progression of resistant varieties must be developed. The potential at this time for biological control seems limited, but certainly worthy of continued research effort.

ALTERNATIVE AND RENEWABLE SOURCES

Ironically, agriculture offers unique opportunities to produce renewable fuels to maintain production. I personally believe that sometime in the future we may see some farms that are essentially independent of outside energy sources.

Biomass can be recovered from crop residues and animal manures or produced as a crop. A summary of the biomass available from crop residues and animal manures is presented in table 15.2. On a dry matter basis, the total biomass available is estimated to be about 800 million tons. (12) If all the biomass could somehow be collected and converted to energy the energy yield would be equivalent to about a billion barrels of oil annually. Even if only 15 percent of the potential were recovered, the yield of 150 barrels of oil per year is substantial.

Table 15.2. Biomass from Crop Residues and Animal Manures

Biomass Source	Dry Matter (million tons)
Crop Residues	
Cereal straw (wheat, rye, rice, oats, barley)	155
Corncobs, nutshells, fruitpits	60
Corn and sorghum stover	100
Soybeans stover and hulls	55
Sugarcane bagasse	5
Other crop residues	95
Sub Total	470
Animal Manures (50 to 80 percent in confinement)	330
Total Crop and Animal	800

The Department of Energy has about a 30 million dollar program in the area of biomass. Some of the technologies are very close to being feasible and ready for commercialization. Researchers at Iowa State University have demonstrated that corn can be dried from heat provided by direct burning of the corn stalks and corn cobs in a furnace. Enough residue is left to return a desirable amount of organic matter to the soil.

Because of the open space and relatively low energy requirements for many operations on the farm, solar and wind power may be utilized most effectively on the farm. Of course, both have been used for decades, to a degree, but new applications are surfacing. Windpower has been an excellent source of power for pumping water in remote locations and is still used for that purpose today. Solar energy collected by plants is captured in the form of energy contained in the grain, produce, and fiber products.

Solar energy may soon be accepted and used widely for drying grains. Inexpensive collectors have been designed and complete systems demonstrated through a joint program sponsored by the Departments of Energy and Agriculture. Other applications include greenhouse heating, heating of livestock shelters, and in food processing operations. The key to success will depend on low cost systems that are economically acceptable.

Wind energy may be further down the road in its application in agriculture. Experiments are underway to heat water directly from a wind turbine using a churning device that converts mechanical energy into heat energy by friction. This work is underway at Cornell University. Other applications for heating, electrical, and mechanical operations are under study.

A combination of alternative sources and new conservation practices can, in my opinion, go a long way toward providing much of the energy needed to supply the need on the farm. My prediction is that within the next decade we will see major new developments in all areas that will be surprising, ingenious, and move us well into viable solutions to the problems of energy supply. Agriculture will play a major role in these solutions.

NOTES

(1) S.H. Wittwer, "The Next Generation of Agricultural Research," Science, 199, no. 4327, (January 27, 1978): 376.

(2) B. A. Stout, et al, "Energy Use in Agriculture: Now and for the Future," CAST Report no. 68, August 1977.

(3) E.E. Gavett, "Can 1918 Farming Feed 1975 People?" The Farm Index, August 1975, pp. 10-13.

(4) "Energy to Keep Agriculture Going," U.S. Department of Agriculture Energy Letter, December 1973.

(5) C. R. Taylor, E. R. Swanson, and P. J. Bloklane "Nitrogen as an Environmental Quality Factor - Economic Considerations," Illinois Agricultural Experimental Station Bulletin, 1977.

(6) "Energy and U.S. Agriculture: 1974 Data Base." Vol. 1, Federal Trade Administration, FEA/D-76/459.

(7) R. G. Hoeft, and J. C. Siemens "Do Fertilizers Waste Energy?" Crops and Soils, 11:12-14.

(8) T. Kurtz, S. W. Melsted, R. H. Bray, and H. L. Breland, "Future Trials with Intercropping of Corn in Established Sods," Soil Sci. Soc. Amer. Proc. (1952) 64:282-285.

(9) G. H. Heichel, "Agricultural Production and Energy Resources," American Scientist (1976) 64:64-72.

(10) H. L. Olson Wittmus , and D. Lane, "Energy Requirements for Conventional Versus Minimum Tillage," J. Soil and Water Conservation (1975) 30:72-75.

(11) D. R. Price et al., "Potential for Energy Conservation in Agricultural Production," CAST Report No. 40, February 1975.

(12) G. R. Stephens and G. H. Heichel, Proceedings of NSF Special Seminar on Cellulose as a Chemical and Energy Resource, University of California, Berkeley, California, 1974.

16 Changing Portable Energy Sources: An Assessment

William C. Burrows
Norman A. Sauter

In the past, and even today, industry and the general public perceived the supply of fuels from petroleum to be infinite and thus demand dominated decisions as to amount, price, and quality. In the future these decisions will be dominated by supply. Interruption of the supply of world crude oil, as in the case of Iran, is perhaps the greatest uncertainty in our energy picture today.

Since portable fuels such as gasoline, jet fuel, and diesel fuel are so basic to energizing the world's mobile equipment and are now totally derived from petroleum, one should start with the outlook for crude oil and then examine possibilities for developing alternative sources of liquid fuels from shale, coal, and biomass.

PETROLEUM

The United States Department of Interior estimates for the period 1960 to 1990 that world petroleum consumption will increase at a more rapid rate than total energy consumption. In absolute terms, total world energy consumption is expected to reach 400 quadrillion BTU or quads in 1990. This is two and one-third times the 1960 level of 150 quads. It is projected that in 1990 petroleum will be used to supply approximately 40 percent of the world's energy needs, a significant increase from 34 percent in 1960. This means that petroleum use will increase over three times the 1960 levels (see figure 16.1).

Estimating the time that liquid hydrocarbon fuels derived from petroleum will be available to meet this projected demand depends on two factors - whether we can reduce our appetite for petroleum, and the extent of world reserves.

In a study made at Deere & Company, three growth rates were selected for crude oil consumption:

245

7½ percent, typifying a maximum rate of increase in consumption based on continuation of past trends;

0 percent, the minimum rate of consumption based on effective conservation efforts and early development of alternative energy sources. Zero growth is probably not attainable.

2½ percent, typifies a more probable but still optimistic rate.

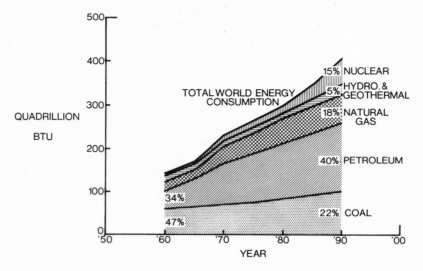

Fig. 16.1.   Total World Energy Consumption by Source, Projected to 1990.

Source: API Special Report, Oil & Gas Journal, November 10, 1975, p. 164.

While projecting rate of consumption is risky, estimating world reserves must be at least an order of magnitude more risky.   Such estimates are viewed with considerable skepticism by the general public and are not even totally accepted by Congress.   The reason may be traced to the rather poor estimates of reserves that have been made in the past, and the general lack of credibility of the petroleum industry which provides much of the data.   Periodic press reports of large finds of oil, for example, describing Mexico as a "nearby Saudi Arabia" suggest that future supply difficulties are only minimal.

M. King Hubbert, an acknowledged authority, points out that there is now a convergence on a range of estimates of from 1,800 to 2,100 billion barrels as being ultimately recoverable.   Ultimate recoverable reserves are defined as the total quantity of crude oil, estimated to be ultimately producible from an oil field, as determined by an analysis of current geological and engineering data. This includes any quantities already produced.

In this study the estimate of 2,000 billion barrels was selected as being most probable, 3,000 billion barrels as the high estimate, and 1,350 billion barrels as the low estimate. Since approximately 1,000 billion barrels have already been discovered, all estimates require new discoveries (see figure 16.2).

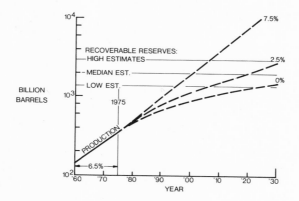

Fig. 16.2. Cumulative World Crude Oil Production in Relation to Estimates of Recoverable Reserves

Source: W.C. Burrows, C.M. Hudson, M.L. Kaesser, and N.A. Sauter, Changing Portable Energy Sources - An Assessment, Deere & Co., Moline, Ill., 1977.

Reserves will probably never be totally consumed because the rate of consumption could reduce appreciably as it becomes obvious that they are close to depletion, and because the rate of crude oil production will likely decrease. but the plot is still useful for applying a time frame for the petroleum era. If the low estimates of reserves are correct, they would be consumed sometime between the years 1996 and 2023. Using the median estimate of reserves and the probable rate of consumption of 2.5 percent, exhaustion would occur in 2019; using the historical growth rate of 7.5 percent, exhaustion could occur as early as 2001. If the reserves turn out to be as high as 3,000 billion barrels, the high consumption rate can only be continued to 2007. Note that there is an increase of only six years when an estimate 50 percent higher is used.

This analysis was compared to a more rigorous one by the Institute of Gas Technology. Both methods predict severe difficulty in meeting the world demand for petroleum very early in the twenty-first century.

The United States cannot become self-sufficient in crude oil (see figure 16.3). A growth rate about one-half the historical demand for refined products could deplete United States reserves as early as 1987, based on the more probable median estimate of reserves and current oil well recovery technology. The problem is that United States demand is currently being met by imports of both crude oil and refined products amounting to about 40 percent of United States petroleum use. Currently, our domestic supply of crude oil has improved due to our Alaskan production. But it must be anticipated that foreign suppliers may decide to limit their production.

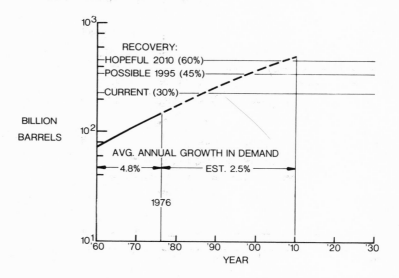

Fig. 16.3. Cumulative U.S. Demand for Refined Products in Relation to U.S. Reserve Recovery

Source: W.C. Burrows, C.M. Hudson, M.L. Kaesser, and N.A. Sauter, Changing Portable Energy Sources - An Assessment, Deere & Co., Moline, Ill., 1977.

COAL

Coal is the most abundant energy resource in many countries of the world. While total coal resources in the United States amount to 3,6000 billion metric tons, the reserve base (the amount economically and operationally feasible to recover) is estimated to be only 396 billion metric tons, or 11 percent of the total resource.

On an energy basis, United States coal reserves are equal to about 2,000 billion barrels of oil. This is about eight times United States oil reserves and about equal to the world's crude oil supply, both that remaining and that already used.

It must be remembered, however, that actual conversion of coal to some form of light liquid fuel, such as methanol or synthetic hydrocarbon, is only about 30 to 60 percent efficient, depending on the process. Therefore while coal is a significant resource, it too is not unlimited.

While hydrocarbons from coal have been commercially produced for about 25 years in South Africa, the process used is less efficient than the direct liquefaction processes which the United States is developing. It has been estimated that 1990 is the earliest feasible commercialization date for coal liquefaction. Regardless of how long it takes for coal liquefaction to reach maturity, there are some formidable obstacles which must be overcome. These include the high cost of plants and equipment, unexpected fluctuations in the price of petroleum, meeting environmental and plant siting regulations, and overcoming the technical problems associated with expanding bench scale processes to pilot and demonstration size units. As high as petroleum prices are now, they would have to increase much more to make coal liquefaction a commercially viable technology. The Department of Energy estimates that petroleum would have to rise from a present $13.50 per barrel to $24 per barrel in 1975 dollars to make synthetic coal liquids competitive with petroleum.

SHALE OIL

The United States has an abundance of oil reserves associated with shale deposits. While 4 trillion barrels of oil equivalent is the total resource in place, it cannot now be recovered economically. Recovery by mining methods will vary depending on the depth of overburden, the thickness of the deposit, the mining system utilized, and many other factors (see table 16.1).

Table 16.1. U.S. Oil Shale Resources

SHALE GRADE LITERS/METRIC TON	BILLION BARRELS OF OIL EQUIVALENT
105-270	620
40-105	1,430
20- 40	2,000
	4,050

Source: Thomas A. Hendrickson, Synthetic Fuels Data Handbook, Cameron Engineers, Denver, 1975.

Additionally, large amounts of water are required for the oil extraction process, and the shale residues have about twice the volume of the material originally mined. Water is not available for on-site processing and dumping sites for the residues are not available in water rich regions.

In-place recovery is being actively pursued by Occidental Petroleum and it may be possible to circumvent the water requirement and shale dumping problems presented by mining methods. Substantial investment is still required and there is a good deal of uncertainty as to when oil from this source will first appear commercially.

BIOMASS

An energy resource of special interest to agriculture is biomass - organic matter that depends on photosynthesis for its production (see table 16.2).

Table 16.2. Biomass Resources

MUNICIPAL WASTE	MANURE
INDUSTRIAL WASTE	ENERGY CROPS
AGRICULTURAL RESIDUES	ALGAE
FOREST RESIDUES	

Since biomass is a renewable resource and is perceived by the general public to be plentiful and low cost, it is attracting considerable attention. Just how much is available and what its cost is, however, are significant questions. Estimates of agricultural residues alone are in the range of 330 to 378 million tons per year. This is about six quads of energy per year. However, a significant amount of this material must be left on the soil. Therefore only an uncertain fraction is truly available, and that is mainly in the Corn Belt. If all of the available residue, say about 120 million tons, could be converted to ethanol, about 12 billion gallons/year could be produced. This is an impressive amount, but in volume it is only about 10 percent of current gasoline demand. Taking into account the lower energy content of alcohol compared to gasoline, it only meets 7 percent of the current United States demand. Looking at it another way, 12 billion gallons of alcohol would meet about 70 percent of the total energy needs of the farm. Thus we have concluded that agricultural residues will not be a significant source of energy on a national basis, but they could make a contribution toward meeting on-farm or some local energy needs.

Forestry residues are considerably harder to estimate, but they are of the order of 4.2 quads. To put this into perspective, this amount is about 28 percent of our 1975 coal production. This also gives some idea of the tremendous job of concentrating diffuse resources such as agricultural and forestry residues into a viable energy source. Vergara and Pimentel of Cornell University recently presented data questioning the promise of biomass as a new energy source. They concluded that earlier estimates of the potential for biomass energy were optimistic for the United States but that it would have potential in countries with small populations, large tracts of unused land, and low energy needs.

HYDROCARBON FUELS: PETROLEUM VS. BIOMASS.

At the present time, only hydrocarbon fuels derived from petroleum are economic (as figure 16.4 shows).

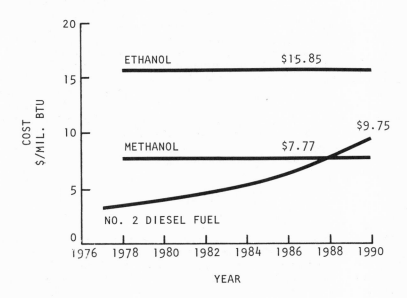

Fig. 16.4. Projected U.S. Energy Cost (In Current Dollars)

Source: N.A. Sauter, <u>Changing Portable Energy Sources - An Assessment</u>, Speech presented at Iowa Section, American Society of Agricultural Engineers, Waterloo, Iowa, Nov. 30, 1978. C. Deere & Company, Moline, Ill.

The prices of ethanol and methanol were projected to remain constant based on producing impure fuel grades at lower cost. It is recognized that the probability of accomplishing this, while introducing new technology at the same time, is very optimistic.

When the energy cost of fuel grade alcohols on the curve is compared with diesel fuel, it is apparent that even the favorable price assumption for ethanol has not really helped that much. In 1990 there is still an energy cost difference of $6 per million BTU, or ethanol is about 60 percent higher than diesel fuel. The future energy cost of methanol, on the other hand, does end up lower than diesel fuel. The normal question is "What difference does cost make if you can't get petroleum?" This is a valid question, but only when in fact petroleum is in short supply, or if it is obvious that our reserves are inadequate for even near-term demand. The answer to the question is that consumers may be willing to pay the cost, but then it may be too late to develop alternative fuels. Development of alternative fuels at any cost will take a long period of time. Early investment in their development will be encouraged only if long-term economics are somewhat favorable. For example, this comparison shows that the economic case for methanol fuel is stronger than for ethanol. In their Alcohol Fuels Program, however, the Department of Energy is estimating R&D costs for methanol from coal at $18 million through fiscal year 1983 and $96 million for ethanol for biomass through fiscal year 1984. The government obviously thinks that ethanol from biomass needs considerably greater support. The technology for producing methanol from coal is already known and there is a strong possibility of converting gas that is now being flared in the mid-East. While ethanol can certainly be produced by fermenting grain, it would appear to be better utilization of our resources to make it from agricultural or forestry residues as proposed by Purdue University. Unfortunately, however, this process is still in the early stages of development.

DEMAND

Having looked at the supply side and having concluded that petroleum based hydrocarbon fuels are really the only viable portable fuels for agriculture for the foreseeable future, the "demand" side will now be examined from the standpoint of various types of engines and the efficiencies they offer.

Powered farm equipment has a useful life of 20 years or more. Tractors presently working in the field range from 1 to 20 years old. Thus the tractors produced now may be expected to be in the field in the year 2000 and after. The engines in this equipment are designed to operate efficiently on today's fuel - predominantly diesel fuel. Developments of both the engines and the fuels of today have been interdependent, and this fundamental relationship will continue. It is easier, cheaper, more energy efficient, and reliable to convert petroleum as opposed to converting coal to a tractor fuel. Kerosene from petroleum, one of the first tractor fuels, was originally produced to fuel lamps, not engines. On the other hand, Rudolph Diesel was attempting to design an engine to be fueled by pulverized coal.

An engine manufacturer would be foolish to manufacture an engine for which an assured supply of the most appropriate fuel is not available at reasonable cost. Similar logic applies to the fuel producer. Both industries have the technical and economic resources to develop efficient engine-fuel combinations for the future. But which of the proposed fuels will be most prominent in the future, and what breakthroughs in engine technology and economics will occur? Current engine technology for farm equipment is based on diesel engines for a very good reason - thermal efficiency.

DIESEL ENGINE

The diesel engine requires a fuel that can be ignited by the heat of compression. Ignition timing is achieved by timing the fuel injection. Power output is controlled by the quantity of fuel injected. Since there is no need to throttle the intake air, even at part load, and because of its high compression ratio, the diesel engine has a high thermal efficiency.

The diesel engine has a distinct advantage in efficiency over other types of engines (see figure 16.5). It is expected to maintain this advantage so long as suitable fuels are available. However, to obtain the greatest work output from an engine with the lowest energy input, devices must be developed to permit the engine to convert what is now lost as heat to useful work.

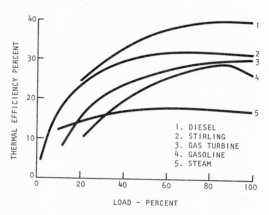

Fig. 16.5. Thermal Efficiency of Various Power Plants

Source: J.H. Pitchford, 1976. The Seventh Annual Fairy Lecture: The Better Conservation of Liquid Fuels for Mobile Use, Journal of Sound and Vibration, 47 (3): 371-285.

STIRLING ENGINE

The Stirling engine is an external combustion engine with the fuel continuously burning. The working fluid is a gas (helium or hydrogen) that is sealed into the engine. Through a relatively complicated arrangement, the pressure of the working gas acts on both ends of each piston at different times. Because of this action, the engines are called "double acting." The pressure is made to act first on one end then on the other of the piston by having one end cold and the other hot. Such an engine requires at least three cylinders, and the optimum is five. The engine operates very smoothly because each revolution is produced by a number of impulses equal to the number of cylinders; and since the fuel burns continuously, operation is quiet.

Stirling engines are, however, complex and expensive. Each cylinder must have a regenerator and cooler to store the heat and to cool the working fuid. Several compact (and expensive) heat exchangers are required. In addition, since the working fluid must not be contaminated, the piston cylinders cannot be lubricated in the usual sense.

Interest in this engine is widespread because the fuel does not have to meet any octane or cetane requirements. It has been demonstrated that the type of fuel used in a Stirling engine operating under load can be randomly switched between leaded and unleaded gasolines; diesel fuel, alcohol; olive, salad, and crude oils; propane; butane; and natural gas. A temporary change in speed occurs during the fuel switch, but the engine quickly recovers and continues to operate smoothly. With a different burner, solid fuels may be used.

The ideal Stirling cycle efficiency is the same as the Carnot cycle which is the highest thermodynamically attainable from heat engines. The maximum thermal efficiency yet attained is 32 percent when using 70c cooling water. This approaches that of today's diesel engines. But when both the diesel and Stirling engines are equipped with waste heat recovery systems, the overall thermal efficiency of the diesel engine system is expected to be greater.

A serious problem with the Stirling engine is that the technology exists mainly in only two corporations, the Philips Company in the Netherlands and United Stirling in Sweden. Excessive license fees could inhibit significant penetration of the Stirling engine into the vehicle industry.

We conclude that the Stirling engine has not reached the stage of being successful commercial venture. Significant unpredictable breakthroughs in both technology and economics must be achieved first.

GAS TURBINE

The gas turbine engine is a continuous flow, continuous combustion engine, and therefore the fuel does not have to meet any octane or cetane requirements. But at present, for practical application in vehicles, the fuel must be a liquid. There are several different configurations of gas turbine engines. Three studies sponsored by Energy, Research and Development Administration concluded that the single shaft gas turbine engine is best suited for variable speed and load vehicular applications. These engines require expensive, infinitely variable transmissions because maximum torque decreases with engine speed. But the gas turbine with an infinitely variable transmission needs only a single engine transmission control system which can be used to operate the engine on the optimum fuel consumption curve.

The gas turbine engine has become a dominant engine for commercial aircraft. Although it can be used for ground vehicles, it is not currently produced for that purpose in spite of the high degree of development. It still cannot compete with advanced diesels for two reasons: Current materials limit the maximum cycle temperature which in turn limits the thermal efficiency for practical uses. Higher turbine inlet temperatures are required to make the gas turbine engine clearly superior to the diesel in fuel economy. Also, reliable effective exhaust heat recovery systems with low pressure losses are necessary for good fuel economy, particularly at part load. This technology is presently too expensive for practical use.

The United Staes government and several private industries have been trying to develop materials and technology for lower cost, more efficient gas turbine engines. Progress has been slow and technical solutions are not likely to be available for commercial applications during the next quarter century.

SPARK IGNITION

The common automobile engine is a spark ignition, gasoline fueled engine. The major difference between the conventional spark ignition engine and the diesel engine lies in the way each converts fuel energy to mechanical energy. The spark ignition engine is low compression, and the maximum energy conversion efficiency (thermal efficiency) of such an engine without exhaust emission controls is about 27 percent. Furthermore, the air and the fuel are drawn into the combusion chamber as a homogeneous mixture and then ignited (this is different from the diesel engine). In order to get the proper mass flow of air and fuel, the amount of intake air must be controlled - that is, throttled - for part load operation. The result is decreased thermal efficiency. Installing emission control devices on the engine further lowers both the power output and the thermal efficiency. Current automotive engines are limited to compression ratios of about 9:1 which require fuels with a research octane number of at least 91.

There are no apparent ways of improving or redesigning the conventional spark ignition engine to achieve diesel engine efficiency. Thus, spark ignition engines will not replace diesel engines as the power plants for farm and industrial equipment.

STEAM ENGINES

Steam engines, both reciprocating and turbine, operate on yet another kind of energy conversion cycle. The fuel is burned in an external chamber. The heat produced is transferred to a working fluid - usually water. Ther mechanical energy comes from the superheated steam. But the cycle requires that heat be rejected for the steam to condense for reheating. The heat rejected during condensation is essentially wasted. Inherently, then, the steam engine has a low thermal efficiency. Efficiency can be improved somewhat by adding reheat cycles, but this adds to the cost which is already significantly greater than the diesel engine

The steam engine is used for large stationary power plants and they have some potential where only solid fuels are available. However, it is not considered a viable alternative power plant for mobile applications.

PORTABLE FUELS

Use of energy resources to fuel the engines of farm equipment requires that the question of portability be addressed. How are energy resources converted to fuels that match engine and vehicle requirements? One must consider fuels from present use to future alternatives in the context of the energy resource from which they are derived.

Petroleum-Based Fuels

Specific requirements for these fuels are based on both the properties of the liquids from the refinery and engine requirements. Both the refining process and the source of crude oil affect the quality and amount of the various end products from the refinery.

Different product yields are the result of using various refining techniques. Typically, a United States refinery produces about 45 percent gasoline and 24 percent distillates (diesel and heating oil). At this point the residual fraction is cracked to increase the yield of gasoline. Overseas, where gasoline demand is not as great and cracking not as widespread, the refineries produce only 13 percent gasoline and 31 percent distillates. However, the trend in non-United States refineries is toward the same product mix as in United States refineries. Two factors are responsible for this trend. One is increased demand for portable fuels. The other is the result of a policy to convert stationary uses of petroleum to coal and nuclear as a conservation measure.

Not only is the quantity of each product influenced by the refinery practices, but also the ignition quality of the fuel. The latter is measured by the cetane and octane level for diesel and gasoline fuels respectively. Most of us know what happens when low octane gasoline is used in the automobile engine. A low cetane level in diesel fuel means long ignition delay. The result, at best, is poor starting, and at worst, misfire or high pressure and temperature rise in the cylinder. Thus, low cetane fuel increases both thermal and mechanical stress on engine components.

Coppoc's plot (see figure 16.6) shows the inverse relation of cetane number to octane number. High cetane fuels ignite readily upon compression while a spark is required to ignite high octane fuels. Much of today's engine research is directed toward using higher octane fuels in diesel engines and higher cetane fuels in gasoline engines. For example, using spark ignition, a diesel engine will run on gasoline; and direct fuel injection with charge stratification allows a gasoline engine to burn diesel fuel.

Combustion research programs and advanced fuel injection systems may enable diesel engines to operate on fuels with a broader range of properties. Spark assistance is another means of solving ignition delay problems due to low cetane fuel usage.

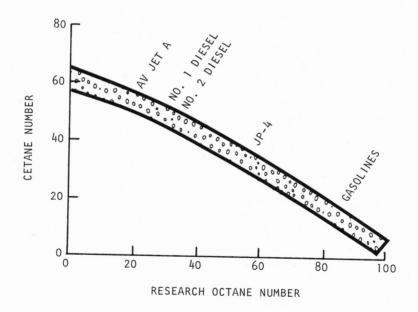

Fig. 16.6. Fuel Octane-Cetane Relationship

Source: Coppoc, W.J., "Fuels for Transportation," 1976, Society of Automotive Engineers, SP-406.

Coal Based Fuels

Coal may be converted to hydrocarbons, methanol, and hydrogen. The properties of fuels thus produced are not as well known as are those produced from petroleum. The reason for this is that only one such coal conversion plant is in operation in the world.

Hydrocarbons   The liquid product of coal conversion is a synthetic crude oil for input to a refinery – not a liquid portable fuel. However, portable gasoline and diesel fuel made from this oil may not differ much from what we know today. More than 150 different processes exist for converting coal to hydrocarbons but these can be grouped into four categories: the Fischer-Tropsch process; pyrolysis; the direct hydrogenation, or Vergius, method; and solvent refining, or solvent extraction.

Methanol: Methanol is produced commercially from coal in numerous plants. The coal is first gasified as in the Fischer-Tropsch process and then methanol, rather than synthetic crude oil, is produced through gas synthesis.

Of the alternative fuels, methanol commands the greatest interest because of its suitability as an alternative for spark ignition, i.e., gasoline engines, for the following reasons:

1. Sufficient methanol is available so that engine/fuel research can be carried out without waiting for the construction of pilot plants as is the case with hydrocarbons from coal.

2. Its high octane number makes it possible to consider methanol as a total or partial gasoline replacement. In fact, pure methanol may present fewer problems than a methanol-gasoline blend.

3. Besides using methanol as fuel directly, recent work by Mobil Oil Company indicates that it may be catalytically reformed to gasoline.

4. Methanol provides and alternative transportable energy form to the liquefaction of natural gas.   Conceivably, North Sea, Algerian, and Mid-east could be converted to methanol, thereby increasing the supply of transportation fuel.

5. Methanol can be produced from forest or agricultural residues, and municipal waste.   As such, it offers the possibility of utilizing renewable resources or waste material for a constructive purpose.

Extensive automotive fleet tests using a 15 percent blend with gasoline have been underway in Germany with apparently satisfactory results. However, low energy density (about one-half that of gasoline) and high cost are specific deterrents to the early use of methanol as fuel.

Methanol does not ignite on compression and thus is not a diesel engine fuel. Scott operated a diesel engine by fumigating the intake manifold with methanol, using injected diesel fuel to provide pilot ignition and correct timing. The results of this research led to the conclusion that methanol used alone was not a natural alternative to diesel fuel. However, in the future it may be economically feasible or desirable, in order to obtain portable fuel, to use additives that will make methanol a diesel fuel or to redesign the engine so that it is alcohol rather than a diesel engine.

Hydrogen: Hydrogen produced from coal has been suggested as a portable fuel. Billings forecasts economical production of hydrogen from coal; however, research and development activity which would substantiate this projection is minimal due to the low priority assigned by ERDA. Ultimately, hydrogen may enter the picture, but will probably not be produced from coal. If fusion reactors for electrical generation ever become a reality, hydrogen could be used as a storage and transport medium to provide engine energy. It is not generally expected that hydrogen for use as a fuel will be available until sometime after 2000, and so its viability as an alternative fuel is questionable.

Shale Oil Fuels

The fuels derived from shale oil will have nearly the same characteristics as those derived from petroleum. However, the nitrogen content may be appreciably higher. With a high nitrogen content in the fuel, changes in the combustion process will not lower noxious emissions as can now be done with low nitrogen fuels. Alternatively, the nitrogen contaminant can be removed in the refining process, but at extra energy and capital cost.

With the technology for extraction not completely known or demonstrated, with capital investment for the technology high and the final costs of actual production uncertain, private firms are not willing to risk the needed investment. The contribution of shale oil to portable fuel supply will be small until well after 2000.

Biomass Fuels

There is a great deal of interest in deriving portable as well as stationary fuels from agricultural residues. Only a few agricultural crops in a few areas produce enough surplus residue to be considered viable sources for energy production. The fuels fall into two categories: Gaseous and liquid.

Producer Gas: Agricultural residues can be converted to producer gas by passing air through a bed of the burning material. Energy content ranges from about 12.5 to 15 percent of natural gas, measured when cold and dry. At the temperatures and moisture contents typically encountered on generation, the energy content is lower. From 65 to 70 percent of the thermal energy of the residue is claimed to be recovered.

Producer gas has been used directly as a fuel in spark ignition engines. But it is not a natural alternative to diesel fuel. Approximately 10 percent diesel fuel is necessary to provide pilot ignition and timing. The producer gas flows through the intake manifold instead of the fuel injection system.

Ethanol: Ethanol can be produced most easily by fermentation of sugar cane, sweet sorghum, or grain (corn, wheat, etc.). Crop residues can be used, but not directly. The cellulose must be separated and enzymatically changed to sugars which may then be fermented. The processes have not been commercially developed as yet.

Ethanol-gasoline blends have been demonstrated to be a suitable engine fuel for existing spark ignition engines without modification. In the production of ethanol by fermentation of grain, more energy is consumed at the distillery than alcohol and residue energy produced. It is believed that ethanol does not have a major potential for fuel except where local economics and resources may favor its development.

Other Fuels: Methane from anaerobic digestion of "waste" material, such as manure, can be used as a fuel. However, significant production is limited to places where the raw material is concentrated - such as feed lots. Like producer gas, the best use of the methane is for stationary, not portable, fuel applications.

CONCLUSION

Modern mechanized agriculture depends on fuels derived from petroleum, and, for the near future, there appears to be no alternative. There is no known substitute for the hydrocarbon fuels now used to power the machines that till the land, plant, cultivate, harvest, and transport the crops that provide food for most of the world's people. Less mechanized methods of agriculture use less fuel but are significantly less productive.

Crude petroleum is a nonrenewable resource and the question of how future needs are to be met concerns not only manufacturers of agricultural and industrial equipment and their current and future customers, but everyone.

17
Biomass Conversion and National Energy Requirements*
Don C. Paarlberg

Recently, a United States study team, comprised of agricultural economists, engineers, and agronomists, visited Brazil to study Brazil's efforts to obtain energy from renewable resources by converting biomass into fuel. Brazil's economic growth and industrialization program was severely hurt by the energy problems starting in 1973. This was so because her industrialization was predicated on imported petroleum. The energy crisis was a real crisis for them. Because Brazil is poorly endowed with fossil fuel resources, she has to import 80 percent of her petroleum needs. By 1977 this amounted to a $3 billion petroleum bill. Moreover, between 1973 and 1976 her foreign debt quadrupled, balance-of-payments problems developed, and the rate of inflation, which had been checked at 15-18 percent per year, was running close to 50 percent per year.

Other energy factors are that while Brazil has hydroelectric power and potential, it is a long way from points of use: Surprisingly, about 25 percent of her fuel needs are currently met by wood and charcoal. Per capita energy consumption is one-tenth that of the United States, with one-half the population.

Brazil, however, is well endowed with solar energy, perhaps more than any other country in the world. Moreover, Brazil has vast undeveloped agricultural areas. The interior of the country is almost totally undeveloped. Today about 12 percent of Brazil's land is in agriculture, with the objective of 25 percent by 2000.

Brazil's best agricultural land today is in the south, from Sao Paulo on down. The state of Mato Grosso, in the interior, has some good agricultural land, and people are starting to move in and develop it. It seems to be the next big area for agricultural development. The

---

* Remarks presented at the Food, Agriculture, & Society Research Program, Lake Bluff, Illinois, November 11, 1977.

Cerrado (savannah), representing some 15 to 20 percent of Brazil's land area, lies to the south of the Amazon jungle. While it is characterized by red and yellow lateritic soils which are deficient in most nutrients, it has some relatively fertile areas which are scheduled for development.

The northeast, the "difficult" area of Brazil, has mostly small farms and is affected by both poverty and drought. The Amazon, as a potential agricultural area, suffers from the popular illusion that it is just one vast area needing only to be cleared of trees to make it viable for agriculture. In many areas such action would only have the effect of exposing the poor quality jungle humus to the sun, burning it up and turning it into laterite. On the other hand, the Amazon is not homogeneous; there are some fertile areas and these are likely to be exploited in the twenty-first century.

As a means of supplementing her limited domestic energy supplies, Brazil has made the decision to obtain a fraction of her fuel needs from agriculture, namely the conversion of sugarcane and cassava into ethyl alcohol. Alcohol is approximately the equal of gasoline in performance, has fewer pollutants, is slower in combustion, and doesn't require antiknock additives. Currently, Brazil blends a small fraction of alcohol with gasoline, but plans to increase this fraction of alcohol with gasoline, but plans to increase this fraction to 20 percent by 1980. A blend of this order can be achieved without carburetor adjustment. Moreover, with a double injection system, diesel engines can use alcohol in conjunction with diesel fuel mixed in the firing chamber. The Brazilians hope to be able to mix alcohol with diesel fuel in this fashion. To meet this objective, there must be a 50 percent increase in the land devoted to sugarcane, or an additional one million hectares. Currently Brazil has 2.1 million hectares in sugarcane. The conversion technology exists and is proven, contracts have been let to build more conversion plants, and the general opinion is that Brazil will meet her 1980 goal. Brazil's stated long-term goal is to eventually substitute alcohol for all gasoline or diesel fuel uses. This would entail a five or six-fold increase in sugarcane production.

Sugarcane is a better biomass producer than corn, especially since the tropics, where cane is grown, have a much longer growing season. The constraints that Brazil faces are not natural, but rather institutional, i.e., the management, infrastructure (especially transportation), and agricultural inputs required to bring about the acreage increase. There is in hand some research to support this acreage expansion. Moreover, Brazil's educational program is strong and in the area of research, work is problem oriented with a focus on what is practical. One principal problem is that of waste from the conversion process. Currently the practice is to dump the wastes into streams. As sugarcane production and conversion increase, this problem is expected to become one of great difficulty.

While the costs of biomass conversion to alcohol in Brazil are hard to obtain, it is estimated that alcohol is currently two to three times as expensive as fuels from imported petroleum. Current economic arguments to the contrary, Brazil's government has made the decision to go the biomass conversion route, expecting that as the cost of fossil fuels increases in the future, alcohol will look increasingly attractive. While Brazil's current strategy has been to grow crops for export to pay her oil import bill, her present and prospective objective entails non economic considerations, namely, not to be dependent on foreign sources of fuel. Since the longer term supply curve for sugar is very elastic, an increase in price would call forth a substantial increase in sugarcane production, say over a five-year period. Thus, the economic sacrifice the Brazilians are currently making would tend to decrease over time. She has long talked of self-reliance, and is even considering the expansion of charcoal as a fuel, based on eucalyptus trees which are ready for harvest in only seven years.

As incentive, the central government makes loans to companies formed to develop rural areas for sugarcane production and conversion at interest rates one-half that of inflation. She also sees this as a prime opportunity to develop her agricultural sector. In microeconomic terms, the scale of operations is largely related to control over the crop variety used and over the movement of the crop to the plant. This calls for a vertically integrated operation, hopefully with a plantation perimeter no larger than 30 kilometers. The Brazilians do not want huge plantations and processing plants.

An important facet of this program is that it will provide the opportunity to correct the severe regional disparity that exists between the northeast and the rest of Brazil. High officials maintain that these new projects will provide employment, stimulate interest, and help alleviate political problems in that area. Industrialization in the northeast will be the prime requisite of job creation.

Brazil is also looking for petroleum both on and offshore. If petroleum is discovered in sufficient quantities the Brazilians will have a real "failsafe" in that they will be able to shift easily from sugarcane to other crops both for export and to improve the diets of their people. With regard to other energy sources, there is some exploration for coal being undertaken. Solar and wind sources are being examined, but these two areas do not look particularly promising. On balance, the study team came away with a favorable impression of Brazil's energy program. The Brazilian public firmly supports the government's energy program. Since the public doesn't know that it is paying more than a competitive price for fuel, the government will be able to phase in alcohol at roughly the same price, and as far as the public is concerned, nothing will have happened except that Brazil will be using its own "materials."

Brazil could be the first country to shift to biomass conversion on any large scale, probably because it is the only country in the world that has the particular combination of circumstances adapted so well to make reliance on energy from biomass feasible. Since our circumstances are so different from those of Brazil, biomass conversion does not at this time, seem particularly applicable to the United States. We have much more natural gas, petroleum, and coal, and much less undeveloped agricultural land than do the Brazilians. Also, our energy needs are enormous compared to those of the Brazilians. With twice the population and 10 times the per capita consumption of energy, we need 20 times the quantity of energy they do. Another way of looking at the difference between countries is that if the price of United States gasoline were to double at the pump, it might be marginally productive to convert grain to alcohol. Some people feel that alcohol production would not only help solve future energy shortages but also would alleviate grain surpluses. The problem is that it would be very difficult to shut down a network of plants during times of grain shortage. Continuous process plants do not operate this way; people who are employed don't, nor do Congressmen who would support only a continuous flow of product and employment. Moreover, it takes an authoritarian government offering widespread subsidies to make something currently as costly (in an economic sense) as sugarcane conversion work. As a dramatic indication of the changeability and perhaps even shallowness of public opinion, just a few years ago people didn't think agriculture could feed people - now people think agriculture should be able to provide fuel needs.

18 Agricultural Chemicals: Boon or Bane?
David P. Harmon, Jr.

This paper addresses the principal issues involved in the use of agricultural chemicals, both pesticides and fertilizers. The objective is to determine how government policy might be used to mold a regulatory/ business environment that fulfills two seemingly incompatible goals: (1) to encourage innovation so that sustainable yield increases are possible in agriculture, and (2) to minimize ecological stress so that the public and the environment are provided high but realistic levels of protection. In order to meet our objective, the various issues and concerns must be set forth, the lack of knowledge must be understood, the atmosphere of emotionalism and hostility must be tempered, and analysis, rigorous yet realistic and given all the "unknowns" and "little knowns," must be carried out.

Questions, such as the effect of regulation (or its absence) on technological development, must be answered, Can a measure of "elasticity" for the agricultural quantity or quality we may have to give up be established? How much should we be willing to give up? If technology is "allowed" to meet the challenge posed by the need for sustainable yield increases, must we sacrifice at all?

THE ARGUMENTS: PRO AND CON

By way of introduction, it is necessary to understand the basic arguments for and against the use of agricultural chemicals. The arguments for the use of agricultural chemicals are economic and social. Some are very obvious, such as increasing yields (growing two ears of corn where one grew before); reducing crop losses to the 10,000 known insect species, the 8,000 fungi species, and the 2,000 known weed species, (1) and the greater availability of cheaper, better quality, diverse foods year round. Table 18.1 is relevant.

Table 18.1. Crop Yield Data, Selected Crops

	Cabbage (pounds per acre)	Tomatoes (pounds per acre)	Broccoli (pounds per acre)	Sweet Corn (1) (pounds per acre)	Corn (2) (bushels per acre)	Soybeans (bushels per acre)
No fertilizer 　No weed control 　No insecticide	0	0	0	9,500	88.5	0
Fertilizer 　No weed control 　No insecticide	0	0	0	14,000	83.2	0
No fertilizer 　Mechanical/hand weeding 　No insecticide	8,300	8,600	500	14,500	116.0	26.6
Fertilizer 　Mechanical/hand weeding 　No insecticide	7,900	11,000	475	15,500	124.5	41.0
No fertilizer 　Herbicide 　Insecticide	15,800	23,500	10,000	18,250	127.4	40.1
Fertilizer 　Herbicide 　Insecticide	16,500	30,000	11,750	21,000	143.7	48.0

(1) Used as a vegetable
(2) Used for oil, meal, and animal feed

Source: Dr. L.A. Anderson, Scan, 1972, The Shell Oil Company.

Less obviously, agricultural chemicals often substitute for the more traditional inputs of agriculture, land, labor, water, and machinery. Furthermore, agricultural chemicals make economies of scale increasingly possible, and make farming more certain for the farmer, which helps make easier credit available. Moreover, some of them, (such as DDT) have another side - providing public health protection. Finally, a steadily increasing amount of food will be needed to meet the twin demands of population growth and rising affluence.

The arguments against the use of agricultural chemicals are largely environmental and social. Economic arguments are fewer and more subtle, but nonetheless important. The principal negative argument is the purported damage to the environment, ranging from the breakdown of soil tilth and the eutrophication of bodies of water to toxicity to beneficial predators, other "nontarget" wildlife, and mammals, including man. The use of chemical fertilizers and pesticides is among the agricultural practices blamed for increasing losses of crops to insects and diseases. The intensive (to some observers, profligate) application of agricultural chemicals, known as the "washday" or "insurance" approach, is blamed, perhaps not without some reason, for the increasing genetic resistance to pesticides of certain pest species and for the breakdown of natural control mechanisms.

The arguments for the use of agricultural chemicals are more persuasive than those against, largely because of the rapid benefits accruing to farmer and consumer, and key instances of public health protection, such as that afforded against malaria by DDT. The arguments against the use of agricultural chemicals are, at this time, less persuasive, partly because of the emotionalism behind them and partly because measurements of environmental effects over an adequately long time span are just starting to become available. Moreover, the assessments of impact on the environment are often ambiguous, and often suspect because of the emotionalism of some groups over environmental matters. The arguments against the use of agricultural chemicals and the background for these arguments are discussed in the next section.

THE INTRODUCTION OF AGRICULTURAL CHEMICALS SINCE WORLD WAR II

Agricultural chemicals are among the thousands of chemical compounds that came into use after World War II. By today's standards, post World War II toxicity tests were inadequate at best, and at worst crude. Moreover, since any possible relationship between human cancer and chemicals was largely unsuspected, no carcinogenicity tests were run.

Today's concern is twofold. The first is that human diseases can be caused by synthesized chemical compounds become increasingly complex, they become more biologically hazardous because the normal chemistry of life will not be able to break them down and they may interact with each other as well as with naturally occurring chemical compounds to form extremely hazardous new chemical combinations.

The main reasons for concern about pesticides are: Limited knowledge of their effects on animals and humans; their widespread use on certain crops, and the varying degrees of their persistence in the environment.

To understand the scope of synthesized chemical compounds in our lives, it is useful to look at some statistics. Some 30,000 synthesized chemicals are now in use; (2) each year several hundred new ones are added. Over the past ten years, their volume of production has tripled, and industry can now synthesize chemicals "to order."

To understand the dilemma of their use is far more difficult. For example, how does one equate the potential threat to human health if a hazardous pesticide is used, versus the potential threat to human health if that same hazardous pesticide is unjustifiably withdrawn from use? The dilemma has many facets, the first of which is the fact that we live in a technologically based, highly complex society with a high standard of living. Our high standard of living has its prices, however. The more obvious portion of the price is exemplified by our conscious decisions to risk death or injury when we drive, or take an airplane, or engage in any one of many activities available because of our high standard of living. The not-so-obvious portion of the price are those elements over which we have little control, such as an increased life span which brings more of us into contact with the degenerative diseases of the heart and cancer, or with chemical compounds, the effects of which are little known today.

THE ANTICHEMICAL MOVEMENT

Fear, specifically the fear of cancer, plays a very important role in the dilemma. This fear is heightened by the realization that we have been widely exposed to an increasing number of synthetic chemical compounds over the past 20 to 25 years, and that cancer has the characteristic of latency. From this, some have drawn the conclusion that we may well experience a blossoming of "environmental" cancer. And as is so often the case when fear is present, rationality can be overwhelmed by the horrors of the unknown.

The horrors of the unknown are well demonstrated by the banning of DDT. The argument behind the ban is well known - that DDT biodegrades very slowly and becomes increasingly concentrated as it moves higher and higher in the food chain - thereby posing a grave threat to the higher orders of life, including man. But how many are aware that human fat, in which DDT concentrates, is rapidly metabolized, thus ridding the human body of DDT? Indeed, there is not one verified case of death or serious illness attributed to DDT, even when having been eaten. Ceylon (Sri Lanka) eradicated malaria with DDT, only to ban DDT and see a resurgence of malaria amounting to a million cases, three years after the ban went into effect. (3)

Pleas for rationality go unheard in the face of industrial accidents involving chemicals and disasters such as kepone, PBB, and DBCP. The uncommon case of company negligence makes it even more difficult to resolve the dilemma. Balance is not permitted. The growing antagonism of the environmentalists for the petrochemical industry is portrayed extremely well by Barry Commoner's comments on the Toxic Substances control Act (TSCA). He stated that this act can

...open what the industry may regard as a political Pandora's box... providing an arena in which the public will be able to intervene effectively in a process that is normally the exclusive domain of industrial managers: Decisions about what to produce and how to produce it. But it (TSCA) will do little to correct the problem at its source which is that petrochemical production is governed not so much by society's need for the products as by the industry's need to make a profit by manufacturing a growing variety of substances in the largest possible amounts. (4)

This antagonism is growing, not only within the ranks of the environmentalists, but also in certain government circles and among the people. When and how did it start?

With the publication of Rachel Carson's Silent Spring in 1962, the antichemical movement was born. The 1960s witnessed the formation and proliferation of both environmental groups and public interest law firms dedicated to "protecting" the public health. While DDT, the subject of Silent Spring, was the first successful scare campaign, the real catalyst for the antichemical movement was the 1969 Santa Barbara oil spill. The harm caused by the spill, and its potential threat to the environment, were visible to all. (5)

Why did the antichemical movement come about? A number of causes underlie this movement. First, and most important, is that our affluence, our longer life expectancy, and our leisure time give us the ability to be concerned with quality of life issues such as the environment. Being able to outlive the infectious diseases, we are now prone to the degenerative diseases (heart and cancer). Ease of earning a good living with a relatively high degree of security means that people can turn to other pursuits and concerns. Mankind is no longer completely subject to the whims of nature; instead he increasingly exercises a measure of control over nature. Nowhere is this clearer than in agriculture. Thus, nature is no longer seen as a tyrant, but as a provider - if only given a chance. Of the reasons underlying the antichemical movement, these two are the most understandable and perhaps even reasonable. The other reasons, however, are less understandable, less reasonable, and potentially very destructive.

For a long time the attitude that business is not socially responsible has grown and spread. The solution, according to some, is greater direction and management of business by government. More pernicious, however, is the viewpoint that there is an inherent incompatibility between the environment and economic activity. The scapegoat is technology, and the solution is to abolish its growth.

Especially where chemicals are concerned, people who are antagonistic toward business tend to operate as follows: They build a perceived problem up to a crisis, and then call for laws to create new government agencies with broad regulatory powers to "solve" the "problem." (6) The crusader mentality to improve the quality of life for the public by substituting government decisions for market decisions, shows little concern for the regulated industries or for the public they are supposed to protect. In some instances little thought is given to the effects of regulation on all aspects of economic activity, including employment, living standards, benefits of economic growth, and provision of essential goods and services. In short, these agencies are not committed to the preservation of free enterprise. In fact, they are antagonistic and in some cases hostile toward business.

SAFETY

The main issue is the safety of human health. Because of advances in measurement techniques, we can now detect chemicals in the environment at very low levels of concentration. The problem is that we are only just beginning to be able to measure their pervasiveness, and we have only rudimentary knowledge of their effects on the environment, including human beings.

The hazard or potential harm of a chemical compound comes from two sources: The use to which the chemical is put, and the inherent toxicity of the chemical itself. Because we have little reliable information on the effects of chemicals on human health, and because such information is value laden, society pays unnecessary expenses in the overly wide margins of safety in protective regulatory standards. It is widely felt that development of an adequate data base, coupled with further research in toxicology, epidemiology, and economic analysis, would be less expensive to society than the ad hoc, "when in doubt don't" type regulation of today.

Hazards may be categorized according to the likelihood that the hazard will occur. Chemicals with high toxicities usually have a threshold at which toxicity effects appear, and the effects usually are reversible. Limitations and control on usage normally are sufficient to control the hazard posed by high toxicity chemicals.

By contrast, chemicals which are carcinogenic or mutagenic tend not to have a threshold level; the likelihood of hazard is low, but difficult to predict. Because the personal cost, for example, of contracting cancer is so high, control must be very stringent; and it therefore is very costly.

Hazards of uncertain likelihood involve those of second and third order effects as one chemical compound interacts with another or others. And chemicals that are not hazardous in early use may become hazardous as they are used more extensively in different ways.

For an effective data base to be accumulated, data on each individual compound, its human and environmental toxicity effects, and its use patterns, present and anticipated, must be continually reassessed. The same is true of predictive toxicological systems. Since the regulator usually is pressed to make a decision, the information derived may never been fully developed. Therefore, a surveillance or monitoring system is needed which feeds back information to reevaluate the first estimates the increase the prevision of these estimates of benefit and risk.

The cost of trade-offs are those of accumulating more complete, precise use and toxicological information versus the costs of more stringent controls arising from a relatively imprecise data base. The problem has been, and will likely continue to be, that ad hoc actions are usually taken under a combination of extreme public pressure and tight deadlines. Thus, the accumulation of more and better information becomes a long run objective.

FERTILIZERS

While most past and current controversy centers on pesticides, fertilizers are receiving increasing attention. The issues range from nutritional qualities of crops grown with chemical fertilizers to possible ozone layer depletion by increased production and use of nitrogenous fertilizers. Fertilizers are increasingly perceived as being important and as requiring the attention of government. These issues are important because they offer the opportunity to clear up certain misconceptions, to point up areas where knowledge is lacking, and to demonstrate how technology can be used to resolve problems.

Increasing concern over food safety and nutritional quality has resulted in an increasingly widespread misconception that organically grown foods are more nutritious, safer, and of higher quality than those grown with agricultural chemicals. Antagonism toward agricultural chemicals and food additives has led some to condemn all chemicals, including fertilizers, and to call for a return to a "natural" system of food production.

Our first step is to look at the facts of plant usage of nutrients and the determinants of plant nutritive value. Plants can only take up elements in their inorganic forms. Therefore, organic matter which is added to soil must be changed by soil microorganisms into their inorganic forms for them to be usable. An alleged advantage of organic materials is that some of them provide a slow, steady release of nutrients over the growing season. Inorganic (chemical) fertilizers, however, are compounded to duplicate the slow, steady releaseof nutrients of organic matter. The nutritive value of a plant is not determined by the type of fertilizer (organic versus inorganic) used. Genetic makeup, climate, light, location, and the kind and amount of basic nutrients available determine nutritive value.

Organic matter added to soil provides many benefits. It makes soil easier to till, increases soil porosity (thereby allowing rain to soak in rapidly), helps maintain moisture so that drought effects are ameliorated, and resists water erosion and "crusting" from heavy rainfall.

To date, there is no evidence to show that foods grown organically are nutritionally any better or worse than foods grown with chemical fertilizer. On the other hand, inorganic fertilizers offer the opportunity, through formulation, to easily provide missing trace elements to plants.

In fact, inorganic fertilizers are incredibly flexible in terms of application. In solid form they can be properly placed in the correct quantities at the right times, and thereby be chemically and cost effective. In liquid form, they can be added to water to be used in the process called "fertigation" - irrigation and fertilization. Organic fertilizers do not offer such flexibility.

Another misconception is that United States soils have been overfarmed, depleted of their major nutrients. It is not true that the use of chemical fertilizers has allowed the soils' naturally occurring trace elements to decline - thus threatening crops' nutritional quality - or that the tilth, porosity, and the nitrogen-fixing bacteria of the soils have been gradually destroyed.

What really happens in agriculture? In a macro perspective, agriculture's history is one of man turning poor soils into productive ones through investment, labor, and better farming practices. The sandy soils of the United States' Eastern seaboard are now among the world's most productive. They were transformed into highly productive vegetable growing soils through the addition of chemical fertilizer, lime, both animal and green manure, and better farming practices. With the exception of "pockets" of soils with naturally occurring high fertility, such as the Po River Valley, the rich soils of Illinois, and certain areas of Argentina, and the Ukraine, farmers worldwide have taken poor, rocky, infertile soils and made them fertile. (7) Such is the case of Western Europe, Japan, and most of the United States.

On a micro scale, Dr. Samuel R. Aldrich, Assistant Director of the Agricultural Experiment Station of the University of Illinois, closely examined trends in soil fertility in that state from 1800 to the present. He determined that over the first 150 years organic matter and nitrogen content of the soil decreased about 40 percent. The decrease was due to conventional early farming practices - "organic" farming practices. Only with the widespread use of inorganic fertilizers were these trends halted, in the cases of nitrogen and organic matter, and reversed in the cases of phosphorous and potassium. Figure 18.1 clearly shows the effects of early versus modern farming practices on soil fertility.

The long-term breakdown of the humus content of the soil (harming tilth and porosity) was stopped by better farming practices. Buildup of humus can be accomplished by returning decomposable crop residues to the soil. This is largely a matter of the farmer recognizing that it is economically beneficial to do so. Moreover, the proper use of chemical fertilizers can correct any potential decline in soil nutrient concentrations.

However, we have less knowledge in two other areas of environmental concern. Initial studies (8) of the effects of nitrogen and phosphate fertilizers on bodies of fresh water show that chemical

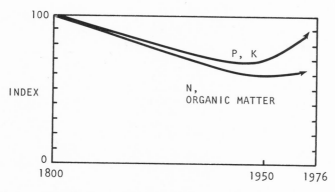

Fig. 18.1. Trends in Soil Fertility in Illinois

Source: Samuel R. Aldrich, "Some Effects of Crop Production
Technology on Environmental Quality," _Bioscience_ Vol. 22, no. 2
(February 1972): 91.

---

fertilizer is unlikely to cause eutrophication - the destruction of the
bacterial action that neutralizes organic wastes. Furthermore, potentially high nitrate levels in water, a threat to human health, do not
appear to have occurred. We lack data on the long-term effects of
natural and chemical nutrients being leached and eroded out of the soil.
We simply do not know what happens to the remainder after subtracting
plant uptake of nutrients.

The most speculative concern is that the increased manufacture and
use of nitrogen fertilizer may cause a significant loss to the earth's
ozone layer over the next 30 to 40 years. The hypothesized harm stems
from the process of denitrification, through which nitrogen is returned
to the atmosphere, partly in a chemical form destructive to ozone
atoms. If this concern is valid, it is far worse than that of fluorocarbon
propellants (aerosols), because nitrogen fertilizer is an essential
product. Fluorocarbon propellants are convenience products, easily
curtailed by substituting other propelling methods. The handling of the
fluorocarbon issue is important because it may presage how nitrogen
fertilizers are dealt with if it should in fact be found that they cause
harm to the earth's ozone shield.

THE "OLD" AND THE "NEW" REGULATORS

As an introduction to government regulation of agricultural chemicals, it is useful to examine the genesis of the current wave of
regulatory activities, the principal characteristics of the regulators, and
obvious and not-so-obvious costs of regulations. The "old" regulators
are economic regulators in a fairly strict sense of the word. They focus
on markets, on rates, and an obligation to serve. The best examples are

the Interstate Commerce Commission, the Federal Communications commission, the Civil Aeronautics Board, and state public utility commissions. In general they tend to protect the stability and the rights of the industries they regulate. By contrast, the "new" regulators concentrate on many different activities of business, and thereby affect many more industries and people. The Food and Drug Administration, the Occupational Safety and Health Administration, and the Environmental Protection Agency are in this category. They concentrate on the effect of business transactions, in its broadest sense - the conditions under which goods are produced, the characteristics of products, consumer ignorance, and the presence of "externalities" such as adverse environmental consequences on society and on the "innocent bystander" from the standpoints of health, safety, and the environment. (9)

Forces Behind the Current Spread of Regulations

The principal force behind today's environmental regulation is not increased deterioration of the environment but rather increased public demand for a cleaner, healthier environment. Our increasing affluence and high standard of living permits us the "luxury" of pursuing numerous social goals, including better environmental quality. In addition, interdependencies in the natural and social sciences are increasingly recognized as these sciences become more sophisticated. Part of this increased sophistication is the heightened ability to detect and measure, but it does not yet extend to understanding the effects on humans of long-term exposure to minute quantities of chemical compounds.

With increased detection and measurement capabilities and increased public interest in environmental matters, industrial accidents involving chemicals such as the Michigan PBB case and, worse, industrial negligence, fan public and environmentalists' demands for regulation of business activities. This movement started early in the 1960s. By the mid-1970s it had grown into a network of government agencies which often compete with one aother. Furthermore, the growth of federal agencies has, in some cases, forced state and municipal government agencies to increase their regulation of local business activities, thus requiring large, more comprehensive bureaucracies. Regulatory agencies have shown little interest in balancing the benefits and costs of decisions. More often than not they resist innovative solutions to problems, and they often make decisions on the basis of extremely inadequate information. These actions, however, are now major factors in determining the cost of many goods and services, and even in the amount of consumer choice available.

The primary justification for the "old" regulation is protection of the consumer from monopoly power. Another important justification is to assure adequate and nondisciplinary service. The "new" regulatory activity, however, aims to protect the public against harm which may arise from many human activities, including those of business. Since the government has an important responsibility for public health, the need for regulation in this area becomes clearer in view of the explosion in organic chemistry, the rapid growth in number of chemical compounds in the economy since World War II, and the kepone, PBB, PCB, and DBCP accidents/disasters.

It doesn't take very many PBBs and kepones to make the public skeptical and suspicious of the chemical industry. It also is clear that legislators will err on the side of safety, since not doing so may prove costly on election day.

Regulation arises because of the fear of the effects of chemicals, the incompleteness of scientific knowledge, and the increasing volume and variety of products incorporating new chemical compounds upon which the public becomes dependent. Furthermore, the increasing ability to detect and measure smaller and smaller quantities of chemical substances without understanding their effects on human health and on the environment add impetus to increasing regulation; this is magnified by occasional industrial accidents such as that involving kepone. Toxicity is considered dangerous to health in the sense of harming well-being, rather than as a definable, measurable, abnormal response. This is consonant with our desire for a better way of life and our tendency to equate good health with happiness. This springs in part from our increased life span, and from having conquered the acute infectious diseases.

The question is: How much control and what kind of control? too much regulation causes society to suffer since innovation may be reduced and the food supply perhaps diminished. Ad hoc control, focusing on individual situations and substances, erodes our ability to protect the environment and human health because it offers loopholes, undermines the protection given by sound general principles, and makes national policy making very difficult.

Characteristics of the New Style Regulators

The new style regulatory agencies are created to deal with highly controversial and difficult issues. They are expected to operate in the "public interest", an often elusive concept whose meaning varies with the interest group defining it and the industry involved.

Regulatory agencies are never subject to the discipline of the marketplace. No economic incentives guide their decisions, and they can seldom be sued. The only potential competition facing an agency is that another agency may take over its prerogatives. Poor management, inefficiency, or lack of capital rarely put an agency out of business. Even worse, regulatory agencies tend not to be subject to the system of checks and balances that guides the rest of government.

Regulators tend to move very slowly and are characterized by a very rigid attitude toward solving problems. It is no wonder that innovative solutions are avoided, caution is the watchword, and "the squeaky wheel gets the oil." An atmosphere of compromise and "splitting the difference" characterizes the old style regulator. The degree of difference splitting is determined by the economic and political strength of the industry in question. The choice is between economic efficiency and fairness to all parties involved. Economic efficiency is losing out. In the decision-making process, economic benefits and costs are often secondary considerations, at best, in the minds of many regulators.

COSTS OF REGULATION

The most obvious costs of regulation are the direct ones - the burden of collecting data and the costs of complying with government regulations. The indirect costs are less obvious. They affect industry and society as a whole, and may be higher than the costs of compliance and red tape. Moreover, they have the dimensions of subtlety and a certain degree of perniciousness. For instance, regulation, or even the threat of regulation, introduces uncertainty into normal business transactions. As a result, new technologies may not be pursued, new ventures may not be undertaken, and alternative suppliers may not be sought. The risk of new endeavors or breaking continuity in the event of policy intervention may become unsupportably high.

Institutional relationships, such as management/labor bargaining, may be altered by regulation. Industry cost structures may be changed by regulations. Compliance with regulation may force large increases in capital investment in plant and equipment to achieve minimum overall economies of scale. For example, water pollution controls in the metal finishing industry may dictate up to a fivefold increase in scale of plant to achieve reasonable efficiency. The characteristics of production may also be affected. Efficiency may now require a reorganization of the production process, possibly requiring seasonality to one of continous flow, for example. This is a case of the regulatory tail wagging the industrial dog.

Worse still, increased capital costs caused by regulations can effectively raise barriers to entry, thus reducing competition. Trends toward oligopoly and increased industry concentration invite increased regulation. The lower cost sector of an industry will of course gain competitive advantage at the expense of the higher cost sector Furthermore, the degree of cyclicity of an industry's activities may be heightened by both "lumpy" capital expenditures engendered by regulation and by diversion of limited capital from planned-for expansion into compliance expenditures, thus bringing about short-term, often large, product price increases. High costs of compliance, along with rising capital and energy costs, tend to change decreasing cost industries into increasing cost industries, thereby fueling inflation. Increases in production capacity lag behind demand because of higher costs, and management's reluctance to create any appearance of windfall gain on existing plant as product prices are raised to cover higher costs of incremental capacity, since such sudden excess profits tend to attract attention. (10)

Several indirect costs of regulation directly affect society. The choice of products and services is reduced for the consumer. The tempo of technological innovations may be slowed for the reasons cited above with consequences for society that are unknown and therefore not measurable. Certain groups in society will benefit at the expense of others. All automobile owners pay for mandatory pollution control equipment while the inhabitants of congested urban areas benefit from the added cost. Optimal social welfare is rarely attained since the balance of costs and benefits across different segments of society is so hard to achieve. On a political scale, the state's power is increased at the expense of the individual's autonomy. Increasing the state's power involves a potential that the power will be abused, that private initiative will be weakened, and that a "dependent" citizenry will be created. (11)

The inability to place a figure or a range of figures on the indirect costs is best demonstrated by the wide range of estimates for compliance costs (a "direct" cost of regulation) that the Toxic Substances Control Act will entail. The estimates range from a low of $100 million to a high of $2 billion. (12) These indirect costs even extend to academic research facilities where the pace of research may be slowed by compliance requirements.

REGULATION AND AGRICULTURAL CHEMICALS

The reasons behind the increasing regulation of agricultural chemicals have been set forth above. Fears (justified or not) of the unknown and somewhat known, industrial accidents, occasional industrial negligence, and a society made increasingly aware of the complexities and possible hazards of modern life all underpin the spread of regulation of chemical substances, including agricultural chemicals. Because the use of agricultural chemicals and fertilizers is so widespread and so important to agricultural productivity, it is clear that regulations should be administered in an orderly effective manner, and that regulators should be cognizant, not only of the risks, but also of the benefits associated with agricultural chemicals. In short, a thorough balancing of societal risks and benefits based on all available scientific and economic data is called for. Only then can reasonable decisions be made whether to continue, suspend, or ban current agricultural chemicals, and whether to permit the introduction of new agricultural chemicals.

Unfortunately, the record to date is not encouraging. It is replete with emotionalism, speculation, and use of sketchy evidence. DBCP (dibromochoropropane) caused some cases of sterility and raised the fear of cancer among male workers blending the compound. This recent case raises the legitimate question, in an emotion charged atmosphere, of how many other DBCPs are in the environment waiting to strike with unknown consequences and damages. Unfortunately, the increasing ability to detect and measure dosage does not extend to measurement of effective human health; under current circumstances, this often leads to costly, ineffective, unreasonable regulation.

COSTLY REGULATION

It is estimated that it takes, on an average, 11 years and $10 million to introduce a new pesticide. Few companies, save the largest, have the resources to justify such an investment. The increasing, often excessive, costs of compliance slows pesticide development as firms shift their resources to the defense of their current products. In 1966, sixty months were required on average, between product discovery and label clearance. Today, about 100 months are required. (13) A recent estimate of how much Dow Chemical spends annually to comply with Environmental Protection Agency regulation of its pesticide products follows:

Testing	$29.5 million
Reporting	5.5 million
Delayed Production and Marketing	6.0 million
Abandoned Plant and Equipment	40.0 million
	$81.0 million

The $40 million abandonment figure is telling.

INEFFECTIVE REGULATION

The regulation of products, services, or business activities, when based on ineffective laws or even on effective laws which are poorly administered, does not serve the public's best interest. The regulation of agricultural chemicals is often indicative of poorly served public interest. Moreoever, such regulation is counterproductive when inadequate thought has been given to its consequences. As pointed out earlier, the time and expenditure required to get a new pesticide on the market can be afforded only by large companies with adequate resources. The obvious effect of this is the withdrawal of smaller firms from pesticide production.

Not so obvious, however, is the counterproductivity which regulation causes for itself when it is inadequately thought through. Being "location specific," agriculture often requires inputs that are tailored to specific local conditions. For example, a particular pesticide which is very effective in one geographic area may not be as effective for the same pest in another area. Such "location specificity" calls for "narrow spectrum" pesticides, which small and large companies can make. Furthermore, "narrow spectrum" pesticides can be formulated, or tailored, to maximize impact on the target pest while minimizing impact on non target beneficial organisms. The lengthy time and high expense of regulatory compliance preclude the development of such chemicals because the smaller firm cannot afford it and the larger company can only afford to develop and market broad spectrum pesticides. The market must be sufficiently large for the company to recoup its investment and make a profit. In addition, broad spectrum pesticides often lack selectivity in 'targeting;' i.e., they kill nontarget organisms as well as target ones. Part of the intent of the regulation is protection of the environment in all its aspects.

After five years of legislative debate the Toxic Substances Control Act went into effect on January 1, 1977. Disasters and accidents involving mercury, asbestos, vinyl chloride, PCBs, kepone, and various carcinogens found in drinking water supplies led to the adoption of this act. Its purpose is to identify and prevent environmental dangers before new chemical compounds and new uses of existing compounds become established. Few would dispute the intent of this act.

Its effectiveness, however, is another matter. The act provides for the screening and testing of new chemical compounds prior to their entry into the marketplace. Existing chemicals, which are suspected of being hazardous, are also to be tested. First, the large number of chemicals to be tested cannot be adequately handled, given the scarcity of funds budgeted by the government and the shortage of private and public testing facilities and competent personnel. Rudimentary comparison techniques and lack of data will preclude the environmental- economic cost-benefit analyses called for by the act. Furthermore, it makes industry responsible for the generation and validation of toxicity data. One may justifiably ask whether industry is likely to generate data that will be detrimental to the success of its products. How will accountability be created, apportioned, and enforced in an economy and environment in which there are already thousands of chemical compounds in widespread use, with little known about their effects, current and potential? While their presence is detectable, their effects at low concentrations are extremely difficult to measure, even to anticipate.

REASONABLE AND UNREASONABLE REGULATION

The Federal Environmental Pesticide Control Act of 1972 (amending and expanding the Federal Insecticide, Fungicide and Rodenticide Act of 1947) includes provisions which add some degree of balance to it. According to FEPCA, any ban on individual pesticides, whether total or partial, must not result in undue hazard to public health and welfare. Use of unregistered (prohibited) pesticides is provided for in the case of emergency situations. The act offers incentives for research and development on new pesticides by giving a degree of protection to the investment a manufacturer makes in generating the data to obtain registration.

Unfortunately, emotionalism and a highly politicized atmosphere seem to prevail. A list follows of actions by the Environmental

Protection Agency which have drawn severe criticism.

1. Abandonment of the unreasonable risk standard, and adoption of the "any risk" standard for current and new registrations of pesticides. (15) Under this standard, the presence of any risk is sufficient to suspend the use of or ban a pesticide. Such a standard is contrary to law (FEPCA1972), and contrary to common sense.

2. Abandonment of the threshold exposure level concept. The Aldrin/Dieldrin cancellation order led the EPA administrator to conclude that there was no "safe" level of exposure for humans to these chemicals, and that the threshold exposure level concept had no relevance in the case of carcinogens. This action also affronts common sense. After all, humans are constantly exposed to low levels of naturally occurring carcinogenicity - ultraviolet from the sun, carcinogens in the air and food, and even manufactured by their bodies in the production of sex hormones. It would seem reasonable that the population could be protected from unacceptable carcinogenic hazards by establishing satisfactory tolerance levels, both through laboratory tests of animals, as well as through human experience with high levels of exposure by occupation and by geographic area.

3. Distortion of the risk/benefit balance. The tendency is to give maximum weight to the risk side of the equation and minimum weight to the benefit side. Moreover, likelihood of occurrence is given only slight consideration. This distortion is evident in the equating of benign tumors found in test animals with malignant ones (Aldrin/Dieldrin) in the acceptance of single laboratory animal tests as conclusive proof of hazard to man (Aldrin/Dieldrin decision), and in rejection of epidemiological studies demonstrating absence of risk to humans (Aldrin/Dieldrin and DDT actions). (16)

To be effective and reasonable, regulation must recognize that technology is crucial if society is to flourish. The objective is not less technology, but better technology. Methods must be developed to help anticipate the effects, both positive and negative, of the application of new technologies and knowledge. The control of pests is necessary in all parts of the world because pests are a serious threat to crops, livestock, and humans.

The final section of this paper will examine technological and farm management advances that will help achieve the dual objective of increasing agricultural productivity and maintaining reasonable levels of environmental protection.

In summary, almost everyone agrees that the regulations cause a great deal of red tape, higher costs, and fewer choices. The more serious side is its often high costs to society in terms of economics and contitutionality. Many feel that the regulators with judicial, legislative, and executive powers violate our system of checks and balances.

TECHNOLOGICAL ADVANCE MAY LESSEN
THE NEED FOR REGULATION

Three broad interrelated areas of technological advances have the potential of significantly reducing the need for agricultural chemicals and providing sustainable rates of <u>increased</u> agricultural productivity. All three have the very interesting characteristic of being apolitical. They are photosynthesis, biological nitrogen fixation, and genetic improvement. If one keeps in mind that agriculture basically processes solar energy and that green plants are net renewable <u>producers</u> of food and energy, it becomes evident that expertise and technology should be directed toward exploiting these characteristics of green plants and agriculture. This is called mission oriented basic research.

Potential advances in the area of photosynthesis range from photosynthate partitioning, i.e., the control of the plant mechanisms that distribute the products of photosynthesis that regulate yield, to improving plant architecture and anatomy for better "harvesting" of the sun and better utilization of carbon dioxide to promote growth. Biological nitrogen fixation, the assimilation of atmospheric nitrogen by soil organisms, accounts for about 70 percent of the total nitrogen fixed on earth. The other 30 percent is fixed industrially, i.e., nitrogen fertilizer, for crop production. A major limiting factor in biological nitrogen fixation is photosynthates. (17)

Greater agricultural productivity appears to be possible with carbon dioxide enrichment of plant leaf atmospheres. Moreoever, atmospheric nitrogen fixation is enhanced. Breeding crops with increased nitrogen fixing abilities is another area offering good chances for success. 18)

The third interrelated area is genetic improvement. Standard plant breeding techniques have already accounted for vast improvements in crop productivity. Changing plant architecture so that more solar energy is harvested, thus leading to increased phyosynthate production, is only one example of current successes. The possible transfer of the biological nitrogen fixing capacity of the legumes to non legumes offers stunning potential. Breeding in pest, disease, and environmental stress resistances, as well as genetic manipulation for improved nutritional qualities, are examples of "better technology."

It is clear that the development of crops with the aforementioned characteristics will reduce dependence on agricultural chemicals. As need for agricultural chemicals declines, the need to regulate them should also diminish. Obviously, the development of such technologies and techniques will require time, years or perhaps decades. How do we span the gap? How do we get from here to there? This is the topic of the final section of this paper.

EDUCATING THE REGULATOR

Industry can influence regulation in several ways. Lobbying and public relations efforts are the most obvious. It can also attempt to educate specific "audiences of interest" within the general public. Education of this sort is a long-term, continuous undertaking, requiring a large commitment of personnel and finanacial resources. Audiences of interest range from employees to homemakers, from shareholders to educated laymen. The payoff is slow, hard to measure, and may seem tenuous; nevertheless, substantial efforts can produce results.

Industry can adopt a policy of "self-realization," ranging from the adoption and monitoring of product and safety standards to the organization of health, safety, and environmental research. The idea here is to take the initiative away from the regulator on the grounds that the industry often has better expertise and more physical and financial resources available than the government regulator. In a less emotional and politicized atmosphere, a well-conceived self-regulation policy would probably be fairly successful in minimizing government regulatory activities. But today the problem is one of industry's credibility. Will the public and the government believe that the industry is truly policing itself?

The most productive short-term strategy, however, entails the recognition that the level and degree of regulatory activity are not likely to diminish; they are almost certain to intensify instead. Recognizing the inevitability of increasing regulation, the Weyerhaeuser lumber firm initiated a strategy of "seizing the data base," which involved the interaction between company technical personnel with their regulatory counterparts. This interaction helps to increase the regulators' understanding of the technical factors inherent in products and processes. Weyerhaeuser's philosophy is quite succinct: An informed regulator produces more reasonable regulations. (19)

RECOMMENDATIONS OF THE NATIONAL ACADEMY OF SCIENCES

In 1975 the National Academy of Sciences published a study entitled Decision making for Regulating Chemicals in the Environment. (20) This study is particularly relevant in light of the increasingly preeminent role the Federal government is taking in the regulation of toxic substances. Its principal findings and recommendations for intelligent and reasonable regulation of chemical substances follow:

1. Information

Improvement in both quantity and quality. Because of inadequate investment in the toxicological, epidemiological, and economic data base, society pays an unnecessarily high cost for an imprecise determination of hazard. Since information is inadequate, the safety margin must be greater and the controls more stringent if society is to be protected.

Early and open exchange of information by all affected parties before and during decision-making processes. The objective is to reduce dependence on lengthy judicial processes to resolve disputes. Moreover, courts are not as knowledgeable as regulatory agencies and companies regarding the scientific and economic aspects of chemicals and their regulation.

Development of an equitable, "secure" means of divulging proprietary information for use in the decision-making process, without compromising the information's competitive aspects.

Better use of available information packaged in a form that is relevant to, and usable by, the decision maker; e.g., to speak in terms of billions of dollars of cost to the economy has less impact on the legislator (who is very accustomed to dealing with "astronomical" sums) than does speaking in terms of dollars of cost impact per household in his district; better coordination and use of available information systems.

2. Decision-Making Process

Open to participation by all potentially affected parties.

Improved quality of information so that decision-making implementation and acceptance are facilitated.

Explicit disclosures of all factors upon which decisions are based.

Use of cost/benefit analysis to increase the amount of informed judgment (decrease the amount of uninformed intuition), recognizing however that highly formalized cost/benefit analysis is seldom satisfactory in evaluating all the costs and benefits of regulatory decisions. An integral part of the decision-making process is the good judgment of an experienced decision maker. Recognition that costs and benefits will be different, depending on whether the focus is the chemical or the regulatory action. For example, to focus on regulatory action makes hazard reduction a benefit and benefit reduction of the chemical a cost. The decision-making process must allow for consideration of trade-offs, uncertainty, alternatives, decision points, and lack of information.

Recognition and appreciation in regulatory standards that chemical substances often appear in different mediums (air, water, green plants, workplace, home, products) with different types and levels of exposures for humans. For example, no single agency has responsibility for possible synergistic effects of chemical compounds.

It should be clearly recognized that factors such as aesthetics, human health, life and equity, involve value judgments which should be dealt with explicitly.

To reduce the degree of sociopolitical biases in the regulatory decision, the members of the regulatory agency should be free of political accountability.

The pressure of unnecessarily tight deadlines should be eased.

Uniformity in standards of evaluation may not be totally desirable; essential tests for some chemical compounds may be missed, while unnecessary tests may be required for others.

3. Other Elements

Recognition of the difficulties and the disadvantages of carrying the burden of proof that new use or continued use (after hazard has been established) is desirable for society. Precise scientific evidence of health and environmental effects is difficult to obtain, data collection costs are extremely high, and the burden of proof can change, as to degree of proof required and responsible party.

Acceptance of the concept of "socially acceptable risk." This concept is particularly valid for dealing with agricultural chemicals which involve substantial benefits to society..

THE "SCIENCE COURT" AND MEDIATION (21)

Because of the scarcity and poor quality of information needed for effective public policy decisions, and the controversy, emotionalism, and politicalization which accompany the debate about chemical substances, the concept of the "Science Court" has been suggested. Since the effects of chemical substances on the environment and on man are part of the frontiers of today's scientific knowledge, much disagreement and controversy characterize the debate. Nevertheless, public policy decisions must still be made. The purpose of the "Science Court," a body of scientific experts, would be to assess evidence and arguments about controversial scientific issues. Such courts would hold adversary proceedings that are now the domain of the judicial courts at a much earlier stage than is now the case; these proceedings are now often very lengthy, imprecise, and uncertain. Once evidence and arguments have been weighed, the Science Court would then pass on its assessment of the facts to legislators, regulators, and the public. The principal arguments for and against Science Courts and one alternative which has been suggested follow:

Strengths

1. Policy would be based on scientific evaluation rather than clever legalistic arguments. Scientific evaluation would be superior to the judicial process of conflicting appeals to laymen.

2. Hard facts would provide a stronger foundation for discussion.

3. Uncertainties would be reduced, and in some cases, eliminated.

4. The tentativeness of scientific truth would be emphasized by a review process of policy issues which remain controversial.

5. The sophistication and expertise of the Science Court would severely discourage factual distortions.

6. The Science Court would permit the scientific community to fulfill a very basic and moral responsibility to the public - the provision of a factual basis on which to make public policy decisions.

Weaknesses

1. In public policy issues, facts and values can't be totally separated.

2. In areas where there is little available scientific information, the adversary nature of the Science Court may increase public confusion about the facts and lead to further mistrust of the scientific community and technology.

3. The Science Court, encompassing the prestige of science and the fairness of due process, could slip into the trap of making value judgments on the issues.

4. The adversary process could be the Science Court's undoing. It is a polarizing process which emphasizes winning rather than the discovery of truth. Its objective is to resolve disputes, but the objective of science is the discovery of truth. Truth is only one factor in the adversary process.

5. The technical dimensions of issues may be overemphasized to the detriment of social, economic, and political factors.

6. Safeguards would have to be found for protecting confidential product data.

7. Certain organization requirements must be met for a Science Court to be truly viable in the public interest:

   (a) The Court's primary obligation would be to the public.

   (b) The client agency would not define the issues beforehand, determine who comes before the court, or make the decisions.

   (c) The Court would not limit itself to the technical or scientific aspects of the issues.

As an alternative to the "Science Court" concept, mediation has been suggested. A mediator who was felt to be thoroughly trustworthy by all parties would strive to elicit the facts through a rather special communications process. Each party, after reviewing data, summaries, and reasonings from the other interested parties, would then argue the others' positions to ensure better understanding of what each thinks he is fighting for or against. The process would culminate in a joint paper which states original position, points of difference, what has changed during the process, and the remaining differences and the reasons why. The objective is not conflict resolution by compromise, but rather conflict resolution by better communication and understanding.

The prime requirement is a highly ethical, skilled mediator who will not allow conflicting parties to stray too far from their basic positions. The process allows scientific facts as well as values to be treated, brings opposing parties together, and supposedly results in an effort on all sides addressing the same questions in the same language, fully aware of each other's arguments.

GETTING FROM HERE TO THERE

How do we bridge the years between today and the future, when mission oriented basic research in photosynthesis, biological nitrogen fixation, and genetic improvement will have significantly reduced our dependence on agricultural chemicals? It is encouraging to note that technology and management techniques today offer us the means of spanning the gap. Technological advances coupled with improved farming practices should permit the maintenance of a satisfactory environment and high levels of agricultural production. The key will be a reasonable regulatory environment that will, by virtue of its reasonableness, permit innovation to continue.

The most promising means of ecologically and economically acceptable pest control is integrated pest management (IPM). IPM has four basic components: Resistant plant varieties, agricultural chemicals, biological controls, and improved cultural practices. As a system, it involves the coordinated use of many technologies and farm management techniques. IPM ranges from appropriate cultural practices, simple pest prevention, and appropriate timing of agricultural operations to judicious use of agricultural chemicals, coupled with sophisticated biological means such as insect attractants, sterile insects, and plant growth regulators. Its objective is to optimize pest control during the entire growth to market cycle, and to minimize the adverse impact of pesticides on non target organisms. It aims at reducing the pest population to an economically acceptable level. By understanding how and when to intervene in order to prevent or reduce pest losses, the cost to the environment and to the farmer can be reduced, while yields can be increased.

The principal requirement for success of integrated pest management is increased education of an incentive for the farmer to use it more widely. Because pest populations and types vary according to area, crop, stage of growth of crop, weather, and farming practices, pest control is exceedingly complex. The educational/informational requisites are well-trained people to carry out "on-time, on-line" pest management. Furthermore, predictive pest management models must be developed, available to all growers, with provision for widespread information feedback from growers. A system of timely advice and help to farmers, improved feedback from them, and increased knowledge of environmental processes should permit pest problems to be anticipated before they occur.

CONCLUSION

Pesticides and fertilizers should certainly be used cautiously. As knowledge of their effects on health and the environment grows, pest and disease losses can be safely decreased, yields increased, and the quality of food improved. More importantly, however, if technological advances are not stifled by unreasonable regulations, they will permit food production with little adverse impact on the environment. As we become more affluent, we can afford to impose higher standards on ourselves. We must not forget, however, that since we are better off than we have ever been, we have more capability to identify and forestall any serious environmental problems which agricultural activity may entail. Foresight, appropriate research, and the application of the results should ensure a better, healthier environment and a high level of agricultural productivity.

The spectacular gains in United States agricultural productivity since World War II would not have been possible without the use of agricultural chemicals, and chemical fertilizers in particular. If in fact the "wash day" approach to application of agricultural chemicals has harmed the environment, the answer is better technology (not less technology), better management techniques, not a return to axe and hoe agriculture. More readily degradable pesticides, controlled release fertilizers, judicious application of chemicals, and the concept of integrated pest management are only a few of the means at hand. Man does have the ability to use technology to benefit both himself and the environment.

NOTES

(1) A.W.A. Brown, et al., eds., Crop Productivity-Research Imperatives (East Lansing: Michigan Agricultural Experiment Station, 1975) p. 275.

(2) "Controlling Toxic Substances," Resources, Resources for the Future, January-March 1977, p. 1.

(3) Rita Gray Beatty, The DDT Myth, (New York: John Day, 1973) p. 12.

(4) Barry Commoner, "The Promise and Perils of Petrochemicals." The New York Times Magazine. September 25, 1977.

(5) Raymond M. Momboisse, "Where We Were, Where We Are, Where We Are Going." Paper given at the Chemical Specialties Manufacturers Association, Inc., Hollywood, Florida, December 12-18, 1976, p. 4.

(6) Ibid., p. 5.

(7) Theodore Schultz, Agricultural Economics (Chicago: University of Chicago, 1974)

(8) George H. Enfield "Water Quality in Midwest Streams." Paper presented at the Midwest Fertilizer Conference, Chicago, February 17, 1970.

(9) William Lilley III, and James C. Miller III, "The New 'Social Regulation,'" The Public Interest, Spring 1977, pp. 52-53.

(10) Robert A. Leone, "The Real Costs of Regulation," Harvard Business Review, November-December 1977, pp. 461-464.

(11) Peter H. Schuck, "Why Regulation Fails," Harpers, September 1975, pp. 24-26.

(12) Jean A. Briggs, "Toxic? To Whom?" Forbes, September 1, 1977, p. 66.

(13) Momboisse, "Where We Were," p. 6.

(14) Briggs, "Toxic?" p. 66.

(15) Chapman Chemical Co., et al. Consolidated Mercury Cancellation Hearing, 41 Fed. Reg. 16497, 16499, as reported by Raymond D. Momboisse, "Where We Were," p. 11.

(16) Ibid, pp. 12-13.

(17) Ralph W.F. Hardy and V.D. Havelka, "Nitrogen Fixation Research: A Key to World Food," Science 188 (1975): 633-43; "Photosynthate as a Major Factor Limiting Nitrogen Fixation by Field Grown Legumes with Emphasis on Soybeans." In Contributions to the Scientific Literature, Sect. IV. Biology Central Research and Development Department, Experimental Station, E.I. Du Pont De Nemours, Wilmington, Delaware (1975), pp. 58-76.

(18) Peter J. Dart and J.M. Day, "Nitrogen Fixation in the Field Other than Nodules," in Soil Microbiology, ed. n. Walker. (London: Butterworth Scientific Publications, 1976).

(19) Leone, "Real Costs of Regulation" p. 65.

(20) Decision Making for Regulating Chemicals in the Environment, National Academy of Sciences, Washington, D. C., 1975.

(21) Arthur Kantowitz, "The Science Court Experiment: Criticisms and Responses," Bulletin of the Atomic Scientists, April 1977. Nancy Ellen Abrams and R. Stephen Berry, "Mediation: A Better Alternative to Science Courts," Bulletin of the Atomic Scientists April 1977.

BIBLIOGRAPHY

Allaway, W. H. 1975 The effect of soils and fertilizers on human and animal nutrition. Agricultural information bulletin no. 378. U.S. Department of Agriculture, Washington, D. C.

A plan to test "science courts." Business Week, January 17, 1977.

Carter, Luther J. 1976. Pesticides: Three EPA attorneys quit and hoist a warning flag. Science Vol. 191, pp. 1155-8 March 19, 1976.

McCraw, Thomas K.   The controversial world of the regulatory
    agencies. American Heritage, April 1977.

Speer, Edgar B. Are the regulatory agencies changing our government?
    Paper delivered before the Economic Club of Detroit, Detroit,
    Michigan, March 15, 1976.

Weaver, Paul H. Unlocking the gilded cage of regulation. Fortune,
    February 1977.

19 An Assessment of Future Technological Advances in Agriculture and Their Impact on the Regulatory Environment
Sylvan H. Wittwer

INTRODUCTION

Today's greatest challenge is to provide an adequate food supply for a rapidly expanding world population. This nation, with its great human and natural resources, occupies a key position. A food production, processing, handling, and distribution system has been designed to create a nutritional abundance, the like of which the world has never known. The ingredients of that system consist of labor-saving technologies, generally stable production at high levels, progressively larger scale operations, and massive inputs of capital, management, and resources. The focus is on single crop or livestock systems.

Our food production technologies have had an important impact not only at home, but also abroad. World food supplies heretofore have kept ahead of population. There is now more food per person, on a global scale, than at anytime in recent history. It is well recognized, however, that food production alone is not enough. It is distribution, delivery, and income. It is getting the food where the people are, and providing them with the purchasing power to buy it. Only poor people go hungry. India today is the classical example; it now has 20 million tons of surplus grain - not because everyone is well fed, but because the poorest people have no money with which to purchase grain.

It is time for reassessment of our technologies for food production. It is no longer sufficient to produce two ears of corn or two blades of grass where only one grew before. One must consider the resource (land, water, energy, fertilizer, pesticides, human labor, machinery) inputs, their costs, availability, and renewability. We in the United States must irreversibly follow a transition from nonrenewable to renewable resources. This may not be true of many agriculturally developing countries where there could be a golden opportunity to skip, at least in part, the fossil fuel era. (1) Major national policy decisions are forthcoming which will outline the role of the United States in the alleviation of world hunger and malnutrition, and help us to marshall our resources to do so. (2)   Food remains our most important renewable resource.

The United States and Canada now stand as the bastion against hunger with a near monopoly of the world's surplus food.   This far exceeds that of any nation in recent history.   The disparity of surplus food among nations exceeds that of oil.

Never has any country exported so much food or been so generous. Current agricultural exports exceed those of any other goods or commodities and approached $25 billion in 1977.   These exports contribute heavily to our national economy and a favorable international trade and balance of payments.   It is estimated that 84 percent of the food sent to starving nations during the past 25 years has come from the United States.

This antion and the world have benefited mightily from its investments in agricultural food producing technologies.   Production has risen rapidly.   There have been large inputs of water through irrigation, fertilizer, pesticides, machinery, and capital.   The result has been a bountiful food supply at low cost.

A dramatic change is now occurring.   Yields of all major crops in the United States (corn, wheat, sorghum, potatoes, cotton, sugar beets, field beans, peanuts, soybeans) have plateaued.   World grain yields are declining.   Prices for farm products have become volatile, unstable, and more uncertain than at any time in recent history.   Four years ago there were shortages, and prices rose precipitously.   Today there are gluts and surpluses with low prices, and a nationwide "farmers strike" labeled "The American Agricultural Movement."   Meanwhile, energy intensive farm inputs have risen sharply with a continuing upward trend.   This has placed American agriculture and the farmer in a uniquely vulnerable position with no counterpart in history.   Increased profitability for the farmer and reasonable prices for the consumer are both predicated upon sustained increased production.   These two complementary objectives, profit for farmers and reasonable food prices for consumers, underscore the need for reassessment of technologies for agricultural production.

What are the forces that increasingly impinge on the productivity of our food systems?   The plateauing and decline in agricultural productivity, as expressed in yields per unit land area per unit time, need careful analysis.   There are many contributing factors, but the magnitude of each is not known (see table 19.1).   Chief among the depressants of productivity are the regulatory constraints (see table 19.2), which remain an unknown factor in both the development of new technologies and their adoption.   The spiraling costs prompted by regulatory activities are also among the most inflationary in our total economy.   This brings us to the next generation of agricultural research. (3)   There are technologies that will result in stable food and fiber production at high levels; are both cost effective and more environmentally benign; that will add to, rather than diminish, the earth's resources; are sparing of capital, management skills, and non-renewable resources; and are scale neutral (see table 19.3).   New technologies, resource inputs, and economic incentives are the para-

Table 19.1.   Causes of Decline in Agricultural Productivity

    Soil erosion - Loss of Topsoil

    Loss of organic matter - Soil compaction

    Chemical soil residues - Air pollution

    More less-productive land under cultivation

    Increased pressures on productive land base

    Fewer options for water, fertilizer, pesticide uses

    Climate and weather fluctuations

    Increased regulatory constraints

    Decreased support for agricultural research

Table 19.2.   Recently Imposed Regulations upon Agricultural Research and Productivity

    Occupational safety and health

    Human subjects requirements

    Personnel relations

    Union/management relationships

    Affirmative action

    Waste handling and disposition

    Chemicals handling and disposition

    Laboratory animals

    Building codes, ordinances, standards

    Accountability

    Budget management

    Freedom of information

    Acts - Clean Water, FIFRA, Toxic Substance, Clean Air, RPAR

meters which will determine future agricultural productivity. This paper provides an assessment of technological advances that are likely within the next 10 to 15 years, and a discussion of how they may impact on the regulatory environment.

GREATER PHOTOSYNTHETIC EFFICIENCY, IMPROVED BIOLOGICAL NITROGEN FIXATION, AND GENETIC IMPROVEMENTS BY NEW TISSUE CULTURE TECHNIQUES.

These have been designated as high priority areas of mission oriented basic research for enhancement of food crop production, (4) along with alternative strategies for improved pest control that have been specifically identified and are now targets for increased support from federal funds (see table 19.3). This is reflected by a $10 million competitive grant program in the Cooperative Research Unit of the United States Department of Agriculture for fiscal 1978, with a doubling of this amount projected for fiscal 1979. Most efforts in these areas should result in technologies which are sparing of resources, cost effective, and may diminish some projected environmental problems and, thus, decrease the need for regulatory action. Specific examples follow.

Table 19.3. Next Generation of Agricultural Research

Greater photosynthetic efficiency

Improved biological nitrogen fixation

Genetic improvement and new cell fusion technologies

Greater resistence to competing biological systems

More efficiency in nutrient uptake and utilization

Reduction in losses from nitrification and denitrification

Greater resistence to environmental stresses

Identification of hormonal systems and mechanisms

Genetic changes in plant architecture and leaf display, to create improved light receiving systems for greater capture of sunlight, should not impact on the regulatory environment. This is a research initiative for improved phyosynthetic efficiency that is being pursued with rather immediate results. Reduction genetically in light and/or dark respiration and a delay in leaf senescence of economically important food, feed, and fiber crops would also be environmentally sound, and would increase photosynthetic efficiency. (5) With all legumes, there would be the added advantage of increased photosynthetically produced energy for improved biological nitrogen fixation.

Rising food demands and the enormous fossil fuel input for chemical synthesis of nitrogen fertilizer (30 cubic feet of natural gas per pound of nitrogen), couples with rising costs (now an annual expenditure in the United States of $2 billion) and potential environmental problems associated with the use of chemically fixed nitrogen, will surely force alternative technological developments for nitrogen fixation. Biologically fixed nitrogen is slowly released, and losses from nitrification and denitrification are minimized. There will be less likelihood of regulatory constraints. Furthermore, the development of small on-farm units for abiotic generation of nitrogen fertilizer powered by solar, wind, or water is being actively pursued. Solar cells that could produce ammonia from nitrogen and water would be a revolutionary and (in regard to the environment and resources) sound new development, in the creation of a technology that would complement current efforts in biological nitrogen fixation.

A likely means for increased photosynthate, now a reality for sugarcane, will come from chemical regulation of crop growth and metabolism. Sugarcane ripeners now give yield increases of over 10 percent. (7) The projected use of chemical ripeners for control of biological processes may, however, invoke additional regulatory constraints.

Reference is made here to the carbon dioxide in the atmosphere as a part of the resource base for crop production. Carbon dioxide concentrations ambient to plant foliage remain the single most important rate determinant for further increases in photosynthesis. No exceptions to increased growth from carbon dioxide enrichment have yet been reported. It works for all the major food crops, and elevated levels will accelerate the growth of forest trees and their seedlings. It is no longer necessary to design and conduct experiments to establish the efficacy of carbon dioxide enrichment for increasing yields in commercially grown greenhouse crops where the atmosphere can be contained. All respond with generally greater production and enhancement of quality, especially during early seedling stages. The magnitude of the response is light dependent, but beneficial effects are derived over a wide spectrum of light intensities, either daylight or artificial. Many experiments have now demonstrated that the optimum carbon dioxide concentration ranges between 1,000 and 1,500 ppm. This is three to five times greater than the current atmospheric level. (8)

A threefold increase (330 to 1,000 ppm) in the levels of atmospheric carbon dioxide will greatly increase photosynthetic productivity and, at the same time, prevent losses from photorespiration (photorespiration is essentially eliminated). With legumes (soybeans), this also results in an almost sixfold increase in nitrogen fixed per hectare. (9) While these beneficial effects have been recorded, they have been difficult to apply as yet on a large scale, other than in commercial greenhouse crop production, although models have been suggested. (10) There is a continuing challenge here for plant biochemists, geneticists, and physiologists to find ways of increasing photosynthetic effeciency by reducing photorespiration, whether it be through carbon dioxide enrichment, chemicals, or breeding. Translation of increased photosynthates into increased nitrogen fixation in legumes, and possibly other plants, needs further exploration. The rewards would be a greatly enhanced food supply and other renewable resources with a minimal regulatory infringement.

Somewhat converse to the well-documented beneficial effects of elevated levels of carbon dioxide on crop productivity are a series of recent reports (11) projecting acceptable to catastrophic consequences that will result from heating of the atmosphere if carbon dioxide continues to increase at the current rate. It has even been suggested that the carbon dioxide gas released by the fossil fuel-burning industry should be heavily taxed.

Few of the conclusions that have been drawn, including the effects of carbon dioxide on the atmosphere, are clear. While the available records indicate that from 1949 until now the carbon dioxide concentration in the atmosphere has increased, there is little evidence for an increase in global temperature. The reverse has, in fact, been true.

Contrary to the above uncertainties, we know that improved plant growth and crop production require more carbon dioxide. Agricultural, forestry, and food production research should concentrate on (among other things) developing methods to enable plants to increase their carbon dioxide fixation. One thoroughly demonstrated approach is to increase the carbon dioxide content of the atmosphere. If there are substantial increases in atmospheric carbon dioxide with resultant adverse environmental effects, serious efforts should be made to optimize this resource through enhancement of food and biomass production. (12) Other research efforts that would slow the increase of a presumably high atmospheric level of carbon dioxide would be reduction in soil losses from water and erosion, (13) conservation or zero tillage, wider use of soil improvement crops to raise organic matter levels in soils, and reforestation of now barren landscapes. Such technologies would preserve, protect, and add to the earth's resources and should not require additional regulating inputs. In the presumably undesirable effects of rising levels of atmospheric carbon dioxide can be validated, we can expect firm technological advances to incorporate more carbon into the biosphere. Such efforts should not encourage but decrease regulatory constraints relating to food and fiber production.

PEST CONTROL

Field losses from pests (insects, diseases, weeds, nematodes, rodents, etc.) for the world's major food crops are truly enormous (14) and approximate 35 percent (see table 19.4). All major crops suffer losses before harvest that exceed 20 percent. Chemical pesticides have played a dominant role in the control of pests. Approximately 1.4

Table 19.4. Losses from Pests in the World's Major Crops

| Crop | Losses (percent) | | | |
	Insects	Diseases	Weeds	Total
Rice	26.7	8.9	10.8	46.4
Wheat	5.0	9.1	9.8	23.9
Maize	12.4	9.4	13.0	34.8
Sorghum/Millet	9.6	10.6	17.8	38.0
Potatoes	6.5	21.8	4.0	32.3
Cassava	7.7	16.6	9.2	33.5
Sweet Potatoes	8.9	5.0	11.7	25.5
Tomatoes	7.5	11.6	5.4	24.5
Soybeans	4.5	11.1	13.5	29.1
Peanuts	17.1	11.5	11.8	40.4
Palm Oil	11.6	7.4	9.6	28.6
Copra	14.7	19.3	10.0	44.0
Cottonseed	11.0	9.1	4.5	24.6
Bananas	5.2	23.0	3.0	31.3
Citrus	8.3	9.5	3.8	21.6

Source: World Food and Nutrition Study, vol. 1 (19).

billion pounds of synthetic organic pesticides were produced worldwide in 1976. The United States expended $1.8 billion for pesticides in 1975. (15) Chemical pesticides have accounted for 20 percent of the increase in farm output during the past 25 to 30 years, during which time production has doubled. Since World War II, there has been an ever increasing dependence on pesticides. Historians will likely refer to the latter half of the twentieth century as the "organic pesticide era." Meanwhile, reliance on this single line of defense has introduced problems of pesticide resistance, destruction of natural enemies, outbreaks of secondary pests, reductions in pollinators, potential environmental contaminations, and health hazards. (16) Regulatory constraints and costs relating to the use of pesticides have multiplied exponentially. Nevertheless, regulatory inputs relating to the use of pesticides have given us more information about their health effects than for any other group of chemicals.

Future alternative strategies for integrated pest control, as now being developed by teams of scientists, if implemented will likely result in the use of more pesticides in agriculturally developing nations, and less in the more developed. (17) For small farm peasant agriculture, it is not a future option but an immediate urgency. The intent of the projected widely used systems approach in pest management will be to reduce costs for pest control, impose less of an environmental insult, create greater production dependability, and increase yields. This will come through the use of natural enemies and parasites, identification and creation of genetically resistant varieties, improved cultural practices, environmental monitoring, and more timely and efficient use of chemicals (see table 19.5). Till now, agricultural crop protection technology has become obsolete at an alarming rate. It will continue to do so, but there will be progressively greater efficiency in the use of chemicals because of economic costs, their environmental impacts and because of their failing reliability in view of acquired resistance of the pests to chemical control. The anticipated more judicious use of chemicals in integrated pest management systems should result in gains for food safety and fewer regulatory constraints. Whereas the possibility may exist for some agriculturally developing nations to bypass the fossil age, it is not likely for them to bypass the chemical pesticide era. (18) It is, however, strikingly significant that most developing countries have not yet been caught in the treadmill of pesticides and pesticide resistance, and have thus far largely escaped the pesticide syndrome. Meanwhile, significant progress with integrated pest management programs has, however, been achieved for some insects on cotton, alfalfa, soybeans, citrus, apples, and greenhouse grown tomatoes. (19) There are yet many challenges ahead for these crops and others such as potatoes and onions. Success, now and in the future, will reside with interactions of scientists from many disciplines, and a greatly expanded technically educated extension service. One of the big steps in the next 10 to 20 years will be real time management of agricultural systems, including pests. In an era of few stable resources, we must develop integrated pest control measures. It is mandatory that we do so. But it will require a change of attitude for scientists to look beyond their own narrow field of interest. There is the opportunity to replace chemicals with information, and to put people with technical information back on the farm.

Table 19.5.   Systems of Integrated Pest Management

Inputs	Outputs
Natural enemies	Increased production
Resistant varieties	Production stability
Cultural practices	Improved environment
Chemicals (pesticides)	Cost reduction

Considerable evidence has now accumulated to implicate secondary plant metabolites as defensive agents in plant to plant relationships. Studies of allelopathy in crop plants have revealed toxic compounds in asparagus and sorghum roots and shoots, and the fruits and seeds of the cucumber. Residues of sorghum plants and sudan grass have provided excellent control of annual grass weeds in both the greenhouse and field. Allelopathy is a widespread phenomenon among crop plants. (20) It may provide an interesting alternative to the use of chemical herbicides, now the most extensively used of all chemicals for agricultural production. No significant breakthrough for field application of allelopathy has yet occurred with any of the major food crops. The rapid obsolescence of current crop protection technology, however, suggests some possibilities that should be explored. Regulatory constraints in the use of this new technology would have to focus upon possible toxic plant components.

IMPROVED EFFICIENCY IN NUTRIENT UPTAKE BY PLANTS.

The most important industrial input into agricultural production is fertilizer. It accounts for about one-third of the total energy input, and is responsible for at least 30 to 40 percent of total crop productivity achieved during the past 40 years. Nitrogen fertilizer alone is credited with providing one-third of the productive capacity of crops. Over 10,000 metric tons of industrially fixed nitrogen, approximately one-fourth the world's total, is added annually for crop production in the United States. Half is applied to a single crop - maize. The annual

United Staes investment for nitrogen fertilizer on maize is $1 billion, compared to approximately $1.5 billion for all grain crops and $2 billion for all crops. Yet only 50 percent of the nitrogen and less than 35 percent of the phosphorus and potassium applied as fertilizer in the United States are recovered by crops. The recovery of fertilizer nitrogen in the rice paddies of the tropics is only 25 to 35 percent. The balance is lost to the environment. Denitrification loses nitrogen to the atmosphere. Nitrification encourages losses in the soil from leaching. Food production could be greatly improved if these enormous losses, particularly of nitrogen, could be reduced in the warm soils of the tropics. Equally important benefits could be ascribed to an environmentally sound technology with less pressure from regulations. A worldwide loss of 12 to 15 million tons of nitrogen fertilizer per year can be ascribed to denitrification alone. (21) Losses from nitrification are equally as great. Nitrification inhibitors, both natural and synthetic and applied with ammonia or urea, are effective deterrents to leaching and atmospheric losses of nitrogen. Their use is just beginning on a global scale and research in this area should be of the highest priority. Substantial progress could be made in 10 to 15 years. The results could be a significant reduction in fertilizer cost and usage; nonrenewable resources would be preserved, our food supply would be improved, and an environmental hazard reduced. The net effect from all directions would be a lessening of the regulatory impact on the food system.

Research emphasis on reduction of losses of nitrogen fertilizer applied to crops (22) should hold equal priority to that for devising new means of nitrogen fixation utilizing renewable rather than non renewable resources.

An equally exciting approach to greater efficiency in nutrient capture from soils is to alter the crop genetically to get more yield from soils which are infertile, too acid, toxic, or saline for varieties now in use. Vast land areas of the earth including the United States are either not utilized or under utilized for agricultural production. For this technological approach, the cost should be relatively low: It would greatly expand the resource base, energy inputs would be reduced, and the reliability of crop yields improved, in both developed and developing countries. Few if any regulatory constraints would be imposed, and significant results should be forthcoming in 10 to 20 years. The results of a major workshop on Plant Adaptation to Mineral Stress in Problem Soils have been published. (23)

MICROBIAL FACILITATION OF NUTRIENT UPTAKE BY PLANTS

The facilitation of nutrient uptake by microorganisms (fungi) in symbiotic associations with the roots of higher plants is emerging as one of the most exciting frontiers for enhancement of food crop production. Mycorrhizae, particularly the endomycorrhizae and the subgroup referred to as vesicular-arbuscular, may result in large increases in the uptake of phosphorus and other poorly mobile nutrients. Almost all food crops respond. Vesicular-arbuscular mycorrhizae can be viewed as fungal extensions of roots. They help roots absorb fertilizer and can stimulate growth and nitrogen fixation by legumes, especially in phosphorus deficient soils. There are superior strains of mycorrhizae, and crops can be inoculated with them. Mycorrhizae fungi have been reported to significantly increase the yields of both legumes and cereal grains. The profound effects of these fungi have only recently been appreciated. (24)   They facilitate nutrient uptake by changing the amounts, concentrations, and properties of minerals available to plants both in forestry and in agriculture. The potential is not only for a substantial increase in conventional crop production, but to expand productivity of economic plants in areas which now have an unfavorable climate and nonproductive soils.

If the recent rates of progress that have occurred in research with mycorrhizae can be sustained, substantial impacts in crop productivity through inoculation of superior strains of mycorrhizae could be realized within 10 to 20 years. The results would be nonrenewable resource conservation, enhancement of crop productivity, and expansion of the land resource base, and the use of a technology not likely subject to regulatory constraints. This approach would be a prime example of optimizing the natural environment for improved crop production.

TECHNOLOGIES FOR IMPROVED MANAGEMENT OF LAND, WATER, AND ENERGY RESOURCES.

We have no viable option for the immediate future, other than to create more energy efficient land and water use and conservation strategies. New soil and water conservation and management technologies can be developed to increase yields of both large and small holdings. To introduce the science of resource conservation into farms of all sizes would be to exploit one of the greatest opportunities for the enhancement of global food production. And it can be done without a negative impact on the regulatory environment.

The problems are massive. There are increasing constraints on the substitutability of energy, land, and water in agricultural production. First, prime agricultural land is disappearing on a global scale because of irreversible use. Second, that which is left is being seriously degraded by compaction, loss of organic matter, and by wind and water erosion. As the land resource base is driven harder, the options in meeting regulatory constraints in the use of water for irrigation, energy, mechanization, and human labor become less.

Problems of soil erosion are global. For 40 years the Soil Conservation Service of the United States Department of Agriculture has promoted sound conservation practices, supported by technical and financial assistance, education, persuasion, and appeals to good land stewardship. It has not been very effective. After more than 40 years, no more than 25 percent of our farmlands are under approved conservation practices.   Meanwhile, we continue to lose enormous amounts (8.3 tons per hectare per year, for a total of 2.8 billion tons) of topsoil from our best lands.   This continues to pollute and sediment our lakes, streams, and estuaries, and invoke additional regulatory actions.   This situation, coupled with massive deforestation, is even worse in many tropical developing countries. (25)

APPROPRIATE TECHNOLOGY - SMALL FARMS.

In the United States, a series of agricultural technologies has been developed with labor-saving equipment for large-scale units, with huge inputs of capital, management, and resources. It is sometimes referred to as hard-high technology.   Much of the world may not want nor be able to handle such technologies if energy, land, and water are in short supply; if unemployment is rampant; and if capital and management skills are lacking.   Food-producing technologies should be sought that are scale neutral, labor intensive, and that result in stable production at high levels with a minimum of capital, management, and resource inputs.

Not apart from the resource inputs (land, water, energy) for food production is the current rhetoric and growing interest focusing on the salvation of the family farm and farmers with small holdings.   Most international development programs now look to the small farmers the central figure.   Technologies will be increasingly addressed to small-scale, labor intensive, and capital and resource sparing farming.   The small farm can be an economically viable unit.   It must be so since the incomes of a billion people on earth depend on farms of five hectares or less.   The output per unit land area per unit time on these mini holdings can significantly exceed that of the large United States farms.   Small increments of fertilizer, water, or pesticides, or other technologies or social or economic incentives in Southeast Asia, Latin America, or Africa would have telling effects on enhancement of agricultural productivity.

The issue of the small-scale or limited resource farm is not foreign to the needs of the United States.   According to 1976 data, 72 percent of all United States farms grossed less than $20,000 and are classified as small farms.   Yet most all United States agricultural research efforts are still directed to large-scale commercial or modern agricultural needs.   Technologies that are conservative of resources and useful for small farms will receive increased emphasis in the years ahead.

Here are some important considerations relating to technological developments for farmers with small holdings.   They are a hetero-geneous not a homogeneous group.   Financial and household manage-ment inputs, including the family labor force, are of high priority. Special attention needs to be directed toward equipment needs and market potentials.   Development of these technologies would have little regulatory impact.

Reduced tillage is an example of an important resource conservation technology. (26)   The moldboard plow, long a symbol of American agriculture, has created insolvable losses from wind and water erosion. The use of appropriate chemicals for weed control has now established the reality of improved crop productivity without plowing the land. The plow is gradually being retired. Over 3 million hectares (corn, soybeans, wheat) in the United States were planted in 1977 without tillage and on over 20 million hectares, tillage was reduced from the conventional level. Reduced tillage is the most significant technology yet developed for the control of soil erosion, maximization of cover on the land, and for the conservation of energy, labor, water, soil fertility, and organic matter for the main food-producing areas of the earth. (27) In addition, a higher proportion of sloping land in hilly areas can be brought into production or planted with more profitable crops.

Successful conservation tillage requires two important inputs: first, an appropriate herbicide, and second, specially adapted seed drills for use on sod or nontilled soil. Use of herbicide mandates registration and clearance by regulatory bodies. The development and release of appropriate chemicals for killing of sod and subsequent weed control will continue to impact on the development and speed with which zero tillage and reduced tillage can be used in both American and world agriculture. There is the potential, however, of bringing into food production tens of millions of hectares of land heretofore not suitable for agricultural purposes, and for reducing soil erosion to essentially zero levels. Many crops on many soils should be adapted to this method of culture on both mineral and organic soils that are eroding badly.

Water is a key issue in future agricultural development. Food production suffers from some degree of water deficiency over the entire globe. Irrigated cropland constitutes about 15 percent of the total under cultivation. The higher productivity of irrigated land, however, results in 30 percent of the world's food.

World food production goals must face the water limitations and optimize the management of the water resources that now exist. The water resource base of the earth, however, is enormous. Seventy percent of the earth's surface is covered with it. Most of it is salty; only one percent is fresh water, and 99 percent of the fresh water is underground. (28) Most of the fresh water (80 to 85 percent) withdrawn in the United States is consumed in agricultural production, the primary volume going to irrigation.

The number of kilograms of water needed to produce a kilogram of food is an important variable. Practically no research has been done in this area, although numerous symposia have been held on irrigation and the efficiency of water use. (29) Large differences in transpiration losses exist among species, varying from a scale of 100 for pineapple, to 400 to 500 for cereals and seed legumes, to over 1,000 for some fruits and vegetables. The water requirement of sugarcane per unit land area in Hawaii is five times that of pineapple. A report from Israel (30) indicates that crops vary widely in their efficiency of water use. Sorghum will produce 1.72 kilograms of grain per millimeter of water applied, compared with 1.23 for wheat, 0.65 for peanuts, and only 0.24 for cotton.

Equally important are new water management technologies for food crop production. Making more efficient use of available water supplies offers the greatest technological opportunities least encumbered by regulatory constraints. The efficiency of using conventionally applied irrigation water varies from 20 to 40 percent in the United States to 80 to 85 percent in Israel.

Drip or trickle irrigation is sometimes referred to as the "Blue Revolution." It was first developed for large-scale crop production in Israel, and may reduce by 50 percent the water now used in conventional irrigation systems (flooding, sprinkling, furrow) for food crop production. Worldwide, there are now 162,000 hectares of cropland equipped with drip irrigation systems. Three times this amount is projected for 1981. California has 15 percent of the total. (31) There are many other concurrent advantages of drip irrigation for high value crops. It reduces operating costs, soil erosion is reduced to a minimum, and no land is wasted to build irrigation ditches. There is no leaching, runoff, or drainage water pollution. Weed control and distribution of fertilizer can be optimized, and crop and soil management and harvest operations can be conducted without interference. Water of higher salinity than would be acceptable with other methods can be utilized. (32) The prospects for high frequency irrigation on some crops hold even greater promise for efficient water use with less capital investment, resource inputs, and management. (33)

Water management schemes adapted to the semi arid tropics have been given little attention. There is an ever widening gap between the productivity of irrigated and nonirrigated agriculture. This is being accompanied by increasing population pressures on the land and recurrent cycles of drought. There is a serious lack of technology to insure dependable harvests, the magnitude of which approaches in importance the enhancement of production itself. (34)

One of the most promising methods for increasing our usable water resource is precipitation augmentation through cloud seeding. There is, however, no area of technology so vulnerable to regulatory (environmental, legal, social, political, and economic) constraints.

A predicted increase in winter snowpack from cloud seeding in the Colorado River Basin would provide an increase of 2 million acre feet of water with no new water resource management facilities. The annual benefits for the West would be approximately $13 million. A benefit of $30 million could be expected with the construction of new basin facilities. Additional water from snow augmentation in the western mountains would cost $1 to $1.50 per acre foot. This can be compared with costs of $25 to $50 for providing additional water by interbasin transfers. It would be considerably cheaper than other augmentation procedures such as desalination of saltwater and condensation of geothermal steam.

Recent precipitation enhancement research in Florida, based on new cloud seeding technologies, suggests very positive results. (35) Dynamic seeding of cumuliform clouds increased aerial rainfall. A high degree of significance was obtained with a capability of enhancing summer rainfall by 25 percent over total target areas. A 50 percent increase was obtained with a single floating target. Many of the types of clouds found in Florida in the summer are similar to those in the Midwestern corn belt. The potential for precipitation enhancement in the Midwest, the major food-producing area of the nation, has not been scientifically determined. Herein may reside the most significant contribution that research can make toward increasing the water resources in the United States during the next 10 to 15 years. (36) Any successful technologies for rainfall enhancement must also include an evaluation and assessment of weather modification related to socioeconomic, legal, and environmental impacts. It is an enormously complex package to assemble for a viable approach to a major technological achievement; and it has great potential for an enormous breakthrough in not only increasing agricultural productivity, but also in enhancing its dependability.

The freshwater resources of the earth are not being efficiently utilized in irrigation for agricultural production. China, India, the Soviet Union, Pakistan, and the United States account for more than 70 percent of the world's total irrigated land, in the order listed. The total irrigated land in the United States increased from 8 to 17 million hectares from 1939 to 1969. There were 23 million in 1976. China has more irrigated land than any country in the world, with one-third of the total (41 percent of its cropped area). India, Sri Lanka, the Soviet Union, and Bangladesh expect to double the amount of irrigated land they now have, and they have the water resources to do it. This will not only increase the productivity of a given crop, but will enable year-round production. Irrigation will also greatly increase food security through greater dependability of supply, and with less vulnerability to climate and weather uncertainties. Largely through irrigation, new seeds, and fertilizer China has doubled the yields of the major food grains in two decades despite recurring droughts. The Planning Commission of India, the Soviets, and the new Prime Minister of Sri Lanka look to vast new irrigation schemes as the primary catalyst for renewed agricultural development and food security.

Expansion of irrigated agriculture will have an impact on the regulatory environment. Sprinkle irrigation systems require more energy but may be less subject to regulatory constraints than surface systems. With expansion of irrigation must come total water management systems including drainage. Disposal of waste waters must be regulated. While the land resource base can initially be made more productive, there are increased hazards of salinization, and new breeding grounds may be created for insects that serve as vectors for human disease. Legal, social, and environmental problems can multiply.

There are vastly under-utilized freshwater resources that could, with modern technological input, be used for agriculture. One example will suffice. The boundary waters of Minnesota and Canada abound with indigenous stands of wild rice. About 10,000 hectares are harvested annually in Minnesota, with 8,000 hectares cultivated in artificial paddies. Wild rice is a uniqud food. The demand in recent years has forced the price to eight dollars or more per pound of processed grain.

Recent developments relating to the creation of shatterproof varieties and mechanical harvesting could open a vast new food resource from the lakes and streams of the North. (37)

An even greater potential exists for salt and brackish waters. The recent genetic breakthrough for the adaptation of crops to grow in seawater is a remarkable development. (38) Marketable yields have been obtained with a salt-tolerant research line of barley irrigated with water from the Pacific Ocean. This genetic approach to saline crop production has been proven with barley, and is applicable to other crops. Barley grown with seawater was found to be satisfactory as a feed, and yields were appreciable. This development could be the first step in opening up a vast new water resource for food production, heretofore not accessible for agricultural purposes.

Further technological advances utilizing the genetic approach to saline crop production can be expected.   The potential is enormous. Work with other saline tolerant crops (alfalfa, sugar beets) will undoubtedly follow. An entirely new set of regulatory parameters may arise relating the food safety and minimal nutrient composition of crops grown in seawater. Conversely, genetic selections of crops, which would flourish under highly saline conditions, may offer new and exciting frontiers to utilize waste waters in the food system.

IMPROVED LIVESTOCK PRODUCTIVITY.

An increase in livestock food resources can come from improved production and utilization of feeds, disease control, and genetic improvement. The greatest potential resides with large ruminant livestock. (39) The single goal is increased productivity. Here, there are three major interrelated research inputs which must be pursued simultaneously: Improved production and utilization of feeds, better disease control, and genetic improvement. All are of equal priority. Little progress in better utilization of feeds can be achieved without timely inputs for disease control, genetic improvement, and increased reproductive efficiency. Similarly, research on animal disease control would be of little value unless accompanied by better feeding. In fact, improvement of the breeding stock of animals may be impossible in some agriculturally developing countries until certain diseases are controlled and some nutritional disorders alleviated.

Enhancement of productivity through animal health must include control of major epidemic infectious diseases, minimizing losses from many other epidemic diseases, control of endemic diseases, studies of the economic impact of animal diseases, and fundamental research on the biological factors relating to host resistance to disease and parasite infections. World mortality losses from diseases and parasites annually exceed 50 million cattle and buffalo and 100 million sheep and goats. A loss of $20 billion occurs annually from animal diseases in the United States. Reduction in the loss from epidemic and infectious diseases up to 50 percent is a possible and realistic goal. Such expectations should be realized within two decades. (40)

Substantial gains in the utilization of feeds in genetic improvement and in increased fertility can come from developing genetically superior animals for low quality diets, increasing the availability of lignin and cellulose which are the major feedstuffs of many developing countries, improving the use of nonprotein nitrogen for conversion by ruminants into protein, improved feeding and management at critical times in the life cycle, and eventual development of the rumen bypass for increased protein utilization and appetite stimulation. Special feed additives may also result in remarkable increases in feed efficiency and rates of gain. (41)

Improved fertility will come from estrus synchronization or control of the reproductive cycle, semen preservation, improved pregnancy detection, multiple births, and superovulation. All can be maximized to increase the number of offspring per breeding unit. Low reproductive efficiency of livestock now results in a 50 percent loss of potential animals. Twinning in dairy and beef cattle can become a reality through hormone treatment for superovulation, controlled breeding, recovery of fertilized eggs, and nonsurgical embryo transfer to recipient females of lesser breeding value.

The above technological achievements in the United States will impact on the regulatory environment. Chemical control of the reproductive cycle may be thwarted by regulatory constraints. Similarly, chemical treatment for diseases, including antibiotics, is now under severe scrutiny. Antibiotics may be transmitted by food animals to people, and there is the hazard of induced allergies from residuals in meat, milk, and eggs. Toxic chemicals in the environment that may enter the livestock food chain will be increasingly scrutinized and subject to increased regulatory action. (42)

Controlled environments constitute a realm of technology scarcely tapped for livestock production. They are widely used now for poultry and swine, and are under test for lambs and beef cattle. Programmed lighting (photoperiod) and temperature regulation can have marked effects upon crop productivity. Similar variables should be vigorously pursued relative to their effects on dairy and beef cattle productivity, feeding efficiency, rates of gain, hormonal relationships, and reproductive behavior. There is a significant report on the promotive effects of supplemental lighting on growth and milk production of dairy cattle. (43) No serious regulatory or financial constraints should be imposed upon technologies relating to improved environments for livestock.

The results can be phenomenal when modern livestock production technology and improved forages, such as hybrid Napier grass and pearl millet, are introduced into a developing country. Such is the "white revolution" which is emerging in the Punjab and Gujarat states of India. A million farmers with water buffaloes have formed cooperatives for collection, processing, marketing, and distribution of milk and milk products to the almost unlimited markets in Bombay, New Delhi, and other large cities. Milk production at the farm level is enhanced by genetic improvement through artificial insemination, better forages for feeding, and the latest in disease control. The result is a steady cash income, better utilization of wastes and by-products, improvement of the nutritional status of poor people, and an enterprise which is labor intensive at the production level. Modern technology can be adapted to farmers of limited resources. (44)

Livestock in agriculturally developing nations serve as important sources of food, fiber, dietary improvement, income, power, fuel, and fertilizer. They are also a living food reservoir that is mobile. It equals the present worldwide grain reserves and is not concentrated in a few surplus nations. Significant advances in technology can be expected in the combined areas of better feeding, genetic improvement, regulating the environment, and disease control. Poverty, malnutrition, and safe water supplies are still primary concerns in developing countries compared to possible food safety relating to traces of toxic chemicals in the environment and in the food chain.

FOOD HANDLING AND PROCESSING

Food production alone is not enough. Extending the life of perishable products by 3 to 4 days without a refrigerator could greatly improve diets, expand markets, and increase the availability of food to people. Similarly, appropriate storage of indigenous production would provide production goal incentives, family food security, opportunity to manage a part of the market system, and a means of improving and preserving desirable seed stocks. It is not likely that development of these techniques will have a major regulatory impact.

There are options for new technological developments in food processing and preservation. (45) As with food production technologies, many previously discarded in the United States as too labor intensive need to be reevaluated for the labor intensive countries. (46) There are developed technologies which in the future, with additional experience and knowledge, should require little regulatory constraints. One is ionizing radiation to preserve food. It has implications in the United States as well as abroad. Irradiation can control spoilage, micro-organisms, and insects. It is now being used commercially in Japan to control storage sprouting of potatoes. With fresh fruits, it will control insects, mold growth, and delay spoilage due to aging. If approved for use, it would allow some fresh fruits to move into new markeys now prohibited because of insect transfer. Irradiation would significantly reduce the levels of nitrate/nitrite required to maintain color in cured meats. Technological breakthroughs in the use of irradiation during the next two decades could have a remarkeble impact in food handling and storage.

A second opportunity is the potential for dehydration and other effective methods of moisture removal such as compression. Any regulatory constraints would be minimal. Solar energy for drying needs to be further explored. It is now used directly in many developing countries. Research will be directed toward converting solar energy to forms that can be applied to a variety of processing technologies.

The potential use of the retortable pouch is a third option. It is a multilayer, adhesively bonded pouch that will withstand thermoprocessing temperatures. The advantages of the metal can and the plastic boil-in-the-bag are combined. It appears to offer savings in energy over containers for frozen and canned products. This product is reportedly superior to foods retorted in conventional cans, and may approach the quality of frozen foods. While questions of labor relocation and food safety may be raised, there should be little regulatory concern.

The increased use of mocroorganisms in fermentation for food preservation will likely occur. It is adapted to batch processing, requires simple equipment, the technology is scale neutral, and the probability for success is high. Fermentation preservation permits distribution without refrigeration and it is applicable to many foods, including those in the tropics. Limitations in the progress of fermentation technology will reside in consumer acceptance and in the regulatory constraints imposed on such food properties as the salty taste, the acid content, and possible microbiological standards.

The future development of extruded or engineered and formulated foods will likely be constrained because of concerns relating to nutrient equivalency and safety.

SOLAR ENERGY

There is a growing interest in the United States and developing countries in the use of solar energy. Technologies extend from nitrogen fixation to greenhouse heating, livestock housing to crop drying, and to food processing. They lend themselves to a decentralized society. Sunlight is usually plentiful year-round in the tropics. It is safe, nonpolluting, without noise, renewable, and free of regulatory constraints. The current energy establishments in the United States tend to downplay solar energy. This is to be expected of organizations that would be threatened by the success of the new technologies. (47) Nevertheless, we should see exciting new developments for the use of solar energy in the food system within the next 10 to 15 years.

MAXIMIZING AGRICULTURAL PRODUCTIVITY

Many have speculated as to the food producing capacity of the earth. As grain equivalents, it has been computed at 40 times its present level. (48) Biological limits have not yet been reached for the productivity of any of the major food crops or animal products. Average and record yields have been recorded for the chief crop and livestock commodities consumed, and, with one or two exceptions, a great gap exists between the two (see table 19.6). The exact inputs for maximum productivity of a given crop are not known, and are apparently very site specific. It is not likely that these will be provided free of regulatory constraints. The real technological advances in food production for the future, however, will focus on the management of the entire complex of systems (land, water, energy, pest, tillage, fertilizer, climate, waste, mechanization, etc.) which go into optimizing total production and delivery. Any but not all of the precise conditions for the world records of wheat and corn production have been recorded. (49) The world record for corn production now stands at 353 bushels per acre, or 22,139 kilograms per hectare, with a theoretical maximum yield of 1,066 bushels per acre (see table 19.7). Yet unknown growth factors and those now identified will continue to stretch the biological limits of crop and livestock productivity. There is the hope that regulatory constraints will be waived for a naturally occurring compound that increases crop yields when applies in miligrams per hectare. (50)

SUMMARY AND CONCLUSIONS

Future increases in agricultural productivity will come from combinations of new technologies, resource inputs, and economic incentives. Technological inputs must be sought after that will result in stable production at high levels, are scale neutral, and sparing of capital, resources, and management skills. The impact on the regulatory environment must also be minimal.

Technological developments that would likely diminish environmental problems and human health hazards and be nonpolluting would include all genetic improvements for increased productivity, yield stability, and greater resistance to competing biological systems and environmental stresses. Greater photosynthetic efficiency and biological nitrogen fixation, as well as solar energy generated abiotic nitrogen fixation, would also be regulatory neutral. Improved nutrient recovery by crops from the soil generated by reductions in nitrification and denitrification and microbial (vesicular-arbuscular endomycorrhizae) facilitation would lessen regulatory constraints against fertilizer usage, enhance food production, and at the same time preserve nonrenewable resources. Greater photosynthetic utilization of atmospheric carbon dioxide would eliminate photorespiration, increase yields, and lessen a potential environmental hazard. Integrated pest management systems should reduce losses from pests, be more environmentally sound, less polluting, more cost effective, and should help stabilize production at high levels. Greater efficiency in the use of land, water, energy, and atmospheric resources (carbon dioxide) should lessen the regulatory impact. Classical examples are conservation tillage and drip irrigation. Any technologies dependent on solar energy would be dispersed, non polluting, add to the earth's resources, and preserve the non renewable

Table 19.6.   Average and Record Yields

Food	U.S. Average 1975	Best U.S. Farmers	World Record	Ratio: Record/ Average
Maize (kg/ha)	5,398	14,123	21,216	3.9
Wheat (kg/ha)	2,085	6,725	14,526	7.0
Soybeans (kg/ha)	1,883	4,371	7,398	3.9
Sorghum (kg/ha)	3,295	16,813	21,521	6.5
Oats (kg/ha)	1,722	5,380	10,617	6.2
Barley (kg/ha)	2,367	8,070	11,405	4.8
Potatoes (kg/ha)	26,632	67,252	94,153	3.5
Milk (kg/cow)	4,725	13,500	22,500	4.8
Eggs (per hen)	230	275	365	1.6
Cassava (kg/ha)	8,000*	40,000*	60,000	7.5
Rice (kg/ha·per crop/112 days)	2,500	8,000	14,400	5.8
Sugarcane (kg/ha/yr)	50,000	100,000	150,000	3.0
Sugar beets (kg/ha/yr)	50,000	80,000	120,000	2.4

* Data for Colombia.

Source: Marylin Chou, David P. Harmon, Jr., Herman Kahn, and Sylvan Wittwer, World Food Prospects and Agricultural Potential N.Y.: Praeger, 1977).

Table 19.7.   World Record Corn Yields

Year	Yield (Bu/acre)	Person	Location
1955	304	L. Ratcliff	Mississippi
1973	306	O. Montri	Michigan
1975	338	H. Warsaw	Illinois
1977	353	R. Lynn, Jr.	Michigan

Theoretical Maximum Yield: 1,066

energy resources we now have. Technologies for farmers with limited resources should have minimal regulatory constraints. Finally, the new food processing technologies relating to dehydration, compression, food irradiation, and retortable pouches would have minimal regulatory impacts.

Conversely, other technological developments may encounter moderate to severe regulatory problems. These would include precipitation augmentation through cloud seeding, any introduction of toxic chemicals in the environment for disease or pest control, chemical or hormonal regulation of biological processes, and increased irrigation by conventional systems. Food processing technologies likely to be objects of additional regulatory attention would be all aspects of fermentation preservation and any developments related to extruded, engineered, or otherwise formulated foods.

NOTES

(1) N. L. Brown and J. W. Howe, Solar Energy for Village Development, Science 199 (1978): 651-657.

(2) Reference is made to the Food and Agriculture Act of 1977 (U.S. Congress): and the U.S. Senate proposal (act) to create a new federal agency to be called the International Development Cooperation Administration.

(3) S. H. Wittwer, "The Next Generation of Agricultural Research," Science 199(1978): 375.

(4) Orgainizing and Financing Basic Research to Increase Food Production Office of Technology Assessment, U.S. Congress, Washington, D. C. 1977.

(5) S. S. Abu-Shakra, D. H. Phillips, and R. C. Huffaker "Nitrogen Fixation and Delayed Leaf Senescence in Soybeans," Science 199 (1978): 973-975; D. J. Oliver and I. Zelitch, "Increasing Photosynthesis by Inhibiting Photorespiration with Glycolate," Science 196 (1977): 14501451; P. R. Day, "Plant Genetics: Increasing Crop Yield," Science 197 (1977): 1334-1339; and H. W. Woolhouse, "Senescence Processes in the Life Cycle of Flowering Plants," BioScience 28 (1), (1978): 25-31.

(6) See Chemical and Engineering News, Oct. 3, 1977, pp. 19-20; and Personal Communication, William Shaw, Charles F. Kettering Research Laboratories, Yellow Springs, Ohio.

(7) L. G. Nickel, "Chemical Enhancement of Sucrose Accumulation in Sugarcane," Advances in Chemistry Series No. 159. Plant Growth Regulators. C. A. Stutte, ed., 1977.

(8) B. R. Strain, Preliminary Report - Workshop on Anticipated Plant
     Responses to Global Carbon Dioxide Enrichment. Department of
     Botany, Duke University, August 4-5, 1977; and S. H. Wittwer,
     "Carbon Dioxide Fertilization of Crop Plants," in Crop Physiology
     ed. U.S. Gupta (New Delhi, India: Oxford and IBH Publishing Co.,
     1977) pp. 310-333.

(9) For a review see R. W. F. Hardy and U. D. Halvelka, 1975. Science
     188:633.

(10) J. A. Bassham, "Increasing Crop Production through More
     Controlled Photosynthesis," Science 197 (1977): 630-638.

(11) C. F. Baes, Jr., H. E. Goeller, J. S. Olson, and R. M. Rotty, The
     Global Carbon Dioxide Problem. Oak Ridge National Laboratory
     Publication ORNL-5194 (Oak Ridge, Tennessee, 1976); G. M.
     Woodwell, "The Carbon Dioxide Question," Scientific American 238,
     no. 1 (1978): 34-43; U. Siegenthaler and H. Oeschger, "Predicting
     Future Atmospheric Carbon Dioxide Levels," Science 199 (1978):
     388395; and M. Stuiver, "Atmospheric Carbon Dioxide and Carbon
     Reservoir Changes," Science 199 (1978): 253-258.

(12) E. S. Lipinsky, "Fuels from Biomass: Integration with Food and
     Materials Systems," Science 199 (1978): 644-651; R. Radmer and B.
     Bok, "Photosynthesis: Limited Yields, Unlimited Dreams," Bio-
     Science 27 no. 9 (1977): 599-605; and Bassham, "Increasing Crop
     Production," pp. 630-638.

(13) R. A. Brink and G. A. Hill, "Soil Deterioration and the Growing
     World Demand for Food," Science 197 (1977): 625-630.

(14) "Crop Productivity," Supporting Papers: World food and Nutrition
     Study, vol. 1, pp. 76-77. National Academy of Sciences,
     Washington, D. C., 1977.

(15) Assessment of Alternative Pest Management Strategies in Food
     Production. Office of Technology Assessment, U.S. congress,
     Washington, D. C., 1978 and Contemporary Pest Control Practices
     and Prospects. Report of the Executive Committee, National
     Academy of Sciences, Washington, D. C., 1975, p. 1.

(16) J. B. Kendrick, Jr., "Agriculture's Most Important Battle," Cali-
     fornia Agriculture 32, no. 2 (1978): 3.

(17) E. H. Glass and D. H. Thurston, "Traditional and Modern Crop
     Protection in Perspective," BioScience 28 (1978) 109-115.

(18) Ibid.

(19) M. J. Way, "Integrated Control - Practical Realities". Outlook on
     Agriculture 9 no. 3 (1977): 127-135; P. T. Haskell, "Integrated Pest
     Control and Small Farmer Crop Protection in Developing Countries,"
     Outlook on Agriculture 9 no. 3 (1977): 121-126; C. B. Huffaker, and
     B. A. Croft, "Integrated Pest Management in the USA - Progress and

Promise," in Environmental Health Perspectives 14, National Institutes of Health, Washington, D. C., 1976, pp. 167-183; B. A. Croft, Integrated Control of Apple Mites. Michigan State University Extension Bulletin 825, 1975; H. Riedl and B. A. Croft, Management of the Codling Moth in Michigan. Michigan Agricultural Experiment Station Research Report 337, 1978; and The Biological Control of Tomato Pests. Growers Bulletin no. 3, Glasshouse Crops Research Institute, Littlehampton, Sussex, England, 1976.

(20) E. L. Rice Allelopathy (New York: Academic Press, 1974); A. R. Putnam and W. B. Duke "Biological Suppression of Weeds; Evidence for Allelopathy in Accessions of Cucumber," Science 185 (1974): 370-372; and D. F. Rhoades, "Herbivore Outbreaks," Submitted to Science, 1978.

(21) J. M. Tiedje, Meeting World Nitrogen Needs - Problems and Perspectives. Paper presented at the Annual Meetings of the American Association for Advancement of Science Symposium on Biological Transformation of Inorganic Nitrogen, Washington, D. C., 1978.

(22) D. H. Huber, H. L. Warren, D. W. Nelson, and C. Y. Tsai, "Nitrification Inhibitors - New Tools for Food Production," BioScience 27 (1977): 523-529.

(23) M. J. Wright and S. A. Ferrari, eds., Plant Adaptation to Mineral Stress in Problem Soils. Proceedings of a Workshop, November 22-23, 1976. Beltsville, Md. Office of Agriculture Technical Assistance Bureau Agency for International Development, 1977.

(24) M. R. Tansey "Microbial Facilitation of Plant Mineral Nutrition," in Microorganisms and Minerals, ed. E. D. Weinberg (New York: Marcel Dekker, Inc., 1977), pp. 343-385 and G. R. Safir "Vesicular-Arbuscular Mycorrhizae and Crop Productivity," in Biology and Crop Productivity, ed. Peter Carlson (New York: Academic Press, 1978).

(25) E. P. Eckholm Losing Ground, Environmental Stresses and World Food Prospects (New York: W. W. Norton and Co., 1976); D. Pimental, E. C. Terhune, R. Dyson-Hudson, S. Rochereau, R. Samis, E. A. Smith, D. Denman, D. Reifschneider, and M. Shepard "Land Degradation Effects on Food and Energy Resources," Science 194 (1976): 149155; and Brink, Densmore, and Hill, "Soil Deterioration," pp. 625630.

(26) Conservation Tillage: Problems and Potentials. Special Publication no. 20. Ankeny, Iowa: Soil Conservation Society of America, 1977.

(27) G. B. Triplett Jr. and D. M. VanDoren "Agriculture without Tillage," Scientific American 236, no. 1 (1977): 28-33.

(28) K. Shoji, "Drip Irrigation," Scientific American 237 no. 5 (1977): 62-68.

(29) R. M. Hagen, H. R. Haise, and T. W. Edminster, "Irrigation of Agricultural Lands," Agronomy, Series no. 11. Madison, Wisconsin: American Society of Agronomy, 1967; W. G. McGuinnies and B. J. Goldman eds, Arid Lands in Perspective. American Association for the Advancement of Science, Washington, D. c., and University of Arizona Press, Tucson, 1969; W. H. Pierre, D. Kirkham, J. Pesek, and R. Shaw eds. Plant Environment and Efficient Water Use (Madison, Wisconsin: American Society of Agronomy and Soil Science Society of America, 1967); and Proceedings of the Water Harvesting Symposium, March 26-28, 1974.   Phoenix, Arizona: United States Department of Agriculture, 1975, 329 pp.

(30) J. Shalhevet, M. Mantell, H. Bielorai, and D. Shimski, Irrigation of Field and Orchard Crops Under Semi-Arid Conditions, IHC Publication no. 1 (Bet Dagan, Israel: International Irrigation Information Center).

(31) C. D. Gustafson, Drip/Trickle Irrigation for Growing Agricultural Crops.   107th Annual Report of the Secretary of Horticultural Society of Michigan for the year 1977, 1978, pp. 63-76.

(32) K. Shoji, "Drip Irrigation," pp. 62-68.

(33) S. L. Rawlins, "High-Frequency Irrigation and Green Revolution Food Production, in Food and Nutrition in Health and Disease, H. Henry Moss and Jean Mayer, eds. Annals of the New York Academy of Sciences, vol. 300, 1977, pp. 121-128.

(34) Climate and Food.   Climate Fluctuation and U.S. Agricultural Productivity.   National Academy of Sciences, Washington, D. C., 1976.

(35) W. L. Wooley, J. A. Jordan, J. Simpson, R. Biodini, and J. Flueck, NOAA's Florida Cumulus Experiment Rainfall Results, 1970-1976. Washington, D. C.: National Oceanic and Atmospheric Administration, 1977.

(36) F. A. Huff and J. L. Vogel, Assessment of Weather Modification in Alleviating Agricultural Water Shortages during Droughts. A Report to the National Science Foundation from the Illinois State Water Survey of the University of Illinois, Urbana, 1977.

(37) W. A. Elliott and E. A. Oelke, "New Era for Wild Rice," Crops and Soils Magazine 29, no. 9 (August/September 1977): 9-11.

(38) E. Epstein and J. D. Norlyn, "Seawater-Based Crop Production: A Feasibility Study," Science 197 (1977): 249-251.

(39) T. C. Byerly, "Ruminant Livestock Research and Development," Science 195 (1977): 450-456.

(40) Supporting Papers: World Food and Nutrition Study, volume 1, Livestock Productivity. Washington, D. C., National Academy of Sciences, 1977, pp. 196-234.

(41) W. E. Wheeler and R. R. Oltjen, Cement Kiln Dust in Diets for Finishing Steers. ARS/USDA Publication NE-88, 1977.

(42) Assessment of Environmental Contaminants Present in the Food Supply. Office of Technology Assessment. U.S. Congress, Washington, D. C., 1978.

(43) R. R. Peters, L. T. Chapin, K. B. Leining, and H. A. Tucker, "Supplemental Lighting Stimulates Growth and Lactation in Cattle," Science 199 (1978): 911-912.

(44) S. H. Wittwer, Observations Relating to Travel in Southeast Asia October 20- November 12, 1977 (East Lansing, Michigan: Michigan Agricultural Experiment Station, 1977).

(45) J. R. Kirk, "Research Priorities in Food Science," Food Technology, July 1977, pp. 66-70.

(46) Supporting Papers: World Food and Nutrition Study, volume 3, Food Availability to Consumers. National Academy of Sciences, Washington, D. C., pp. 30-52.

(47) R. W. Peterson, "All in the Boat Together" (Remarks to the National Audubon Society Annual Dinner, New York, November 9, 1977).

(48) P. Buringh, "The Food Potential of the World," World Development V (5-7), 1977, pp. 477-485.

(49) R. H. Hageman, Factors Affecting Yield of Cereal Grains via Physiological Processes (Proceedings of the Fourth Annual Meeting of the Plant Growth Regulator Working Group, Hot Springs, Arkansas, August 9-11, 1977) pp. 14-42.

(50) S. K. Ries, T. L. Richman, and Violet F. Wert, "Growth and Yield of Crops Treated with Triacontanol," Jour. Amer. Soc. for Hort. Science, 1978.

BIBLIOGRAPHY

Chou, Marylin; Harmon, David P.; Kahn, Herman; and Wittwer, Sylvan H. World Food Prospects and Agricultural Potential. New York: Praeger Publishers, 1977.

Crop Productivity - Research Imperatives. Proceedings of an International Conference, Boyne Highlands, Michigan, October 20-25, 1975. Michigan Agricultural Experiment Station and Charles F. Kettering Foundation, 1976.

Enhancement of Food Production for the United States. Report of the Board on Agriculture and Renewable Resources, World Food and Nutrition Study. National Academy of Sciences, Washington, D. C., 1975.

National Academy of Sciences. 1977. World Food and Nutrition Study.
    Potential Contributions of Research. Report of Steering Commit-
    tee. National Academy of Sciences, Washington, D. C.

Proceedings, The World Food Conference of 1976, June 27-July 1, 1976.
    Iowa State University, Ames, Iowa, 1977.

IV
World Outlook

Introduction

    In the final section we turn to broad issues that will be of concern to both the United States and the rest of the world. The first paper by David Harmon treats two emerging trends in world agriculture: The increasing emphasis on agricultural self-sufficiency by many developed and developing countries and the growing momentum by certain countries to increase agricultural exports to pay for oil imports and economic development. He describes the structural changes that have occurred in United States agriculture and how these changes tie into the two emerging trends.

    "Conventional wisdom" states that foreign demand for United States agriculture will increase steadily over the next ten years, and is buttressed by the growing importance of the centrally planned economies of the Soviet Union and Eastern Europe, as well as that of the advanced developing countries - notably Taiwan and South Korea. Moreover, since 1974 more than half of the world wheat imports have been made by the developing countries. Mr. Harmon examines the "minority" view that agricultural trade patterns for the United States will change as foreign countries with self sufficiency and agricultural export objectives "compete" more heavily with the United States, as well as what the likely impact will be on United States agricultural policy.

    Following Mr. Harmon's paper are three presentations on the topic of world grain surpluses, given at the March 1978 meeting of the Food, Agriculture and Society Research Program in Washington, D. C. The first presentation is an outlook for the world grain situation in the 1980s by Dawson Ahalt of the U.S. Department of Agriculture. Mr. Ahalt points out the new and very complex nature of world markets for the United States and the consequent policy requirements imposed on the United States. For the short run he forecasts a relatively close balance between supply and demand for grains with fairly volatile prices. For the longer term he foresees a growing gap between developing country food needs and productive capacity, with the United States and the other grain exporting nations being called upon to meet these expanding markets. He concludes that, on balance, the outlook for world grain production in the next decade is optimistic.

Philip Sisson of Quaker Oats takes the opposing view that the current situation is one of "plentiful supplies" rather than of surpluses. He reminds us that what is true of the United States may not be true for the rest of the world. Furthermore, he makes the case that technological development in United States agriculture has plateaued in the past few years. Mr. Sisson supports his case with several charts showing that world wheat production has slowed, wheat stocks have leveled off, and United States feed grain inventories as a percentage of consumption have declined almost continuously since 1960.

Thomas Saylor of the United States Department of Agriculture points out that the long-term grain outlook will be increasingly affected by the dependency of foreign consuming nations on external food markets. While effective demand (demand with money behind it) will be met through normal market distribution channels, it will be difficult to meet the additional potential demand brought on by domestic pressures to reduce our production so that it better matches effective demand and by foreign efforts to insulate domestic markets from volatile price and supply movements of the world market. Moreover, the Peoples' Republic of China, having pushed traditional intensive agriculture to its limits, will likely turn to world markets to cover its own needs while the modernization of its own agriculture proceeds. The net effect will be increased vulnerability of consuming nations to the vagaries of world markets and a sharing of the adjustment by both producing and consuming nations.

Shifting from the "macro" needs of the developing countries, David Harmon addresses the role that the multinational corporation (MNC) could play in offsetting developing country vulnerability to the vagaries of weather and climate, and the policies that these countries should adopt to enhance MNC participation in agricultural and economic development. Drawing on the experiences of Algeria to establish a framework for how MNCs could act as agents of growth, providers of technology, and "buffers" in the food-climate system, he differentiates between the role of government and the MNC role in the early stages of a country's agricultural development.

Mr. Harmon examines Algeria, a "crucible" for MNCs beset with climate and institutional problems where it is very difficult for a MNC to operate. He uses Algeria to help us understand the need for technology appropriate to a country's stages of development and he cites both failure and success. He gives us an introduction to the requirements imposed on both developing country government and MNCs if there is to be a climate conducive to MNC participation.

Following Mr. Harmon's paper is a report of how one developing country in collaboration with a United States multinational is exploiting the flow of MNC generated technology for the benefit of its people. Robert Cotton and Steward Flaschen of ITT describe how Chile is attempting to take advantage of this MNC global commercialization and transfer capacity by the creation and operation of Foundation

Chile, a joint Chilean government-ITT organization. The foundation is the mechanism that takes up agricultural and nutritional innovations and adapts them to Chilean conditions and needs. Although still in its early years, Foundation Chile has both improved Chile's ability to feed itself and to provide different food items for export with a high percentage of Chilean contributed value. Foundation Chile thus allows Chile's public and private sectors to respond to the benefits of technology, and it draws on the technologies and expertise of one of the world's largest MNCs for increased food production, better nutrition, and less vulnerability to weather and climate.

The last section concludes with Don Paarlberg's paper which deals with the question of United States agricultural overproduction. Several factors that are responsible for a tendency toward overproduction (on the parts of both the United States and other large grain producers) are the advance of agricultural science, the fact that aggregate demand for food is inelastic, governments' emphasis on boosting domestic food prices and income, and their disinclination to apply effective production controls. These factors cause the world food system to be "biased" toward oversupply. He notes that since World War II there have only been three short periods of time when the world has departed from the norm and has experienced scarcity.

Mr. Paarlberg examines two policy alternatives for the United States to use to avoid once again becoming grain warehouseman for the world. He discusses the benefits and difficulties inherent in a return to fully competitive markets versus internationalizing the world food system, and he concludes with a strategy and a warning for United States agricultural policymakers.

20 Return to World Grain Surpluses: Trends and Implications
David P. Harmon, Jr.

INTRODUCTION

The purpose of this paper is to link an apparent short-term grain surplus situation with two emerging trends in world agricultural production - an increasing emphasis on agricultural self-sufficiency by many developing and developed countries, and a growing momentum on the part of certain countries to increase agricultural exports in order to pay for oil imports and economic development. These trends, given the changing United States agricultural policy in a time of growing world grain surpluses, have serious longer-term implications for both United States and developing country agricultures and economies.

SURPLUS - BACKGROUND

As recently as seven years ago, adverse weather simultaneously affected grain production in the Soviet Union, India, Southeast Asia, and the Sahel. Output of cereal grains dropped for the first time in 20 years. This decrease in world production coincided with ongoing United States and Canadian supply management programs designed to reduce large grain surpluses, as well as with very large Soviet purchases to cover its own production shortfall. At the same time the anchoveta "disappeared," putting increased pressure on already scarce feed grains. Wheat stocks of the major exporting countries dropped from 49 million metric tons to 29 million tons in 1972 to 1973, and to 21 million tons by 1973 to 1974. On the economic side, 1972 to 1973 was marked by the synchronization of an economic boom in the developed world, an increase in inflationary forces worldwide, monetary instability, an energy crisis, commodity speculation, increases in ocean freight rates, and a cyclical production shortfall in fertilizers.

This economic situation, coupled with tight food supplies, led to a steep increase in world cereal prices in 1972 and even higher prices in 1973. Fertilizers were in short supply and high in price, thereby constraining developing countries from obtaining vital supplies of fertilizer. The increased prices of petroleum and other goods led to developing country difficulty in financing food imports. All in all, it was a bleak picture. But it was short term. The 1973 to 1975 price boom, coupled with a return to reliance on market mechanisms, led to large American crops and even bumper crops in 1976 and 1977. In 1977, both United States corn and soybean crops were at record levels, and the wheat crop was the third largest ever. The world situation was similar - on balance, 1977 was the second consecutive bumper harvest year. Brazil had an excellent soybean harvest, while Argentina had a large corn harvest and a record sorghum crop. India had favorable monsoons for the third consecutive year and accumulated a grain surplus of 22 million tons. Carryover stocks of the four major grain-exporting countries were just slightly more than twice what they were at their low in 1974. Although Canada suffered from wet weather and Australia from drought which cut into their respective wheat harvest and although the Soviet and Chinese harvests did not live up to expectations, on balance, the world grain situation was similar to that of the United States - the second consecutive bumper harvest year.

1978

What of 1978? In the United States the Midwest got substantial rain at the end of August and during the first half of September 1977, replenishing soil moisture enough to ensure good starting conditions for crops. The drought in the West ended. Acreage set-asides for wheat and feed grains for 1978 have had a minimal effect on production. Farmers set aside their marginal lands and planted fence post to fence post on the remainder. Moreover, the announcement of the acreage set-aside came too late because many farmers had already planted their winter wheat. As of November 10, 1978, both corn and soybean production was forecast at new record levels, 6.89 and 1.81 bushels respectively, with the total feed crop at 211 million metric tons - a new record.

STRUCTURAL CHANGES IN U.S. AGRICULTURE

It is also instructive to take a brief look at the structural changes which have taken place in United States agriculture over the past two decades, and at what these changes have meant for the United States and for the developing world.

The 1950s and 1960s were marked by a need to maintain United States farmers' income under the conditions of continuing agricultural surpluses. Income maintenance was accomplished by government storage of grain, supply management programs, export subsidies, and PL 480 - to dispose of a portion of that excess grain to developing countries. In short, our farm policy was still largely a domestic matter.

United States Food Aid under Pl 480 could be characterized as a mixed experience. It did help to meet emergency needs after crop failures and provided food to countries that were short of dollars. Its availability allowed some governments to undertake agricultural reforms. On the other hand, the principal charge levied against food aid was that in some countries it allowed cheap food policies to keep urban populations appeased while reducing rural incentives to expand agricultural production. It also permitted countries to use limited resources in capital intensive development strategies, some of which have had only limited success, while agricultural sector development received lower priority.

By 1975 we had a different situation. The government surpluses of the 1950s and 1960s were largely gone. In early 1978, however, we found ourselves with large wheat surpluses and increased stocks of corn and soybeans.

The United States farmer produces almost half the volume of the world's major export crops and is our major source of export earnings. Our agriculture has become increasingly dependent on foreign markets, and our agricultural sector is thus more "open" in the sense that domestic agricultural and food prices are increasingly responsive to foreign demand. In the 1930s our role in world grain trade was minimal; today we are the single largest supplier in the world. Over the past two and one half decades the export coefficient for United States agriculture was doubled. This sensitivity is heightened by importing countries which are now less inclined to absorb their own shortages by going through the traditional process of belt tightening. Rather, they depend more on world markets to meet food goals. The Soviet Union is the prime example of a country bound to maintain domestic food consumption levels. Fortunately, some of the unpredictability of the trading actions of the Soviet Union has been alleviated by our five-year grain contract with the Soviets.

The 1970s witnessed a leveling off of United States yields. High energy prices, high fertilizer prices, unfavorable weather, and the inclusion of 35 million marginal acres in the United States agriculture land base brought about the current "flat" yields.

With the advent of large grain surpluses, our domestic farm policy has changed from one of encouraging maximum food production under freer market conditions to one of increasing government activity in the agricultural sector. We now have acreage set-asides for wheat and for feed grains. The government is paying farmers to store wheat in their own bins. Our policy initiatives are being taken at home and abroad.

What must be remembered, however, is that the yearly agricultural situation is extremely dynamic. Both Argentina and Australia were knocked out of the world wheat market in early 1978 by drought; Canada was sold out, and only the United States had wheat. A poor year in India, China, or the U.S.S.R. could reduce the wheat surplus very rapidly. A poor worldwide harvest could turn the surplus into a shortage. While we held some 1.2 billion bushels of wheat at mid-1978 and will probably have half the world carryover of grains (75 million tons) by the end of the 1977 to 1978 marketing year, these quantities translate into approximately seven percent of world grain utilization. (1)

AGRICULTURAL SELF-SUFFICIENCY

The much written about interdependent community of nations has undergone more rapid expansion of trade than of output, with the result that today many countries depend more on foreign trade than on their own production for markets and for sources of supply. (2) On the other hand, slow economic growth is causing protectionism in trading relationships. A related phenomenon is the move toward agricultural self-sufficiency and its subset, the use of agriculture as a means of financing petroleum imports.

As a result of the grain shortages of 1973 and 1974, the concurrent higher prices of both grains and agricultural inputs, and the embargo places on the export of United States soybeans, many countries have felt the need to attain a greater degree of agricultural self-sufficiency or, in certain cases, to assure themselves of alternate (i.e., non-U.S.) reliable sources of supply. This perceived need is heightened by the changing dietary demands concomitant with economic growth in the developing world. In fact, developing country economic growth with its attendant increases in per capita income; migration from rural to urban areas; and changes in diet toward increased consumption of meat, milk, and eggs may make the financing of oil imports via agricultural exports more difficult as crop production is shifted toward domestic needs. Such a shift is now occurring in Brazil where (with expanded livestock and poultry industries) the corn export policy is under review. Because of economic growth, an increasing yearly share of corn production is going to her mixed feed industry. It is likely that her export expansion drive will be partially subordinated to domestic needs for the next few years - even with the expected growth in corn output.

Furthermore, the developing country movement toward agricultural self-sufficiency is likely to be fairly slow, uneven, and in some cases unsuccessful. This unevenness is seen in Brazil's drive for wheat self-sufficiency where climate, weather, lack of appropriate varieties, and extremely tight soybean-wheat scheduling of planting dates all conspire to make a good wheat crop fairly chancy. Egypt may be the best example of an unsuccessful case where agriculture is definitely unable to meet domestic food needs. Food imports grew from $300 million in the early 1970s to $1.6 billion in 1976. Lack of land, lack of infrastructure, high soil salinity of irrigated land, and insufficient incentives for farmers are conspiring to make Egypt the failure case.

We are probably all familiar with the fact that China has given increasingly high priority to agriculture as a major foundation of economic development. China has recognized that a secure agricultural base is needed in order to have modern industrial development. In fact, her emphasis on the agricultural sector appears to have paid off because she has attained a fairly high degree of self-sufficiency in agricultural production - in years of good weather. Continuing poor weather since 1976 has contributed to China's purchases of grain from abroad which are expected to reach 10 million tons in 1979.

India, with a predominant agricultural sector, a large, relatively unproductive labor force, a large domestic market, and with the potential to meet the demand of that market from within, finally recognized that a strategy of increased agricultural production would both increase employment throughout the economy via increased wages goods. In 1976, India instituted policy changes in an effort to provide an economic climate for farmers that would be more conducive to increased production. Specifically, India raised state prices for farm output, dropped the prices charged farmers for fertilizer, instituted an irrigation program which stresses projects with a quick return, and removed interstate barriers to private trade in grains. Her 1978 wheat crop is reported at 31 million metric tons, up 50 percent from 1974, and her rice crop is up 10 percent over 1975. India will be a food grain exporter in 1979.

In 1976 Algeria raised state prices for farm output in an attempt to increase agricultural production. Under more enlightened farm policies, Tunisia her neighbor in the past experienced per acre yields for wheat of up to three times those of Algeria.

Colombia plans to expand her output of African palm oil in order to be self-sufficient in the production of edible oils. Malaysia and Indonesia are planning for large increases in production of palm oil with most of the increases destined for export. Currently these two countries represent 60 percent of world production of palm oil and 90 percent of world exports. By 1985, world production of palm oil is expected to double to 6 million tons.

Interest in agricultural self-sufficiency is not limited to developing countries. The Soviet Union has embarked on a three-pronged plan of self-sufficiency comprised of the U.S.-U.S.S.R. five-year grain contract, a storage facility building program to help tide the country over in bad years, and a slowdown in the rate of expansion of livestock production - to let grain production catch up with demand.

Japan, on the other hand, unable to become self-sufficient in grain production and shaken by the 1973 United States soybean export embargo, is using both conventional (long-term contracts) and novel means of assuring herself of dependable grain supplies. Japanese investment in agricultural projects extends to soybean production in Maxico and Brazil; corn production in Thailand, Indenesia, Mexico, Argentina, and the Philippines; and beef production in Australia, the Malagasy Republic, and Indonesia. (3) Under the "Develop and Import" program Japan introduced corn production into Thailand. Approximately 80 percent of the corn grown there is exported to Japan for feed. With the "Export Corridor" program in Brazil, grain storage and refrigeration facilities for food exports to Japan are being built. In the "cerrados" (savannah) region of Brazil, the Japanese are carrying out experimental farming operations. With improvement in soil fertility and proper development, the "cerrados" offer great agricultural potential. The Arab world is reported to be planning a total investment of $3 billion for the agricultural development of the Sudan, in order to turn that country into the breadbasket of the Middle East. (4)

AGRICULTURAL EXPORTS TO PAY FOR OIL IMPORTS AND ECONOMIC DEVELOPMENT

The second emerging trend is that of certain foreign countries producing crops for export in order to offset the higher costs of oil imports and economic development. Brazil and Argentina are perhaps the most important examples. The principal effect on the United States has been the decrease in our exports of the same grains resulting from this competition.

With changes in policy beginning in the mid-1960s, Brazil put increasing emphasis on her agricultural sector. Until 1964 her development policy had been one of import substituting industrialization. In 1964 Brazil opened up her domestic economy with policies favoring domestic technological growth and the transfer of technology from industrialized countries. To offset a growing trade gap caused by the import of capital goods and growing debt service requirements (currently over 40 percent and expected to rise to 50 percent by 1980) occasioned by heavy borrowing abroad, exports were and are strongly pursued. Most recently, the high price paid for oil imports has exacerbated her trade gap. What makes Brazil so interesting is her shift from a two-cash crop (coffee and sugar) exporter to a multi-crop/food exporter with an increasingly ambitious agricultural sector development program. Figure 20.1 and table 20.1 highlight this facet of Brazil's development.

When viewed in the light of her growing oil import bill her limited short-term ability to secure sufficient sources of domestic oil (whether from increased offshore exploration or from exploitation of her huge - second only to the U.S. - shale oil deposits), and her transition from a developing country to an industrialized one, a strategy of increased agricultural exports is of prime importance. The large current account deficit of $6.3 billion in 1976 dictated that exports be expanded.

Argentina is also promoting agricultural exports, and it appears that Argentina is following much the same strategy as Brazil in expanding from a one or two cash crop exporter to a multi crop exporter - differing from the past because the crops are also tied to the country's economic development. Argentina is fast becoming the third largest exporter of soybeans after the United States and Brazil. A brief overview of Argentina's agriculture in 1978 can be seen in figure 20.2.

Table 20.1. U.S.-Brazil Comparisons (million metric tons)

Production: Soybeans

	United States	Brazil
1975-76	30.7	1.5
1976-77	44.3	11.6
1977-78	48.0	9.9
1978-79	49.3	13.5 (estimated)

Exports: Soybeans & Soybean Products

	United States			Brazil		
	Soybeans	Soybean Meal	Soybean Oil	Soybeans	Soybean Meal	Soybean Oil
1975-76	12.5	3.8	.365	3.5	3.5	.32
1976-77	15.1	4.9	.510	3.6	4.3	.498
1977-78 (est)	19.1	5.4	.9	2.6	5.4	n/a/

Source: USDA data, World Agricultural Situation, USDA, October 1978.

AGRICULTURAL PROFILE

1. World leading producer of:

   coffee   edible beans
   cane sugar   cassava
   bananas   oranges

2. World's largest exporter of:

   coffee   orange juice
                       concentrate

3. Soybeans:
   world's second largest exporter (after the U.S.)
   world's third largest producer
      (after the U.S. & China)
   in 1974 and 1975, Brazil's top foreign
      exchange earner

4. Fertilizer:
   450,000 metric tons used in 1967
   2,600,000 metric tons used in 1977
   Usage still small by developed country standards

5. Corn: Production increased from 12 to 19 million
   tons during the period from 1965 to 1977 and exports were in excess of one million tons annually
   by 1977. Corn export policy is under review,
   however, as domestic demand for mixed feeds
   grows. In fact, 1978 may see corn imports up
   to one million tons.

6. Wheat: Brazil hopes to become self-sufficient
   in wheat production in the 1980s, partly through
   a strategy of subsidizing wheat prices at a high
   level and partly by the possibility of double
   cropping with soybeans in southern Mato Grosso
   and Western Parana. Even so, it is likely that
   Brazil will have to import wheat in substantial
   quantities one out of every three years due to
   the uncertainty of the weather. In addition,
   wheat production is expensive due to infertile
   and acidic soils requiring relatively expensive
   manufactured inputs, sufficient scientific
   and technical support, and a lack of appropriate
   varieties for Brazil's tropical and sub-tropical
   climates. Her goal of wheat self-sufficiency
   is a long way off. For example, her domestic
   needs of 200 million bushels were only frac-
   tionally met in 1977 by a poor harvest of 70
   million bushels (vs. the planned for 120
   million bushels)

7. Cocoa Beans: By the early 1990s, Brazil hopes
   to produce 700,000 tons of beans which, it is
   estimated, would make Brazil the world's principal exporter of cocoa beans. Currently, she
   produces in the neighborhood of 250,000 tons
   of beans annually.

8. Tobacco: Both production and exports have
   been growing, with the former amounting to
   approximately 300,000 tons annually and leaf
   exports around 100,000 tons. Government
   production and EEC preference duties enable
   Brazil to sell leaf on the world market at
   approximately one-half the U.S. export price.

9. Orange Juice: In 1963, a Florida frost
   launched Brazil's orange juice industry.
   While the larger U.S. orange juice industry
   primarily serves a much larger domestic market,
   Brazil in 1976 exported three times as much
   orange juice concentrated as did the United
   States (181,000 metric tons vs. 66,000) with
   21,000 tons shipped to the U.S.

10. Beef Cattle: Brazil has the world's fourth
    largest beef herd numbering 100 million
    head - twice the size of that of Argentina.

11. Agricultural exports: In recent years,
    Brazil's agricultural exports accounted for
    50-60 percent of total export earnings.
    Exports of soybeans, coffee, sugar, and
    cocoa have helped keep the balance of trade
    deficit under control.

Source: Foreign Agriculture, U.S. Department of
Agriculture, January 16, 1978, February 20 and
27, 1978, May 15, 1978, June 12 and 26, 1978.

Fig. 20.1. Brazil's Agriculture - An Overview

THE SOYBEAN BOOM - ORIGINS AND OUTLOOK

Origins:

1. A spinoff of Brazil's domestic wheat expansion
   program (started in late 1930s). Improved cultural
   practices, and an existing producer cooperative network (wheat) developed certified soybean seed and
   diffused the new (soybean) technology. Increased
   availability of low cost agricultural credit, government price support program and continued high world
   prices for soybeans and soybean products provided
   the incentives for farmers.

2. Climate, favorable growing conditions and increasing
   profitability of soybeans led to double cropping
   with winter wheat.

3. Program to eradicate low yielding coffee trees
   and reduce Brazil's dependence on coffee as the
   major foreign exchange earnings gave incentive
   for farmers on larger, outlying farms to switch
   from labor intensive coffee to mechanized soybean-wheat production. Having made the equipment investment, it is now unlikely that these
   farmers will switch back to coffee.

Outlook

1. Future high production levels depend primarily
   on continuation of present high yields. Smaller
   farmers have shown willingness to use modern
   agricultural techniques and inputs.

2. Government policy likely to seek expanded production of soybeans since it is a strong
   foreign exchange earner.

3. In an effort to maintain as much as possible of
   a product's "value stream" in country, Brazil
   is expanding its soybean crushing capability.
   Export emphasis will be increasingly on soybean
   products.

4. Brazil's government attempting to establish
   long-term arrangements for guaranteed markets
   with individual countries.

5. Demand for soybeans and soybean products should
   continue high as diets in many countries shift
   toward greater consumption of meat.

6. Her export policy vis-a-vis soybeans and soybean
   products appears to be to move as much as fast
   as possible to prop up her weak foreign exchange
   position. U.S. exports of soybeans to Europe have
   steadily lost ground to Brazil. Only because of a
   comparative advantage in freight and a slight
   quality advantage has the U.S. market share in Japan
   remained stable. While Brazilian soybean growers
   pay higher internal transportation and handling
   charges than do U.S. farmers, land prices in
   Brazil are significantly lower. This, coupled
   with the higher proportion of double cropping in
   Brazil accounts for a per acre cost in Rio Grande
   do Sul about one-half the estimated average U.S.
   cost.

Sources: Foreign Agriculture, March 15, and 22, 1976,
March 21, 1977; Vivian E. Morgan "Agriculture - A Vital
Input to Brazilian Industrialization" Vivian E.
Morgan, "Brazilian Industrialization," Wall Street
Journal, September 15, 1977, pp. 22-23.

PRINCIPAL ELEMENTS OF BRAZIL'S AGRICULTURAL DEVELOPMENT STRATEGY

Improvement of sector productivity including the modernization of marketing
channels.

Opening large, unexploited tracts of land in the north, center-west and
western part of the north-east.

Providing an economic climate which will give continuing incentives to
farms to produce via fiscal, credit and insurance measures as well as the
extension of the full benefits of labor and social security legislation to
producers and rural workers.

Expansion of agro-industry, especially for sugarcane and other tropical
products.

A yearly growth rate of 7 percent for her agricultural sector.

Source: David P. Harmon, Jr. and Andrew Caranfil, "Brazil: The Economy,"
HRS-135-CC, Hudson Institute, July 1977.

Fig. 20.1. Brazil's Agriculture - An Overview - Continued

Increase in soybean production with a record crop of 3 million tons (1976 crop = 1.4 million tons; 1971 = a mere 78,000 tons) of which 1.3 million tons are expected to be exported.

Record corn crop of 9.5 million tons and sorghum harvest of 6.9 million tons.

A poor 1977-78 wheat harvest of 5.2 million tons due to drought at planting time, dry spells and low prices, but 1978-79 crop expected to reach 7.4 million tons.

Expansion of cottonseed, flaxseed and peanut growing area.

Record sunflowerseed harvest close to 1.3 million tons.

With only 13-15 million tons of storage capacity, Argentina has embarked on a storage expansion and modernization program which should mean growth in her exportable surplus of grain.

Livestock production and export of livestock products are being expanded.

Expansion of area planted to grain sorghum since it is extremely adaptable to Argentina's climate is complementary to cattle raising.

Source: Foreign Agriculture, U.S. Department of Agriculture, April 14, 1977; June 19, 1978; p. 5; July 10, 1978, p. 7-8. World Agriculture Situation, U.S. Dept. of Agriculture, December 1978, p. 29.

Fig. 20.2. Overview of Argentina's Agriculture in 1978

CHANGING TRADE PATTERNS

Forecasting foreign demand for United States farm commodities is a difficult task because foreign markets are the most uncertain variable elements in any estimate. We feel that it is safe to say, however, that United States agricultural exports will not grow at the phenomenal rates of the early mid-1970s. As to the course of agricultural trade over the next decade, observers differ even to the end of the century. Many seen to feel that on the average foreign demand for United States agricultural exports will increase fairly steadily. The reasons given for this anticipated increase are growth in world population, economic growth leading to increasing affluence and changing diets, and fewer restrictions on trade. Moreover, we have the best resource base in terms of varied climate, fertile land, and all the elements of agricultural infrastructure to supply increasing demand for food. Furthermore, as our oil import bill mounts, it becomes increasingly imperative that we export agricultural products.

However, others feel that the United States under the pressure of increased "competition" from foreign country self-sufficiency objectives and competitor grain export nations, will suffer a decline in agricultural exports, particularly the grains.

The effort to promote United States agricultural exports is being given renewed emphasis and an additional focus. "Rapid growth" markets such as the stable developing countries, the Middle East, and North Africa are the object of new market development activities. Heavily populated countries such as Iran and Egypt are looked to as promising markets for food and feed grains as well as bulk products. The centrally planned economies of Eastern Europe and the Soviet Union represent rapidly growing markets for feed grains, feed grain products, and breeding stock. Over the period from 1970 to 1976, United States agricultural exports to this area grew from $200 million to $3 billion.

The key to how the Soviet market develops is the weather, foreign exchange availability, her agricultural policies, and her success in managing her enormous state farms. Plans to double fertilizer application by 1980 (1971 to 1975) are not likely to succeed because of lack of production facilities, fertilizer application machinery, and high losses of fertilizer in transportation and storage. (5) Weather, however, is the major factor in Soviet agriculture. From a 200 million metric ton average yearly production base, her output can swing 40 million tons either way, depending on the weather.

The transfer of technology, provision of credit facilities, and most favored nation treatment to the developing countries are seen as primary requirements of ensuring economic growth, which concomitantly means increased demand for feed grains and associated products as well as for nongrain agricultural goods.

This is not to say that our more traditional customers, the developed countries, will be ignored. On the contrary, they will continue to be important to us and will receive the attention of our promotional efforts.

What has been recognized, however, is the growing importance of the U.S.S.R., Eastern Europe, and certain higher income developing countries (notably South Korea and Taiwan) as feed grain markets. Also recognized is that since 1974, more than half of the world wheat imports have been by the developing countries. Moreover, the concessionary sales of the 1960s gave way to cash sales in the 1970s, and rapid expansion of the Asian wheat market is expected over the next few years. This growing interdependence between the United States and many other countries thus requires United States agricultural and food policies that are multidimensional. Only in this way can the United States meet its various objectives ranging from financing oil imports to providing an emergency grain stock to help developing countries in times of disaster.

But what of worldwide sluggish economic growth, the new pattern of protectionism that is emerging, and the moves toward agricultural self-sufficiency and increased agricultural exports as a means of paying for high priced oil? And what of our competitors in agricultural trade? Australia, Argentina, Brazil, South Africa, Israel, and the EEC outspent us seven to one ($146 million vs. $21 million) in the promotion of farm products in 1976. (6)

Our share of soybean meal exports to Eastern Europe dropped from 41 in 1973 to 35 percent in 1976. Better Brazilian prices, Brazilian lines of credit, and United States quality problems were the cause of the decline. Brazilian soybeans offered for export are the top of grade, while ours tend to be at the bottom of grade.

Brazil's export efforts are also in the direction of trying to guarantee markets for its agricultural export through bilateral agreements with large importing countries, e.g., Iran, Japan, and Western European nations. As Argentina becomes increasingly important in soybean markets, she too is likely to follow the same path.

The movements toward self-sufficiency, toward agricultural exports for oil, toward economic growth, and toward increased competition will require a much more complex United States export strategy. Demand for agricultural products will increase, but in different ways and rates for different commodities. (7)

How we sell a commodity will be as important as where we sell it. This is key to the recognition that enhancement of developing country economic growth will help ensure a market for United States goods. United States strategy must be flexible enough to deal with emerging short- and long-term trends; and, most importantly, it must not allow us to become once again the residual supplier to the world.

MORE MANAGED GRAIN MARKETS?

In the United States higher price supports for wheat and corn and acreage set-asides for wheat and feed grains are a reality. Furthermore, the government is paying farmers to keep wheat and other grains in their bins so that the government does not have to go back into the storage business. Secretary of Agriculture Bergland's agrument for these policies is that it helps the consumer by assuring supplies year to year, helps the government avoid embargoes in times of very short supply, and has enough flexibility in terms of the target, loan, and government resale provisions that farmers can only gain.

Another factor in the policy making is that for the first time in several years the livestock sector is making money as a result of lower feed grain prices. Also, dairy farmers are making money. Of course, these groups want to maintain lower feed costs. These measures were taken to curb production just enough to stabilize falling farm prices, but not so much that grain prices will take off and trigger increases in food prices.

SUPPLY MANAGEMENT

Because short-term aggregate demand for grain tends to be inelastic and because grain-exporting countries have been following "bare shelves" policies, a small change in global grain supplies will have a disproportionately large effect on world prices. Thus we have the perceived need for international grain reserves.

Food-deficit developing countries are less able to import grain and ensure internal food price stability when world grain prices are unstable. Food-exporting developing countries depend on foreign exchange earnings to help finance their development and therefore suffer under unstable prices. Moreover, when grain supplies are tight, less grain is available for aid and developing countries tend to divert resources from economic development objectives toward grain purchases. Proponents of international grain reserves cite the following objectives:

1. to promote price stability, and a smooth flow of food when needed, for developing countries

2. to smooth out short-term variations in food supply and the attendant problems

3. to prevent irreversible inflationary effects of large increases in grain prices - especially where higher food costs get locked into wage and price structures which only have upward flexibility

A COMPROMISE BETWEEN MANAGED SUPPLIES AND
FREE TRADE

With the United States agricultural sector more "open" in the sense that domestic agricultural and food prices are increasingly responsive to foreign demand, the appropriate farm policy is crucial. This recognition has led to a lessening of the polarization between the advocates of firm government control on agriculture and the advocates of free market reign. As early as 1974 the Committee for Economic Development set forth guidelines which demonstrate the convergence of the two positions. These guidelines were designed to take advantage of export opportunities, to be able to meet short-term emergency needs, and to mitigate the exposure of farm prices and supplies to external forces. The following are CED's principal recommendations:

1. primary reliance on free market forces

2. Government policies aimed at:

   a. reducing price and income instability
   b. assuring adequate grain supplies

3. standby authority to

   a. take land out of production to prevent accumulation of large crop surpluses
   b. institute a crop loan program which backstops a market characterized by declining demand

4. closer linking of domestic farm policy with trade policy so that farmers are encouraged to grow those commodities which meet both domestic needs and foreign trade requirements while at the same time retaining the ability to change both trade and agricultural policies according to national interest. (8)

The intent of the program is to provide United States farmers with protection against very low prices, to encourage them to produce, and to socialize the cost of maintaining production flexibility with the authority to take land out of production and offer crop loans.

Furthermore, reliance on the operation of the free market offers both farmers and private traders incentive to carry grain inventories, thereby fulfilling the price stability objective for consumers. (9)   If effective, such private stocks would simultaneously allow the United States to reap its comparative advantage as an efficient, large-scale grain producer and offer protection against widely fluctuating world prices. The program's objective is to permit a maximum amount of free market operation for the private sector and a minimum public role while at the same time permitting the expansion of agricultural exports without serious income effects on consumers.

The structural change caused by the dollar devaluation of the early 1970s allowed our comparative advantage to work, and thus we were able to capitalize on our investments in agricultural technology. (10) This is one of the advantages of allowing the marketplace to operate. While there is a short-term redistribution of income away from consumers as the domestic terms of trade shift in favor of agriculture, technological advances in agriculture, increased capacity in production of agricultural chemicals and other inputs, as well as economic growth, should permit the long-term downward trend in real agricultural prices to continue. Furthermore, prices in the long-term tend to decline with increasing availability of substitute products, processes, and new sources of supply.

The argument for free trade is that farmers and private industry operating in a free market will respond to price signals and provide what is necessary. Freer trade in agricultural products should be beneficial to both the grain-exporting countries and to developing countries. Freer trade between the United States and the rest of the developed world allows the United States farmers' comparative advantage to operate, thus leading to increased production. (11)

Developing countries, where they have comparative advantage, will find it easier to export. They tend to have a comparative advantage in the areas of unsophisticated manufacturing and processing, the areas in which today's developed countries have imposed tariff barriers to protect the same relatively high cost industries. A prime example is that of sugar production where they are the lowest cost producers, and developed countries maintain high cost sugar industries. Furthermore, it is very often these industrial crops that are important foreign exchange earners for them and which, if freer trade prevailed, would permit them to cover more of their grain shortfalls by purchase on the world market. (12)

The gain in ability to trade will strengthen them and provide a time and earnings "buffer" by permitting them to develop where they have a comparative advantage. And the developed countries need each other and also the developing countries as reliable markets.

Further advantages of a free market are:

1. Increased price stability as the private sector, both farmers and traders, holds its own reserves to take advantage of temporary market opportunities or as protection against temporary shortfalls.

2. Reliable trade channels alleviate the need for expensive national reserves of grain to offset production fluctuations.

3. Unsubsidized, unregulated grain sales for cash to such countries as the Soviet Union increase both United States wealth and the strength of the dollar. A stronger dollar means that the United States pays lower prices for imports. (13)

A policy of freer trade also enhances the image of the United States as a reliable supplier, alleviates the fear of United States government cut off of exports, and gives the United States farm producer incentives when he sees the increasing development of foreign markets. Government controls, on the other hand, bolster the farmer's fear of a consumer oriented government and blocked export markets. United States export controls on soybeans in 1973 convinced Europe and Japan that dependence on United States soybeans as feed grain had to be reduced.

Our agricultural sector has a great deal to gain from accelerated economic growth and increased foreign exchange earnings in the developing world. Overly regulated commodity production, trade, and prices, however, could spell long-term danger for the potential of United States agriculture. Only if American farmers are permitted to use their resources efficiently will they be able to meet future export demand and export competition.

NOTES

(1) J. Dawson Ahalt, Presentation of " World and U.S. Agricultural Outlook" at 1978 Food and Agricultural Outlook conference (USDA), Washington, D. C., November 15, 1977.

(2) G. Edward Schuh, Food and Agricultural Policy. Conference sponsored by the American Enterprise Intitute for Public Policy Research, Washington, D. C., 1977, p. 157.

(3) ForeignAgriculture, U.S. Department of Agriculture, October 3, 1977.

(4) Foreign Agriculture, July 18 and 24, 1977.

(5) The Impact of Fertilizer on Soviet Grain Output, 1960-1980. National Foreign Assessment Center, Central Intelligence Agency, R77-10577, November 1977.

(6) Foreign Agriculture, February 13, 1978, p. 7.

(7) Thomas Saylor, 1978 Food and Agriculture Outlook. Committee on Agriculture, Nutrition and Forestry, U.S. Senate, November 14, 17, 1978, p. 83.

(8) Committee for Economic Development. A New U.S. Farm Policy for Changing World Food Needs, New York, October 1974, pp. 24-28.

(9) K.L. Robinson, "Unstable Farm Prices: Economic Consequences and Policy Options," American Journal of Agricultural Economics 57, no. 5 (December 1975): 775-776.

(10) G. Edward Schuh, "The Exchange Rate and U.S. Agriculture, " American Journal of Agricultural Economics 56, no. 1 (February 1974): 11.

(11) Wayne Moyer, "Iowa Dateline: A View from the Cornfields," Foreign Policy, no. 19 (Summer 1975): 187-188.

(12) James Vermeer, David W. Culver, J. B. Penn and Jerry A. Sherples, "Effects of Trade Liberalization on U.S. Agriculture," Agriculture Economics Reaearch 27, no. 2 (April 1975). U. S. Department of Agriculture, Economic Research Service, pp. 24-26.

(13) D. Gale Johnson, "Population, Food and Economic Adjustment." Speech presented at the annual meeting of the American Statistical Association, New York, December 27, 1973, p. 93.

BIBLIOGRAPHY

Bacha, Edmar L. "Issues and Evidence on Recent Brazilian Economic Growth." World Development, 5, nos. 1, 2 (1977).

Banco Real. Economic Letter, April 1977.

Brazil 1976. Associacao de Exportadores Brasileiros, Rio de Janiero.

The Economist Intelligence Unit, Quarterly Economic Review.

Fontaine, Roger W., and Theberge, James D. Latin America's New Internationalism. New York: Praeger Publishers, 1976.

Foreign Economic Trends and Their Implications for the United States-Brazil. U.S. Department of State and U.S. Department of Commerce, December 1976.

Furtado, Celso. Economic Development of Latin America. Cambridge University Press, 1976.

Latin American Commodities Report 1, no. 15, April 22, 1977.

Latin American Week 7, No. 355, April 1, 1977.

London Times. October 25, 1976.

Looney, Robert E. Income Distribution Policies and Economic Growth In Semiindustrialized Countries. New York: Praeger Publishers, 1975.

New International Realities. April 1977.

Science 196, April 29, 1977 and March 4, 1977.

Syvrud, Donald E. Foundations of Brazilian Economic Growth. Stanford University, 1974.

Tyler, William G. "Brazilian Industrialization and Industrial Policies: A Survey." World Development, 4, nos. 10, 11, (1976).

Webb, Kempton E. "World Food Distribution and the Great Brazilian Time-Space Machine." Unpublished paper.

21 A World Grain Outlook for the 1980s: Three Viewpoints*

J. Dawson Ahalt
Philip Sisson
Thomas R. Saylor

J. DAWSON AHALT

The 1970s have been an awakening for many people concerned with agriculture. We have lived through periods of very tight supply, and others of excess when stocks could be built while prices drop.

The situation in 1978 reflects this delicate balance between too much and too little. Because demand is so inelastic, the agricultural plant can overproduce in the short run and depress prices. The problem for the near term is how to deal with instability.

The present administration has tried to tackle this (for the first time) putting together a deliverage reserves program. Instead of accumulating stocks through a program of loan rates, the effort is to isolate a relatively small reserve with specified release levels - to lessen some of the instability of the marketplace. The hope is that this will permit us to devote more attention to other pressing agricultural issues, domestic and international.

We have tended to look at United States agricultural problems in isolation, to jack up support programs through domestic loan rates, and so on. In the meantime, world markets have become so important to the United States, and vice-versa, that United States policy must take account of a very complex international picture. Some of those major markets, including Japan and the European Common Market, isolate their markets by various devices. The United States, as the world's supplier, tries to operate a relatively open policy. The result is that the United States becomes the shock absorber for the rest of the world. The fluctuations in Unites States supplies and prices thus become more

---

* Remarks presented at the Food, Agriculture and Society Research Research Program Meeting, Washington, D.C., March 28, 1978.

magnified than they would be in an open world system. Some developing countries which must import food also must absorb some substantial adjustments.

In terms of the future, we will probably remain in a situation of relatively narrow balance between supply and demand. Years of excess supply and years of shortages lie ahead; prices will be pretty volatile. This is our best guess for the next two or three years.

In the longer run, the outlook is quite different. The gap between what the poor countries can produce and what they need will grow. The exporting countries will have to devise ways of financing the deliveries of supplies which these countries will need.

In terms of progress, some of these developing countries have been growing faster in food production during the past decade than the developed world. On a per capita basis, their progress is less impressive. In terms of per capita volume increase in the last 10 years, the poor countries have gone up an average of 2 pounds of additional grain per person per year. This has been added to an average level of 420 pounds per person. In the developed world, the rate of growth has been about 20 pounds per person, added to about 1 ton per person per year. This includes grain consumed directly and indirectly through livestock.

The nutritional gap between the haves and the have-nots is likely to widen further. More focus will be needed on policies to stimulate production in the developing world. What should be done varies by country.

In Southeast Asia some countries are making progress, notably Malaysia. This nation will probably not need a great deal of outside help in the future. By contrast, Indonesia has enormous problems and will have to rely on the outside world for concessional sales.

The United States and other exporting nations can look forward to expanding markets for food exports in these countries and the developing world. Our effort should be directed toward stimulating production in the poor countries which must import food. They have problems of infrastructure and problems of energy.

But, in general, one can be relatively optimistic about the decade ahead. Although tough periods due to bad weather are always possible, progress can be greater than in the past decade. But we must do the right things, and this won't be easy.

PHILIP SISSON

It is advisable to talk about plentiful supplies rather than surpluses, since what the United States has may not be indicative of the situation in the rest of the world. We certainly have evidence from the past five or ten years that the world may be reaching the limits of its capacity to produce. This may be due to weather or other growing conditions. During 1977 fairly significant problems occurred all over the world. The total usable supply of grain from the U.S.S.R. and Eastern Europe will be below expectations, even if the Russian crop reaches 195 million tons. Australia encountered drought last year; Brazil and the southeast United States also ran into some trouble. Central Iowa also had some drought conditions. The United States, however, still ended up with very large crops.

The impact of weather often shows up more in United States exports than in total production. The agricultural outlook in the first quarter of 1978 reduced expectations for potential United States exports in 1977 to 1978. A good argument can be made that United States technological development has slowed. Regardless of whether this is brought about through reaching the limits of our capacity to expand through fertilizer use or through improved seed varieties, there is reason to believe that future gains will be harder to attain than they have in the past.

The projection beyond 1977 in figure 21.1 is based on the 1960 to 1977 trend, adjusted for population. Over the past decade, production growth has certainly slowed down. Figure 21.2 certainly does not suggest that the world is in a situation of surplus.

When we talk about the United States as a residual supplier, figure 21.3 should be kept in mind. It shows the fantastic adjustment in United States coarse grain production which occurred in the 1974 to 1975 crop year. This occurred because we do not isolate our supplies from the rest of the world, and thus our domestic consumption fell off. This has to have a bad impact on the livestock and poultry producers in this country.

Figure 21.4 shows that, at the end of 1978 stocks should be at their lowest level since 1970. this may not be a major problem, but it could become serious if some legislation passed by the Senate is turned into law. Thus the Talmadge Act could lead to some fantastic swings in demand for United States grain or in its price. This could hurt United States grain consumption for our livestock and poultry.

THOMAS R. SAYLOR

The United States accounts for roughly half the wheat and coarse grains moving in world trade, and the United States market share tends to be cut before other exporters in a situation of oversupply. Since the United States is the dominant supplier in world markets, the term "residual supplier" may not be very apt. The United States is seeking to attain better coordination so that the major suppliers can compete on somewhat equal terms. Since the other major wheat exporters sell through some sort of state trading operations, they have more flexibility to try to outguess the United States as the price leader. But if the United States were to change its marketing system, no better adjustment might result. If the United States were to intervene more directly in export markets, the only result might be for governments to try to bid the price lower.

The margin between global production and annual requirements has

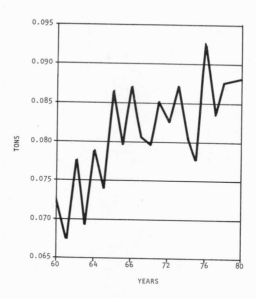

Fig. 21.1. World wheat production per capita, excluding U.S.

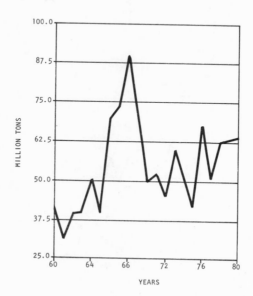

Fig. 21.2. World wheat stocks, excluding U.S.

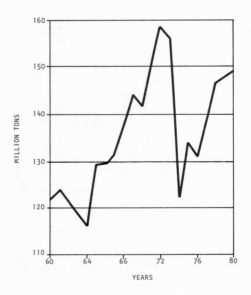

Fig. 21.3.   U.S. coarse grain consumption

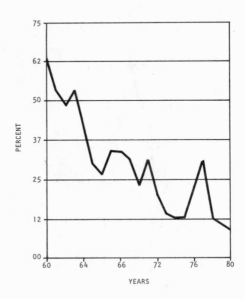

Fig. 21.4.   U.S. coarse grain - ending stocks as a pct. of consumption.

narrowed considerably. This is basic for the long-term world grain outlook. There has been a trend for consuming nations to seek to meet these requirements externally. Exports now account for about 15 percent of utilization, compared to 11 percent 5 to 10 years ago. Trade and dependency on external markets have clearly grown, and consuming nations are now more vulnerable than they used to be.

Another major factor is the increasing problem of food distribution as opposed to the absolute availability of supply. For the near and intermediate term, we can extrapolate a situation where production increases can expand at a rate which matches trend line growth of consumption. In terms of population growth, however, a disparity between potential and effective demand will certainly grow and it will thus be difficult to meet potential demand though normal market distribution channels.

Some national policies will have a major impact on the long-term outlook. In the first place, the production policies of the major producing regions will be critical. A great concern over excess supplies is already being expressed in the United States, and pressure is growing to bring our production more in line with effective demand. Large surplus stocks like those which accumulated in the 1950s and 1960s are unlikely to recur.

Second, a worldwide movement toward a larger portion of the diet based on livestock seems irreversible. The Soviet Union has committed itself to this goal and similar policies are emerging in Eastern Europe and the Middle East. During the 1963 to 1973 decade, Soviet grain utilization rose from about 150 million to 250 million tons for this reason.

Third, in the intermediate term, the instability implied by the narrowing margin between global production and annual requirements will probably result in efforts to insulate domestic markets from the volatility of world markets. Certainly the richer countries which can afford such policies will be moving toward more trade barriers. This transfers the burden of adjustment to other countries, consumers and producers alike, including the United States. This is well illustrated by the experience of 1973 and 1974 when a drastic reduction, about 130 million tons, occurred in United States feed utlization. Meanwhile, the European Community has effectively isolated its markets. Their feed utlization remained about constant; they even increased their coarse grain stocks marginally, despite pressing world needs.

Finally, the situation of The People's Republic of China will have a major impact on future world grain availability. Several things are happening there which will have a significant impact on China's participation in world grain markets. China may have pushed traditional intensive methods pretty close to their limits. Given the limitations on further expansion on her arable land, some major structural changes are likely to take place in Chinese agriculture unless large amounts of capital are applied. In view of the efforts toward increased mechanization which are under way, intercropping and the structure of small plots may have to be compromised. Second, the introduction of such things as new varieties will require a supportive infrastructure in terms of fertilizer and other imports. This will take time and involve further capital investment. Substantial efforts of this kind are under way, but they have not yet had a broad impact. The upshot of these developments is that China will probably be turning to world markets on a fairly large scale to meet its own needs. Since the Chinese economy consumes about 270 million tons a year, shortfalls in domestic production could bring about fairly substantial participation in world trade.

In terms of meeting the food needs of develping countries, a tripartite strategy was outlined by the Rome World Food Meeting. This strategy involves increased assistance for the agricultural production of developing countries, attention to their special trade problems, and stabilization effects. Substantial initiatives have been taken to put additional resources into food production, but their financing has been scaled down. Efforts are being made to make food aid flows more stable, but this addresses only a small part of the problem. Thus, aid may be maintained at 9 or 10 million tons annually, while the needs of developing countries have sometimes reached 40 or 50 million tons. The belies the effect that increased prices have had in denying many potential participants in the marketplace from meeting their full requirements.

The rationale behind food aid is to recognize that some part of effective demand must be met through extramarket channels. The largest share of aid is concessional assistance, through loans or special arrangements or on a government-to-government basis. A second form of aid is distribution programs within countries; these can be more effective than foreign aid in reaching people who might have limited access to food supplies even on a subsidized basis. But, since the infrastructure needed to do this is costly, it will remain limited.

Stabilization is the third area of food aid. This effort is being negotiated in Geneva. Past international wheat agreements have usually been arrived at in a context of surpluses. The current discussions have been dominated by the concept of providing mechanisms to ensure a balance between excess and tight supply. The primary mechanism has been stock accumulation when supply is ample, and release of stocks when supply is tight. No consensus is visible as yet on how to approach this problem, largely because of the politics of multilateral trade negotiations. But the political will exists to try to construct a mechanism for greater stabilization of world wheat trade.

Finally, efforts are also being made to reduce or eliminate trade barriers, despite the tendencies by some countries to turn inward. Multilateral trade negotiations are the main forum of efforts to maintain an outward direction in adjusting to world supply problems.

22 The Multinational Corporation: A Buffer in the Food-Climate System*

David P. Harmon, Jr.

INTRODUCTION

The role that multinational firms play in reducing developing country vulnerability to the vagaries of climate and weather and the policies that are adopted by developing countries to provide both an economic and political atmosphere conducive to multinational participation in agriculture and economic development will become increasingly important in the 1980s. Since climate and weather are still the most important factors in food production, and since they cannot be directly controlled nor confidently forecast within a narrow range, it behooves man to insert "buffers" in the food-climate system to protect against the system's inherent year-to-year and within-year variability and vulnerability. The reduction of climate induced vulnerability is also important because it can influence the adoption of new technologies. In a farming area of high weather/climate risk, a farmer will be very cautious in adopting new technologies because of the perceived risk of failure and because of difficulties in assessing benefits and costs. The experiences of Algeria and of Chile (in the following paper by Robert Cotton and Steward Flaschen) with multinationals and economic development will be drawn upon to portray the efforts that multinationals might make as agents of growth, providers of technology, and "buffers" in the food-climate system.

---

* Paper presented at Food and Climate Program, Aspen Institute for Humanistic Studies, Aspen, Colorado, June 8-9, 1978.

"BACKSTOPPING" AGRICULTURAL DEVELOPMENT

The Real Problems - Institutions

While the availability of resources and technology over the long term leaves little doubt as to the potential of both conventional and unconventional agriculture, it should not be taken as an invitation to complacency. Necessary for the task of feeding a growing population is the ability of individual governments to marshall their resources and to design and implement the appropriate policies to capitalize on the resources. The solutions to tomorrow's "food problem" must come in large part from the problem countries themselves.

The requirements of agricultural advance are comprised of not only physical inputs - labor, seeds, and agricultural chemicals - but also of an institutional infrastructure which permits these physical inputs to be supplied at the required time and place and in the required form - an infrastructure which is built on the provision of research, education, credit, availability of supplies, transportation, and marketing networks.

Implementation of agricultural advances are impossible if the farmer cannot obtain seeds, does not have the transportation facilities to market his produce, or lacks credit to purchase fertilizers or pesticides. Although the peasant farmer is often considered illiterate and conservative, his willingness to adopt high yielding varieties has proven that, given adequate incentives and opportunity, the small farmer is willing to change and adopt new techniques. The problems, therefore, are not with the farmer but rather with inadequate government priorities and policies for agricultural development. Incomes create <u>effective</u> demand, that is, demand with money behind it. <u>Effective</u> demand calls forth supply and this is the key economic fact of development. (1)

Government's Role

In the early stages of a country's agricultural development, the country is especially vulnerable to climatic fluctuations. It does not have the productive capacity, the grain reserves, nor the complex infrastructure and other buffers to tide it over periods of shortage. It is here that the United States and other governments could "backstop" the developing country and at the same time provide the type of assistance that will permit the private sector to flourish. Only in such circumstances can the multinational play an effective role - even if only a collaborative one at this stage.

The need for food aid is present in the short term when there is either lack of food or lack of money to buy food, since increased agricultural production takes time. However, limiting food aid to emergency situations lessens dependence on the United States and gives governments the will to emphasize the development of their own agricultural sectors.

In the short term foreign assistance would serve the dual purpose of alleviating the stress of current and near term debt service problems and financing capital intensive intermediate products such as fertilizer, thus conserving domestic capital for other needs. Longer-term food aid, however, can have undesirable effects. For example, our past food aid to India took pressure off the government to accelerate agricultural development, and allowed the allocation of limited capital to the industrial sector to meet industrialization goals. In retrospect, India would have been better off had she first established a firm agricultural base from which to industrialize. India also reduced food prices, which had the effect of reducing the farmer's incentive to increase his output. (2)

The longer-term role of foreign aid would be to assist the rapid development of the agricultural sector by provision of both the requisite capital goods and technical assistance for the early stages of development. It would also decrease agriculture's vulnerability to weather by guaranteeing food and thereby not letting development falter. (3)

Moreover, the United States should attempt to influence developing countries to encourage the efficient production of food by facilitatory rather than regulatory policies. Specifically, developing countries must understand the essential need for both private and public sector participation. In the early stages of agricultural development and for certain activities in the agricultural sector, government has a definite role. For example, research and development activities would be a public responsibility since industry would not be able to capture enough of the gains to justify the investment and efforts required. The private sector, on the other hand, should be encouraged to create and operate production and distribution facilities. This, in fact, happened in the Pakistan Punjab with the introduction of high yielding varieties. Spontaneously, small manufacturing firms sprang up to fill the need for diesel motors, pumps, tubewells, and other irrigation equipment.

As developing countries try to increase their agricultural productivity today, they are benefited by the availability of existing technology. What has taken years of research and development and a sizeable investment by one nation or research center is available for their use and adaptation. Today we tend to transfer only the skills that have been developed in the expansion of temperate country agriculture. In the future the development of adequate infrastructure and institutions in tropical climates and the ability to adapt agricultural technology to specific area conditions should permit the actual transfer of temperate country technology to the developing world. The multinational has an important role to play in both the early and later stages - that of transferring skills and technologies. But this will be possible only if the economic and political climates are conducive to multinational participation. Once these institutional mechanisms are established to facilitate this transfer, developing country farmers will be able to increase their productivity at a relatively minimal cost and at much faster rates than the farmers in countries who had to cope with the problems of the new technologies and refine and adapt them to their needs.

A prime characteristic of scientific agriculture is that it requires inputs which complement one another.   Lack of one or more complementary inputs may well cause the mrginal productivity of a new input or an entire package of inputs to drop below its marginal cost. If there is a limited market for increased production due to lack of effective demand, or if the benefits of using yield-increasing technologies does not sufficiently exceed the costs, then adoption of scientific agriculture will be slowed.

Fortunately, most developing countries have made efforts to increase agricultural production and some of the "nontraditional" inputs have been made available, consequently reducing the number of inputs currently limiting production.   Since the limiting inputs differ from agricultural area to area and when available usually yield prompt and large returns, accurate diagnosis of current and future input needs of scientific agriculture is crucial. The requirement is to identify the key limiting input(s) and remove or circumvent the limitation.

Where there is a high degree of input complementarity coupled with variability in both input needs and availability, potentially high returns accrue to a limited number of inputs.   Therefore a highly flexible agricultural development program is required wherein it concentrates on the inputs which are limited at any one place and time.

Moreover, a technological change, such as chemical fertilizer, can serve to increase the productivity of existing traditional factors of production, draw more of them into production, and also allow substitution of inputs with relatively high elasticities of supply for those with low elasticities - e.g., agricultural chemicals for labor.

Since farmers are unable to provide the inputs for yield-increasing technological change but are efficient resource allocators once the inputs are provided, the diagnosis must be made as to: 1) the total amount of scarce resources to be provided; 2) the optimum proportions of scarce resources for given levels of output; and 3) the precise form or organization and institutions required to make the resources available on a timely basis. (4)

Since agriculture is highly location specific, the effectiveness of assistance would be greatly enhanced if the aid were tailored to specific local conditions and aimed at removing the limitations caused by missing or insufficient key factors.

TECHNOLOGY - SIDESTEPPING LIMITING FACTORS

One of the most important goals of developing countries is to give their citizens a diet which is adequate nutritionally. Expressed in the simplest of terms, the goal is to put the necessary quantities and qualitites of nutrients into the mouths of people. This objective is important not only for "humanitarian" or "moral" reasons, but also for very realistic reasons. If people are malnourished, they are less productive and the potential time spent in productive employment is reduced. Children who are malnourished offer less potential return to the investment in their education and other skills. (5) Furthermore, the successful exploitation of new agricultural methods increasingly demands understanding of sophisticated techniques, correct timing of application of inputs, and, at certain times, great physical dexterity. (6) Thus a skilled, well-nourished labor force is a key requirement for both agricultural and general economic development.

Insurmountable institutional obstacles may prevent a country from developing the necessary physical and institutional infrastructure for agricultural development. Such obstacles may include not only physical and financial deterrents, but also resistance to change from those who stand to lose it. Climatic obstacles, such as the failure of the monsoon two years out of five in India, may also exist.

In the case where there are serious institutional and/or climatic obstacles hindering agricultural development, what are that country's alternatives? Technology offers peoples and governments the means of achieving at least some of the pressing objectives by sidestepping (rather than head-on meeting) some of the more serious institutional obstacles that exist.

Technology offers such alternatives at three important points in the field-to-table food chain. The first point is "in the field" and involves mission oriented basic research in three promising areas: Photosynthetic efficiency, biological nitrogen fixation, and genetic improvement. Better "harvesting of the sun" and subsequent partitioning into the plant's harvested parts, enhancement of biological nitrogen fixation of legumes, and the genetic improvement of plants are of great interest because they represent means of greatly increasing agricultural production while at the same time being apolitical, scale neutral, nonpolluting, and easily transferable.

The second point occurs post harvest and entails the technologies of loss prevention, of both quantity and quality, at numerous points from the field to the table - storage, intransit, processing, packaging, and distribution. Post harvest losses worldwide are estimated at 10 to 20 percent of the harvested crops, and it is reasonable to assume that such losses are higher in the developing world. "Loss" prevention technologies are available, easily adaptable (especially as a country's industrial sector modernizes), and apolitical, but entail capital, management expertise, and skilled personnel and training - areas in which multinationals excel.

The third point occurs in the processing stage and entails fortification of food. The enrichment of common foods such as bread, fats, salt, tea, and cereals offers an inexpensive and rapid way of reaching large numbers of people without the massive socioeconomic changes that occur when eating habits change. It would also offset the nutritional loss that tends to occur in the early stages of economic development as people switch to aesthetically more pleasing, but often less nutritious, foods.

Amino acid enrichment of bread offers one of the least expensive means of improving its quality. Listed below are the requirements, benefits, and limitations.

Requirements

●   Modest changes in milling processes to accommodate addition of amino acids.

●   Modest increase in storage and transportation costs, since only small quantities are needed.

Benefits

●   Possibility of a vitamin and mineral amino acid "package" in kernel form being added to whole grains.

●   No alterations in eating, cooking, or buying habits required; no alteration of color, texture, or taste of grain to which they are added.

●   Faster reaching of target populations than devising new foods or new seed varieties, or nutritional education.

●   Very little need for bureaucracy to put a food fortification effort into operation.

●   Especially suitable for urban areas where large concentrations of people have nutritional deficiencies.

●   The cost of synthetic amino acids approaches that of oilseeds, the world's least expensive, most available protein source; furthermore, synthetic amino acids have none of the toxicity, taste, and digestibility problems of oilseeds. (7)

Limitations

●   Finding a common food, or "carrier," that will reach a maximum of target people is subject to large scale production in a small number of plants.

●   Use of foods that are processed limits the target to those who buy and eat processed foods; if a cereal grain is the "carrier," people who grow and mill their own grain will be missed.

    In summary, synthetic nutrients can be added to the flour-milling process, and can give the bread-eating population the equivalent of the nutrients contained in fruit, vegetables, and milk. Food fortification has been successfully used since the 1930s in the United States, where bread and iodized salt, among other foods, are enriched and fortified.
    Of the principal factors of production, technology is special because it not only has a heavy impact on productivity in the short run, buy also has the attribute of rapid mobility. To be applied directly, however, it must be commercialized or adapted into a useful product or productive capability.

THE MULTINATIONAL: CREATOR AND TRANSFER AGENT
OF PROPRIETARY TECHNOLOGY

One of the prime roles of the multinational is the transfer and commercialization of the technologies it creates. It is the most important institution with a global capacity to apply science and technology to both production and marketing and to transfer technology across national borders. (8) It is potentially the most important channel of technology transfer. Technology is transferred by the multinational in a range of simple to rather sophisticated forms such as :

1. products

2. technical assistance to customers, users, and local suppliers of materials and components

3. local service facilities

4. local production facilities and associated training of personnel

5. long-term arrangements (produit-en-main type contracts) which include local production, facilities and training of personnel, as well as orgainizational form, management expertise, internal accounting systems, and access to new technological developments over a specified period of time.

This institution (the multinational corporation) is indispensable for the agricultural and industrial development of latecomers. There is such a rich flow of technology across borders that the "wise" developing country would design its trade and investment policies to exploit this flow rather than try to keep out foreign technology or duplicate what has been or is being done in the developed world. (9) Moreover, because of the very rapid advances in science and technology, developing countries are simply unable to generate enough scientists of sufficiently high quality themselves. And rapid adaptation to change is something that business does well. In a competitive market environment the reward/penalty "system" ensures efforts to exploit technologies. The need for the multinational corporation as the agent of technology transfer to the developing world is perhaps best seen in the words of Fernando Monckeberg, Chile's foremost nutritionist:

> When the scientific and technological level is low, so is the educational level, the organization of the community is ineffi-cient, and productivity is low, all of which leads to stagnation and poverty. (10)

ALGERIA: A CRUCIBLE FOR MULTINATIONALS

Algeria is examined as a developing country whose agricultural production is constrained by climate, and whose agricultural and industrial sector development has been constrained by both political philosophy and institutional obstacles. For purposes of developing a strategy to stimulate multinational participation in developing countries' food and agriculture sectors and to transfer technology, Algeria is an "ideal" country to consider because it is:

1. young (17 years old), outwardly socialistic, but basically nationalistic, with heavy residue of "free enterprise spirit" among the people;

2. politically left on the world scene; fairly radical in the Arab world; trying to take the leadership of the "Third World";

3. a nation with real potential for development:

   a. large national gas reserves; significant oil reserves

   b. eight to nine month growing season

   c. hard working, relatively capable labor force

   d. potentially large supplies of non fuel raw materials

   e. a growing economic infrastructure;

4. an extremely difficult place in which to operate - even as an Algerian organization:

   a. differences in business practices, "mores," and ethics

   b. deep suspicion of outsiders

   c. shifting requirements for foreign companies planning or doing business in Algeria

   d. joint ventures possible (51 percent or more Algerian ownership mandatory) but with constant threat of nationalization.

Algeria gained its independence from France in 1962 after an eight-year-long struggle in which 1 million people were killed. As one might imagine, it was flat on its back economically. Ninety percent of its 15 million people live along the littoral, which supports the bulk of Algeria's agriculture with the exception of wheat and sugar beets. Its principal food grain crop, wheat, is susceptible to drought, desertification, and to the sirocco - the hot, dry wind that blows north off the Sahara desert just before harvest time. The author spent a total of 4 months in the field with an Algerian counterpart in 1973 and 1976, personally visiting the headquarters and plants of 10 of Algeria's 20 "national" companies, including all those involved in the food sector. The purpose was to determine strengths and weaknesses in each national company. Of the 10 companies, 7 operated in the food and agriculture sector: milling, food processing, agricultural machinery, oilseed products, beverages, tobacco, and forest products. Because of the organization of Algeria's industrial sector, other ministries and agencies were involved, including agriculture, livestock, viniculture, forestry, and soil conservation. Algeria is fairly typical of developing countries which have an important government component in the economy; which are left politically; and which need multinational expertise and participation, but which make this participation extremely difficult.

It is a country of contradictions: Suspicious of outsiders (sometimes to the point of paranoia) and politically hostile to the United States, but aware of the benefits multinationals can bring and relatively eager to do business with United States firms; nationalistic, but filled with Arab-Berber factions and jealousies; and socialist in government, but with a population that is basically capitalistic. It is one of the most difficult countries in which a multinational might do business; one reason is the European/American difficulty in understanding the Arab mind, and vice versa. Because of these contradictions and the difficulties they imply, it is a crucible for those multinationals which operate there, and good lessons can be drawn from the "Algerian experience."

1. Overemphasis on Production: The country, within the past ten years, has embarked on a real economic gamble - that of starting many technologically complex and capital intensive industries as well as a visible economic infrastructure practically overnight. In the founding period of the national companies, production was stressed to the exclusion of all else. To a greater or lesser degree, depending on the activity, nonproduction requirements (for example, planning, marketing, distribution, management, and personnel) are being recognized, but due to lack of prior planning, serious bottlenecks have arisen.

2. Bottlenecks: The public industrial sector, with generally satisfactory production activities, suffers serious supply and distribution bottlenecks. The bottlenecks are largely due to the administrative separation, by the government, of functions properly belonging to the national companies. In many cases, agencies of the Ministry of Commerce are responsible for the supply of raw materials and for the marketing of final products; in other cases an agency of the Ministry of Transportation is responsible for the transport of goods both in intercompany sales and to the retail level for final sale to consumers. Other bottlenecks arise due to lack of coordination between agricultural agencies and particular national companies; or in some cases, other ministries' agencies and national companies do not even communicate with one another when, in fact, the closest of cooperation is vital. The necessity for cooperation is evident when one understands that Algeria has as little as ten days of wheat reserves in storage and suffer from extreme port congestion. Because of climatic and political (to be touched upon later) conditions her wheat crop does not meet its potential one year out of two. The power accorded various ministries and agencies to determine prices, terms of payment and quantities and qualities of goods which they will purchase from some of the national companies have reduced particular companies to the role of production entities, rather than companies responsible for the entire spectrum of normal business activities. This emasculation means that these companies cannot function efficiently, that discord and friction arise between the companies and agency/ministry, and that the economy suffers.

3. Long-Range Planning and Investment: In many national companies, as well as in many ministries, there is a severe lack of long-
range planning. Lack of planning, failure to consider alteratives, and a
lack of broad view cause misplacement of investment funds through
faulty investment decisions. For example, often factories are built to
replace old plants, when in fact the old plants should merely be shut
down.

In the past 10 years the economy has grown in size and complexity
to the point where adminstrative and structural bottlenecks can
strangle, and investment mistakes can have very serious repercussions.
There is a critical need not only for "strategic" planning but also for
"tactical" planning and redefinition of areas of responsibilities. For
example, the national companies should be allowed to perform the full
gamut of normal business activities including marketing, supply,
distribution, and the ability to make contracts enforceable by law. Such
allowance would go far in enabling the national companies to plan for
the future, to optimize production and usage of production facilities,
and to alleviate the stranglehold of the current major bottlenecks.

Technology Appropriate to Stages of Development

The foregoing background comments on Algeria's economy are
essential to understanding the need for technology appropriate to a
country's (and its various sectors,) stages of development, both present
and future. In the eleven years between independence and 1973, Algeria
had risen from a devastated country to one having to come to grips with
some very sophisticated questions such as a development policy of
industrialization or of agricultural sector led growth; capital rationing;
the acquisition of technology and how to meet the nation's current and
future food and nutritional requirements in the face of severe climatic
difficulties. Examples of failure abound. In many cases, the Algerians
(and the Europeans and Americans) failed to understand that it is also
essential to have an appreciation of the economic and political climate
in which multinationals have to operate. Technology transfer entails
more than just the transplanting of equipment, a plant, or a technology
itself. It involves planning, managerial expertise, cost accounting and
measures of performance, education, and understanding that
development is both a dynamic and iterative process. Two examples
will serve to point up the failure side for Algeria's development. The
national food (vegetables and fruits) processing company, Sogedia, built
a beet sugar refinery in the town of Guelma (in the East) on the premise
that the sugar beet was a "national" product and would provide
agricultural employment. While this was true, refined sugar from the
sugar beet was more than two times as expensive as refined sugar from
raw cane sugar in 1973 - both of which raw materials were processed at
the El Khemis sugar refinery (in the West). Comparative cost and yield
figures follow:

Cost of 1 ton sugar beets delivered El Khemis	= 190 DA
Cost of 1 ton raw cane sugar delivered El Khemis	= 680 DA
Average yield of refined sugar from 1 metric ton sugar beets	= 120 KG
Average yield of refined sugar from 1 metric ton raw cane sugar	= 900 KG
Cost per kilo refined beet sugar 190/120	= 1,58 DA
Cost per kilo refined cane sugar 680/900	= 0,76 DA

Of course this calculation did not take into account the processing costs of both raw materials at El Khemis, but the disparity in the cost per kilo of cane versus beet sugar would have been even greater since beets require more processing (washing, stem cutting, beet cutting, grinding, etc.) before they reach the stage comparable to raw cane sugar. In addition to the per kilo cost of beet sugar must be added amortization of all the extra equipment needed to process the beets. The totality of sugar beet processing equipment was approximately three times as expensive as the cane sugar processing equipment. On top of all this must be added the costs of eight or nine months maintenance on equipment, owing to the extremely corrosive nature of sugar beets and the fact that the equipment is only operative three months of the year due to the size and timing of the beet crop, while cane sugar processing goes on all year. Of course the argument in favor of self-sufficiency in sugar was raised, but with a well-developed international market (supply) for sugar, one must ask if further investment in sugar beet processing facilities was truly justified given not only the high cost of beet sugar, but also Algeria's pressing needs in other areas.

The second example involved the construction and operation of a plant to turn out a high vegetable protein food, Superamine, comprised of chick peas, lentils, soya, and wheat. While the idea of increasing the availability of proteins via locally grown products with foreign technology was certainly laudable, poor planning, financial constraints, and severe contamination problems led to the project's demise. On the other hand, three industrial flour mills (to be located in the east, center, and west of Algeria's littoral - covering 90 percent of her population) have been in the planning stage for the past ten years! Algeria is a nation of eaters of bread and cous-cous - both wheat products, most of which she grows herself. In this case, however, technology offers a low-cost effective solution to much of Algeria's nutritional deficiencies, and secondarily places a needed buffer in the food climate system.

Since nutrition, like agriculture, is "location-specific," fortification of wheat flour, a food eaten regularly and in consistent quantities throughout the year by all age and economy groups, could help achieve Algeria's nutritional objectives. (Industrial countries take fortification of foods for granted. Their citizens assume that salt is iodized and bread and milk fortified. This is a case of an on-the-shelf technology that is directly transferable from developed to developing countries.)

Fortification technology would also allow Algeria to partially sidestep the political problems inherent in her agriculture. Algeria's political development has a heavy Trotskyite influence which manifests itself in the agricultural sector in the form of worker-managed state farms. The results of this influence may be seen in years of good weather where Algeria's neighbor, Tunisia, records wheat yields three times as large as that of Algeria.

The success side is perhaps best typified by Algeria's automotive industry, which includes agricultural machinery. Sonacome, the national automotive company, identified important interrelationships between various national needs as well as between company needs. Sonacome's tractor-producing facility at Constantine not only satisfies Algeria's needs for tractors, but also has given Algeria the expertise of manufacturing diesel engines which she will produce in greater quantities for the buses, trucks, vans, and industrial vehicles to be built at other Sonacome facilities. Since the Constantine plant is the first fully integrated Sonacome operation (by the end of 1973, 85 percent of the value of each tractor produced was Algerian, with only 15 percent foreign, i.e., rubber tires, carburetors, and other small items), Sonacome has benefited by having run an extremely complex manufacturing operation which will be translatable immediately into the planned automobile production facilities. It is a self-sufficient source of supply for all diesel motors in Algeria and, coincidentally, has met Algerian agriculture's need for tractors. Sonacome's strategy entailed the use of the "produiten-main" (literally translated, product-in-hand) concept of acquiring foreign technology. The use of this concept was forward thinking on Sonacome's part because not only did it entail the construction of the tractor plant and associated training of technical and work staffs, but also involved the acquisition of a management organization, internal accounting and performance measures, and guarantee of output under full operating conditions, and a ten-year access to technological innovations in all aspects of tractor design and construction from the constructor firm, DIAG (West Germany). Sonacome demonstrated that it understood how to respond to and take advantage of the benefits of technology. The tractors produced are simple, unadorned, durable, and appropriate to Algeria's stage of agricultural development. They are also suitable (and exportable) for other countries of the Maghreb and the Middle East.

The Sonacome strategy certainly sounds ideal for many other sectors of activity in Algeria. The problem is that there is a high degree of political and economic risk in Algeria for the multinational firm. At best, most firms will go no further than turnkey projects and much prefer straight sales of equipment and production lines for hard currency payable elsewhere. Thus it is not surprising that there are very few joint ventures operative in Algeria, and little multinational activity in the agricultural sector where long-term commitment is necessary. The country just poses too many obstacles and risks. Its political and economic environment for multinationals, however, is similar to that of other developing countries and therefore it is a good springboard into the development of appropriate multinational/developing country strategies to improve agricultural and food sector development, to speed the transfer of technology, and thereby to reduce climate related vulnerabilities.

MNC PARTICIPATION IN AGRICULTURE AND FOOD SECTOR DEVELOPMENT

The Problem - Lack of Incentives and LDC Fears

In the August 1977 issue of Fortune magazine, Sanford Rose (author of the article "Why the Multinational Tide is Ebbing") gave two views of the multinational corporation - the "New Bully on the World Block," and "one of the greatest forces for progress yet devised by man." Whichever view is ascribed to, it is clear that there is increasing MNC reluctance to move into any but the most stable of developing country markets. While MNCs have little security of tenure in the developing world, the United States Congress is whittling away at their current tax status. Between 1971 and 1975, in low technology and in highly competitive areas, approximately ten percent of all United States foreign subsidiaries have been sold off. (11) There is little commercial bank funding of projects to increase agricultural production in developing countries because earlier loans for similar projects have been found to be shaky and the projects have been lacking in both management and technical feasibility. (12) Multinational firms are also often loath to get involved in projects to increase agricultural production or to provide low cost, nutritious food because of past bad experiences - many with formulated protein-rich foods. They were simply too costly for the market, and in many cases the companies involved did not even recoup their investments.

Multinationals face many restraints in developing countries, although since the oil crisis some capital-poor LDCs have softened their opposition. The restraints range from control over allowable license fees, royalties, dividends, and branch earnings that a subsidiary may remit to its parent, to outright expropriation. One insidious form of restraint is the process of "unbundling" whereby the developing country seeks technologies through licensing, financing through international banking channels or domestic savings, and management expertise locally or from abroad. Thus the developing country attempts to get the benefits of the MNC without actually admitting the MNC to the country. Another form of restraint is that of creeping expropriation where the subsidiary is forced to give up increasing amounts of control. (13)

On the other hand, how are MNCs viewed by developing countries? Many governments are uneasy about MNCs because they are unable to predict (and control) their behavior - even if the subsidiary is completely willing to adhere to the laws of the particular country.

Their unease also stems from the following:

1. Some multinationals have more economic power than the developing country itself.

2. Short-term capital movements by multinationals can create balance of payments problems for a country. For example, the timing of payment of intercompany accounts can be adjusted to take advantage of potential currency devaluation.

3. Political pressures, fears of neocolonialism, North-South frictions and developed country trade restrictions on developing country manufactured goods add to the uneasiness. (14)

The First Step - Incentives for the MNC and a Spirit of "Pro Bono Publico"

The developing country must recognize that multinationals simply will not operate in situations where risks and restrictions, both commercial and political, are too high. Second, multinationals can only make a difference in food supply in money economies. Third, developing countries must recognize that private enterprise is and will be the predominant creator and transferrer of industrial technology. Developing country public institutions are only capable of modest contributions. The specific measures that the developing country can take to create an environment conducive to MNC participation start with the country knowing its needs and making them known to potential foreign investors through planning and enabling legislation. Other measures are the classic ones of investment guarantees, tax concessions, reasonable currency repatriation allowances, a viable legal system - in short, fundamental and permanent assurances of a reasonable business climate in order to obtain foreign capital and technology. (15)

The multinational, for its part, could enhance chances of long-run success by adopting a sprit of "pro bono publico" in its initial endeavor in developing countries. The multinational and the host government must work in a complementary fashion with specific agribusiness and food industry projects that fit into overall government programs. The multinational can take a portion of the "backstopping role" that it normally ascribed to foreign grain exporting countries - usually the United States. It can do this by using its "comparative advantage" in transferring resources (capital, management expertise, and technology) and in commercializing technology.

Developing Country Response to Technology - The Multinational as the Mechanism

While there are several organizations, some private, and some quasi-private, which act as "synchronizers" of agribusiness and governments in the developmental process, little attention has been given to the possibility of the multinational as the "mechanism" which could enhance public sector response to technology. As indicated earlier, the multinational firm is an agent of change, is eminently qualified to react rapidly to change, and is highly capable of transferring and communicating technology and expertise. What are the general requirements?

1. Both the multinational and the government share equally in the operation of and the funding of the "institutional mechanism." Funding by the government is critical in order for the government to have a stake (which it could lose) in the institution. Both parties share the risk and rewards equally.

2. Recognition that most of those suffering from malnutrition will benefit from expanded food production if they are brought into the money economy.

3. To as great an extent as possible, local resources should be used to fulfill local needs. This requirement is consonant with developing country desired to keep as much of the "value-stream" of a product in the country as possible.

4. Technologies appropriate to the country's/sector's stage of development be used. Too often developing country planners want to "catch up" immediately and are mesmerized by economies of scale.

5. Recognition that food, from production to diet, is a dynamic area and therefore requires flexibility in policy and project planning and implementation.

6. Realistic evaluation of a country's current and likely future agricultural potential, and recognition that a successful food production system cannot be bought, but rather it must be developed - as part of a country's overall economic development.

7. Recognition of the developing country's need to develop its own technology if it is to be competitive in domestic as well as in international markets.

8. That government/multinational collaboration enables a domestic scientific/technical infrastructure capable of generating knowledge.

Specific Requirements

To meet the objective of blunting climate induced variability in food supplies, developing country/multinational collaboration should fulfill certain requirements, such as:

1. Projects to increase food production and agricultural and food processing must produce for the marketplace - which means price incentives must be present. Farmers and multinationals alike need economic incentives to increase production. Moreover, such projects translate into employment and value added.

2. Maximum advantage of science and technology must be taken in the design of projects - especially where the country is poor in natural resources.

3. More than one crop/one enterprise must be emphasized in order to cushion against adverse crop developments.

4. Improvement of existing infrastructure, especially water supplies, communications, and transportation/distribution networks, is of key importance.

5. Clear definition of market opportunities, both domestic and foreign.

6. Existing technologies should be tailored to the country's specific requirements and its comparative advantages - raw materials, labor skills, natural endowment, etc. This must be done with care so that the multinational is not open to the charge of having provided second rate technologies. (16)

The area in which the multinational corporation can have the greatest impact is in the provision of a reliable waste-minimizing distribution system from the farmer to the consumer. Both in post-harvest food conservation and in human nutrition the MNC can truly be a "buffer" to climate caused variations in food supply.

Effective central storage of grains is one of the most important ways a country can protect itself against fluctuations in agricultural production. Even though the required capital investment is high, the returns (social) are high and the facilities are long-lived. Moreover, the need for improved handling and distribution techniques runs all along the farmer-to-consumer food chain. No organization is better versed in training and application of safety, food purity, and sanitation standards in food processing than a multinational food corporation. Another area that is a "natural" for the American multinational is food research, since most of this work is done in the private sector in the United States. Further along the food chain, a particularly effective area in which effort should be placed in in food service for the developing country's institutional market. By concentrating on providing a balanced diet from local foods and on decreasing food waste, pressure can be placed on the food chain, from farmer to processor, to supply foods in required quantities and of requisite quality.

CONCLUSION

The multinational corporation is one of the most powerful agents of change, transferrers of technology, and potential creators of income. All three facets are important points of intersection of the developing country and the multinational. If a foreign subsidiary is successfully established, it becomes an appropriate conduit for the transfer of innovations. Moreover, it is part of the international marketing network of the multinational, a network which is extremely difficult to duplicate. (17)

For a multinational to enter a developing country and develop a viable business, the climate - economic, social, and political - must be conducive to meeting the objectives of both the country and the multinational. Laws and regulations affecting foreign investment must be reasonable and stable, and there mst be a market for the multinational to serve. Moreover, the developing country must be committed to the success of projects entailing MNC participation.

For its part, the multinational must be as apolitical as possible, (18) be willing to accept a minority position in created subsidiaries (provided the returns are adequate to justify investment), be prepared to reinvest earnings locally, and even be willing to shift part of all its equity to local ownership as the business and local capital markets evolve. (19)

In its normal areas of activity - production, marketing, and transferring technology and expertise - the multinational firm can bring significant opportunities to the agricultural and food sectors of developing countries. These opportunities can help protect the developing country against the vicissitudes of climate. Enlightened developing country leadership will take the words of Fernando Monckeberg seriously.

> Changes are happening too fast - to ignore them, to try to change their nature or to minimize them means missing opportunities that may not come again. (20)

NOTES

(1) Marylin Chou, David P. Harmon, Jr., Herman Kahn, and Sylvan Wittwer, World Food Prospects and Agricultural Potential (New York: Praeger, 1977) p. 213.

(2) John W. Mellor, Thomas F. Weaver, Uma J. Lele, and Sheldon R. Simon, Developing Rural India (Ithaca, New York: Cornell University Press, 1968) p. 354.

(3) John W. Mellor, The New Economics of Growth - A Strategy for India and the Developing World (Ithaca, New York: Cornell University Press, 1976) p. 294.

(4) Chou, World Food Prospects, p. 223.

(5) Alan Berg, The Nutrition Factor - Its Role in National Development (Washington, D. C. : The Brookings Institution, 1973) p. 14.

(6) Ibid, p. 21.

(7) Ibid, pp. 110, 124, 140.

(8) Rutherford M. Poats, Technology for Developing Nations (Washington, D. C. : The Brookings Institution, 1972) p. 64.

(9) Ibid, p. 67.

(10) Fernando   Monckeberg,   Checkmate   to   Underdevelopment
(Washington D. C. : Embassy of Chile, 1976) p. 83.

(11) Sanford Rose, "Why the Multinational Tide Is Ebbing," Fortune no.
2 (August 1977): 111.

(12) Ernest C. Charron, "Financing Food Production in the LDCs,"
Chase   Manhattan   Bank.   Paper   presented   at   conference   on
Agribusiness 1977 and Beyond, Chicago, Illinois, April 25-26, 1977.

(13) Rose, "Tide Is Ebbing," p. 114.

(14) Robert B. Stobaugh, "A Proposal to Facilitate International Trade
in Management and Technology."   Paper completed under the
auspices of New York University Graduate School of Business
Administration project: The Multinational Firm in the U.S. and
World Economy, 1973.

(15) Arnold W. Sametz, "The Decline of Private Foreign Investment in
the LDCs - Causes and Cures of the Widening Gap."   Salomon
Brothers, Center for the Study of Financial Institutions.   Working
Paper no. 2.   New York University Graduate School of Business
Administration, April 1973.

(16) Charron, "Fianacing Food Production," p. 5.

(17) Rose, "Tide Is Ebbing," p. 116.

(18) Wall Street Journal, November 10, 1977.

(19) Sametz, "Decline of Private Foreign Investment," p. 70.

(20) Monckeberg, Checkmate, p. 47.

BIBLIOGRAPHY

Dunlop, Pierre R.   "Institutional Obstacles to Expansion of World Food
Production." Science, No. 4188, May 9, 1975.

Enzer, Selwyn.   The Twenty Year Forecast Project - Impacts of the
World Food Supply Problem on American Society.   Center for
Futures Research, Graduate School of Business Administration,
University of Southern California, Los Angeles, California, June
1975.

Gasser, William R.   World Climate Change and Agriculture.   Paper
presented at Conference on Agribusiness 1977 and Beyond, Chicago,
Illinois, April 25-26, 1977.

Hudson Institute. General Remarks on the Algerian Industrial System.
Croton-on-Hudson, New York, November 1973.

Lu, Yao-Chi, and Quance, Leroy. "Outlook for Technological Change and Agricultural Productivity Growth Through the Year 2000." Paper presented at the National Center for Productivity and Quality of Working Life's Symposium on the Future of Productivity, Washington, D. C., November 16-17, 1976.

MacDonald, R. B., and Hall, F. G., LACIE: A Look to the Future. National Aeronautics and Space Administration, presentation at the Eleventh International Symposium on Remote Sensing of the Environment, Environmental Research Institute of Michigan, April 25-29, 1977.

McHenry, Donald F., and Bird, Kai. "Food Bungle in Bangladesh." Foreign Policy, no. 27, Summer 1977.

National Academy of Sciences. Climate and Food. Washington, D.C., 1976.

Office of Technology Assessment. "Organizing and Financing Basic Research to Increase Food Production." Washington, D. C., June 1977.

Orr, Elizabeth. The Use of Protein-Rich Foods for the Relief of Malnutrition in Developing Countries: An Analysis of Experience. London: Tropical Products Institute, August 1972.

Pearson, Jack W. "New Ways to Bring Technology to the Marketplace." Technology Review. March/April 1977.

Pimental, David, ed. World Food, Pest Losses, and the Environment Boulder, Colorado: Westview Press, 1978.

Rasmussen, Wayne. "The Past 200 Years of American Farming." Agricultural Outlook 12, Washington, D. C., July 1976.

Ross, Douglas N. Partners in Agroeconomic Development. New York: The Conference Board, 1977.

Rotty, Ralph M. Energy and the Climate. Oak Ridge, Tenn.: Institute for Energy Analysis, Oak Ridge Associated Universities, September 1976.

The Wall Street Journal, May 4, 1978.

23 Foundation Chile— A New Strategy for Industrial Development *

Robert H. Cotton
Steward S. Flaschen

A unique opportunity to provide technical assistance to a developing country presented itself to International Telephone and Telegraph, Inc. (ITT) in 1974 when the present Government of Chile (GOC) came into office. As part of an overall agreement concerning property expropriated by the previous regime, ITT and GOC decided to establish a nonprofit orgainization with the primary purpose of advancing industrial development in Chile through research and development and education and training programs. Because of ITT's experience and expertise, these programs focused on Chile's food and nutrition problems and developments in electronics and telecommunications..

"Fundacion Chile," as the organization is known locally, was established in August 1976 by an official decree signed by the President of Chile. The Foundation is funded for its first ten years by grants of $25,000,000 (U.S.) from both the Government of Chile and ITT. Since its inception the Foundation has become a functioning and viable entity, and it shows promise of making important contributions to the industrialization of the country.

It seems appropriate to tell the story of Foundation Chile - its mission, organizational features, current program, and future plans -to illustrate a unique approach for private industry to help developing countries achieve industrialization. Hopefully this success story will encourage other multinational firms to explore similar possibilities for helping developing countries and perhaps will significantly speed up industrial development in them.

---

* Cereal Foods World, July 1978, Vol. 23, No. 7. Copyright 1978 American Association of Cereal Chemists, Inc.

BASIC FACTS ABOUT CHILE

To begin our story, let's review some facts about Chile. The country is very long and narrow and extends north from cold Cape Horn, for more than 2,600 miles, to a tropical valley. It is bound on the east by the Andes Mountains, and on the west and south by the Pacific Ocean. Chile consists essentially of a valley between two mountain ranges.

Water resources in Chile run from nil in the northern regions to plentiful in the south. In the central valley considerable water is available for irrigation from the eastern mountains.

Chile's agricultural potential varies tremendously because of its climatic and geologic diversity. In the south there are fine forests and lush pasture lands; extensive areas for irrigated crops exist in the central valley.

The marine food potential in Chile is fabulous, due to its more than 2,900 miles of coastline. In addition, Chile has considerable mineral resources, especially copper and iron ores and nitrate fertilizer deposits. On the other hand, the country is poor in fossil fuels. Hydroelectric power potential is good, however.

Chile is certainly one of the developing countries of the world. It is not self-sufficient in food, importing wheat from Argentian and elsewhere. Nevertheless it does export sizeable quantitites of fresh fruit and wine, as well as lumber and wood products. Copper, iron ores, and some finished metal products are also exported in quantity.

Over the years Chile has suffered periodic negative balances of payments due to highly volatile copper prices and political instability. However, from negative trade blanaces of $12 million, $45 million, and $275 million in 1974, 1975, and 1976, respectively, a positive balance of $18 million was recorded in 1977. It is expected that a positive balance of payments can now be maintained, and this can certainly be helped by an accelerated industrial development. The Foundation is dedicated to help achieve this goal through its programs of research and education.

All in all, Chile appears to have sufficient natural resources to support a strong, healthy, viable economy if a sustained industrial development can be maintained.

BASIC CONCEPTS AND PHILOSOPHY

One of the first steps necessary to activate Foundation programs was to inventory Chile's natural and human resources that could be used in the development of the food production, processing, and marketing industry, and for improving the electrical communications infrastructure. A thorough survey of government, university, and private industry groups involved in these sectors of the economy was required.

ITT and GOC agreed not to hire highly competent scientists and engineers having a "free rein." Rather, in order to obtain sustained technological progress in meeting the needs of a country, it was considered necessary to have continuous inputs from university, government, and private sector economicsts, and business management and marketing specialists. Otherwise it would be easy for the technical staff to undertake very interesting projects that were not really relevant to the needs of the people, or that were not sufficiently practical to be worthy of commercial development.

Another important consideration in program development was to recognize the importance of cooperation and teamwork in successfully reaching project goals. Not only was it necessary for scientists, engineers, economists, and marketing people within the Foundation to work closely together, but it was also highly desirable to involve concerned industry, government, and university people on the outside. Thus the research and development and the education and training programs are structured and implemented to catalyze constructive joint action by all concerned, thereby multiplying the benefits in relation to costs.

Finally, it was decided to plan for the eventual takeover of the control of the Foundation's activities by Chilean nationals. This requires that continuous effort be made to recruit qualified Chileans, especially for the upper echelons of management, and also to provide in-house training programs so that these people are ready to step into key positions of leadership and responsibility in the future.

FOUNDATION CHILE AT WORK

Organization

The Foundation is governed by a board of directors, with half of the membership named by the Government of Chile and half by ITT. The board is responsible for policy and the allocation of funds for Foundation programs. At present ITT is responsible for the staffing and the Foundation's daily operations.

The Director-General is chief executive officer and is responsible overall for program development and operations. Four executives under him are responsible for carrying out the research and education programs - food and nutrition, electronics and telecommunications, marketing and economic studies, and administrative services and finance.

Ongoing Programs: Research and Development

The primary mission of the Food and Nutrition Department is to carry out projects aimed at the production and utilization of Chilean raw materials for new and improved food products for domestic markets and export. Some special efforts are being devoted to developing products for use in the Government's unique feeding programs for the poor (known in Chile as CONPAN). It is appropriate here to acknowledge the assistance United States AID has given to the CONPAN program and the Foundation in a number of areas.

For many years the GOC has provided food for needy children, especially those attending school. Earlier efforts were only partially effective because of serious problems in supplying schools with the proper foods and because of sanitation problems in food preparation and service in the school environment. Foundation Chile scientists (in cooperation with Dr. Fernando Monckeberg, head of CONPAN and a world-renowned professor at the University of Chile) have developed a wholesome, nutritious, and acceptable biscuit item to replace the ones formerly used for this purpose. (This product is ready-to-eat and can be consumed without any preparation.) This product is now being manufactured by a local baker and is in widespread use in the school feeding program.

A number of other projects involve the development of food products for sale in regular market channels or for export. One of the more important and interesting projects involves the better utilization of raw materials from the sea. The first step in implementing this work has been to survey Chile's marine food resources and their utilization. With the help of expert consultants, the Foundation staff has assembled a directory of the fishing industry - commercial firms, their key personnel, the equipment and facilities used for harvesting, processing and storage, and methods of marketing. This directory will be an invaluable aid in the pursuit of the programs on product development in this area.

An interesting marine product development project involves the use of ground tissue from fish species not commonly used for food. Another project concerns the development of a hatchery program for producing seed stock for clam, oyster, and other shellfish culture. The Universidad Católica and Universidad del Norte are cooperating in this effort. A successful hatchery program would be of enormous help to Chile's declining shellfish industry.

Another commodity area that the food and nutrition department staff is investigating is the utilization of fresh apples unsuitable for export. Most promising is a convenience product manufactured by special preparation and dehydration.

The refining of an edible but crude oil for use in the domestic market is yet another project. Not only has a satisfactory product and a feed supplement by-product been developed, but at the same time a serious water pollution problem has been avoided. Another benefit is a substantial saving in the foreign currency now being spent to import food-grade fats and oils.

On the more purely agricultural side, Foundation efforts have focused on a crop rotation system for wheat and a unique lupine species. (The latter has been specifically bred by a Chilean scientist for human food use and is said to be free of natural toxins.) The rotation system results in higher wheat yields since the soil is richer in nitrogen because of the nitrogen-fixing bacteria associated with the alternately planned lupine (a legume). Other studies have shown that the lupine seed could be used as a protein source in the biscuit used for the school-feeding program.

Other food and nutrition projects are in progress or in the planning stage. However, those discussed give a good representation of the kind of studies that seem to offer promise for sound industrial development in Chile as well as serving certain social needs.

In the electronics and telecommunications program, the basic thrust is to assist the government and private agencies involved to modernize the telecommunication system and to extend services to all regions of Chile. There are a number of projects being pursued under this program to transfer "know-how;" engineering applications; systems, methods, and practices; computer-assisted planning and design; feasibility studies; and network program implementation..

Major efforts are being carried out in planning metropolitan networks, major national networks, and in bringing more rural areas into the national system. Another project is concerned with expanding Telex services throughout Chile. Still other projects are designed to provide additional types of services, including switching systems for data transmission.

Ongoing Programs: Education and Training

An important segment of the Foundation's program is to sponsor education and training activities. These will help provide the skilled manpower required for industrial development as well as the management and technical skills needed by Chilean nationals to carry out Foundation activities.

Chile has a number of excellent universities that offer academic courses and curricula in agriculture, food technology, nutrition, electronics, and telecommunications. Lacking are continuing education and more vocationally oriented programs. There is also a need for "on-the-job in-house training to improve the know-how and skills needed to manage and operate special technical organizations such as the Foundation itself.

In food technology food plant sanitation was identified as an important training need. A successful seminar on this topic put on by the Foundation drew more than 250 participants. This was followed by many plant visits by Foundation experts. Seminars and workshops on other topics are planned for the future. In addition, Foundation staff members are expected to participate in teaching and graduate student training programs offered by Chilean universities.

In addition to the academic programs in electronics and telecommunications sponsored by Chilean universities, the French government, through the United Nations Development Program (UNDP), is providing specialized training for engineers and technicians in industry. The staff of the telecommunications department cooperates with these and other efforts and, where needed, will supplement them where special ITT expertise exists.

FUTURE PLANS

Foundation Chile is now getting into high gear. A full spectrum of programs aimed at promoting industrial development in all areas of its competence can now be expected.

In the area of food and nutrition, the well-balanced staff of scientists, engineers, economists, and market specialists should be able to significantly enhance the technological development of the food industry for the benefit of all the people of Chile. This means better quality food products at reasonable costs for local consumption, as well as items for export to provide a positive balance of payments. In telecommunications, Foundation efforts should help provide the services demanded of a modern industrial nation.

ITT stands ready to make available all of its worldwide experience and expertise in the successful pursuit of Foundation Chile's objectives. And, of course, the Foundation is free to go outside the ITT system to obtain any special assistance it may need.

While there is a small key core of high level, non-Chilean ITT employees currently working in the Foundation, there will be a strong and continuing effort to train and employ Chileans capable of taking over and successfully carrying out its mission. We can already say that the well-trained, highly motivated, industrious Chileans are demonstrating constructive leadership and making solid professional contributions to the Foundation and to their country.

24 Coping with Abundance

Don C. Paarlberg

How can we avoid making a problem of our agricultural production capability? For the sake of simplicity we will concentrate our attention on the cereal grains and the oil seeds. These food and feed crops are the backbone of the food supply, our major export crops, and the principal concern of farm policy.

A standard truth in analytical work is this: Conclusions follow logically from the premises; the results can be no better than the postulates. The propositions which underlie this discussion have been carefully chosen and, to the best of the author's knowledge, are factual. They are first set forth so that the reader may know the basis of the analysis.

1. <u>Long-term weather prospects are unpredictable</u>. We cannot at this time predict what the weather will be a year or more hence. Meteorological science has not yet advanced to a point at which this is possible. Therefore we must discount predictions of "a cooling trend," "a warming trend," "a clustering of drought years," "an increase in year-to-year variability," and like forecasts. Such events do occur, and can be identified after the fact. But in the present state of knowledge they cannot be anticipated with sufficient accuracy to be useful in forward planning. In the present state of knowledge, the best indication of next year's weather is the average weather of the previous decade. Poor world crops from 1972 to 1975 were more an aberation than a new norm.

2. <u>Agricultural science will continue to advance</u>. World expenditures on agricultural research appear to have tripled from 1959 to 1974 - from $1.3 billion to $3.8 billion in constant terms. It may be true, as stated, that the backlog of agricultural science is less than it once was. For one thing, farmers pull it off the shelves faster. Much of the current talk about a lag in the development of new agricultural

372

knowledge comes from scientists who are concerned with obtaining larger research budgets.

There are good practices in use on some farms that are not yet in use on others. There are new methods, proved in test plots, not yet in use on any farm. There are also good new ideas that have not yet been tested. There are young men and women, trained in agricultural science, who have not yet produced new ideas, but will do so. Agricultural science continues to lift our production capabilities approximately in pace with the increasing need for food.

3. Demand for food in the aggregate is inelastic. This is the economist's way of saying that a one percent change in world food production will be accompanied by more than a one percent change in price, in the opposite direction. In general it appears that, other things equal, a one percent change in total world food supply is associated with something like a five percent change in price in the opposite direction. A small world crop costs more money than a large crop.

While this is true in the aggregate, it does not necessarily hold in the individual case. By dropping her export prices for wheat by one percent, Canada very likely can increase her wheat exports by more than one percent. This is the motivation which causes individual countries and individual sellers to push their products into world markets while the United States, the major exporter, is constrained by its price supports and production controls as well as by its concern for price stability to be the residual supplier.

4. Governments in many countries are inclined to boost farm prices and farm income. This is established policy in the United States, Canada, Australia, Western Europe, and many other countries. The result is to overstimulate production and, to some degree, to restrict consumption.

The widely observed tendency for the agriculture of advanced countries to overproduce its markets is not so much a result of agriculture's structural characteristics as it is a reflection of government intervention.

5. Governments are disinclined to apply tough production controls. Production controls, which would be needed to counteract the production-stimulating effect of price and income policies, are generally disliked by farmers and hence, for political reasons, are not fully applied.

6. Because of the foregoing reasons, the food production system has an upward bias. The net effect of strong price and income incentives, coupled with weak or nonexistent production controls, is to push the food system toward output which is high relative to market demand. This has been the situation in the United States during most of the time since the initiation of government programs in 1933, as documented by a number of competent reprots.

There may again come a time during the next decade when there is concern about the adequacy of the food supply. There have been three such periods since World War II: 1) 1946 to 1947, when we discovered the population explosion; 2) 1964 to 1966, when the monsoon failed in South Asia; and 3) 1972 to 1975, when world harvests were poor.

But such events appear to have been departures from the normal rather than the onset of a period of continuing scarcity. If the foregoing assumptions are reasonably correct and if, as a consequence, agriculture is inclined to oversupply its markets, how can the United States cope with the prospect of burdensome supply?

For more than 40 years we pursued policies that made us, unfortunately, the residual supplier in world markets. We held our export prices above world levels. Other exporters priced their products a cent or two under ours and sold their supplies. Buyers would first purchase these bargain products and then turn to the United States to round out their needs. We thus became the residual supplier, and typically were left with unsold stocks which we carried over. When the stocks became excessive we cut back production. In 1972 we held out of production some 62 million acres, 18 percent of our cropland, at a cost of $3.5 billion.

The results of these policies, which we were slow to understand, were as follows:

1. We carried the reserve stock of food for the world, at no cost to the other nations.

2. We carried, almost single-handed, the supply-adjustment role for the world food system.

3. We helped stabilize food prices in the world, at no cost to the other countries.

4. We granted to other agricultural exports most of the growth in world markets.

These policies were much more advantageous to the other exporting countries than they were to the United States, which had adopted them. But our legislators would never admit that the laws they wrote were more favorable to other countries than to ourselves. And the other countries claimed in behalf of their own actions the good fortune that had emanated from U.S. policies.

As a matter of fact, the Canadians and Australians, being good diplomats, seized the initiative and criticized us severely for certain actions in international trade, surplus disposal in particular. The Americans, full of gullibility and good will, were pretty much taken in by this tactic. At numerous international meetings, the American delegates were subjected to severe criticism and in effect pleaded guilty to all sort of transgressions. Actually, the United States was holding an umbrella for the rest of the world. It is possible, in retrospect, to see some wry humor in this situation.

This system came to an abrupt halt during the poor crops and high food prices of 1973 to 1976. We terminated our production controls, competed vigorously in the export market, and sold our accumulated stocks of grain. Farm prices and farm incomes rose, the cost of government programs diminished, and export earnings grew. We liked it!

Now, however, with two good world grain crops in a row, supplies are again becoming heavy, and we appear to be sliding back in the direction of our earlier policies. How can we avoid becoming the residual supplier again? Here are two alternatives, quite opposite in philosophy, representing (for the sake of analysis) the polarized positions.

1. Scrap the government programs and be fully competitive on world markets. If we could avoid the high loans and high price targets sought by grain producers, we could avoid holding a price umbrella for the rest of the world.

Definitions may be needed here. "Loans" and "price supports" are used interchangeably in this statement. What is involved is a nonrecourse government loan on a storable commodity like corn. The government loans would be, let's say, $2.00 per bushel on a farmer's corn crop. If the market price goes above $2.00, the farmer sells the corn, repays the loan, and pockets the difference. If the market price falls below $2.00, the farmer turns the crop over to the government in full repayment of the loan. The effect is to hold the market, in most cases, close to the loan level.

"Target prices" are prices set by government. The market fluctuates more or less freely. If the average market price falls below the target, farmers receive deficiency payments based on the difference; if the market price rises above the target, the farmer owes the government nothing.

If we could avoid high loans and high price targets, we could compete aggressively in international markets and escape the cost and trouble of being the world's warehouseman. We would avert the overstimulation of supply which is part of the problem.

But this strategy encounters some formidable obstacles. First of all, farmers mistrust the competitive market. The lobbying power of the farm commodity groups is great and has substantial political support. Secondly and more subtly, in the event of a large crop, if we were fully price competitive in the market and if the private trade were to push this big crop aggressively in world markets so as to avoid a big buildup of stocks, world prices would be driven to very low levels. This is because of the inelasticity of demand on a world basis, discussed earlier. We would injure all of the agricultural exporters, most of all ourselves because we are by far the largest. So this, the solution of classical economics, does not look good to most farmers or to most politicians.

What of the argument that in such circumstances the private trade would carry substantial stocks, and thus cushion the decline in world prices? There would be some of this. With a large crop both farmers and the trade would increase the carryover. But the carrying of stocks is costly, about 35 cents a bushel for corn. In six or seven years the cost of storage equals the cost of the grain. The private trade would push out grain until the price was depressed below next year's anticipated price by an amount equal to the cost of 12 months storage. This would very likely result in smaller stocks and less price stability than is politically imperative.

The private trade cannot be expected to deport itself in accordance with some allegedly desirable level of stocks or some standard of price stability or farm income objective. Nor can the trade be expected to operate so as to maintain certain desired diplomatic relations with other exporting countries.

The truth is that the body politic now demands of the food system a standard of performance that the private trade and the open competitive system are unable to provide.

2. Get the other countries to join us in a stabilization effort. At the opposite extreme are the proposals for internationalizing the food system. The argument goes as follows. Each country has a stake in reasonably stable world markets. Hitherto the United States has carried the burden almost single-handed; other countries have tailgated. They should pick up their share of responsibility for adjusting production, carrying stocks, and stabilizing the market. Such proposals have strong appeal to those with great faith in government action, particularly to those who believe in international solutions to problems.

The United States has made this argument and has offered specific proposals based thereon. But thus far there have been no takers.

There are two reasons for the nonsuccess of this strategy. First, regulating production, carrying stocks, and adhering to internationally agreed price criteria are costly and burdensome. Few countries relish such ventures. Second, other countries are convinced that despite its protests, the United States will again, in its own interest, undertake to hold a price umbrella, stabilize markets, adjust production, carry stocks, and so again become the world's residual supplier.

The record of international agreements in agriculture is not very good. Many have been started; few are still in existence. Mutuality of interest appears to be insufficiently strong to hold them together and most of them lack the internal discipline that would be required for success when interest diverge. Up to this point, most international commodity agreements have in effect been conspiracies of producers against consumers. Increasing awareness of this fact provides a doubtful climate for such ventures.

As usual in public policy, neither of the idealized positions is viable. What we must do, then, is to find some pragmatic, compromised middle ground, which lacks the clean-cut logic of either polarized position. What follows is a strategy for muddling through, citing tools of proven usefulness.

Keep the Loans and Targets at Reasonable Levels

Preferably this would be lower than the present levels which are already hurting our exports. Certainly it would be far lower than the 100 percent of parity that was demanded by the striking farmers of the American Agricultural Movement. If the loan and target objectives were kept moderate, the problem would be held to manageable proportions.

The writer differs from some of his conservative colleagues because he does not oppose loans, targets, and government-held stocks on ideological grounds. At reasonable levels these programs can indeed reduce price fluctuations, domestically and in export markets. They can provide the world some assurance regarding food supplies.

Total opposition to loans, targets, and government influenced carry-over is not only likely to be a loser, but also is likely to add to the zeal of those who advocate these techniques. And as is often the case with confrontation politics, the victor sees need for demonstrating that he has won. Programs that result from confrontation politics are usually more noteworthy as victory celebrations than as workable operations.

Active Export Promotion

There are legitimate ways to push exports: Use of export credit supplied by the Commodity Credit Corporation, use of the Ex-Im Bank, trade promotion, careful adherence to grades and standards, and the maintenance of good trade relationships with other countries. The rest of the world is receiving the advantage of our stock-holding, price-stabilizing, and agricultural-adjustment efforts. We should not feel guilt ridden about efforts to get our products into the world market in competition with other exporters.

Support for Liberal Trade Policies

If our production is to be heavy and if we are to get this abundance into world markets, these markets will have to stay open. The worldwide trend toward protectionism will have to be resisted. Export subsidies, variable tarriffs, and nontariff barriers, which are increasingly put forward, are inimical to liberal trade policy. So strong is the protectionist mood in the world today that a mere holding to past liberal trade gains may be the best we can do.

Vigorous But Judicious Use of PL 480

The theory of Public Law 480 (Food-for-Peace) is that there is a need for food in the world above and beyond the demand represented by those with the money to buy, and if these nonmarket needs can be sought out and supplied from our burdensome stocks, additional supplies can be moved in a manner helpful both to him who supplies and to him who receives. This program has been in operation almost 25 years. In recent years it has been running at an annual rate of a little more than a billion dollars.

The objectives of PL 480 are not only surplus disposal but also emergency relief, developing markets for United States trade, meeting nutritional needs, promoting economic development, and providing backup support for United States diplomatic and military objectives.

From 1973 to 1976, when food was short and prices were high, use of PL 480 was curtailed. Now that supplies are more abundant, the scale of operations can be increased.

Care must be taken that we avoid pitfalls. First, there is the danger that overaggressive use of PL 480 might result in displacing some product that we might otherwise sell for cash. Another is the danger that pushing too much product into a given country might depress food prices there, inhibit agricultural production, and make the recipient country a subsidized relief client, building a bond of dependency that neither supplier nor receiver could break.

Public Law 480 is not as great a supply safety valve as some people think. It is at least as difficult to give a product away usefully as it is to sell it. Nevertheless, Public Law 480, wisely administered, provides an opportunity to make of our production capability the asset it really is.

Rebuild Stocks

This we are already doing. The hope is that we can hold these stocks at reasonable levels, somewhere between the bin-busting amounts of the early 1960s and the bin-scraping between crops that we experienced during the mid-seventies.

Other countries, on their own and in the absence of international agreement, are rebuilding stocks, notably India and the Soviet Union. There need not be a formalized international stock-holding agreement for stock-building to occur.

Production Controls

This one is listed last, as a technique to which we should reluctantly turn after doing everything else we reasonably can.

The experience with production control from 1933 to 1973, in the judgment of this writer, has been adverse to the long-run interest of the American farmer. These controls have held agriculture in outmoded patterns, increased production costs per bushel, and kept us from exploiting new market opportunities. Restricting production for the controlled crops like cotton, corn, and wheat has resulted in increased production of uncontrolled crops like fruit and vegetables.

We should avoid production controls if we can, and minimize them if we can't. Production control should be a last resort means of coping after all else has been tried. It should not be a first choice way of shorting the market to boost the price.

The price support production control syndrome is what made us the residual supplier in world markets. It is the device that concedes market growth to other countries. It is the means by which, for 40 years, we held the price umbrella for other countries.

We managed, as a result of special circumstances, to dismount from the tiger without getting chewed up; we should be wary of remounting.

Index

About the Contributors

As policy analysts at Hudson Institute, MARYLIN CHOU and DAVID P. HARMON, JR. were Associate Directors of the Food, Agriculture and Society Research Program, a project dealing with current and near term food and agricultural issues affecting the public, the food industry, and the government. Prior to this program they coauthored a study funded by the National Science Foundation and published by Praeger in 1977 under the title World Food Prospects and Agricultural Potential.

Their publications include chapters in The Next 200 Years (William Morrow and Company, 1976) and Food: Nutrition, Preparation and Management (Goodhart Willcox Publishers, 1979), and articles in The New York Times, Family Circle, AgWorld, and Worldview.

In addition to her work in the food area, Mrs. Chou has also been involved in a number of area studies with a focus on China, Japan, and Korea. In 1975 she visited The People's Republic of China for the purpose of observing agricultural communes. Mr. Harmon participated in the development of a management information system for the government of Algeria as well as specific studies on the future economic development of the Republic of Korea, Saudi Arabia, Mauritania, and Iran. Mrs. Chou and Mr. Harmon are principals of the consulting firm Food Advisory Board which carries out policy studies and education programs in the agrifood area.

J. DAWSON AHALT is acting chairman of the World Food and Agriculture Outlook and Situation Board, U.S. Department of Agriculture.

WILLIAM C. BURROWS is Principal Scientist at Deere and Company.

J.B. CORDARO was formerly Group Manager of the Food Program at the Office of Technology Assessment.

ROBERT H. COTTON is retired vice president and chief scientist of ITT/Continental Baking.

RENE DUBOS is Microbiologist, Experimental Pathologist, and Professor Emeritus at Rockefeller University.

STEWART S. FLASCHEN is Vice President and Deputy General Director at ITT/Continental Baking.

WILLIAM W. GALLIMORE is Agricultural Economist at the Economics, Statistics and Cooperative Service, U.S. Department of Agriculture.

STEVEN GOLDBY is President of Dynapol.

WAYNE HENRY is Vice President of Castle & Cooke Foods.

HERMAN KAHN is Chairman and Director of the Hudson Institute.

GRAHAM T.T. MOLITOR is President of Public Policy Forecasting, Inc.

EMIL MRAK is Chancellor Emeritus of the University of California, Davis.

DR. ROBERT E. OLSON is Professor and Chairman of the Department of Biochemistry at the School of Medicine, St. Louis University Medical Center.

DON C. PAARLBERG is Agricultural Economist and Professor Emeritus at Purdue University.

DEAN PETERSON is Director of Economics at Nabisco, Inc.

MICHAEL J. PHILLIPS is Marketing Projects Leader of the Food Program at the Office of Technology Assessment.

DONALD R. PRICE is Associate Professor and Director, Energy Programs at Cornell University.

PEG ROGERS is a Food Scientist and officer of Food Advisory Board.

NORMAN SAUTER is Senior Scientist at Deere and Company.

THOMAS R. SAYLOR is Associate Administrator of the Foreign Agricultural Service, U.S. Department of Agriculture.

ROBERT M. SCHAFFNER is Associate Director for Technology at the Bureau of Foods, U.S. Food and Drug Administration.

PHILIP SISSON is Manager of Economic Research at Quaker Oats Company.

SYLVAN H. WITTWER is Director of the Agricultural Experiment Station, Assistant Dean of Agriculture and Natural Resources, and Professor of Horticulture at Michigan State University.

Pergamon Policy Studies